YOUNG
WINSTONE

'A gripping insight into his youth . . . For fans of his
violent turns in *Scum, Nil by Mouth* or *Sexy Beast*, this is
a perfect literary counterpart. For everyone else, it's an
engaging portrait of a boy done good'
Telegraph

'Brilliant . . . *Young Winstone* is a must-read'
Shortlist

'As much about London as his nascent career. Ray
made such an impression in *Scum* that I still remember
his prison number, and he is just as vivid on his
formative years . . . There'll be another volume, I hope'
Independent

YOUNG
WINSTONE

RAY
WINSTONE

and Ben Thompson

CANONGATE
Edinburgh · London

This paperback edition published by Canongate Books in 2015

First published in Great Britain in 2014 by Canongate Books Ltd,
14 High Street, Edinburgh EH1 1TE

www.canongate.tv

1

British Library Cataloguing-in-Publication Data
A catalogue record for this book is available on
request from the British Library

ISBN 978 1 78211 245 7

Typeset in Bembo by Canongate Books Ltd

Printed and bound in Great Britain by Clays Ltd, St Ives plc

MIX
Paper from
responsible sources
FSC® C018072
FSC
www.fsc.org

CONTENTS

INTRODUCTION

It's early 2007 and I'm standing on a ship off the coast of north-eastern Australia. We're moored right by Lizard Island, named by my fellow Londoner and Great Briton Captain Cook, and I'm making this film called *Fool's Gold* starring Matthew McConaughey, Kate Hudson and my old mate Donald Sutherland, who is a blinding geezer.

Donald is playing an Englishman and I'm playing a Yank, but in hindsight we should've swapped roles because I was fucking diabolical in that film – I should've got nicked for impersonating an actor. Anyway, I digress . . . a big word for me – seven letters.

So there's a bit of a buzz going on with a few people running about on deck, and all of a sudden we're summoned downstairs to this big room with a telly in it. This is the whole fucking crew by the way, with me and Donald hiding at the back like two naughty schoolboys. Then somebody announces it's the 'Most Beautiful Man in the World' Awards.

Well, obviously me and the Don think we might be in the running here, but hold up, the next announcement tells us that our very own Matthew McConaughey is one of the nominees and he's up against that other alright-looking geezer, George Clooney. Anyway, the show begins and Matthew is giving it the old 'Woo! Woo!' like the Yanks do when they get excited. After about five minutes of this bollocks I wanna be somewhere else – anywhere else. Yeah, I suppose I might be a little bit jealous. I mean, he ain't a bad-looking fella . . .

As they're building up to the big moment the television shows this satellite going across the world from east to west. Funny how everything and everyone seems to travel from east to west. Maybe they're following the sun – wanting to find out where it goes before it comes up the other side again – or maybe they thought it went down a hole. Anyway, this satellite is travelling across Europe and as it's getting closer to London, I'm thinking, 'You never know . . .'

Bang! It hits London and with all the lapping up that's going on I can't contain myself any more. I shout out, 'Stop right there, my son! That's me!' The Aussies, who have a great sense of humour – well, they're cockney Irish, ain't they? Or at least the majority are – are all giggling. But as far as the others are concerned, it goes straight over their heads.

Eventually the satellite gets to America and we're into Clooney and McConaughey territory. We creep quietly past George and slip loudly into Texas, and at this point it's announced that Matthew is the winner. He goes absolutely potty – like he's scored the winning goal in the World Cup final and won the Heavyweight Championship of the World in one go.

I'm thinking, 'Fuck me, what a prat!'

The whole thing just seems a bit embarrassing, but then on reflection I start to think maybe this is the big difference between us – apart from my good looks, of course. Maybe this is what makes Matthew a film star, which he is – at the time of writing he's just won an Oscar, and deservedly so.

Anyway, once I finally get back up on deck, the whole thing kinda makes me think about where I've come from. Looking at Australia, 14,000 miles away from home – literally on the other side of the world – I start thinking about me and my mate Tony Yeates as kids in the East End, and I start thinking about Captain Cook. There's a plaque on the Mile End Road which marks the start of his journey to Oz. It's just opposite the place a club called Nashville's used to be, where me and Tony had a few adventures of our own in the late seventies. We'd often find ourselves gazing unsteadily up at that plaque after we'd had a few on a Friday night – dreaming of travelling the world, the places we might see and the people we might meet. And suddenly standing on that ship in the southern hemisphere, it comes to me: 'I've made that journey. I've done what Cook did!'

Alright, he did it on a sailing ship and I did it First Class British Airways, but I've done it just the same. I'm not trying to book myself as being on Cook's level as an explorer, but for someone who comes from where I do, getting to the Great Barrier Reef was still some kind of achievement. That was when the idea of paying my own tribute to the places and the people that made me what I am (I won't be demanding actual blue plaques: 'Ray Winstone narrowly escaped a good kicking here' etc.) started to make me smile. I hope it will do the same for you.

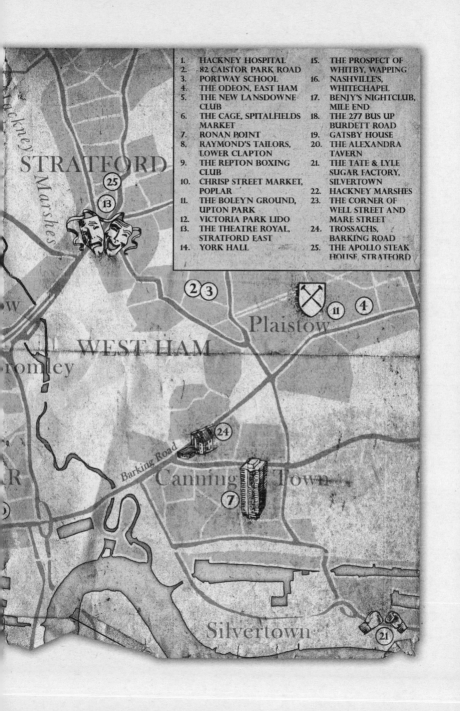

1. HACKNEY HOSPITAL
2. 82 CAISTOR PARK ROAD
3. PORTWAY SCHOOL
4. THE ODEON, EAST HAM
5. THE NEW LANSDOWNE CLUB
6. THE CAGE, SPITALFIELDS MARKET
7. RONAN POINT
8. RAYMOND'S TAILORS, LOWER CLAPTON
9. THE REPTON BOXING CLUB
10. CHRISP STREET MARKET, POPLAR
11. THE BOLEYN GROUND, UPTON PARK
12. VICTORIA PARK LIDO
13. THE THEATRE ROYAL, STRATFORD EAST
14. YORK HALL
15. THE PROSPECT OF WHITBY, WAPPING
16. NASHVILLE'S, WHITECHAPEL
17. BENJY'S NIGHTCLUB, MILE END
18. THE 277 BUS UP BURDETT ROAD
19. GATSBY HOUSE
20. THE ALEXANDRA TAVERN
21. THE TATE & LYLE SUGAR FACTORY, SILVERTOWN
22. HACKNEY MARSHES
23. THE CORNER OF WELL STREET AND MARE STREET
24. TROSSACHS, BARKING ROAD
25. THE APOLLO STEAK HOUSE, STRATFORD

CHAPTER 1

HACKNEY HOSPITAL

When I look back through the history of my family, we've done fuck all for this country. I don't mean that in a bad way. The Winstones weren't villains. We've always been grafters, back and forthing between the workhouse and the public house. But at the time I was born – in Hackney Hospital on 19 February 1957 – the Second World War was still very much on people's minds. It's probably a bit of a cliché to say 'everyone had lost somebody', but in our family, it wasn't even true. Maybe it was more the luck of the draw in terms of their ages than anything else, but there was no one you could put your finger on and say they had sacrificed themselves in any way.

Doodlebugs rained down on Hackney – I remember being told about one going straight up Well Street – but none of them hit my nan and granddad's flat in Shore Place. They had to go in the air-raid shelter round the front a few times, but their three young sons – my dad Ray and his two brothers, Charlie and Kenny – were safely evacuated out towards High Wycombe. The village they were lodged in lost three men on HMS *Hood*, so that was about as close as the war got to them.

Uncle Kenny, my dad's younger brother, got a start as a jockey and rode a few winners for Sir Gordon Richards' stable. I've always surmised that he must've picked up his way with horses when he was evacuated to the countryside, because there weren't too many racecourse gallops in the East End. That said, his dad, my granddad, Charles Thomas Winstone, did work as a tic-tac man, passing on the odds for bookmakers at tracks all around Britain, so horse-racing was kind of in Kenny's blood.

When he got too tall to be a jockey on the flat any more, Kenny became a butcher. I guess that was one way he could carry on working with animals. He ended up with a couple of shops – one in Well Street, and one just round the back of Victoria Park – so he did alright. But before that he'd been a pretty good boxer as well. He boxed for the stable boys, and once fought at the Amateur Boxing Association (ABA) finals against a mate of my dad's called Terry Spinks, who went on to win a gold medal at the Melbourne Olympics aged only eighteen, and would later be known for raising the alarm as the Black September terrorists approached the Israeli athletes' quarters when he was coaching the South Korean team at the Munich Olympics in 1972. Apparently he gave old Spinksy a bit of a fright.

This wouldn't have come as any great surprise in the Winstone household, because boxing was what the men in our family did. My granddad had been drafted into a Scottish regiment and stationed in Edinburgh for a while just to be on their boxing team, and when my dad did his National Service with the Royal Artillery, he spent virtually the whole three years in his tracksuit, boxing out of Shoeburyness. I think Henry Cooper might've been doing his stint at around the same time, and the only actual service I ever remember my dad telling me about was helping out after the great flood of 1953, when all those people died on Canvey Island.

He said he'd got really angry because the Salvation Army wouldn't give him a cup of tea when he didn't have the money to buy one. From then on if he ever saw someone selling *The War Cry*, he'd just tell 'em to go away. He had no time for those people whatsoever, to the extent that I even remember asking him about it once as a kid: 'Surely there must be some good people in the Salvation Army, Dad?' But he just told me, 'Nah, son, they wouldn't give me a cup of tea.'

Hopefully this has given you a bit of an introduction to the kind of men I grew up around. I'm going to have to go back a bit further in time for the women, because I came across a story recently which really answered a lot of questions for me about the way I think, and the way the women in my family live their lives. It all started when the Winstones got turned down by the BBC TV series *Who Do You Think You Are?*

Now, I like that programme – I get right into it (although I have seen some boring ones) – but the first time they asked, I didn't really want to do it. I enjoy watching them go through other people's ancestors' dirty laundry, but when it came to mine, I just didn't really want to know. That's all in the past, and it's the future you want to be thinking about. They kept coming back to me, though, and in the end I thought, 'Do you know what? Maybe it would be good to find out a few things.'

I knew I had a great-uncle Frank – my granddad's brother on my mum's side – who played centre-forward for West Ham. He was at Reading first, and then he moved to West Ham in 1923, the year they got to their first Wembley final. Maybe if they'd bought him before the big game instead of just after it, they might actually have won. As it happens, they got beat, and my great-uncle Frank was a kind of consolation prize, but still, I thought that might be a good starting point.

Unfortunately, it seems that on the show they stick to the direct bloodline, i.e. parents and children only, so an uncle can't be the story, or at least that's what they told me. And after giving due consideration to the mountain of material that their researchers had unearthed, they had come to the conclusion that the various roots and branches of the Winstone family tree were just too fucking boring to make a show out of. They were lovely about it – 'Sorry, Ray, but there's nothing in here we can use' – and I did get the giggles on the phone. That can't have been an easy call to make: 'Listen, Fatboy, there's just nothing interesting about you or your family.'

It's funny looking back, but I was quite depressed about it for a while – not depressed so I wanted to kill myself, just a bit disappointed and choked up. But then I sat down and went through some of the stuff they'd dug up, and I actually got really enlightened by it.

The one thing that did come out of *Who Do You Think You Are?* was that both branches of my family had been East Londoners for as far back as they could trace. Right the way back to the 1700s my mum's side came from Manor Park/East Ham and my dad's from Hoxton and the borders of the City.

OK, my family never changed the world. They never invented penicillin or found the Northwest Passage or won a VC at the Siege of Mafeking. They were basically just people who sometimes fell on hard times and ended up in the poorhouse for a couple of weeks – or longer. But there was one extraordinary thing about them, as there is about any family that's still around today, and this was that they survived. On top of that, it turned out we did have one story worth telling after all, because some time afterwards the same TV company came back to me and said they were making another show that they did want me to be a part of. The subject? There's a thick ear for anyone who's guessed it: asylums.

4

The researchers had discovered that my great-great-grandmother (on my dad's side) was originally married to a Merchant Navy man called James Stratton, who ended up in the old Colney Hatch Lunatic Asylum at Friern Barnet. That was somewhere I'd end up too a century and a bit later, albeit for slightly different reasons – I was shooting the movie version of *Scum* – but poor old seaman Stratton had got syphilis.

I didn't find out until we were researching the programme – they like the historians and other experts to break the news to you as you're going along, so they can catch you looking surprised – just how rife syphilis was in Victorian London. Even before that, going back to Hogarth's time in the eighteenth century, all those wigs they were wearing in his paintings weren't just fashion accessories, they were there to cover the fucking scars.

One strange thing that happened was that at one point it actually became fashionable to be syphilitic, so people would wear false noses and ears to make it look like they had it when they didn't. Wearing a false nose to show you were a proper geezer – how nutty was that? No crazier than covering yourself in tattoos or having plastic surgery you don't medically need, I suppose.

As far as the unfortunate Mr Stratton was concerned, they thought he'd probably picked the syphilis up in the Navy, before he was married, but then he might have had a dabble again, because the sixth of his eight children was born with it too. Either way, he died a terrible death, leaving my great-great-grandmother alone with all those kids, and no real means of support – visible or invisible.

At this point in the story, the odds must've been on her drifting into prostitution. That's certainly what I thought was going to happen. Because all these events were unfolding around Whitechapel, and the name she went by at the time, Hannah Stratton, had a familiar ring to it – like Mary Kelly or one of those other tragic victims – in my head we were heading towards Jack the Ripper territory. Obviously the programme-makers don't tell you what's going to happen because they want you to cry. In fact, they want that so badly they're practically standing behind the camera with a big bowl of freshly chopped onions.

They'd taken me to Christ Church, Spitalfields, the big white church opposite the market my dad used to take me to as a kid when he was in the fruit and veg game. I didn't remember ever having been inside before – me and my family not being churchy kind of people, and in any case it was boarded up and virtually derelict for most of the sixties and seventies – but it looks amazing now it's all been restored. So I'm standing there in this beautiful place, waiting for the bad news about Hannah getting gruesomely done in by the Ripper, and then they tell me that it was in this church that she married her second husband.

It turned out that Stratton wasn't actually my great-great-grandfather at all, because Hannah managed to marry again within a year of his death. She would probably have been ostracised at first because of the syphilis, and could easily have headed for the nearest gin palace and ended up in the gutter somewhere, but instead she thought, 'Fuck it, I'm fighting for my kids.' So she stood her ground and her neighbours rallied round to help her – which was incredible in itself, because that kind of thing doesn't happen so much today, at least not in cities, where no one tends to know who the people living next door to them are any more.

After Hannah remarried and became Mrs Durham, she and her new husband lived round the corner from Christ Church – for a while, and then moved to West Hackney. Her syphilis became dormant and she had more kids, so that was when my granddad's father was born. Her second husband had only been twenty-seven when they married – effectively a toyboy, and she never marked his card about exactly how old she was. So, while he thought she eventually died at the ripe old age of sixty-one, it was probably a good bit riper than that.

You couldn't blame her for dangling the carrot a bit, though, given that she had kids to look after. And if she hadn't done it, I wouldn't be here today, so it was a happy ending for me as well. (And for the programme-makers, because Hannah's story did make me cry. It broke my heart, to be honest, but it also made me very proud of her, and glad I'd done the show as now I can pass the story on down through my family to make sure she's not forgotten.)

All in all, Hannah Durham was an amazing old girl, and I could see a lot of the characteristics of my sister Laura and my auntie Irene, my dad's sister, in her. Not that either of them have ever had syphilis, but I've got a lot of strong women in my family. Obviously my mum's is a different line, but it's the same on her side as well. We'll get to my maternal grandma and her three husbands in the next chapter . . .

In the meantime, the long and the short of it is that the men in my family seem to like marrying strong women, probably because we need them to keep us in line. But the other thing I realised standing in that old Hawksmoor church – and I know this might sound overly romantic, a bit pony even – was the depth of my family's connection to the area.

My dad was born in Hoxton. You could definitely hear the bells of St Mary-le-Bow on Cheapside from there, so that makes him a proper cockney. And as I've said, the family had been basically there or thereabouts since the 1700s, until his generation started to move away in the late sixties. Yet now, just a few decades later, I've got cousins in Dunmow, Braintree, Watford, Bushey, but there's none of us left inside the M25: we've all got let out for good behaviour. How and why that change came about, and what it meant to us and to others, is one of the main subjects of this book.

I still think of myself as an East Londoner rather than a Londoner. And as I was driving in to do that filming in Spitalfields from where I live now, out in Essex, I seemed to pass places that had some relevance to mine or my family's lives every few hundred yards from Whipps Cross onwards. None of the actual people are there any more, but that doesn't make the memories any less vivid. It might even bring them through more strongly – after all, you don't need to remember things that are still happening.

We were a big old tribe, and when I was a kid we used to have a big get-together more or less every Sunday, but now we're much more dispersed, and the unit has kind of contracted much more to immediate family. My cousins all keep in touch, but I've been guilty of letting that go a bit in recent years. The way people perceive you is part of it as well. You start living in a bigger house and they'll tell you, 'Oh, we went past yours the other day', so you'll say, 'Well, why didn't you fucking knock on the door?' But if the door's behind a security gate, then the fact that they don't knock on it is as much your fault as anyone else's, isn't it?

Looking back now, I can clearly see the staging posts by which the old closeness started to leave us. When my mum and dad brought me back from Hackney Hospital in the winter of 1957 (the building's still there, up on Homerton High Street – I think it was the tall Victorian-looking wing to the east, not the lower section where the entrance is – but last time I looked they'd turned it into a nuthouse in my honour), they didn't have a home of their own yet. From what I've gathered, there was never any question but that the three of us would stay in the flat in Shore Place with my dad's parents for a little while after my birth.

At a time when families would generally stay in the same place, nans and granddads were the nucleus of everything – everyone else would circulate around them. Now they just tend to get left where they are when everyone moves away, and then you see 'em when you can. It's no wonder they get a bit grumpy. I feel lucky to have grown up at the tail-end of the old way of doing things, because the world of my childhood could not have wished for a better focus than my granddad Charles – Toffy they called him, I suppose because he was a bit of a toff – and Nanny Maud.

He was a real one-off, my grandfather; an old-fashioned gentleman. I'm sure a lot of people say that about their grandparents, but in this case it was definitely true. Toffy was a short, wiry man who always dressed immaculately and never forgot to lift his hat to the ladies as he walked down the road. By all accounts – at least, all accounts of his own – he was the man behind the modernisation of tic-tacking (the complex sign language for communicating bookmakers' odds which you used to see John McCririck doing on the telly, until Channel 4 Racing gave him the Spanish – as in Spanish Archer, the El Bow). I think he definitely simplified it, him and another fella . . . there's always another fella.

Nanny Maud was a similarly upright individual. I think she'd run a café as a younger woman, but by the time I came along everyone called her 'The Schoolteacher', because she had a lovely proper way of talking. She wasn't all gorblimey, she was much more 'telephone voice'. Even nowadays, when you meet the really old East London boys and girls, I find they have that almost Dickensian style of speaking which is nothing like how I sound. There's still an accent, but it's all very clipped and correct, and it's a beautiful thing to hear.

I don't have any specific recollections of sharing a home with Toffy and Maud as a child, because we moved out of there when I was about a year old. But some of my happiest early childhood memories are of the days when Maud would take me to the toy shop in Mile End – just by the junction where they've put that silly grass roof over the main road – and buy me Airfix kits, or the Batmobile with a Bat-boat that fired little rockets out the back. And in my teens I'd actually end up living with my granddad for a year, which would turn out to be one of the most influential, as well as the funniest, times in my life.

Hospitals take away as well as giving, and in my early teens Nanny Maud would die in the same place I'd been born. She had a fall and never quite got over it, and I don't think the family could ever forgive Hackney Hospital for the feeling that a bit more could've been done. I was a kid on the cusp of being a young man by that stage, and I remember the sombre, grown-up mood of the family gathering in the Jackdaw & Stump – the pub just along the high street from the hospital – when everyone had come up to visit Nan together after her fall.

We were all worried about her, and at times like that you obviously feel an atmosphere of foreboding in the air, but I don't think any of us realised how big a change was coming. People often think of the granddad as being the head of a family, but I think it's the nan, really. Obviously once she's gone, you still go and see him – and Toffy did a pretty good job of managing by himself, he even got himself a nice girlfriend after a while – but you can see how lost the men in the family are once the maternal mainstay is gone. From then on, there's less and less reason for everyone to get together, and the whole family starts to break up.

It was probably a good job I didn't know all that on the day of her funeral, because I was upset enough already. This was the first loss

I was old enough to really feel properly. I remember being outside the flats where all the flowers were laid out ready to be taken to the cemetery, when I heard some local kid ask 'Who's dead?' quite rudely and I lost the plot. I couldn't cope with that at all – it seemed very disrespectful – and things went pear-shaped for a few seconds, before I was told in no uncertain terms to keep quiet and have a little bit of dignity about myself.

'Who's dead?' is never the right question to ask, though, is it? If someone says, 'Who's passed?' you can tell they're making an effort, but 'Who's dead?' is just too brutal. That's not to say there's no room for levity when someone's died. Quite the reverse. I remember it used to be a big event for my dad and his mates and we still do it today – when someone would say, 'There's a bit of underground sports on Thursday.' What that means is there's a funeral, and a funeral means a wake, which means a blinding party.

The funny thing about 'underground sports' is, it's OK for us to talk about them, but we'd still reserve the right to take it amiss if someone else did it at the wrong moment. I love that kind of hypocritical cockney morality. That is very much the tradition I was brought up in, like with the old boys off the docks, they'd be telling you some great stories and effing and blinding all the way through (the expression 'swear like a docker' doesn't come from nowhere), but heaven help you if you swore in front of their wife on the bus: ''Scuse me . . . 'scuse me . . . oi! 'Scuse me! Not in front of the wife.' I do understand and respect that way of doing things – it's kind of my way of doing things too, if I'm honest – but it does have its flaws.

CHAPTER 2

CAISTOR PARK ROAD, PLAISTOW

When I started writing this book the first thing I did was go back to the street I lived on as a kid. I wanted to have a look around to see if people or incidents I'd forgotten would come flooding back to me. What I couldn't get over was how much smaller everything was than the way I remembered it. Obviously when you're little you're down at hedge and gate level, so the world looks massive to you, but there was more to it than that. Going back to Plaistow now, it feels very quiet and suburban, whereas in my childhood there seemed to be people everywhere, and something was always happening.

Of course at that time – in the late fifties – the London docks were still working at full speed and strength. The southern end of our road wasn't far away from the Royal Victoria and Royal Albert Docks, so a lot of the hustle and bustle of the neighbourhood (not to mention the odd bit of unofficial bounty from shipping crates that had accidentally on purpose fallen open in transit) could be traced back to there.

The docks are long gone now, or at least the idea that anyone would use them for unloading stuff from boats is. But my home from the age of one to the age of eight – 82 Caistor Park Road, Plaistow – is still very much there, looking more or less unchanged over the intervening half century.

It's a boxy, two-storey house near the end of a terrace. When we first moved in, we lived upstairs while an old lady and her sister kept the ground floor. Then after my sister Laura came along – in February 1959 – the Winstones took over the downstairs as well. There was never a bathroom (I'm assuming they've got one now). We had an outside toilet in the small back garden, and a tin bath would come out in the front room when it was time for a scrub-up.

In my early years my mum had to keep me on reins, because as soon as I saw daylight, I'd be off like a greyhound out of the trap (my eldest girl Lois was the same). But from pretty much the moment Laura and I were old enough to walk around unaided, we played outside in the street all day. There were very few cars about in those times, and we still had a milkman with a horse-drawn cart. He'd come round the corner at a set time every morning, and since all the kids knew he was coming we'd have plenty of time to put bricks in the middle of the road so he'd have to go round them like he was doing a slalom, shouting, 'You little bastards!' as he went.

At the north end of Caistor Park Road was, and is, the main drag down to Stratford, and beyond that thoroughfare stretches the wide open space of West Ham Park, which is still a lovely bit of grass to have a walk around. Returning to the area now, I can see that the houses at the top of the road tend to be much better finished off, whereas our bit is more of a khazi. Don't go down my end – it's a shithole.

I don't recall it being that way when I was a kid, but then again, in my memories the sun has always got his hat on. Even though my rational mind knows Londoners were still afflicted by deadly pea-souper fogs at that time, all I can remember is clear skies and long days of unbroken sunshine.

In my mind, Plaistow in the early sixties is like one of those adverts filmed in New York where it's a hot day and someone knocks the top of the fire hydrant off, except done the English way – with a hosepipe. Over the years you do colour your memories in a bit (at least, I have done), but I'm going to try and keep them as toned down and close to reality as possible. Obviously you're only going to be seeing things from my point of view, because that's what an autobiography is all about. But I realise there's at least one other side to a lot of these stories – just ask Matthew McConaughey – and if someone's given me another perspective, I'm not going to hold back on it.

For instance, I look back on myself as a little boy and I think I was alright, but my aunties always tell me I was a right little fucker. I'll insist I was a nice kid and they'll say, 'No, you were an absolute fucker – always up to something.'

Now that must be true, because it's not the sort of thing they're gonna make up, so I have to start thinking about how they might've got that idea. I do remember there was a little parade of shops round the corner from our house where I used to sing for the greengrocer and he would give me a banana – well, every showbiz career has got to start somewhere, hasn't it? I was still in the pram, so I couldn't have been that old, but one day I sang for him and he didn't give me one and I told him to fuck off. My mum would laugh telling me that story years later, but she was embarrassed at the time because she very rarely swore, so wherever I'd picked that word up from, it hadn't been from her. And 'No, you'll have no banana' was my first bad review. There've been a few more since . . .

In Plaistow in the fifties and sixties, there used to be a shop on every corner, and the one change to my immediate childhood surroundings which I really couldn't get my head round when I went back on my fact-finding mission was that the old corner shop is now just a normal house. The shopkeeper's name was Mr Custard, which was obviously a gift to us as kids. He had a big shock of un-ruly white hair and looked a bit like Mr Pastry. We used to terrorise him, going in there and shouting 'Cowardy, cowardy Custard, can't eat mustard!' You know what kids are like. I feel quite sorry for him now, as he was probably a nice old boy.

A lot of good people lived on Caistor Park Road. A couple of doors up from us was a girl called Sylvie who lived with her mum – I don't remember a dad, and there might not have been one. She must have been in her mid-teens and she used to babysit for us and take me up the park. One day, before my sister was born, she was pushing me to the swings in my stroller when a geezer jumped out in front of us and flashed her. I was only a baby, so I don't seem to have accrued any deep psychological scars, but when my parents told me the story they were still really impressed that she hadn't just fucked off and left me. She was a lovely girl, Sylvie, and it was very sad that a few years later she committed suicide. I always hoped it wasn't what happened in the park that day that upset her.

Everyone living on Caistor Park Road knew everyone else, and all the stuff you always hear about windows being left open and it being OK to leave a key hanging behind the door was still true. There was even an old girl living on her own over the way who my mum used to cook dinner for. She had no connection with our family, other than that she lived near us. I know this sounds corny, but people looked after people. They really did. Every time you went out of the house in the morning you'd see women doing their steps and their windows. I know that sounds a bit chauvinistic now, but how can it be a bad thing for people to have taken pride in themselves and in their community?

Our home was always spotless, inside and out. My mum made sure everything was in its place and everything was done properly. She'd learnt that from her mother, who was not a woman to be trifled with.

My nan on my mum's side was called Dolly Richardson, but she was always Nanny Rich to me. We called her Nanny Rich because she was . . . rich. By the time I was born, she owned a fair bit of property in the Plaistow, Manor Park and Forest Gate areas, and I think it was down to her that we ended up living where we did. She was a furrier by trade – not a farrier shoeing horses, a furrier making coats – and she'd done well enough to move out of East London to Shoeburyness, just along the Essex Riviera from Southend, after the war. There are a few fur coats left in the family somewhere, but obviously you can't wear 'em any more because someone will throw paint over you. I presume there must have been a few quid poking around when Nanny Rich – God rest her soul – eventually went away in the early eighties, but I never saw any of it.

Nanny Rich was married three times – once more than old Hannah Durham – and she outlived all of her husbands. We'd started to look at her in a different way by the end. Her short-lived first husband, my auntie Olive's father, wasn't my grandfather. That was Husband Number Two. My mum's dad was Mr Richardson (no relation to the notorious South London clan), but he died before I was old enough to really get to know him. By all accounts he was a very tall man, and the only one in the family who ever fought in the First World War. True to form for my family he came out of it in one piece, but it's possible his death in the late fifties may have been caused by the lingering effects of mustard gas forty years before. I remember being in bed one night and hearing my mum distressed and crying, but not really knowing why he'd died or what that meant.

My nan's last husband, Reg Hallett, who she married after a decent interval, was a terrific old boy. I had a lot of time for him. Reg was a mason – a very well-to-do man from Shoeburyness, which sounds like an Ian Dury song. I think he worked in Churchill's Treasury during the war. When I got a bit older he used to beg me to become a mason too, but I wasn't having it.

Whoever she ended up marrying, mason or otherwise, Nanny Rich never stopped being her own boss. I believe she made fur coats for the Royal Family, although that is the sort of thing that sometimes gets said without too much evidence to back it up. She definitely made them for Donald Campbell, though – the Bluebird man who held the land and water speed records simultaneously and died in that terrible crash on Coniston Water – which is no less impressive in a way, as Campbell was renowned for enjoying the good things in life, and no doubt knew a nice bit of fur when he saw it.

This is probably as good a moment as any to tell the story of my childhood brush with another snappy dresser: Ronnie Kray. I think how my dad knew the twins was that when they were kids they'd all boxed at the New Lansdowne, a club on Mare Street in Hackney which my granddad Toffy was on the board of. Reg and Ron were actually pretty good boxers before other more nefarious activities began to take precedence.

I was still a baby the day Ronnie Kray came round to Caistor Park Road to see my dad, but I've been told this story so many times that I can see it unfolding in my head. Obviously everyone's on their best behaviour, but then Ronnie picks me up, and by all accounts I've pissed all over him. He's got a new Mac on, which has probably cost a few bob, and I've absolutely covered it. Everyone's laughing. Well, not at first. At first they're all thinking, 'Fucking hell, he's pissed on

Ronnie Kray!' But then Ronnie cracks up, so everyone else knows it's safe to join in.

Cups of tea get drunk, and him and my dad have a talk about whatever it is they need to talk about, and then everyone breathes a sigh of relief when Ronnie leaves. The Kray brothers hadn't yet reached the peak of their notoriety by that time, but people still knew who they were. The funny thing was that earlier on the same day my dad had got in a row with a bloke who lived up the road, and after Ronnie fucked off to get his coat dry-cleaned, this guy came round going, 'Look, we've only had an argument – there's no need to bring them into it.' Obviously there was no way my dad would ever have done that. If he needed to have a fight with a bloke up the road, he was quite capable of doing that on his own initiative, without calling in the Krays for back-up.

Readers are entitled to a measure of curiosity about what mutually advantageous business Ron and Ray might have been discussing. There was a time while I was still very young when my dad was possibly up to all sorts, with or without Ron and Reg, but I think something happened that he didn't like when he was out with them in Walthamstow once. He only told me this years later – and even then in quite a cryptic, Edwardian kind of way – but I think my dad saw someone get stabbed, fairly brutally, and he just thought it was unnecessary. When is that kind of violence ever anything else? But for my dad I think that was the moment he thought, 'Not only is this wrong, but also it ain't for me.'

He wasn't going to be joining the Salvation Army any time soon, but from the time I was old enough to remember, he was mostly working on the markets. Not only my dad's two brothers but also most of his friends seemed to work in either the meat market, the fish market or the fruit market, so we never went hungry. My dad started off on the meat at Smithfield Market, but then moved to fruit and veg. Either he got caught nicking something, or they were trying to guarantee the family a balanced diet (given that his brother Kenny already had a butcher's).

There was a fair bit of ducking and diving going on in those days. It still wasn't long since the end of the war, and people needed a bit of a lift – especially as even though we'd won, we seemed to be re-building places like Berlin and Munich (which had admittedly been smashed to pieces) before we got started on our own cities. At that time people reckoned that the best job was the bread round, because you'd get your wage and pay your little bit of tax – whatever that was at the time – but you'd also have your own bread. That was your bunce. It was allowed. The company knew it went on but turned a blind eye, and the bread-man lived a good life.

It was the same on the docks, where a few of my dad's friends who didn't work on the markets seemed to earn a crust. There they even had a name for it: 'spillage'. A box would get dropped, and whatever the contents were, the people working there were allowed to keep. I suppose that kind of thing would be looked upon as theft today, but I prefer to think of it as 'garnish' – that little something extra which meant we didn't go hungry and always had a shirt on our back and shoes on our feet.

My dad's eldest brother Charlie was doing a little bit better than that. He'd got a job in the print when he was younger. Those jobs were so well paid that what they used to do was sub them out – some geezer would give you half his wage if you let him take over from you, and that gave you money to go and do something else. Charlie went on to own his own factory which upholstered settees. He was very generous and would always give us a ten-bob note every time we saw him. He usually had nice cars as well – often those big old

Rovers that look like Bristols – and he'd let my dad borrow them sometimes if we were going somewhere nice.

I think Maud and Toffy might've lost as many as three kids (ages ranging from infant to young child, and at least one of them to whooping cough, which was rife at the time) to leave them with just the three boys and my auntie Irene. That was the main reason people had bigger families in those days – to cover themselves, because you were probably going to lose a few.

Laura and I had plenty of other 'uncles' who weren't genetically our uncles to make up the numbers. A lot of them worked in the fish market at Billingsgate, like Frankie Tovey, who was a Catholic, and Ronnie Jacobs, who was Jewish. We were Church of England, but people's religious denomination was something you only tended to find out about later in life. Like with my best mate Tony Yeates: even though we basically grew up together from my mid-teens onwards, I only found out he was a Catholic when he got married. No one ever knew, and I think London's always been a bit like that. It's one of the great things about it in a way. Basically, who gives a fuck?

It was the same with the mate of my dad's who everyone thought was gay. He was a terrific guy, always immaculately turned out, and all the girls loved him, but no one ever worried about who he was having sex with. I'm talking about a load of hairy-arsed geezers here who didn't give a fuck for anyone. They were the chaps – out pulling birds and doing what they were doing – and what my dad's mate got up to on his own time just wasn't a problem for them. When someone's your mate, they're your mate, and that's all there is to it.

I found out some interesting things about the situation with homosexuality in old London – and sexuality in general – when I was making that TV show about Hannah Durham. It turned out that people in those times were much less prudish than we tend to think of them as being, and than we are now. It was only towards the end of the Victorian era that everyone started to get more buttoned up.

In terms of public life, everything was still pretty much under wraps by the fifties, but looking back at the way my dad's friend was accepted by my dad and his mates, it gives you a fresh perspective on people who weren't necessarily highly educated. They weren't moving in the supposedly enlightened circles of the art or literary worlds. These were geezers who worked in markets and had their own street education and would often be presented as quite brutal – shouting 'Fucking poof' at Quentin Crisp in TV dramas or whatever – so it's quite refreshing to realise that they weren't always like that. In fact, it was a shame the people who actually had power in the country weren't as tolerant as my dad and his mates. People who come from where I come from don't get to make the laws, we just get to break them.

There was a tradition on my dad's side of our family of naming eldest sons after their father, so my uncle Charlie's son got called Charlie boy. My dad – as those of you who are on the ball will already have noticed – was Ray, so a lot of my relatives used to (and still do sometimes) call me 'Ray-Ray' to differentiate between us. When I got a bit older, my dad's mates also used to know me as 'Little Sugs', because his nickname was 'Sugar', in honour of the great Sugar Ray Robinson.

There were signs from very early on that I was going to carry on the family's pugilistic tradition. The nursery school I went to was up on the main road on the way to Stratford. I got suspended from it once for having a fight with another kid on a climbing frame. It was only a skirmish, and I don't think I was a generally disruptive presence, although you probably won't be surprised to hear that this was not to be the last educational establishment I would be suspended or expelled from.

I loved that place, though. They used to get us all to lie down and have a kip in the afternoon, and you didn't just get free milk in a little bottle, you got orange juice as well. The only other thing I remember really clearly was that every kid was allocated their own special decorated peg for putting your coat on, and mine was a camel – probably because I always had the hump.

CHAPTER 3

PORTWAY SCHOOL

Our house was a happy house, and it was also a loud house – in good times and in bad. Sometimes there'd be rows, and sometimes there'd be parties, but Sunday mornings were always the same. Dad would go out and get the bagels, and then Laura and I would get into his and mum's bed while she did the breakfast. We had a little pink-and-white Pye record player, and we'd listen to some Frank Sinatra, Jack Jones or Judy Garland on it while Dad read the papers. Then after breakfast we'd get smartened up in our best clothes and head over to Hackney to see the grandparents.

At other times, the family would come to us. When we were in Plaistow, we always used to have a big party on Bonfire Night. My dad's brothers and sister would come round with their kids and we'd make a load of noise in the garden. All the fireworks would be kept in the outside toilet to keep them dry and warm. One time, Uncle Charlie went in there for a more traditional purpose and a Jumping Jack went under the door. We heard a kerfuffle inside and everyone was laughing, then out came Uncle Charlie swearing and running round the garden. The Jumping Jack was in his trousers. He was lucky he'd come out the door because you wouldn't want that blowing up in a confined space.

Another evening – I want to think of it as the same night but it would almost certainly have been a different one – the party was in full flow when a policeman turned up, on a motorbike, wearing one of the old strap helmets like in *The Blue Lamp*. He knocked on the door and asked for Sugar – all the local coppers knew my dad's nickname, not least because about nine out of ten Old Bill in those days came from the area they policed – then told him there'd been a complaint about the noise. This was unusual so it must've been loud. My dad was very polite about it, and invited the copper in and gave him a drink, and by the end of the night he was giving all the girls rides up and down the street on his motorbike.

They were good times, but it was one law for the law and another for me, as my dad would never let me ride a pushbike, let alone a motorbike. I've been a bit the same with my girls – I'll let them ride a bicycle in the garden, but not outside. (Obviously Lois and Jaime are all grown up now, so I can't stop them going out into the world without stabilisers, but Ellie-Rae is only twelve, so she still has to do things my way.) It wasn't an irrational fear on my dad's part – he'd seen a guy on a bike get his wheel stuck in a tram line on Stratford Broadway once, and the tram had done him.

I remember one tricky moment when my dad came out of the house and saw me riding a mate's bike round the corner. I jumped off it and came charging back up the road, vaulting over everyone's fences to come out behind him on our front path, but I still got a clip round the ear to send me back inside. Those little patches out the front of the houses in Caistor Park Road are nearly all gravelled over now, but in the early sixties there were a lot more postage stamp-sized patches of grass.

Once The Beatles had come along, you'd find us standing between the hedges with our plastic guitars and Beatle wigs on, singing 'She Loves You' and making out we were John, Paul, George or Ringo. Another one of my favourite activities was watching the mods and rockers go roaring down the road like the Lancaster Bombers I used to make Airfix kits of.

All the mods seemed to live on our street, and all the rockers came from the next one down (close enough for me to know how wide of the mark my wardrobe of leathers and Liberace haircut was in *Quadrophenia* fifteen years or so later). They were all mates and they'd all been in the same class at school, but they'd get together to go to Margate or Southend and have a fight on a bank holiday, then for the rest of the year it would all be forgotten.

In terms of historic events which made an impact on people, the one that springs to mind for me is the one that springs to mind for most people, but maybe not for the same reason. Even though I was only six years old at the time, I can clearly remember what I was doing when the news of John F. Kennedy's death broke in November 1963 – I was wondering what all the fuss was about.

Obviously it was sad for him and his family, but I couldn't understand why grown adults were breaking down in tears in the street over something that didn't really have too much to do with them, because he was a Yank. For some reason, everyone seemed to see it as being their business. I suppose because he was young and well liked, and people thought of him as more of a celebrity than a politician.

By then I'd left the afternoon kips and free orange juice of nursery behind for the relatively grown-up world of Portway Primary School. As a kid I never thought of it being 'Portway' as in 'you're on the way to the port' – that's the kind of connection which is lodged so deep in your mind it doesn't really occur to you. And by the time I would've been old enough to get them, those jobs in the docks that might once have been waiting for me had all gone.

You can't be hanging around the gates of your old primary school for too long at my age or people will think you're a nonce. But it made me laugh to retrace the footsteps of my walk to school again all these years later – at the time it felt like miles and miles, but in fact it was only a couple of hundred yards. A little group of us used to assemble on the way down there in the morning, and we'd usually meet up with a mate who had a glass eye. His mum used to let us watch her put it in – you can't believe how much space there is in the socket at the back of the eye – and it used to roll around all over the place until it settled in position.

He'd got his real eye poked out by the spoke of an old bicycle wheel on a bombsite on the main road. With the city to the west and the docks to the south, East London had taken a belting during the Blitz – anything the German bombers had left, they unloaded on us on their way home.

Of course we always won in the endless re-run of the Battle of Britain that was being staged by the Airfix kits hanging from my ceiling, but the fabric of the place I grew up in was definitely holed. If the spaces in the city that the bombsites opened up were the war's legacy to young Londoners, it was our duty to make the most of them. Everyone knew they could be dangerous places which we weren't really meant to hang around in, and that was half the appeal.

A copper caught me messing about in one when I was five or six, and took me straight back to 'Sugar's house', where the punishment for my crime was to be kicked straight upstairs to bed and grounded for a week. It's not just your family, friends and neighbours keeping an eye on you which helps set you on the right road as a kid. If policemen, teachers and doctors know where everyone lives too, that helps you grow up with a sense of being part of a community, rather than just a mass of disconnected individuals. Not that this would stop me getting into a fair amount of mischief, obviously.

Another time when I was messing around on a bombsite I found this big kind of metal torch. I think I'd just watched *Spartacus*, so I knew what to do – I got hold of a box of matches and tried to set fire to some straw in it. Nothing's more interesting to you as a kid than fire, because there's such a big warning sign over it as far as adults are concerned. Unfortunately on this occasion things got a bit more interesting than I'd intended, as some of the flaming straw fell down and set fire to a chair. I was shitting myself after that – every time we walked past that bombsite I thought the police were after me. And the next few times I went shopping with my mum I'd duck down in the seat of the car if a police car came past, which I suppose was good training for later life.

All the bombsites are gone from Plaistow now, but you can still see where they once were from where the houses stop. A little block of flats in the middle of a terrace is always a tell-tale sign, and where the gaps have been filled in it's like the street has got false teeth.

Not all the memories prompted by seeing my old primary school again are happy ones. Quite early on in my time there I got six of the best across the arse for throwing stones up in the air. OK, one came down and hit another kid on the head, but he wasn't badly hurt, and it was obviously an accident. The headmaster wasn't having any of it though, and he gave me a caning I can still remember to this day. I was absolutely terrified to tell my mum and dad, and the fact that the weals only came to light because my mum was bathing me shows you how young I was.

She asked what had happened so I had to tell her. When my dad found out he went round to the school to hear the headmaster's side of the story. He sat down calmly and listened to his explanation, then when the teacher had finished talking he said, 'So let me get this straight. My boy is five years old, and you've given him six hard wallops across the arse for something he didn't even mean to do?'

I'm not exactly sure what happened next but the impression I got was it was something along the lines of my dad forcing the teacher's head down onto the desk and trying to shove his cane down his throat. Either way, the headmaster never looked at me again, which was a result as far as I was concerned. I did get caned a few times over the years, and sometimes I deserved it, but that one was a fucking liberty.

When you're five or six years old, the boundaries of your world are very clearly defined. Going somewhere in the car was fine, but if I ever walked further than the school, it was like you were Christopher Columbus and didn't know if you were going to fall off the edge of the world.

Apart from Sunday trips over to Hackney to see Maud and Toffy, the main excursion we used to go on would be out of London to see Nanny Rich, Reg Hallett, Auntie Olive and Uncle Len in Shoeburyness. Those drives along the old Southend road seemed to go on forever, and there were three trips which particularly stuck in my mind.

My dad had an old Austin van. If we were all going to squeeze into it, I usually ended up sitting over the engine, between the passenger seat and the driver, which was not so great in the summer. But in the winter I'd be the only one who was warm, especially while the van was lacking a back window, as happened for a while after it got smashed. One time we were driving east in thick snow when the car broke down near the Halfway House pub. Obviously you couldn't just call the AA on your mobile in those days and there wasn't a heater you could put on in the car, so we were absolutely freezing.

I can't actually remember who rescued us on that occasion, but another time we didn't make it all the way to Nanny Rich's house was when we hit a Labrador which ran out in front of us. The dog flew up in the air and came down in the road with a horrible smack, then just got up, shook itself and ran away, apparently none the worse for the impact. We were alright too – just a bit shocked – but my dad's van was not so lucky. The front of it was severely smashed to pieces and there was steam coming out of the radiator, so we had to wait till someone we didn't know stopped to help us. When this guy found out what had happened, he ended up giving me, Mum and Laura a lift all the way back to Plaistow.

That wouldn't happen now apart from anything else, a woman would be frightened of taking their kids in a car with a stranger – but the geezer genuinely wanted to help and there was a different mentality in those days. I'm not saying there weren't evil fuckers about, because there were, but everyone wasn't so primed by the media always to be thinking about the worst thing that could possibly happen. We didn't have that same fear factor we do now everyone's got Sky News.

In my memory, that change in people's thinking wasn't something that happened gradually. It happened more or less overnight when everyone found out about the Moors Murders. I'm not saying children hadn't been taken away and killed before, but it wasn't something people ever really thought about until Brady and Hindley put it in their heads. In a way, taking away that freedom for parents and children to live without fear was another crime that they committed. Even though it happened all the way up north in the hills outside Manchester, it was such a horrific case and it scared everyone so much that it might as well have happened just up the road. When we got up the next morning after it had been on the news, the streets of East London were empty. A lot of the old freedoms that we used to enjoy had gone out of the window overnight. I must have been eight at the time.

It was a dangerous old road, that one out to Southend. The third – and most dramatic – of the incidents I remember from those drives was the time we drove past a big car crash. There were police everywhere, and as we approached what appeared to be a fair amount of carnage, my mum said, 'Don't look.' Obviously that's the worst thing you can say to a kid – it's right up there with 'Never play with matches'. So by the time we drew level with the scene of the accident, Laura and I both had our faces glued to the window.

I've never forgotten what happened next. Things kind of went into slow motion, as they always seem to at moments of crisis. I suppose it's your body's way of protecting you – the adrenaline speeds up your brain, so whatever else is happening seems to slow down in comparison, which (in theory at least) gives you more time to respond. That's why when we've seen something really horrible, we usually remember every unfolding detail, because it's like we've recorded it so fast that when we try to play it back at normal speed it comes to us in slow motion. Anyway, as we drove past the wrecked car, the back door swung open and a body fell out. I hoped she wasn't dead, but the absent look in that woman's eyes has stayed with me ever since, and there was someone else in the car who looked in a bad way too.

As I'm describing this, I'm realising that it sounds quite like the car-crash sequence in David Lynch's *Wild at Heart*, and probably loads of other films as well. When something shocking's happened to someone and they say it was 'like being in a film', they usually mean it was out of the ordinary. But the reason things happen the way they do on the screen is because a lot of people have got together and done their best to create the illusion of what it actually would be like. So it's no wonder we use those kinds of scenes as a way of understanding reality and distancing ourselves from it at the same time.

I've had similar experiences several times since, of being a witness to really bad things happening. I'm not saying I see dead people like the little boy in *The Sixth Sense* (although I did look a bit like him as a kid), but knowing what death is does change you as a person. And I can understand what they say about people who see a lot of it – whether they be soldiers or doctors, policemen or undertakers – finding that their emotional responses start to close down. We use the word 'deadened' for a reason.

It's the same with me and violence, which I've seen a fair amount of over the years. I've never liked it – and I've liked it less and less as I've grown older – but it doesn't shock me either. I don't see it happen and think, 'Oh, what was that?' I know exactly what it is, and, to a certain extent, I understand it.

CHAPTER 4

THE ODEON,
EAST HAM

When we first arrived there, in the late fifties, Plaistow was in Essex, which used to reach as far into London as Stratford. But from the day they changed all the boundaries around (1 April 1965, and I think we know who the April Fools were – us), the Essex border got pushed back to Ilford, and Plaistow was bundled up with East and West Ham to become part of the Frankenstein London borough of Newham. Why? What did they want to go and do that for?

Essex is one of the great counties of England. You just have to say the name to know what sense it makes: Wessex was to the west and Essex is to the east, with Middlesex somewhere in the middle. But some soppy cunt who sits in a council office somewhere has a bright idea, and all of a sudden something which has worked very well for hundreds of years has got to change, just so he or she can pat themselves on the back for inventing 'Newham'.

Ever since I was a little kid, I've always been really interested in the mythology of East London – the kind of stories which might or might not be true, but which help to define the character of the place either way. One of my mum and dad's best friends was a Merchant Navy man who we called Uncle Tony. I learnt a lot from him – he told me all about his voyages round the world as a young man, which probably helped encourage me to want to travel, as that wasn't something people in my family had tended to do much before. He also had a lot of great stories about the games they used to play in the docks.

For instance, there was one fella whose party piece was to bite the head off a rat. Everyone would bet on whether he could do it or not, then he'd get the rat and put his mouth all around its neck . . . apparently the secret was that you had to do it cleanly, just pull it by the tail and the backbone would come out. Now I'm not recommending anyone try that at home, but being a kid of six or seven and listening to a story like that is certainly going to have an impact on you. As I grew older I loved all the tales about 'spillage' – for some reason, the closer you got to Christmas, crates of whisky would get harder to keep a firm hold of – and the canniness of the docklands characters.

There was one about a geezer who owned a pub that used to do lock-ins for the dockers. They'd stay in there all night and then when it got light the next morning they'd go out and go to work. Obviously he didn't want them to leave, so first he took all the clocks out and then he painted the windows black. They're all in there having a booze up and since it never gets light, he's got them in there forever. Looking at that written down, it seems more like a fairy tale than something which actually happened, but I love the dividing line where something would be on the edge of being made up for the sake of the story.

When I was a bit older and started going to Spitalfields Market with my dad, people used to tell me how all the bollards around Gun

Street and through the old city of London were made from the old cannon that had helped us win the battles of Trafalgar and Waterloo. Now I don't know if that was true or not, but either way it gave me a sense of the history of the place. And if we had any reason to be down in the Shadwell or Wapping areas – where the Ratcliff Highway murders took place more than 200 years ago – I'd usually get told how if you'd gone down there at that time it was like some kind of zoo, because sailors would bring back baby giraffes or lions or monkeys as pets, and by the time they'd get them home they'd be fully grown.

Even as a small boy, I was never averse to a bit of make-believe. I had two little girlfriends called Kim and Tracey who lived just up the road from me. They were twins, and we used to play doctors and nurses together (I think I peaked too soon as a ladies' man). I was always the soldier who came back from the war injured and they had to kiss me better. That was where it all started for me as far as acting was concerned.

Another place that helped incubate the bug was the Odeon, East Ham. There were a couple of local cinemas we used to go to, but this was the main one – it was just near the Boleyn Pub as you go around the West Ham football ground. Do a left onto the Barking road at the end of Green Street and you're there, down by the pie and mash shop (which we never ate at, because my dad hated pie and mash almost as much as he hated the Salvation Army).

It was a beautiful cinema which had opened just before the Second World War with a live show called *Thank Evans* starring Max Miller. You'd go in and the organ would come up from the floor and you'd all have a little sing-song. Then you'd get the B-movie before the main picture – you weren't just in there for a couple of hours, it was the whole afternoon. The first film I ever went to there was *101 Dalmatians*, which came out in 1961, so I must have been four.

My mum took me, and by all accounts I got quite angry with Cruella deVil, because she was bullying the doggies. Apparently I got out of my seat and ran down the aisle towards the screen waving my fists and shouting 'Cruella de Vil, leave them puppies alone!' I don't actually remember doing this myself – the red mist must've really come down – but Mum told the story so many times I can't forget that it happened.

The slant she put on this incident was that I was so trappy as a kid that I 'even wanted to have a fight with a cartoon'. With hindsight I suppose you could also take it as evidence of how willing I was to get caught up in a drama even then.

Although my mum was the first person who ever took me to the cinema, my dad soon took over the reins. Obviously he had to rise very early to work on the markets. The upside of that was that he tended to be free in the afternoons, and every Wednesday from the age of five onwards he'd pick first me and later me and Laura up from Portway and take us to the pictures. There's a few stories later on that'll show Ray Winstone Senior's harder side, but he was a great dad to us, and I might not be doing what I am now if he'd decided to go down the pub instead of taking his kids to the cinema every week.

Of course, part of his motivation was that he fancied an afternoon kip, but if it was a good film – like 633 Squadron – he'd stay awake to watch it. I remember him falling asleep in Jason and the Argonauts, though, and by the time he'd woken up I'd watched it all the way through twice. We used to see some pretty adult films given how young I was, but the only one I ever remember us being turned away from was a war film called Hell is for Heroes with Steve McQueen and James Coburn in it. I think it was an X, which at the time meant sixteen and over, and I remember the ticket-seller (who knew us) very politely telling my dad, 'Sorry, Ray, your boy can't come in.' With hindsight, I can't really fault the guy from the Odeon for that. It is quite a violent film – especially the bit where the guy gets shot and you see his glasses crack – and I was only five years old.

Going to the movies wasn't just a local thing. About once a month, usually on a Sunday afternoon, we'd go up the West End. Cinerama was a big draw then, and we'd go and see big, grown-up films like *Lawrence of Arabia* or *Becket* with O'Toole and Burton – which I loved, even though I was only seven when I first saw it.

My nan and granddad took me to see *How the West was Won* in 70mm, and I had the poster up on my wall with a big map of America and pictures of Annie Oakley on it. Even though grand historical epics were the films I felt most strongly drawn to, I liked stuff that was meant for kids as well. Probably my favourite film of all when I was a youngster was *Mary Poppins*. Where else do you think I got the accent from?

The Sound of Music was good as well – that was definitely one for the West End.

The only small dampener on going to the cinema with the whole family was Laura saying, 'I wanna go toilet.' Sometimes she wouldn't even last till halfway through, and because Mum would have to take her, we'd all have to stand up so they could make their way out into the aisle.

Even though we went up West regularly, sometimes it felt like people there would dig us out a bit. The first time we saw *Zulu* was one of those occasions. It's probably the best film ever, and I know it more or less off by heart now, but the day we went up to Leicester Square to see it has stuck in my mind for a different reason. It's one of the earliest memories I have of people trying to make us feel like we weren't good enough to be somewhere.

We're all sat down, we've got our popcorn, sweets and drinks, and the music's playing. The film hasn't started – I don't think the trailers have even started – and obviously there are a few crackling noises as the bags are opening. But this woman sitting behind us with her Old Man almost barks at us, 'Could you keep the noise down, please?' My mum twists round with a polite half-shrug and explains, 'The film hasn't started yet, darlin' – we're just opening the popcorn and some sweets for the kids.'

Obviously a few more sweet-wrappers get rustled over the next couple of minutes, but no one's making a noise deliberately, and it's still a while before the film's due to start. But the woman can't help herself – she decides to have another go. This time she practically hisses, 'Keep the noise down', and the 'please' is nowhere to be heard. Now my mum's had enough. She stands up, turns round to look the woman straight in the eye and says, 'Do yourself a favour, love, or you'll be wearing it.'

At that point, the pair of them got up and moved. My dad hadn't even said anything – because it was a woman causing the trouble and he would never have a go at a woman. He was probably waiting for the bloke to start and then it would really have gone off. I clearly remember the feeling of 'Oh, sorry, are we not allowed to be here?' Just because we're off our manor, suddenly everyone's going to have something to say about it. This was a feeling I would grow quite familiar with over the years, not just in day-to-day life, but once I started acting as well.

As a small child looking up at that big screen, the idea that I might one day be up there myself would have seemed completely ridiculous. Of course a kid might say they'd 'like to be in a film', in the same way they might want to fly a space rocket or captain England at Wembley, but it wasn't something that was ever going to happen. One of the big differences in those days was you didn't have the Parkinsons or the Wossies – let alone the internet – so film stars were fantasy figures. That was your two hours of escape, and you believed who they were on the screen was who they were in real life.

That said, we did have one film star in the family already. My cousin Maureen, Charlie-boy's sister, was an extra in a Charlie Drake film once. It was set in the Barbican, which was where they lived at that time, and when the film came out we all had to go to the pictures to see Maureen in a big crowd of local kids chasing Charlie Drake down the road at the end. Good luck to anyone trying to get a load of local kids together for a crowd scene in the Barbican these days – you'd have to contact their agents first.

The Odeon East Ham's been through a few changes over the years as well – which one of us hasn't? The last film they showed with the place as an Odeon was Walt Disney's *Sleeping Beauty* in 1981, but then fourteen years later it reopened as the Boleyn Cinema, which was one of the biggest Bollywood cinemas in Britain. They'd have all the dancing films on, and I'd often go past it on the way to and from West Ham games. But when I went back there specially to have a nose around for this book, I saw it had closed down again. Who knows what'll happen next? Maybe someone will buy the place up and re-open it screening Polish art films . . . you never know.

Going back to the Plaistow area in 2014, there's no doubt about what the biggest change is: it's the shift in the ethnic backgrounds of the people who live there. In the space of a couple of generations, it's gone from being the almost entirely white neighbourhood my family moved into, to having the predominantly Asian feel that it undeniably does today. Anyone who thinks a population shift of that magnitude in that short a space of time isn't going to cause a few problems has probably never lived in a place where it's actually happened.

I remember the first black man who came to live on Caistor Park Road. He was a very smart old Jamaican gent who always wore a zoot suit and a hat with a little turn in it. In truth he probably wasn't all that old, he just seemed that way. But he was so novel to us that we just used to stare at him and sometimes even (and I realise this isn't something you'd encourage kids to do today) touch him for luck. He'd just smile and say, 'Hallo, children', in a broad Caribbean accent. He knew we didn't mean any harm by it – we were just kids who hadn't seen a black man before.

I say that, but in fact we had, in the familiar form of Kenny Lynch, who knew my dad. Lynchy had been on the fringes of my dad's world for a while – he was a regimental champion boxer in the Army and went on to have a few hit singles (as well as writing 'Sha La La La Lee' for Newham local heroes the Small Faces) and sing in the kinds of clubs that the Krays used to run – but I'm not sure if he really booked himself as a black man, or wanted anyone else to for that matter.

When the first West Indian and then Asian people moved in, people weren't worried about them; they were a novelty. But as more and more came, a feeling began to develop – particularly with regard to the new arrivals from Bangladesh and Pakistan – that they wanted to just stay in their own community rather than joining in with ours. That was what caused the problems: people sticking with their own.

In a way, you couldn't blame them. They tended to come more from rural areas and maybe had more of an adjustment to make to living in London – if someone from your village goes and lives half-way across the world and they're your mate, then if you do the same thing, it's inevitable you're going to want to join them. And under the pressure of trying to establish yourself in a new environment – especially when what makes you different is visible to all – it's only natural to close ranks. Looking back now, I can understand the fears they must have had, but there were fears on both sides – fear of losing jobs to people who would work longer hours for less money, fear of the manor you'd lived in all your life being taken away.

Going back to East and West Ham now, they're not just 'cosmo-politan', they're probably more Bangladeshi and Indian and Pakistani than they are anything else. The positive thing I can see happening in the playground of my old school is that maybe the younger gener-ation are kind of educating us. Whether one side is becoming more Anglicised or the other is becoming less so – or most likely a bit of both – what they've got to do is learn to meet in the middle.

Whatever happens, it's probably not going to be anything that hasn't happened along the banks of the River Thames plenty of times before. The other side of all those dockyard traditions that have always given the inner London section of the East End its exotic edge is that it's also always been the place that immigrants have come to first, whether that's meant the Huguenots or the Chinese or the Jews or the Hindus or the Muslims or the Poles or the Romanians. The docks might be gone now, but the tide still goes in and out.

CHAPTER 5

THE NEW
LANSDOWNE CLUB

The years just before and after our move away from Plaistow are marked out in my mind by three huge moments in football history. In May of 1964, West Ham won the FA Cup for the first time ever. Dad, Mum, Laura and I walked down the bottom of Caistor Park Road (in those days you could still get straight out onto Plaistow Road) for the parade.

They couldn't even afford a double-decker. West Ham's idea of an 'open-topped bus' in those days was sitting on the roof of a coach, but that didn't stop us having a great time. We blew all our bubbles and had a little party afterwards. You don't get many days like that (at least, West Ham fans don't) so it's best to make the most of them when they do come around.

A year later, the good times miraculously continued as West Ham won the UEFA Cup Winners' Cup at Wembley. My dad had been thinking of getting us tickets for that one, but sadly decided not to take me with him in the end because he thought I was a bit young to be in such a big crowd (he probably had a point, as almost a hundred thousand turned up to see us beat Munich 1860 2–0). We were only the second English team to win that competition. I can't remember who the first mob were.

Luckily, by the time the World Cup came round a year later, my dad had decided that at nine I was now old enough for Wembley. So he called in some favours from people he knew in the fruit and veg trade and we ended up getting tickets to every game England played. Full match reports are coming later in this chapter for anyone who doesn't know how the tournament ended. But before that, there's another landmark to be negotiated – nothing to rival Bobby Moore bringing the World Cup home in terms of historic significance, but an event which probably defined the course of the rest of my life.

If the Winstones had just stayed in Plaistow, that probably would've been it for me for the duration. But in the year between those two Wembley finals our family had made a move which brought us much closer to the twin towers, but took us what felt like a long way from the place I'd always thought of as home (and probably continue to think of that way, despite all physical evidence to the contrary). It's not like my dad sat us down and told us we were moving to Australia – it was only Enfield, or to be more precise 336 Church Street, on the Winchmore Hill side of the A10 – but it might as well have been the furthest shores of the Antipodes as far as I was concerned.

North London is a foreign country, they do things differently there. I couldn't really even book Enfield as being in London, any-way (it is now, but then it felt more like Middlesex). From being a kid with a very clear idea of who I was and where I belonged, I sud-denly found myself moving to another place where the only things anyone at my new school knew about me were that my accent was different, I didn't really have any friends, and I seemed to be a couple of years behind where I should've been with my education.

I don't think I was fully dyslexic, but when I wrote something my eyes tended to move around the page, and I'd have to check over what I'd done at the end to make sure that the thought which had left my mind had actually reached the paper. It's the same with emails even now – I have to go through them at the end to make sure I haven't got distracted and left something out. I wasn't a great one for reading at school, either, and it's probably only having to learn scripts that has brought my spelling up to a level where I can just about get by.

As a defence mechanism to protect me from the things about my new life that I was finding difficult, I became a bit of an inverted snob. In my eight-year-old mind, I was a proper Plaistow geezer and all this country-bumpkin business wasn't for me, but that probably made life more difficult rather than easier. It's hard for any kid to move away from their mates and everything they know and love, and when you go into school for the first few times, you just feel like an alien. I'm not saying I know what someone who comes here from Poland or Pakistan goes through, because obviously the language is more of a factor there (although they do talk funny in Enfield), but if there'd been a ready-made community of East End kids for me to join up with at my new school, I'd have been in there in the blink of an eye.

I know what you're thinking: 'Enough of this bollocks about you being a sensitive cockney flower that should never have been trans-planted up the A10, Ray, just tell us about the football.' The great thing about going to the 1966 World Cup was that even though my dad managed to get two tickets for every game, he made it a surprise every time. It was really good of him to take me because deep down he wasn't even that much of a football fan – he'd supported Arsenal when he was younger, so he can't have been.

43

A lot of people of my age or older will tell you that their memories of these matches are in black and white, because that's how they saw the games on TV at the time. My recollections are a strange mixture of Technicolor from actually being there – the light blue of Uruguay's kit, or the green of Mexico's – overlaid with the monochrome of endless subsequent viewings. The commentaries have seeped in too at some key moments, even though I only heard them afterwards.

The first game was Uruguay at Wembley. Geoff Hurst didn't play, but I've got a feeling Greavesie did. He was a fantastic player, and we had Terry Payne from Southampton on the wing, but that didn't stop it being a boring 0–0. England weren't expected to do too much in the World Cup and Uruguay were a tough nut to crack.

The one thing I'll never forget about that day is, you know how at the beginning of the game they'll have all the teams coming out represented by schoolchildren as mascots? With the World Cup now it'll be all fireworks going off and balloons going up, someone sings a song and it's a big show. But then it was just a few kids coming out with sticks – like people would use to make a banner for protesting outside an embassy – with the name of the team written at right angles on a piece of wood.

My dad bought me a 'World Cup Willie' pennant and also a West Ham one which I've still got to this day. With those lucky charms in place, the following two games went much better. Bobby Charlton scored a screamer against Mexico, and Roger Hunt got one too, then Hunt scored both our goals against France.

Next up were Argentina. Geoff Hurst played in that one and Antonio Rattín got sent off. We did well to hold our tempers as Argentina were scrapping like animals, but then Bobby Moore put the ball down quickly and flicked it up for Geoff Hurst to nut it in, and Argentina were history. It was almost like a dress rehearsal for our first goal in the final. By then a measure of optimism had really started to take hold, but Eusébio's Portugal were still favourites to knock us out in the semis. They were blitzing everyone, but Geoff Hurst and Bobby Charlton both scored and now England were in the final.

When that great day came I had more than a vague idea of what being 1–0 down to the German machine meant, because I could still feel the clip round the earhole I'd got off the copper for playing in one of the bombsites they'd left. There was a lot of historical friction and a real sense of them being the old enemy, so going 2–1 up just set you up for the emotional sucker punch of them equalising. I remember almost crying when they pulled that goal back which wouldn't have been the done thing then, although you see dads doing it as well as kids on *Match of the Day* all the time now.

The sense of pride when we finally did them at the end of extra time was amazing (that's where the voice of Kenneth Wolstenholme butts in, even though I wasn't listening to him at the time), especially as three of the most important members of the team – the captain Bobby Moore, Geoff Hurst who scored a hat-trick and Martin Peters who scored the other goal – were West Ham heroes. To see Bobby Moore holding up the trophy with his chest puffed out at the end of that gruelling game was an experience I'll never forget.

The funny thing is that when you're nine years old, the euphoria of actually being World Champions seems perfectly natural. We're British and we won the war, so it's sort of expected that we should win the World Cup as well. Forty-eight years later, I can look back on that feeling from a more worldly-wise perspective. I suppose the era I was brought up in was basically the end of the British Empire, but we still felt like a force in the world. We had The Beatles, we had the World Cup. We were kind of alright.

Times were still hard for a lot of people, but the economy was doing pretty well. Our family's improving situation was probably a good example of the way people from working-class backgrounds could get on in the mid-sixties. Although I was pissed off to have had to leave Plaistow, I had a lot to be thankful for.

We'd moved into a really nice four-bedroom George Reid house. My parents had paid four and a half grand for it, which was a lot of money at a time when the average weekly wage wasn't much more than £16. It was the equivalent of buying a house for £750,000 today, which was obviously a bit of a stretch, but my mum and dad were, for the moment at least, on a much sounder financial footing than they had been. On top of that, they'd gone thoroughly legit.

Ever since the nasty incident in Walthamstow with the Kray brothers, my dad had backed away from the ducking-and-diving side of things. That can't have been easy, because there was quite a romantic image to it in those days, but I think there comes a time when you've got a family that you don't want to be shitting yourself every time there's a knock on the door. He stepped back from all the other bollocks and concentrated on going to work, to the point where he'd been able to step up to running his own grocer's.

His first shop was in Bush Hill Parade, just outside Enfield, which was why we ended up moving there. The impetus for the move came from Mum. She'd got Nanny Rich's genes after all. Whereas my dad – no disrespect to him – was quite set in his ways, and if left to his own devices might have been happy staying in a council flat in Hackney all his life. Although I didn't know this at the time, my sister told me recently that my mum just sold our home in Plaistow without asking him. Some blokes came around making offers on a lot of people's houses for buy-to-let and she just turned it over to them and went off and picked out the house in Enfield without saying a word to Dad. Then again, if she had asked him, he probably would've said no.

Either way, Mum was the motivator, and even though I wasn't too happy about the move at the time, there was no denying we'd gone up in the world. We had a nice bit of garden now, and after we'd been in Enfield for a few years we got a bar installed in the front room – the forerunner of Raymondo's, whose doors are still always open in my house to this day – with one of those Bobby Moore World Cup ice buckets. Everyone had one of those, or at least every West Ham fan did. Bobby was standing on the brown-coloured ball holding the World Cup, then you'd lift him up and all your ice would be in there.

We got a dog as well. He was a Boxer (I suppose that ran in the family) called Brandy. He was soppy as a bag of bollocks with us – you could do what you liked with him – but if anyone else came within range, he'd mullah 'em, even when he got so old he only had one tooth left.

They say your porn name is your first pet and the first street you can remember, which makes mine 'Brandy Caistor'. I reckon I'd do alright with that, then if I wanted to redefine myself as an actress and go a bit respectable later on in my career, I could always change it to 'Brandy Caistor-Park', which sounds much more distinguished. Brandy was a clever old bastard as well. The dustmen used to tease him in the alley where the bins were, so he worked out how to back up and make it look like his lead was tighter than it was, then when the dustman came to torment him, Brandy had him on the penny and gave him a right good biting.

When we'd lived in Plaistow, one of the things I'd liked doing best was driving over to Hackney to see Maud and Toffy on a Sunday. There were all sorts of different cars we'd go in – they weren't necessarily ours. In those days if you wanted a car, you just had one. You could do that then – thank God you can't any more, because I don't want anyone just taking mine. One of my dad's cars (well, I say it was his . . . we certainly used it a lot) – a black Ford Zephyr – ended up in a pond at Victoria Park once after someone had nicked it and used it on a blag.

We'd jump in the car (whichever one it was) all suited up and looking nice to go off and meet the cousins while Mum would stay at home and cook the dinner. Even the mums who wore the trousers had to miss out on a lot of fun in those days, on account of their place still being in the home. My aunties Irene, Barbara (Charlie's wife) and Joycie (Kenny's wife) would all be back in their kitchens cooking up a storm, while their kids Scott, Spencer and Becky, Charlie and Maureen, and Tracey and Melanie came down to Hackney to meet us.

We'd go up to the flats first to see Granddad and Nanny. Obviously she'd have to stay at home to cook the dinner as well, so it would just be Toffy who came down to the New Lansdowne Club with us. It was a proper old East End gaff – a working men's club with a snooker table and a boxing gym. My granddad had been on the committee so he had a lot of mates there, like Archie who could hit you with either hand. A few of them and maybe some of Charlie's pals would come and join us until there was quite a gathering.

All the fellas would have a drink and a chat and the kids'd be fucking about and getting up to mischief, messing around on the drumkit. Someone might even get up and sing a song – me and my sister would do 'Cinderella Rockefella' or Sonny and Cher's 'I Got You, Babe', and one of the uncles might give us a bit of Sinatra. Then we'd all head home in time for our separate Sunday dinners at three or four in the afternoon – there was never too much traffic on the roads on a Sunday.

I had a few tussles at the Lansdowne with my cousin Charlie's sister Maureen, who was a couple of years older than us and even trappier than I was. She's my cousin and I love her to death, but we did used to bicker a lot. That said, I remember one time when we were visiting her mum and dad in the Barbican, and me and Charlie were getting bullied by a gang of older kids, Maureen went and sorted them all out – shut them right up with a couple of swift right-handers. It's a good job she wasn't born a geezer because then she'd have been even more dangerous.

After we'd moved, being in Enfield exile made those weekly trips to the Lansdowne something to look forward to even more. It wasn't actually much further to bomb down the A10 than it had been to drive over from Plaistow, anyway, and going there to see all the family felt like going home. When I went back to have a look at the old place again recently the building was still there – walk south down Mare Street past the Hackney Empire and the town hall and it's on your right – but there were boards up all around it.

I'm hoping someone's got some Lottery funds to restore it, because I know it had fallen into serious disrepair. There were a load of depressing photos online showing how it had been squatted by some junkies who'd made a horrible mess of the place, but you could still see the beautiful interior underneath. If I had the money, I'd do it up myself.

CHAPTER 6

THE CAGE, SPITALFIELDS MARKET

My new primary school in Enfield was called Raglan, and as I may already have mentioned – probably three or four times – I didn't like it much there at first. Things only began to look up once I got into the school football team. We were a pretty good little side and managed to get to a regional cup semi-final. We lost 2–1 in that but my mate Colin Bailey scored.

Even as young as nine or ten, I was already looking for any excuse to get back to East London. So when my dad asked me if I fancied getting up early and going down to Spitalfields Market with him before school, I jumped at the chance. It wasn't really to work at that age, it was more just to meet his mates – they'd all bring their boys down to see how life was and show them there's a great big world out there. This was at the time when he had the shop in Bush Hill Parade, so we'd be back for Dad to open it and for me to get to school. The other kids would be at home having their Ready Brek and I'd be down the market, drinking in the local colour – a commodity of which there was not a shortage, in fact 'colourful' is the politest word you'd use.

Spitalfields Market was as formative an educational experience as any boy could hope for. I used to shadow-box down there with a real gentleman called Sammy McCarthy, who had boxed as a pro and will turn up in the story again later on in somewhat less happy circumstances. There were a lot of old fighters around who my dad had known as kids, and I'd have a spar with them all. My dad's pal Archie Joyce's older brother Teddy would throw a few imaginary right hands for me to fend off, and that's when the 'Little Sugar' nickname really started to stick.

Another thing I loved down there was the special market coinage which you could only spend in A. Mays, the big shop on the corner. It came in triangles and 50p shapes, but before the 50p had even come out – I suppose they were tokens more than anything – and I saved loads of them when I was little. Until recently I still had thousands of them in boxes and tins in the garage that I was going to polish up and get framed, but then when I was having some work done at home the fucking geezer threw them on the fire and they all melted. I could've killed him.

The breakfast you'd have on that market early in the morning would taste better than you could get anywhere else on earth. To this day I still love a bacon roll – a good crusty white one with brown sauce in it – and the place we'd get them was the Blue Café. It's not there any more, but it was just up from Gun Street, along the south side of the market, and it was owned by Vic Andretti's dad Victor – we called him Uncle Victor. His son, who was a mate of my dad's, won a European boxing title, and gave me the gloves he wore, which still had the claret on 'em.

By coincidence it was outside Uncle Victor's café that I saw the longest street-fight I've ever seen in my life. Two fellas had what we used to call a 'straightener', which is like a formal stand-up bare-knuckle fight where someone's got a grievance and everyone backs off to let them sort it out. I know it sounds like I'm exaggerating – and I probably am a bit, because I was only a kid – but I swear this fight went on for twenty minutes. Now, that might not seem like a long time to you if you don't know anything about boxing, but if you think that even a fit professional fighter will be blowing after a three-minute round, then you can imagine that twenty minutes without a break feels like a lifetime.

Not that they didn't have the odd pause for breath, because when one of them knocked the other down, he'd stand and wait for his adversary to get back up. Every time someone got knocked over it was almost like the end of the round. There was no kicking anyone in the head or anything like that – it was all very courteous and old-fashioned. All the guys were standing round watching, and I was there with them, a small boy with a bacon roll.

By the time those two were done it didn't even seem to matter who won any more. At the end they both shook hands and went in the café to have a nice cup of tea, and everyone was clapping them and saying, 'Blinding fight.' Obviously this is a very romantic notion of what violence should be like, but that only made it more impressive to see it actually happen. In a strange way it was a beautiful thing to watch – two men just being men – but it was also pretty scary. I wasn't much more than ten years old at the time, and they were really going at it: I mean, this was a severe tear-up, but it was still some way short of being the most unnerving thing I saw happen in that market.

Across the way from the Blue Café was a place called 'the Cage', which was where all the big lorries pulled up to load in and load out. That was also where the methers – the tramps – used to burn the bushel boxes to keep warm. They'd all be sleeping around the fire in the winter with big old coats on. You don't see meths drinkers so much now – it's like it's gone out of fashion. I suppose they'd be crystal methers now. Maybe the news has finally broken that drinking methylated spirits is bad for you – I think the clue was in the way they coloured it blue and purple.

The meths drinkers used to have their own hierarchy, with different pitches and guv'nors who sometimes used to fall out among themselves and have a ruck. I don't know if it's still like that among the homeless today, but you're going to get that kind of thing going on wherever people are under pressure, and I don't suppose changing the intoxicant of choice will have ushered in a new era of peace and harmony.

My dad used to bring them in old coats and shoes sometimes, but you could guarantee that the next week they wouldn't have them any more, because they'd have sold them to buy meths. He wasn't the only one on the market who used to do this, either. Other people would bring them out a bacon sandwich or an egg roll. The methers did get looked after, they just didn't look after themselves.

I remember standing by the Cage once with my dad and Billy and Johnny Cambridge. They were two of his mates from over the water not the Irish Sea, the Thames – and they used to have a painted cab with horseshoes on it. Quite a few of the South London greengrocers were a bit gypsy-ish, and the Cambridges were wealthy fellas and grafters with it. I remember Billy having a row with a one-armed mether once – the geezer pointed to the stump where his arm used to be and said, 'If I still had that, boy, I'd put it on ya!'

Anyway, Billy and Johnny were nice guys, from a really good family. And we were just standing there having a fag (well, the men were – I'm not sure I'd've been allowed one at that age) when an articulated lorry drove into the Cage without looking carefully enough and ran straight over one of the tramp's legs in his sleeping bag. The worst part of it was, this old boy was so cold and rotten with meths that he never even woke up. Hopefully that meant he didn't feel the impact, but it was a horrible thing to see – never mind hear. He was still alive when they took him away in the ambulance, but he was in for a nasty surprise when he eventually woke up. I've had some pretty serious hangovers in my time, but nothing on quite that level.

Spitalfields in the late sixties and early seventies was a rough, noisy old place, but it was definitely alive. When I first started going there I was only a kid, so I wasn't really old enough to understand the politics of it all. Everyone would make a fuss of you, but sometimes you'd get a sense that there was a bit of an edge to it when someone from a different firm came over.

I was walking down the market with my dad one day when a fella went to doff his cap to us. Bosh! My dad knocked him out. My jaw was on the floor – just like the other geezer's was, but for different reasons. I was thinking, 'What's he done that for?' But it turned out a lot of the lorry drivers from up North used to carry a razor blade in their cap, and if you crossed 'em they'd whip it out and cut you with it. Obviously something had gone on between them before and my dad needed to get his retaliation in first.

Apparently they used to hide razors in their lapels as well, so if you grabbed their jacket and went to nut them, the blade would cut your hands to pieces. I think it's an old Teddy Boy thing, but the lorry drivers used to do it too. All sorts of nasty things could happen if you got on the wrong side of the wrong people in that market. I never saw this done myself but I heard about people getting their legs held down across the kerb and broken the wrong way, or someone getting a pencil through their eardrum. It wasn't like there was any reason for that to be happening to me, but the fact that some real tough guys worked on that market was definitely a big part of the character of the place.

If you go to Spitalfields now, the atmosphere could hardly be more different. There are new shops, which certainly don't take triangular tokens, where A. Mays and the Cage used to be, and while there's still a market, it now sells clothes to tourists on one day and antiques or artworks on another. The basic layout of the whole covered section is pretty much unchanged, but it's all been tidied up so much that it's hard to believe it's the same place. It's kind of recognisable and unrecognisable at the same time – like a big crab shell that a smaller sea creature has moved into after the former resident has departed.

The same thing's happened at Covent Garden, the old fish market at Billingsgate was moved out to the Isle of Dogs years ago, and it won't be long till the meat market at Smithfield follows. Sometimes it's a shame things have to change. Many of those men I met at Spitalfields as a kid were members of families who'd passed stalls down from father to son since the time of Henry Mayhew's costermongers and before, and yet now all those traditions which have come down across the generations have disappeared.

I'm not one of those people who believe nothing new should ever be allowed to happen, though. And some of what went on in that place we're probably better off without. I never actually saw my dad come off worse in any of the tussles he had, but everyone does some time, and it's much better to be coming home from work without lumps and bumps all over you. I wouldn't want to paint a picture of him as someone who was constantly having rows, but those are the stories you tend to remember.

When my mind turns to happier times, there's a holiday in Bournemouth that always comes back to me, for some reason. One day – I think it was a bank holiday Monday – we got the boat across to the Isle of Wight. Dad was never great on boat trips and when we got to the other side where there was a coach waiting to take everyone round the island, he said, 'We're not getting on a coach, let's walk round the island.' He had no comprehension of how big it was – I think he thought it was like the Isle of Dogs – 'Of course we can walk round the Isle of Wight. It's a dot on the map to us. You get on your coach and we'll have a little bit of proper . . .'

We were only kids at the time, and the minute the coach drove off, the realisation hit us that this place was not only huge, it was also pretty desolate. What's more, nothing was open 'cos it was a bank holiday, so we were basically going to be stuck there for the next seven hours. As it turned out, we ended up having a blinding day. We found this little hotel which was willing to take us in and give us a bit of dinner. We played football and flew a kite. I think it was that make-the-best-of-it attitude that the English have when we're not moaning about everything which saw us through.

All nearly didn't end so well, though. We had the dog with us, and at one point we were walking along the top of some cliffs when Brandy came to a hole in the sea wall and jumped right through it. I looked over the edge and I could see him disappearing like in a cartoon – sailing through the air to land on his chin with his legs splayed out all around him. I knew he was dead – there was no way he could've survived that fall. But just like that indestructible Labrador on the Southend road a few years earlier, he got up, shook himself and found a path to run all the way back to us. It was fucking unbelievable – who did he think he was, Superdog?

Some other holidays I look back upon really fondly were with my nan and granddad. I was probably nine or ten when they took us to the Ocean Hotel in Brighton, which was like Butlins' flagship hotel. There was a fancy dress competition and I went as a billboard – it was my first big advertising job – while Laura was the Queen of Hearts. We watched *She Wore a Yellow Ribbon* at the cinema club in the afternoon (I've always loved John Wayne and I still think he's a very under-rated actor). And I remember Maud and Toffy dancing together in the evening – my granddad was a terrific dancer and loved spinning Nanny Maud round the floor.

A couple of years later – it must have been right at the end of the sixties – they took us on our first foreign holiday. We went to Arenal in Majorca, and I loved the freedom of being abroad right from the off. You can get the paella, but if you don't fancy it, they still eat egg and chips just like us. Granddad would still always have a tie on when he was on the beach – they would, the old guys, they always looked immaculate – and he couldn't pass a woman without lifting his hat, even if she was only wearing a bikini.

CHAPTER 7

RONAN POINT

Early on the morning of 16 May 1968, an old lady who'd recently moved into a newly built East London block of flats lit a match to get the stove going for her morning cup of tea. The gas explosion that followed sent her flying across the kitchen and left her shaken but miraculously unharmed. That should've been the end of it, but weaknesses in the just-completed building caused the whole south-east side of the block to collapse with a human toll – four dead and seventeen injured – that would have been much higher if most of the flats hadn't still been unoccupied.

This disaster made a huge impression on me at the age of eleven because it happened on our old patch – just down the road from Plaistow, on the way to Custom House. Looking back, I can see it also had a wider significance. It was certainly poetic justice that the block concerned had been named after a former chairman of Newham council's housing committee (I didn't know that at the time, I just Googled it), because the now infamous Ronan Point became a symbol of the huge mistakes that were made back then in building the new accommodation that East London, and Britain as a whole, so desperately needed.

We wanted homes building – and quickly – but instead of houses, they gave us prisons in the sky. I realise that some of the architects and town planners responsible were probably quite idealistic people, but it was easy for them to be idealistic when they didn't actually have to live in these places. Those gaps where the bombsites were should have been filled with the kind of properties that would have enhanced the communities that already existed. Instead, whole streets of perfectly good houses were demolished and everyone was shipped off into these fucking great big concrete tower blocks.

Not only did these new high-rise buildings split up communities and separate people from the neighbours they'd lived with all their lives, they also – as the Ronan Point disaster demonstrated – weren't very well built. However idealistic some of the original plans might have been, a lot of the good intentions got lost in the transition from two-dimensional drawings to three-dimensional reality. It wasn't just government cost-cutting that did the damage, there was a lot of skulduggery going on as well, with a lot of the money going into the wrong people's pockets via the old secret handshake.

Obviously this wasn't bothering the Winstone family too much in our nice new house in Enfield, but when I'd go back to Plaistow to visit my old mates, I could feel the landscape changing. My memories of growing up there were very much low-rise – you could see the sky, it wasn't all huge blocks looming up over you, and there was much more of a village mentality. But once they started turfing people out of their old terraced houses and moving them into these new flats, no one knew who lived next door to them any more. Sometimes it almost felt like a divide-and-conquer thing.

Going back there started to get depressing as more and more people moved on. The last time I went back there on a Red Bus Rover I was probably thirteen. By that time I only had one mate left living on Caistor Park Road. His name – and I'm not making this up – was Micky Ghostfield. A field of ghosts was what that place was starting to feel like to me, and when I went back to knock for him, the fucker lived up to his name by blanking me. He might as well have answered the door with a white sheet over his head. I guess he hadn't seen me for a while and didn't want to know. I suppose I can understand it in a way, but then again, if you're reading this, Micky, fuck you.

One place out East I never got tired of going was Shoeburyness. In the summer holidays we would basically be shipped off there for six weeks. My mum would come with us and then my dad would drive down for the odd weekend because he'd be working. I remember going up the OAPs' club with my nan quite a lot. Sometimes me and my sister would get up and do a song to entertain the troops. You've got to have your party piece, and we had some great parties at home and at our aunties' and uncles' houses at that time, when everyone would get up and sing.

After a few years in Bush Hill Parade, my Old Man progressed to a bigger shop up in Watford. My dad was always known for having a great flash. I'm not being personal, that's what they called the display of produce you'd use to entice the punters into your shop. The apples would all be beautifully polished, and he found a way of putting mirrors in at the back of the shelves to make the fruit look massive, so people would come in just to look at it. It was like fruit and veg CGI.

As his operation got bigger his overheads would've gone up too, but as kids we never felt we were going without anything. He must've felt pressure to pay the bills and put food on the table, and we could tell by the way he walked up the front path if he'd had a bad day. He didn't get the hump with us as much as with himself, but I remember one night when he came home and we'd already got the message that he was in a bad mood. Then Mum put his dinner on the table and he just threw it straight out the window.

There is an anger in our family, which for my part I like to think I've learnt to control much better these days, but it's taken me a long time. We're argumentative and stubborn and tend to have short fuses. My mum was the exception to that – she was very good at letting Dad have his tantrum while never letting there be too much doubt about who the real boss was. They did have rows, but it never got physical or violent.

Well, I suppose it depends on how you define violence. Some people think shouting and screaming or throwing things is violent, but I don't. It's what you're used to, isn't it? If you live in a quiet house, then someone raising their voice can be more shocking than a full-scale barney would be somewhere else. I think our way of doing things was quite healthy, really, because nothing got bottled up. There'd be a huge slanging match and next thing you knew we'd all be on the sofa, hugging each other and crying at the Sunday afternoon film.

My dad only properly hit me once in my life, when I was caught cheating in a school exam. I had done it, so they'd got me bang to rights. I came home from school to see the letter on the mantelpiece, so I had it on my toes rather than face the music. Obviously that only made the situation worse. By the time I finally got up the courage to go back home it was about ten o'clock at night. My dad opened the front door, and before he'd even finished asking me where the fuck I'd been, he'd gone bosh, and chinned me. I probably deserved it, and the message his punch delivered has certainly stuck with me: 'If you're not good at it, don't fucking do it.' That's a very pragmatic moral code: not 'don't do it because it's wrong', rather 'don't do it because you're not good enough at it not to get caught'.

Now that I think about it, this was probably a bit later on, maybe more into my mid-teens, but I might as well do the other big family row while I'm at it. There was another incident when my mum and dad were having a barney and I thought I was becoming a man so I should probably intervene. I stepped in and said, 'Why don't you leave her alone?' But it wasn't my dad who reacted – he just looked at me as if to say, 'You really don't know what you've done here' – it was my mum. She didn't just tell me to mind my own business, she threw the gin and tonic she had in her hand at me to underline the point.

I think she'd have hit me with it if she'd wanted to, but the glass smashed against the door close enough to my head to send me ske-daddling out the door. I'm getting quite into these stories now, but maybe I should save the one where my sister stabbed me with a fork for a bit later on.

The fact that I've gone on so far ahead of myself in time probably gives you a fair idea of how interested I was in my secondary school. Because I was still quite different to a lot of the other kids there, in terms of how I talked and how I carried myself, I did get picked on a little bit. At that point, if you're not going to be someone who gets bullied throughout your time at the school, you have to kind of design a way to survive. Whether that means having a fight and taking a belting, or just trying to stay out of certain bigger kids' way is up to you.

When I first went to Edmonton County, a big change in the British education system had just shifted it from a grammar school to a comprehensive. On a practical level, this meant kids who wanted to learn were suddenly finding themselves in classes with kids who didn't. No prizes for guessing which side of this line I was usually on. On the downside, this meant I could now experience the dubious pleasure of holding my brighter classmates back. On the upside, contact with kids who saw things a different way to how I did would actually have a beneficial impact on me.

There was one boy called Stewart West, who was a big dumpy kid and a bit of a schoolboy philosopher. He said something once which really stuck with me, about life and death being like a cassette tape: once you get to the end it rewinds and plays again. I haven't explained it as well as he did, and at the time I had absolutely no idea what he was talking about, but it certainly left an impression.

Now I think about it, maybe someone had taught him the idea of reincarnation – perhaps his parents were Hare Krishnas. Either way, this was something that caught my interest, and it fed into the two subjects at school that I'd really started to get into, which were history and physics. I ended up getting more than ninety per cent in the end of year exams in those subjects because I liked them so much.

Obviously history and physics is quite an unusual combination, and my enthusiasm for them didn't stop me being shit at chemistry and geography. The reason I paid more attention in those classes was mainly because we had great teachers in them. Mr Povey, who was the physics teacher, was one of those mad professor types who capture your attention by being as nutty as a fruitcake. He threw a kid called Chamberlain out the first-floor window once, just to see what would happen.

I was not immune to the joy of doing things for that reason myself. The Enfield ABC, which was the cinema where I went to the Saturday morning pictures, used to get a load of young rockers in, sitting downstairs. Me and my mates would lurk up in the circle, pouring drinks down on them over the balcony and generally causing murders. They'd try and run up the stairs to get us but we'd have it on our toes before they could catch us.

The other big draw at the Saturday morning pictures was that every week would be your birthday. OK, maybe not quite every week, but they had this thing where if it was your birthday you would get called up onstage and be given candyfloss. I've always had a bit of a sweet tooth and I really liked candyfloss so I made sure I had as many different birthdays as possible under a variety of different names. I suppose I'd bought that East Ender's scamming culture with me to a certain extent – either that or I was already testing the boundaries of my dramatic range.

There was another cinema in Tottenham called the Florida which operated an unofficial open-door policy. Well, I say they operated it, really it was the creation of a new mate of mine called Alan Hewitt. This kid could climb anything – we used to call him Thomas O'Malley after the streetwise one in Disney's *The Aristocats*. We'd be about four- or five-handed, and Thomas would shin up a drainpipe round the back, in through a window and down to open the exit door and let us in. The Florida still got our pocket money in the end, we just got some sweets for it.

The cinema was still a big deal at that time, but TV was starting to make more of a fight of it. *Steptoe and Son* was quite popular in our house, and I remember pestering my mum and dad to be allowed to stay up to watch Roger Moore as Simon Templar in *The Saint*. I didn't even particularly like the programme, but I'd beg to watch it just so I could stay up a bit later on a Sunday night. Somehow the counter-argument, 'No, you've got school in the morning', never quite swung it for me.

The first colour TV in the family was my granddad's. He got it just in time for the 1970 Cup Final. Chelsea versus Leeds at Wembley was a bruising encounter (it finished 2–2, with Chelsea eventually winning the replay) and now we could see those bruises in all the colours of the rainbow. That was when football was football. Norman 'Bites yer legs' Hunter and Ron 'Chopper' Harris – they wouldn't have nicknames like that now. The sponsors of the Premier League would never allow it.

CHAPTER 8

RAYMOND'S TAILORS, LOWER CLAPTON

Every year in the run up to Christmas we'd go to my dad's tailor to get some clothes made. You had to have a special bit of clobber made for Christmas and Easter – it's something I still do today.

This geezer's shop was up beyond the north end of Mare Street, past the centre of Hackney that you have to drive round instead of through now, going towards Clapton Pond. I went back to have a look for the exact place recently but the shop was gone. I'm pretty sure the guy who owned it was called Raymond though, so when me and my dad came round we were three proper little Rays of sunshine.

One particular time we were in there – it was when I was getting my first pair of long trousers made (so I must've been in my very early teens, as we mostly used to be in shorts before then) – I remember my dad buying a very smart but conservative suit, the kind of thing Sean Connery used to wear as James Bond. My choice was a little more flamboyant. I had a pair of grey flannel trousers made for me, along with a blue mohair blazer that had my initials embroidered on the pocket. My middle name, which I never use, is Andrew, so the initials spelt out R.A.W, which looked pretty good, though I say it myself. If your name is Colin Roland Arthur Patterson, I would advise you to give this gimmick a wide berth.

My dad was always a snappy dresser, and I guess some of that rubbed off on me. When he was younger, he had a little bit of a quiff thing going on with his hair. He was never a Teddy Boy or anything, but that kind of Edwardian style sent its roots quite deep. That didn't mean there wasn't room for the odd moment of experimentation, though. I've got a great picture from the late fifties or early sixties somewhere (which sadly I've not been able to find to put in this book) of my dad and his mates all done up in these stripy jumpers with tapered trousers and pointy shoes.

They saw a fair bit of dirt in their working lives (especially the ones who worked on the fish market, who would definitely need to come home and have a scrub up at the end of the day, because the smell was terrible) but when they went out at night they were immaculate. You'd never know they'd even been to work, let alone lugged sides of beef or bags of potatoes or big vats of mackerel about since the early hours of the morning. I suppose that's half the point, really. You'll often find it's people who keep their hands clean all day who don't feel the need to worry too much about how they look in the evening.

It wasn't just my dad and his mates' fashion sense which harked back to Edwardian times. Their emotional lives had the same buttoned-up quality that their clothes did. To put it in a nutshell, they didn't let a lot go. This wasn't so much the case when I was little, when my dad was happy to be quite affectionate and even tender. But I remember a very clear cut-off point when I reached a certain age and the hugging stopped. I suppose you get to thirteen or fourteen and suddenly your balls drop and you become a man, and men don't cuddle each other (or at least they didn't in the early seventies). So one day your dad would get hold of you and give you a squeeze, and the next day he wouldn't.

This is an experience that a lot of men of my generation – or at least, a lot of the men I know – seem to remember. That's probably why now we're older we like to get hold of our mates and give them a cuddle, because we're trying to fill that gap. This doesn't always apply in other cultures, though. I say that because of an unfortunate incident with a younger American actor I was working with a few years back. I won't name him, because he's a big star and that would be a bit unfair, but it wasn't Leonardo DiCaprio. Oh alright, then, it was Matt Damon.

A lot of different people I'd worked with had told me about him, saying what a great kid he was, and he is a great kid – don't get me wrong – but I'd heard so many good things about Matt that when I met him, I felt like I knew him, so I gave him a big hug and said, 'Hello, kid, how are you doing?' and he went as stiff as a fucking board. I said, 'Oh, OK.' I guess I'd kind of got into his space – which is an unusual thing for an Englishman to do to an American, because they're notorious for doing it to us – but the poor fucker nearly had a heart attack. He probably thought I was trying to roger him.

There's a lot to be said for the modern way of doing things, where people are more open about their emotions, though. Especially when it comes to being a dad. Because sometimes as a kid you see things that trouble you, and if you can't talk about them, they play on your mind.

I'm not saying I'm bad luck to be around but, as I've mentioned before, I've seen a number of people killed or injured, especially in car accidents. It always seems to happen when I'm on the plot. There was one time when I was up in Southgate, helping my dad sell stuff out of a lorry. I must've been in my early teens, and I'm doing one side of the road for him, knocking on doors and saying, 'Hello, we've got this or that to sell', whatever it was. I've finished my section of the street, so I'm coming back down the road to find my dad, but I can't see him anywhere.

At this point I have a little sit-down on a low wall by a junction – one of those ones where it's almost like a roundabout but it ain't a roundabout – and I'm going into a bit of a daydream about what a nice area it is and what it would be like to live there. At this point a car comes down the road, but when it gets to the curved bit it never slows down. Well, it tries to at the last minute, but it's too late by then.

The car clips the kerb, and I know things are pretty serious because everything goes into slow motion, like that time when Laura and I saw that woman's body slide out of the car when we were on our way to Southend. The car takes off – not high enough to be actually flying, but certainly as high as in the film *Bullitt* – and as it goes flying through the air, the boot opens and the spare wheel falls out and starts bouncing down the road. Even as that's happening, the car smacks against a wall – there are bricks everywhere – and a woman's thrown out of the passenger side where the door's burst open. I can see her arm's bent round under her back at a bad angle, and even as I'm noticing that, what remains of the car comes flying back from where it's hit the wall and rolls over on top of her.

All this hasn't taken more than a couple of seconds. At this point, the guy who was driving, who seems to be OK, gets out and runs round to the other side of the car looking for the place where she's fallen. I'm trying to shout out, 'She's stuck underneath!' but I can't actually speak. I suppose I'm in shock – I was only a kid at the time.

I want to go and help but basically I'm still rooted to my spot on the wall thinking, 'Fuck me!'

Before I've even had the chance to get myself together the guy – all on his own, it was amazing the strength that came to him in a crisis, because he wasn't a big man – somehow lifts the car up and pulls her out from under it. By that time I've finally regained the power of movement, so I run up to him asking if they're alright. At this point, my Old Man turns up, sees what's happened, and instead of getting involved or seeing if there's anything we can do to help, he takes me straight up the road, puts me in our motor and we're gone.

It's what's called a 'stoppo' – where your first priority is to get the hell out of there. He said it was because he could see I was in shock, but I thought afterwards maybe we were selling something we shouldn't have been and he didn't want me to get in trouble as an accessory. Either way, the right moment never came up to ask my dad why he did what he did, even though I would've liked to know.

I was lucky that just at the point in my life where I maybe needed a bit of guidance – something to set me on the right road – boxing came along. Given that my dad and my granddad had both boxed before me, and my dad's mates had been calling me 'Little Sugar' and mock-sparring with me for pretty much as long as I could remember, it was inevitable that I was going to give it a go at some point. What I could never have predicted was how much I would take from it into the rest of my life. I honestly think I learnt more that was useful to me from boxing than I did from over ten years in the British education system (though I'm not blaming my schools for that – it was my doing more than anyone else's).

Something happens to a boxer when they get in the ring that changes their whole lives. I think it's mostly that you're frightened, and in the process of having to overcome that fear you find a deeper humanity in yourself. Everyone is scared when they step through those ropes – I don't care who you are, even Muhammad Ali used to be – because you know you're going to get some pain, and if that doesn't frighten you, you're a psychopath. But what boxing gives you is an understanding of your own capacity for fear, and a structure within which to deal with it.

Beyond that, it's not just the discipline of boxing which stands you in good stead, it's the morality: the respect you have first for the people who are training you, who you really don't want to let down, and then for your opponents. I've transferred so much from that into acting, where you've got to have respect for whoever's playing opposite you, because you can only be at your best if you're bringing the best out of them too. When I've talked before about the parallels between boxing and acting, people have sometimes thought I'm seeing other actors as my competition, but they're not the opposition you've got to find a way to overcome (well, not usually – all that scene-stealing stuff doesn't happen nearly as often as you might think), your adversary is the script.

When I was growing up, I often heard it said that when you come from the East End you talk about boxing and birds, but when you come from North London you talk about football and birds. I don't know how true that is in general, but I took my first tentative steps in the fight game as an East Londoner in exile at the New Enterprise boxing club in Tottenham. It was a good club, despite its unfortunate location in the heartland of an inferior football team.

I went along with a couple of guys from my school, Charlie Woods and Jeff Coward. They were both better boxers than me. Not just technically, they were much fitter as well. I was a skinny little runt – a long way from the more expansive frontage I offer the world today – and the first time you walk into a gym as a raw kid of twelve years old and see a load of grown-up fighters training, there's something wrong with you if you don't feel at least slightly intimidated. I remember a big boxer at that gym at the time was a black kid called Battleman Austin. I know, it's a great name, isn't it? More like something out of a Marvel Comic than an actual person.

Luckily for me, Battleman was up in the heavier weights (he was more of an Austin Maxi than an Austin Allegro), so there was no danger of me having to fight him. And obviously they don't just put the gloves on you and throw you out there the moment you arrive. They have a look at you first to see how you shape up, and then you're in the ring, sparring. That's the moment when you find out the difference between messing about with your dad's mates down the market and doing it for real.

Jeff Coward, the first kid I ever properly sparred with, is one of the many people I met through boxing who I still see today (when he comes back from Cyprus, where he lives now). His granddad, who my granddad knew, was Charlie Coward, a very brave man who was famous for having smuggled prisoners out of Auschwitz in the war and was later played by Dirk Bogarde in the film *The Password is Courage*. Not living down to their surname seemed to be a family tradition, as Jeff was as game as a bagel too.

Charlie Woods was the first person I had to have an actual formal boxing match with. It was only an exhibition bout, which means there's no decision at the end. That was probably good news for me, as I don't think I did too well. Number one, Charlie was still probably a better fighter than me at that point. Number two, he was my mate and I felt a bit weird about giving him a clump. It's a strange thing about the friendliness of the boxing world, that all the real camaraderie you share – and it's more real than any I've come across in any other walk of life, with the possible exception of the armed forces – is based on having to hit people who haven't actually done you any wrong.

Charlie was a lovely bubbly kid, and I was really sad a few years later when I heard he'd committed suicide. Another tragic young life gone, just like that lovely babysitter Sylvie. His body was discovered in a shed, where he'd covered himself with hay because he didn't want to be found. It was heroin that did it, and this would be the first time – but sadly not the last – I'd see what the effects of hard drugs can be. We'd kind of lost touch with one another by this time because he was in the drugs world and I wasn't. Obviously, people have to choose their own route through life, but there are some roads you really don't want to go down.

After I'd been going to the New Enterprise for about a year, I switched to a club in Enfield because it was nearer home. There was another kid from my school who went there who turned out to be a terrific fighter. His name was Chris Hall and he ended up as an ABA champion before becoming a trainer, which I think he still does today.

If you'd met this kid, you'd never have thought he was a boxing champion in the making. Not only was he very tall and gangly, but he was also quite a loner and had a tendency to hoard things. I remember him opening my ears to all these different kinds of music, though. It was bands like Yes and Genesis and Jethro Tull that he was into, and I remember thinking, 'Fucking hell, what is all this hippie shit?'

We'd never have listened to that kind of thing at school. It would've been considered more as music for posh people: 'We don't touch that. It's not for us, it's for kids who are going to university.' The funny thing is, now it only seems to be people who've gone to college who tend to progress in the music business, but in those days that was more of a stigma to be overcome. Maybe Chris was ahead of his time in that regard, but he was a really game fighter either way. Bam! Bam! Bam! He'd just march forward, and he was very hard to stop.

CHAPTER 9

THE REPTON
BOXING CLUB

A couple of years of training and fighting at gyms in Tottenham and Enfield probably did help cure me of some of my inverted snobbery about North London, but it couldn't stop me yearning to be back in the East End. I was thinking of switching to West Ham boxing club for a while, as that had a good reputation and it was on my old plot, but it would've been a big journey to do to get over there three times a week.

It was probably my dad who said, 'If you're going to box, you might as well do it at the Repton', which was much closer and easier to get to. Going there was the best decision I've ever made. Not only did it give me the chance to mix with champions on a regular basis, it also gave me a base back in the area I still thought of as home.

No disrespect to Enfield, but I always felt like a fish out of water there. The Jesuits do say, 'Give me a boy until he is seven years old and I will give you the man', and I'd lived in Plaistow till I was a year older than that, so it was no wonder I thought of myself as an East Londoner through and through. Obviously I live in Essex these days, but there are probably more East Enders of my age in that county than there are left in London. Everyone I knew when I was young seems to have moved out, and maybe once you realise that, you start to see it ain't the places you love so much as the people.

Moving from one boxing club to another is not like a transfer in football – no actual money changes hands – but you do have to sign forms and all that kind of stuff. The Repton was (and still is) definitely somewhere near the top of the premiership in boxing terms, so places there were quite sought after. I think you have to go through a three-week trial period before you can join now, but in those days the fact that I'd won a few fights in Enfield by that time probably got me in.

The Repton moved premises not long after I stopped boxing. It's now in the Gary Barker gymnasium in the old bathhouse on Cheshire Street, just east of Brick Lane. Darren Barker was a world champion whose brother, also a great fighter, was sadly killed in a car crash, so they named the new gym after him. The old place I used to go to was in Pollards Row, in the basement under the Bethnal Green Working Men's club. It's just a few hundred yards away. Go up Vallance Road – past the new house built on top of where the Kray brothers used to live at number 178 – do a right, then a left and you're there. Someone told me there's a vandalised Banksy on the wall outside now.

The first time I went to the Repton, my dad drove me. But given that I was thirteen or fourteen by then, I was soon old enough to get the train down to Bethnal Green from Lower Edmonton on my own. I used to love that journey – it really felt like going back home, and sometimes I'd be counting the hours till the time came to go. Even though it was a bit of a walk down Bethnal Green Road to the gym, through what was a rougher area in the early seventies than it is now, I never felt nervous or ill at ease about it. I didn't feel like I was entering potentially hostile territory, I felt like I belonged there.

As a young kid, the thing about Bethnal Green was its synonymousness – is there even such a word as 'synonymousness'? I'm writing a book now, so I feel I've got to stretch myself – with the Kray twins. Detective Superintendent Leonard 'Nipper' Read had finally got Ron and Reg banged up for the murders of George Cornell and Jack 'The Hat' McVitie in 1969, so even though they weren't physically around any more, the place still kind of smelt of 'em.

Whether this was right or wrong – after all, a lot of people did get hurt – they still had that aura about them of being Robin Hood characters. Hard evidence of the Krays robbing the rich and giving to the poor might have been hard to come by, but the mythology of 'nothing bad ever happened when the twins were about' (except the stuff they did, obviously) was still very powerful.

Now I'm a bit older and wiser, the idea that nobody ever broke into anybody's house in Bethnal Green in the sixties because Reg and Ronnie would sort them out is not one I really buy into any longer. But when you're young it's easy to get caught up in the romance of that way of thinking, and as far as people in general were concerned, I suppose another side of it was that when there's a bit of a reign of terror going on, it's only human nature to try to put a positive spin on it. I bet there are parts of Belfast where they'll still tell you you could leave all your windows open when the IRA were running things, however ridiculous the evidence of innocent people kidnapped and murdered might make that suggestion look.

One of the mistakes people often make when they talk about 'glamorising violence' is to think that this glamour is something that's only projected from the outside. It's on the inside as well. Just as it'd be crazy to assume policemen never watched *The Bill* or

The Wire (which I was going to be in originally, but I couldn't face the idea of living in Baltimore for six months of the year), so it is easy to under-estimate how much gangsters think about their public image. The traffic between myth and reality is not one way – life copies films almost as much as films copy life. And being a successful gangster is just as much of a performance as making it big in films is.

When you think about the way their interests overlap, it's no wonder there's such a big crossover between showbiz stars and the criminal underworld. Both sides need to get the balance just right between everyone knowing who they are and no one getting up in their face too much. That's why those relationships which used to shock everybody, say Barbara Windsor and Ronnie Knight or Diana Dors with Alan Lake, always kind of made sense to me.

The big stars in the sixties would always be in the clubs in the West End, and a lot of those clubs were owned by the Krays and whoever else was about. The glamorous people got looked after – 'cos obviously it's good business for the management if they're in your gaff – and all of a sudden they're in this world of intrigue and it's very exciting. The gangsters have got some style and they know how to turn on the charm. Plus anyone else gives you a problem and they're out on their ear sharpish.

With David Bailey and Diana Dors doing the business for them, the Krays couldn't have had better PR if they'd employed a firm (rather than simply being The Firm). And all these stories you'd hear about George Raft coming over and being with the boys and them having major connections in the States only kept the pot boiling even more. Obviously the pot was well and truly off the stove by the time I got to the Repton, but the reality that the twins wouldn't ever be cooking with gas in E2 again took a long time to sink in.

Luckily, joining the Repton gave me access to a glittering array of more suitable role models. Going down the stairs to the gym I'd look at the pictures on the wall and think, 'Every one of these boxers is a champion.' Looking back now, the Repton roll-call was amazing: Maurice Hope – Olympic champion, going to be a world champion; Billy Taylor – what a fighter!; Graham Moughton, captain of the Olympic team; John H. Stracey, another world champion; Johnny Whitehorn; Dave Odwell, another Olympic team captain . . . It was quite daunting to walk into the Repton and see those pictures, especially at first, but once I found my feet I soon realised how lucky I was to be at such a special club, because if you're training alongside these guys, you can't help but learn.

You walk down those stairs for the first time and straight away the place smells of blood, sweat and tears. What I didn't understand at the time was that a lot of the really important things the Repton was going to teach me wouldn't be about how to handle myself in the ring, they'd be about ethics – having respect for myself and having respect for humanity. It was only years later that I began to look back and think, 'Fuck me, I learnt a lot more than boxing.'

The boxing had to come first, though, and I had some great teachers there. The head coach was a guy called Tony Burns. Burnsy was the Repton, and for me he epitomises what's good about boys' club boxing trainers the world over. He never once trained you as a boxer – although he was more than capable of doing that – his greatest gift was as a matchmaker. A lot of them will overmatch you to try to move you up the ranks too fast, but Burnsy would always do his best to make any imbalance in your favour. If he thought there was any chance of you getting hurt, he just wouldn't put you in there.

Another guy I owe a lot to was Billy Howick, who taught me ringcraft, which is basically how to unbalance your opponent while staying within the law, or at least within the law in the referee's eyes. Billy's big thing was that if you make your opponent miss you the whole fight but you hit him once, then you've won the fight (I suppose he was the Sam Allardyce of his day in that regard). This always seemed pretty logical to me. Also at the Repton I was able to watch a lot of boxers like Dave Odwell and Billy Taylor, who were tremendous counter-punchers, so I styled myself that way too.

Amateur fights last for three rounds of three minutes each, which might not sound like much, but believe me it's long enough when someone's trying to hit you in the face from start to finish. Nowadays they force you to wear head-protectors, but I never did and I still wouldn't want to if I was starting out now. I think they make boxing more dangerous, rather than less. Head-protectors are there predominantly to stop you getting cuts, but the cuts aren't really the problem in terms of the long-term damage people sustain from boxing. It's the shaking of the head and thence the brain which is the worst thing.

If you haven't got a head-guard on, you can see everything. The most fundamental technique in boxing as far as I'm concerned is the slip and miss, which is the way you pull your head inside or outside your opponent's punches. Once you've put your head-guard on, you may have covered your brow and your chin, but at the same time you're a bigger target, so even when you slip, you're still getting hit. What that does is shake your head, which is the one thing you really don't want to happen. I've thought this for a long time and a lot of people agree with me, but unfortunately not the ones who make the rules. If it was down to me, I wouldn't even use head-guards for sparring. I think they do more harm than good even then.

A lot of the boys who started at the Repton around the same time as me I still see to this day. Among my group were: Billy Jobling, a great fighter who came out of the Isle of Dogs; Glenn Murphy, who became an actor on *London's Burning*; my mate Tony Yeates, who came over to the Repton from the Fitzroy Lodge club, which is south of the river; and a guy called Tony Marchant, who ended up as a writer. We had some brilliant moments together, and you don't keep people as friends for forty-odd years unless you have a special bond with them. For me it's a kind of moral code that they all share – boxing taught them to be old-fashioned gentlemen.

When the club was originally founded, in 1884, it was more or less a missionary outpost for the Derbyshire public school it was named after. The idea was to come to the East End, which at that point was considered a dangerous slum, and impart Victorian discipline to the lawless inhabitants by teaching them the Marquess of Queensbury's rules. Obviously there's a paternalistic element to that, but paternalism is not necessarily a bad thing. Especially when it gives you tools you can use any way you want. It was no coincidence that so many of my mates from the Repton went on to succeed in other fields, because our time there gave us psychological resources we could fall back on for the rest of our lives.

In a way, the impact the Repton had on us was very similar to the one Anna Scher's children's theatre (which she started up the road in Islington in the late sixties) was having at around the same time on another bunch of unruly Londoners – Ray Burdis, Pauline Quirke, Phil Daniels, Perry Benson, Tony London, Kathy Burke – many of whom are still my mates to this day. Anna would take kids who were maybe lacking a direction in life and getting in a little bit of trouble and give them something creative to focus on. The only difference was that she was doing it from a left-wing political perspective, which wouldn't have got you very far in the fight game.

Obviously people tend to think of a boxing club as a violent place, and the Repton's Latin motto, 'Non Viscera, Non Gloria' ('No

Guts, No Glory'), would do nothing to change their mind. But the club crest doesn't have a dove of peace with an olive branch in its mouth by accident, because one of the main things going there taught me was how to mix with a group of people as a unit, even as a community. Those who try to put boxing down as more brutal and less evolved than other pastimes have a hard time explaining away the fact that it was probably the first sport where there was no colour bar.

That's not to say Jack Johnson aka 'the Galveston Giant' had an easy time of it after becoming the first African-American world heavyweight champion in 1908. Obviously his marrying a white woman went down like a sack of shit, but no one could take away from him the fact that he had been World Champion. And when I think back to being fourteen years old in London in the early seventies – how things had changed over the course of a decade or so from the first time I saw a black man in the street who wasn't Kenny Lynch, to maybe a bit of a feeling of 'them and us' developing – I know how much I've got to thank boxing for. Because once you're mixing with people on the same wavelength, what used to be 'them and us' suddenly just becomes 'us'.

Boxing certainly showed football the way in terms of being the first truly integrated sport. In fact I think it's only just about catching up now. To say West Ham crowds did not always extend the friendliest of welcomes to visiting black players in the seventies would be putting it mildly, but at least we were the first British team ever to field three black players at the same time, when Clyde Best, Clive Charles and Ade Coker all played against Spurs in 1972.

I was at Upton Park a few years later to see West Brom's more celebrated black trio – Brendon Batson, Laurie Cunningham and Cyrille Regis – who the Baggies' then manager Ron Atkinson famously, if perhaps unhelpfully, dubbed 'The Three Degrees'. That day I saw one of the best examples I've ever seen of someone defusing a situation, which is not a skill I've always – if ever – had. Brendon Batson was down in the corner at the South Bank end when someone chucked a load of bananas on the pitch. He simply picked one up, peeled it, and ate it, and the whole stand clapped him.

That sort of thing used to happen all over the country, but Chelsea was the worst place I ever went for it – I suppose they've always been a bit less cosmopolitan in West London. Their fans used to call it 0–0 if one of their black players scored, 'cos a black geezer shouldn't be playing for them. His own fans! I remember going there with a mate of mine once when they were playing Leicester and a whole stand stood up and Sieg-Heiled. There were grown men of fifty doing it who were old enough to have fought in the war. It was fucking disgraceful.

Boxing was the first sport that, I believe, dealt with the problem of racism without even consciously approaching it; it approached itself, in a way. No one ever said, 'There will be no discrimination in boxing', it just kind of happened. I suppose because people were constantly in a one-on-one situation, or just training together in the gym, they couldn't help finding out, 'Hey, you're just like me.' Maurice Hope was older than me, but he was someone I really looked up to, and boxing opened up all our minds by sending us out into the world with a common identity to take with us.

CHAPTER 10

CHRISP STREET MARKET, POPLAR

When my dad had his grocer's shops – first in Enfield, and then in Watford – my mum used to come in and work with him. I'm pretty sure she lost a couple of kids during that time – not because she was working so hard, it was just bad luck. There was definitely one morning when she had to be taken home from the shop in Bush Hill Park because she'd miscarried, and I had a sense of it happening another time as well, even though it was never talked about. Dwelling on such things was not encouraged in those days, and even though she must have felt sadness about this loss, she never shared it with us.

The Old Man had a good spell with the shops and we lived well for a few years, but the fruit game was changing, with the supermarkets squeezing out everyone else. I was still only a kid but I think what made his business start to go tits up at the shop in Watford was when they put a new one-way system in so no one could park nearby any more. My dad probably hung in there for a bit longer than he should've done, because that shop was his pride and joy and

Now and then – outside 82 Caistor Park Road in 2014 and as a bouncing baby 57 years before.

My mum with Nanny Rich and the first of her three husbands.

My mum and dad together before Laura and I came along.

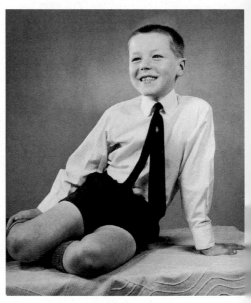

Me posing on a blanket like a dog at Crufts.

At another wedding with my cousin Charlie-boy (I'm in the middle, he's on my right). Not sure who the hatless kid was . . .

Cowboy-style this time in hat terms – with Laura in Nanny Rich's garden.

Early morning – the Cage with the sun rising in the east behind Christ Church, Spitalfields.

Old Spitalfields Market as it was – good luck finding a sack of King Edwards in there these days.

My dad looking suave on the market.

Spitalfields life before the clean-up, with The Cage, A. Mays and
Christ Church in the background.

West Ham bringing home the 1964 FA Cup on their luxury single-decker. All four of the
Winstones are in that crowd somewhere.

Repton boys at the London Feds . . . (I'm the one bang in the middle).

With my dad after beating David
Heyland (the tall one on the left)
who was Essex champ. Although I
won, I gave David the bigger trophy –
winning was enough for me,
and he was a nice kid.

Ready to rumble.

In *The Sweeney* in 1975, shortly before making my unauthorised escape.

Me in *Minder* – with George Cole on the right
and my fellow Corona old-boy Dennis Waterman between us.

he'd got a good living out of it. So in the end it totally ironed him out. He had no option but to go back out on the markets.

He had some mates who still had stalls so he started off working for them on various different markets – which wasn't something he'd had to do much before – until he got back on his feet. Me and Laura never went hungry, but there must've been a couple of years when the family was a bit financially challenged. My mum put a shift in too. She got a job collecting the money from fruit machines – not in a strong-arm kind of way, she was meant to be doing it – and inadvertently she taught me a useful scam.

On the old big machines, when you got a 'hold' you could fuse them out by pouring your Coca-Cola or lemonade over the buttons, and then they'd just carry on paying out until the machine was empty. This was something else I never looked upon as thieving. It's not as if the fruit-machine business is run on principles of good will to all men, anyway – it was just another kind of spillage. The money did come in handy, but you couldn't do it too often in the same pub, and sadly it doesn't work on the new machines . . . not that I've ever tried it, obviously.

The areas my mum was working in, mainly Hoxton and the bottom end of Islington, were quite rough at the time, so someone from the pub would usually escort her to the car. The sort of woman my mum was, if someone had come up to her and demanded the money, she wouldn't have been the one to risk her life by not giving them the bag. She'd probably have said, 'Here you go, son, take it', because money's not that important – at least, it's not when it's not yours. I guess there's always an element of danger any time you're collecting cash, but it's the cash that makes it dangerous, not the place you're picking it up. That said, in somewhere like Hoxton, life might actually be more dangerous for the person who's trying to nick it, because they don't know whose fucking place they're ripping off.

Returning to the markets was obviously a bit of a needs must for my dad. It wasn't a world he'd totally left behind, but he'd got pretty respectable with his shop in Watford and now he was having to go all over the place just to make a crust. Chrisp Street in Poplar is not necessarily somewhere you'd be setting up if you had any choice. But I was delighted, because I was old enough to go and help him now – on Saturdays, and maybe a day or two in the week sometimes as well – and as far as I was concerned, we were going home.

Obviously, you've got fewer overheads in that situation because you're just buying daily and selling what you can. Well, usually you're buying daily. If things are really tight, you might have to nick a bit of stock here and there to make up a deficit. I remember once we were a bit short of cash so we had to steal some tomatoes at Spitalfields Market. We had to have them away or we'd have had nothing to sell.

My dad kept the guy busy while I loaded the big old barrow with Canary tomatoes. Unfortunately I piled it too heavy at the back – I was only about fourteen at the time, and I suppose my eyes might've been bigger than my arm muscles. When the time came for me to have it on my toes, I came out of the market at top speed with the barrow behind me, hit the cobbled street, and the weight of it threw me what felt like twenty or thirty feet in the air. I seemed to be up there for ages – I was waving to the man in the moon – and by the time I finally landed in a heap with tomatoes splatting on the ground all around me I was lucky I hadn't burnt up on re-entry.

There would have been murders if we'd been caught, so we made as rapid an exit as possible, and I probably got a clip round the ear for my foolishness afterwards: 'If you're not any good at it, son, don't do it.' The way I was brought up was that if you owe someone some money and you're too skint to pay 'em back, you should usually front up and go and talk to them, but I suppose there were times when you have to find a way of earning the money to pay off the debt and you just have to do what you have to do. I remember us going to Covent Garden instead of Spitalfields to buy stock once or twice, which seemed perfectly natural at the time, but looking back it probably meant there were people on our usual plot we didn't want to run into.

These occasional incidents of ducking and diving probably gave me a head-start when the time came for me to play a gullible mechanic in *Minder* a few years later, but as a general rule my dad was no Arthur Daley. He was a grafter and he expected me to be the same, so when we arrived at Spitalfields at four in the morning there was a strict rule that we'd have to buy all our bits and get the lorry packed and tied up before we could stop for a nice cup of tea and a bacon roll.

Then we would head off to Chrisp Street or Roman Road or wherever we had a pitch and we'd have to pull the stall out and dress it. Cutting the cauliflowers was the worst job, especially in the winter. It used to get so cold that to this day I find I can't wear gloves in normal life, because if I put them on, my hands just start sweating.

Obviously, working on markets is no picnic. Sometimes you can stand around freezing your arse off all morning and come home with absolutely nothing. When I used to go to work with my dad, I knew that if we had a bad day I wouldn't get paid. Those were the rules of the job and I had no qualms about them. Well, I say that now – at the time I probably thought, 'Fuck it, I was going out tonight', but I knew that was the way things were done when you were part of a family business, and every now and then when you had a blinding day you would definitely get looked after.

The principle of 'fair's fair' also covered giving my mum house-keeping. 'Raymond, you've gotta do the right thing' were words drummed into me from an early age. Even if sometimes you bor-rowed it back by the end of the week, it was the gesture that counted – showing you knew you shouldn't take your food and lodging for granted, just because it was your parents who were giving it to you. My mum and dad shared that work ethic, and they've passed it on to me.

I remember falling back to sleep once after my dad had woken me up early to go to the market and getting a bucket of cold water thrown over me to make sure it didn't happen again. That gets you out of bed pretty sharpish, I can tell you, and it's another one of those childhood lessons that's stayed with me. I'm a stickler for time-keeping to this day. If I'm going anywhere I have to be punctual, if not early – it's almost an illness. And even if I've not gone to bed till four in the morning, I'll still be up with the sun. It's unheard-of for me to be asleep after nine in the morning.

Although as I said I was really pleased to be working at the mar-ket again, sometimes I used to moan about getting up early for work – especially if I'd got a bit of a hiding in the boxing ring the night before – but once we got there I loved getting to grips with the var-ious personalities of the different markets we used to go to. Roman Road in Bow, for instance, was a funny old market, because it was only on Thursdays and Saturdays, not Fridays. It could be desolate there sometimes on a Thursday, especially because we were stuck at the Old Ford end, which is quieter than the Bethnal Green end.

We had a yard there just round the back of a little kids' clothes shop called 'Trendy', and there was a blinding old boy who used to work with us called Sammy Keyworth. I think he was Jewish and he'd make this kind of ehhh noise when he spoke, a bit like Blakey from *On the Buses*. One of my jobs at Roman Road was to take the orders to the other stalls. I'd have a big bag to carry with potatoes, carrots and cauliflowers on the bottom, softer fruit and veg higher up, and grapes on the top.

One time I'd taken them all up the road and delivered them when I saw from the look on my dad's face as I returned that I must've taken them to the wrong people. As I turned to walk away and give him a chance to cool down, a cauliflower hit me full bore on the back of the head. I was laid out sprawled across the middle of Roman Road – I know cauliflowers aren't normally thought of as weapons of mass destruction, but you know about it when one of those fuckers hits you on the canister. It was a bit harsh, but I never made the same mistake again, and I'll always have these two cauliflower ears to remember it by.

There was a nice girl who worked on one of the other stalls. Our eyes used to meet across the Roman on a regular basis, but I was a bit too shy to talk to her. Then I met her one night out and about somewhere and we had a lovely little evening together. It was weird though, because the next time I saw her on her stall we both went back to being exactly how we had been before. We liked each other too much to actually have a conversation.

Rathbone Market in Canning Town was a rough old place – not much chance of romance there, especially as our pitch was opposite the fish stall. Luckily we didn't hang around for too long, although I used to like the fact that we still knew a few people in that manor, because it was just down the road from Plaistow.

Chrisp Street in Poplar was a bit further from where we used to live, but that didn't stop it becoming my gateway to Upton Park. We used to work there quite regularly with Terry Brown, who was one of my granddad's tic-tac mates. All those families knew each other, and me and Terry's son Billy would take it in turns to go up to the Boleyn Ground for West Ham home games. I'll save that for the next chapter though, to give fans of lesser teams a chance to prepare themselves for the thrill of another visit to the Academy of Football.

This market offered a further exciting diversion in the form of a stall where I bought my first ever records. 'Speed King' by Deep Purple was one of them. I don't know why, 'cos I was never really into heavy metal. I just thought the song was alright. Then there was 'The Resurrection Shuffle' by Ashton, Gardner and Dyke – I still love that to this day – and 'Banner Man' by Blue Mink, whose singer was that black girl with big teeth, what was her name? Madeline. I think that was the other side of 'Melting Pot'.

While we're on the subject of melting pots, I'm not a Catholic – although my wife Elaine is – but there was a young priest who used to walk through the market wearing a West Ham scarf. He used to have a rabbit with everyone, he was a real character. The thing about working on markets is, even when you've had to get up at two or three in the morning at the end of a week of school with a couple of nights of boxing training thrown in, you can't help noticing people. You're in a unique position in a way. It's very much a man's world, but at the same time you're having a lot of conversations with women, because they're the ones buying your produce.

You've got to learn how to talk to people the right way, or you're never going to sell anything. So when it got towards the end of the day and I'd have to 'bang up' some cauliflowers – which basically means shouting and screaming to let everyone know you're taking the price down – the pressure would really be on. You know you've got cauliflowers left that will go pear-shaped before you get another chance to sell 'em, and no one wants a pear-shaped cauliflower, so you've got to holler, 'Come on, girls, lovely big juicy ones, two bob a time', and you've got to make it sound convincing.

If you're ever on a market and you hear people doing this, you'll probably notice the way their voice sounds, which is usually like they've just taken a deep breath, even if you know they haven't. That's because you need to puff out your chest like it's full of air as a way of showing confidence, the same way a robin does if it's having a fight in your garden.

Banging up is not an easy thing to do as a teenage boy, especially if you're at that age when you're not exactly sure which way your voice is going to go at any given moment, and you've got all these girls looking at you waiting for you to make a mistake. You know what they're like, women. 'Ooh look, he's made a mug of 'isself' – they love that 'cos it gives them one up on you. Once you know you can do it, though, it gives you confidence in other areas of your life. I suppose it's a bit like boxing in that way, or at least it was for me.

When I was fourteen, there was a girl I really fancied at school, a lovely little Jewish bird. I won't name her, because she'll know who she is and it'll be embarrassing for her, but when I found out she was doing a school play I thought, 'I'll have a go at that – get in there.' The play was *Emil and the Detectives*, and I played the newspaper boy. On paper, this was a nothing part, but it turned out to be a first step down a happy path of doing exactly what I'd normally do and calling it acting. I'm not saying I'm still on that path today, but it certainly took me a fair way in the right direction.

All I had to do was walk through the audience acting like I was selling them papers. This gave me the perfect opportunity to have a pop at the headmaster, Mr Hudson. I could dig him out by saying that he looked like Hitler dressed in his baggy suit – 'You wanna sort yourself out, son', something a bit saucy like that – and he couldn't do anything but pretend to find it as funny as everyone else did.

The whole place was laughing and I remember thinking, 'Oh, I like this.' My mum and dad came as well, and I think it was probably seeing how much I was into it that gave them the idea of me going to drama college. But I still had another year or so of banging up, doing the markets two or three times a week and generally being up and down the A10 like a whore's drawers before that would happen.

CHAPTER 11

THE BOLEYN GROUND, UPTON PARK

The first football match I went to that wasn't the 1966 World Cup was to see Southend play at Roots Hall with my uncle Len. I was always mad for West Ham – still am – but I look for Southend's results to this day, and not just because I live in Essex.

I don't have any specific recollection of the earliest times I went to Upton Park (or the Boleyn Ground in Upton Park, as it's officially called). I suppose it's like with a car or train journey that you've done your whole life – all the repetitions blur the edges of the pathway to the memory in your brain. I used to love the atmosphere of the night games, though. There was always a real buzz about the place. And the time I started going regularly, or at least to every other home game, was when me and my mate Billy Brown would take turns on the Saturday afternoons we worked at Chrisp Street Market.

It was only a bus-ride up the road, and I'd sit on the step on the side of the South Bank. Sometimes if it was quiet our dads would let me and Billy go together, and later on I started going with my mate Tony Yeates from boxing. But I never minded going on my own either. I've always been a bit of a loner, and you were part of a big crowd, anyway.

There was much more of a fun atmosphere at the Boleyn Ground in the early seventies than you get today. I find football fans in general nowadays are much more cynical and angry than they used to be. I don't know why, but I presume it's something to do with the Premier League, because it's only happened over the last twenty years or so. West Ham used to get beat a lot in the past as well, but then some of the abuse you'd hear them getting would make you laugh, whereas now there's a rage in it that makes you catch your breath.

I remember when Alan Curbishley was manager a few years back. He'd been a great player for us, and was a West Ham boy through and through. He comes from a big Canning Town family and his brother Bill was manager of The Who and producer of *Quadrophenia*. There was no reason for people not to like him. OK, Alan had been at Charlton before, but that's not exactly the crime of the century and he'd done a good job there. And yet the coating he'd get off the crowd used to stop you in your tracks. I remember thinking, 'Fucking hell! That's a bit strong', and it wasn't just me. It got to a point where one guy was giving him so much abuse that all his mates had to tell him to sit down and shut his fucking noise.

You never really got that at football years ago. People would make the odd funny remark and everyone would be laughing, and then you'd get all the firms having little rows, but that would be it. Maybe it's stopping the violence at football that's made it more miserable, because the anger's got to come out somehow.

Even though I was going to Upton Park regularly throughout the seventies and eighties – what you'd probably consider the 'golden age' of football violence, if football violence could have a golden age – the hooligans and all that never really interested me. I suppose the ideal thing would've been the Inter City Firm (ICF), but I didn't know anyone who was in it because I didn't live round there any more – a lot of them were Canning Town boys too – and I don't think I'd have been involved, anyway. I had too many other things I wanted to do.

The funny thing is, I do know a couple of those old ICFers now. They're wealthy businessmen, because they got in on the rave scene in the early days and made a lot of money. I think they're mostly in clothing these days, so at least something good came out of it all in terms of economic benefits for the area, and there's no denying they were a proper firm in their prime – better than Tottenham, anyway.

The main thing about football violence is that it's very territorial, and I never really saw things that way. Maybe if we'd stayed in Plaistow it might've been different, but by the time I was in my early teens I was so used to bombing around London on trains or Red Bus Rovers that the idea of defending one bit of turf against another didn't really make much sense to me. I was never really one for being part of a gang, either in or out of school. Obviously there were gangs about, but I tended to knock about with two or three geezers, and if we were going somewhere, it was usually because we knew someone, so I never remember thinking we'd better watch ourselves in this place or that place, because there might be trouble (except in South London, obviously).

I suppose in a way – although I never saw it like that at the time – my parents did me a favour by moving us out to Enfield, because that stopped me putting my roots down so deep in one part of East London that I couldn't go anywhere else. Me and my mates didn't really have any boundaries we wouldn't cross over. It was never like that with us. We weren't really affiliated with anyone except each other, so we were at liberty to come and go as we pleased.

Tony Yeates was a good example of how freely we moved around, because when I first met him he was boxing for the Fitzroy Lodge club in South London, but then he moved over to the Repton because that was the place to be. He's going to be cropping up a lot in this book from now on, because he's one of my best mates. In day-to-day life I usually call him Yeatesie, but that looks a bit pony written down – if he was Yates instead of Yeates it would look better – so in print I'm going to refer to him by his full name for the purpose of guaranteeing him literary immortality.

Anyway, Tony Yeates came from Bow Common, which is between Bow and Poplar. They had a famous battle there once where a firm came out of the station carrying pick-axe handles and a load of Old Bill were waiting there with shooters – I think it was one of the first few times police had been armed like that on the British mainland. They shot one of the guys in the head and the bullet went between his skull and his skin and came out the back. It was all kept very quiet at the time. The official line was that the robbers had the guns, but I've spoken to people who were there and that's not how it went down.

Obviously, none of this had anything to do with Tony, who was every bit as squeaky clean as I was. One of the great things about boxing was that it didn't just give you a legitimate outlet for any tendency towards physical aggression which might have got you into trouble otherwise, it also gave you discipline, which stopped you doing the things that make teenage kids more likely to get into strife, like taking drugs or drinking heavily before you're old enough.

Tony and I made up for lost time later of course, but when we were in our mid-teens we were too dedicated to our training to be falling over drunk or getting into fights outside the minicab office like a lot of the kids we knew from school would've been. Even a few years later when the boxing had dropped off a bit and the lure of other distractions had begun to get a bit more powerful, we'd still meet up at West Ham gym for an hour before going out for a drink.

Looking after yourself is a habit that's hard to break, and so is getting out and about. Boxing meant we had mates from all over the East End. A lot of people have their one precise patch they'll hang around in – whether that be their street, their estate, or just a particular area or neighbourhood – but we used to go everywhere. West Ham, Stratford, Bethnal Green, Hackney; it was all the same to us. We'd even go somewhere like the Isle of Dogs (which should in theory have been totally off our plot, because it was Millwall) to see my mates Billy Jobling or Russell True.

Once we'd got a bit older, in our late teens, and were young men knocking about having a drink, Moro's and the Two Puddings in Stratford and the Charleston out towards Maryland Point would become our main haunts. But sometimes we'd go further afield – even as far east as Southend or Canvey Island – to nick a bird. I know this sounds ridiculous, but at that age it felt like travelling the world. And once we came back to town, the whole of East London felt like home to us.

Back at school in Enfield I still wasn't one of those kids who knocks around in a gang – I don't mean big horrible gangs like the Crips or the Bloods, I just mean a big load of mates. It's not for me to say whether that's because I didn't want to be, or because there was no larger group that would have me. But even when it came to school trips, it'd usually just be me and a couple of mates hanging around together. I suppose because I was always off training and had my own mates from boxing, I must've seemed like I didn't really want to be part of the normal social life of the school.

I remember one skiing holiday, which my parents had kindly got the money together to pay for, when I looked around and saw that, well, it's a little bit unfair to say it was me and the nerds, but I can't think of another word that sums 'em up. All the kids who wanted to be off drinking and getting in trouble, which wasn't really my cup of tea yet, were back at home doing whatever it was they were doing. I suppose going somewhere with a load of teachers didn't seem cool to them any more. Luckily for me there was a rather nice girl called Suzanne who hadn't got that memo either, so she'd come on the trip too and all the real competition had stayed at home.

The whole lone-wolf thing would stay with me once I became an actor too. Obviously there are people in the business I'm mates with, but from the moment I got cast as Carlin in the TV version of *Scum* with all the Anna Scher boys ranged against me, I don't think I'd ever be thought of as being in a gang of actors. I think the reason why is that – without sounding too Californian about it – I kind of know who I am. I've never really reinvented myself, so I don't need the reassurance of a lot of other people being like me to tell me that I've made the right (or the wrong) decisions.

No disrespect to 'em, but a hell of a lot of actors choose to go down this particular career path because they don't like who they actually are. This isn't something I've deduced, it's something they've told me. I speak to many of them who feel that way. Don't get me wrong, they're nice kids, but they've got no history from before they became an actor, or if they have got history, it's not something they want to take with them. They're only interested in where they're going or where they are now, not where they started out.

Life's never been like that for me, because I'm proud of where I come from. But that doesn't mean I never want things to change. For instance, on the controversial subject of West Ham moving to the

Olympic Stadium in Stratford in 2016, a lot of people who ask me about it expect me to get really upset, but I don't think it's a shame at all. I will miss Upton Park, but it's always been hard work to get to. And if we want the club to progress, we've got to take the chance of a proper stadium with better transport links and parking facilities, as that's the only way to attract better players. On top of that, to be honest, the whole thing has probably been worth doing just for how much it's pissed Tottenham off.

Obviously, it was a bit of a touch for West Ham's owners, Sullivan and Gold, because they got the government to pay for the transformation of the Olympic stadium to stop it becoming a white elephant, and then sold off Upton Park to property developers. But that's business, and they're entitled to prosper so long as the club benefits in the long term.

The 2012 Olympics certainly changed the view from the end of Caistor Park Road, but the building of the actual stadium was a complete fucking con. I got myself in a lot of trouble at the time because I was asked to carry one of the flags round in front of the Coldstream Guards at the opening ceremony and I said no. I was gutted to have to do that, because obviously it was a huge event and it would've been great to be a part of it, but I'm a bit trappy sometimes. I get these bees in my bonnet and I have to let them buzz.

It wasn't the Olympics themselves I objected to – I really admire the athletes and the effort and dedication they put in – I just looked around at East London and thought, 'When we've built the hospitals and paid the teachers to be teachers and stopped closing all the fire-stations down, maybe then we can afford this, but at the moment it's an outrageous fucking liberty.'

The Olympic organisation isn't really about the sport, it's about the building, and when I see the people who run the Committee

– not so much Lord Coe, but he's a puppet, anyway – they look like white-collar gangsters to me. The corruption isn't just a side issue, it's at the heart of the whole enterprise. And FIFA are even worse.

They're a law unto themselves, and the government allow them to come in and basically rape the country that's hosting, then move on somewhere else four years later and leave the people who live there to clean up the mess. I went to the World Cup in South Africa in 2010 and had an amazing time (that was actually the biggest group I've ever been away in – we went forty-handed and stayed in Mauritius). But I also saw the way they built walls around the shanty towns and tried to sweep all the poverty under the carpet. I love sport as much as anyone, but to me there are things which are more important. It would've been an honour to carry the flag in front of the Coldstream Guards, who I love to pieces, but I had to say no, otherwise I'd have been a hypocrite for supporting something I didn't believe in.

I think you owe it to yourself to be true to your own moral code, however much flak it brings you. It's like with the Bet 365 adverts I do. People ask me why I do them. And I tell them: number one, it's very, very good money, and number two, it's for gambling which people have a choice about whether they do it or not. If you wanna gamble, you gamble; if you don't, you don't. I like gambling – I have a little flutter myself every now and again – so I have no qualms whatsoever about advertising it. But I'd never do a bank commercial or something for an insurance company, because that's something you're forced to do and it's a rip-off. They fucking slaughter you and I don't agree with that. No doubt there are plenty of people who'd see this completely the other way round – they'd be happy to take the banks' money, but wouldn't touch Bet 365 with a barge pole – but good for them if that's how they feel. It takes all sorts to make a world.

When it comes to West Ham leaving Upton Park behind, I say bring it on. If you look at the magnificent World Cup heroes' statue, just across the Barking Road from the Boleyn Cinema, it kind of makes sense that the team who won us those medals in 1966 should move to the stadium where Britain did so well in 2012. None of us live round that way any more – at least, no one I know does – and unless the younger generation of Bangladeshi kids who live there now are really into football, I don't see what good it does them to have a match there on Saturday afternoons when they're trying to run a business.

You do see a lot of the sari shops on Plashet Road will have saris in claret and blue at the right-hand end of the window (the one nearest the Boleyn Ground), but I'm not sure that's to support the team. I think that's more to stop a passing thug smashing their window. Now, I'm not saying I won't ever turn up to watch West Ham in a sari, because you never know where the tide of fashion is going to carry you. Obviously, David Beckham's tried it, but I did beat him to the punch by wearing one out in the Maldives years ago, although to be honest it probably looked a bit better on him than it did on me.

CHAPTER 12

VICTORIA PARK LIDO

I lost my virginity when I was fourteen years old. I was staying at Nanny Rich's in Shoeburyness and I met a girl on the beach. She must've been a raving lunatic because it was a freezing cold winter's day and she only had a bikini on.

There was no one else about. One minute I was just having a chat with her, and the next thing I knew I was in the woods by the mini-golf, losing my virginity standing up. I thought I'd done myself some damage afterwards.

I think she was eighteen, and I wasn't one of those kids who look older than they are. When I was fourteen, I looked it, maybe even younger. Bearing in mind our ages I suppose I was less a sexual partner and more a (willing) victim of abuse, but it didn't feel that way at the time, God bless her! I don't remember the girl's name – if I ever knew it – but I know her initials were 'GG', because she had them on a gold chain around her neck. Of course, I've loved the gee-gees ever since.

There'd always been girlfriends in my life, right back to when I was a little kid in Plaistow playing 'put a big bandage on the war hero' with the twins Kim and Tracy and Jeanie Green from down the end. Obviously the sexuality part of it is new from twelve or thirteen onwards, and it was different in those times – kids didn't mature as early as they do today.

Bikini-clad lunatics aside, the first port of call in the courtship process would usually be taking a bird up the pictures. The trouble was – aficionado of the big screen that I was even then – I always wanted to watch the film. If it was more a cuddle and a handful that you were after, you were better off taking them to a poxy movie you weren't interested in. It would probably be *Love Story* with Ryan O'Neal, and there's only one reason any heterosexual teenage boy would go and see that.

I'm not sure if it was *Love Story* (although the dates are about right, as I was thirteen when it came out) but I remember being sat in the cinema once with my arm round a girl and thinking my hand was on her threepenny when it was actually on her shoulder. She must have thought I was very sensitive to be paying so much attention to that particular area of her body – a shoulder massage would've been considered wildly metrosexual in Enfield in 1970.

By the time I got properly into my mid-teens, I'd probably be going out to a club once a week. I couldn't afford to do it more often than that, but it was possible to go up the Tottenham Royal and pull a bird on a fiver in those days. The bus-fare alone wouldn't be far off that now.

I still looked young, so I was always being asked my age on the door, but I overcame that obstacle with the same strategy which worked so well when it came to getting in to X-rated films. I used to say I was a jockey up at the Crews Hill country gallops at Enfield. It worked every time, probably because it had the element of surprise about it, as it didn't seem like the sort of story anyone would bother to make up. Even once I'd grown quite tall this ruse didn't stop doing the job for me. The only time I ever got turned away from anywhere was a few years later when I actually was eighteen. At that point I parked the jockey story, and they refused to believe I was old enough, even after they'd seen my driving licence. Sometimes it's easier to look like you're in the right when you're guilty than when you haven't actually done anything wrong, because that way your mind is properly focused on what you need to do, and innocence can breed complacency.

Once inside the Tottenham Royal, what we were all looking to do was get on the last-dance express. We weren't really much for dancing, we just used to chat with the birds and have a look about, then, when the night started to wind down, we'd be in like Flint.

I remember 'Love Train' by The O'Jays was a song that was very good to me. 'Slow one?', 'Alright, then', 'Where d'you live?', 'Stamford Hill', 'Sorry, wrong way'. If there was someone going back towards Enfield, that was perfecto, but you might consider the other direction if she was a really good sort. That's terrible, isn't it? But you know what boys are like . . . and girls ain't too far behind when it comes to being unmerciful.

My way around that was always to start off going for the ones where it looked like you didn't have a chance, because if that didn't work out you could always work your way down the scale a bit. At least that way the other girls would be impressed that you'd had the balls to give it a go and they might think they'd got a catch. It's no good starting at the bottom and trying to work your way up. Sometimes you'd get yourself in trouble by having three or four girls on the go at once and end up with nothing. But that would serve you right for getting too greedy, and next time you'd know that a bird in the hand is worth three in Shepherd's Bush.

A lot of people who get into acting or music do it for the girls (or the boys) they wouldn't have a shot at otherwise. I'm not being flash when I say that this was never what it was about for me. I already knew how to talk to a girl – or pull a bird, or whatever way you want to put it – so I never had that problem.

I'm not saying it was easy, because it wasn't. In fact, it was hard work. Looks weren't my forte. No girl worth having was just gonna see me on the dance floor of the Tottenham Royal and think, 'Oh, he's lovely.' We'd have to have a talk if I was going to get anywhere. That's why going to gigs never appealed to me, because the music was so loud you couldn't talk to anyone, and you (or at least I) couldn't pull a bird if she couldn't hear what you were saying. Me and Tony Yeates or whoever else it was would be more likely to give the big-band night at the Southgate Royalty a try, which was like a throwback to the forties. Or when we were a little bit older, we'd go to the Goldmine on Canvey Island, where they did all the Glenn Miller stuff.

Luckily, I was a bit of a past master at that thing where you and the girl are both looking across the room and you time it perfectly so that just as she catches your eye, you duck your head and look shy. It's the show of vulnerability that's the key. I used to practise on our dog, Brandy. Everyone loved him 'cos he had sad eyes, even though he was vicious. I used to watch him and think, 'Blindin'! That'll do it.' (Anthony Hopkins was the same; he had those big, watery puppy eyes too, especially when he was drinking.) Of course, this tactical approach – Brandy-eyes instead of beer-goggles, or maybe with a beer-goggle chaser – wouldn't always pay off, but I've got to tell you, the old 'Who, me . . . with all my hidden complexities?' routine worked ninety-nine times out of a hundred.

Apart from the Tottenham Royal, another venue with a bit of potential as far as girls were concerned was Victoria Park Lido. You didn't just go there to swim. I'd be down there all the time in the summer when I was fourteen or fifteen – in the morning in the school holidays, or later on for a bit of a lounge about if I'd done a hard morning on the market. There was nowhere better to have a laugh with the chaps or chat to some girls. There used to be a bit of peacocking going on, but I never really had the physique to be swaggering round the fucking pool with my budgie-smugglers on.

The lido's gone now – it was closed in 1986 and demolished a few years later – but Victoria Park is still one of the great parks of London. It used to be called 'The People's Park' because of its strong tradition of political protest, and even though it's not so much talked about as the more well-connected green spaces of West London, the avenues are so grand you could be in Regent's Park, and the boating lake's like the Serpentine, only with fewer tourists.

Everywhere else around it got bombed really badly in the war, but Victoria Park stayed pretty much intact – either because a load of ack-ack batteries were stationed there, or because the Germans wanted to keep it nice just in case they won. The feel of the place goes further back than that, though, at least it does to me. It's a real bit of old London whose bandstands and deer-park reek of the age of Empire (although the deer themselves have their own distinctive aroma).

Part of the reason I associate Victoria Park so strongly with military conquests gone by is the stories my uncle Flabby used to tell me when I'd visit him as a younger kid. Old Flabs wasn't a blood relative – I think my dad had gone out with his daughter before he met my mum – but I used to love going round to his house and listening to his tall tales of when he was in India with the British Army back in the day.

He told me some terrible stories – which are always the kind you're most interested when you're little – about how all the British soldiers in India were given an order that if they were ever in a car accident with a local they had to back up and run them over again to save on the insurance payouts. How true that is I don't know, and the same goes for the story about soldiers going over ravines on trains and deliberately pushing people off the bridges with their boots, but knowing people's inhumanity to people in occupation or wartime situations, they both kind of read as true. And maybe they give you a bit of the historical backdrop to some of the tensions between people of white and Asian backgrounds in the East End in recent years.

Apart from Britain's imperial past, the other thing Victoria Park always made me think of was armed robbery. And not just because of the time some blaggers stole my dad's black Ford Zephyr and drove it into the pond – hardly the best way to avoid drawing attention to yourself. There used to be a lot of talk locally about how many bank robbers used to train in the park. They'd jog around it planning their next blag secure in the knowledge that they were out of the range of flapping ears.

The thing about armed robbers is they're not always the fittest, but they do have that competitive instinct, so every now and then one of them would get a bit carried away with the old running and just keel over – heart attack. Maybe it's true what they say: it's a dangerous life being a blagger, but even more so if you throw a bit of jogging in as well.

Then again, there are a lot of myths surrounding those people. One of them is the idea that they always drive Jags. In fact that's the worst car to use in a bank robbery, because they've got a special switch-off button which kills the engine if you hit a kerb or something. The button is down by your right foot apparently, but you don't really want to be scrabbling around down there to restart the engine if you've gone over a level crossing too fast with the Flying

Squad on your tail. 'No Jags in blags' – that's probably the best way to remember this.

I was always fascinated by stories about the old-school London underworld. I'm not saying I was old before my years, because I wasn't. I was basically a little kid inside for a long time, probably till I was about forty (and Elaine might question whether my passport was properly stamped for the land of adulthood even then). But working on the markets and training and fighting at the Repton gave me a sense of myself as someone who could be accepted in grown-up situations from quite an early age. I was always comfortable in the company of people from older generations – whether it was my nan and granddad, or Uncle Flabs, or even the actors whose films I loved the best, who often tended to be men from earlier times like Jimmy Cagney, James Stewart or John Wayne.

There was something about those three where their flaws were also their strengths. Like in that John Wayne film where he's a bigot who hates Indians because they raped his niece – *The Searchers* – for someone like him to do a film like that was quite shocking. And obviously it's a bit later – I was doing the first *Scum* by then – but John Wayne gives an amazing performance in his last film, *The Shootist*, where he's dying of cancer and he knows it. He's just so naked and open about what his illness is doing to him, and he's not usually an actor you think of as making himself vulnerable.

Alan Hewitt was still sneaking us into the Florida in Tottenham to see X-rated films throughout my early teenage years. I remember seeing a great Italian B-movie there – probably with *Frankenstein* (the film: I wasn't dating the monster) – called *Four Flies on Grey Velvet*, where the last thing the murderer saw was these four flies on a swinging pendant. I think it's the only film I've ever seen that starts with a drum solo.

The idea that I might end up being an actor myself in films of that quality or even higher one day still wouldn't have occurred to me. Even once my mum and dad came up with the idea of me going to drama college, it wasn't something that really connected in my mind with what happened up on the big screen – I just thought of it as something to do.

What with boxing, early-morning starts for the markets, and the girls of the Tottenham Royal and the Victoria Park Lido all competing for my attention, it was no wonder there wasn't much time left for homework. Getting up for school in the morning had already begun to feel like a waste of energy that would be better put to other uses. When you meet the careers adviser and they ask what you want to do, and you say, 'I'm thinking of going to drama college', and they laugh in your face, that does give you a bit of extra motivation. You might not know exactly what your long-term goal is, but you know it's not to sit behind a fucking desk trying to crush kids' dreams.

I held the record for the highest number of detentions at Edmonton County. Detention was a pointless punishment by my way of thinking – I'd choose the cane over detention any day, and did so on a number of occasions. As far as me and school were concerned, the straw that broke the camel's back (or in this case the three-year-old thoroughbred's back) was when my dad took me off for the day to the 1972 Derby to help him sell a load of umbrellas. When the teacher asked where I'd been afterwards I was honest about it, and we got in trouble for telling the truth. My dad explained that he'd thought going to the Derby would be an education for me, but they didn't like that, so they suspended me, and I never really went back.

Whether it actually was an education is debatable – he probably just wanted somebody to carry his umbrellas for him – but it was certainly a blinding day out. At first it looked like we were on a hiding to nothing because it was a lovely sunny morning, but then it pissed down in the early afternoon and so we sold all the brollies. But that was where my dad's luck ran out, as the horse he'd put a nice few quid on in the big one that day got pushed out wide coming round Tattenham corner and Piggott said, 'See you later' on Roberto, timing his run like the master he was.

We still had a great day, though. Granddad got us into Tattersalls and Lester came walking really close to us through the enclosure. It was funny with Piggott – he was the king of Epsom, but people took the mick out of him a bit as well. He was much taller than normal for a jockey, which was why they called him 'The Long Fellow'. The two things everyone knows about him are that he was famous for his love of a pound note, and he talked the way he talked because he was deaf. Someone in the crowd put those two facts together by shouting out, 'Oi! You dropped a tenner, Lester', as he walked past us. Of course the great man turned round to pick it up, and my granddad said, 'Well, he heard that.'

When the school suspended me for taking one day off I just thought, 'Fuck 'em, I don't really need this. I'm not the brightest of sparks and I could probably stay here for the rest of my life without becoming an intellectual, so I might as well go out into the world and find something I can do that's actually going to benefit me.' It wasn't like I was a problem kid – I was doing well with the boxing, and I was always up to something. Maybe that was part of it. My mum and dad saw me in that school play and thought acting might be a way of occupying my mind and keeping me out of trouble.

I know how strange the idea of my parents sending me to a £900-a-term drama college will probably seem, because I still can't believe it happened, and I was there. Money was less tight than it had been by then, but we weren't rolling in it on any level. Maybe it was a bit of Nanny Rich's speculate-to-accumulate mentality coming in – and maybe a bit of her money as well. Or maybe that was just what was going on in my head, and my mum and dad had a different agenda. For all I know, they might've thought I was gay and the boxing was just a cover, so they wanted to get me doing some fencing and ballet to help me find myself.

Either way, at the time I don't remember thinking my dad in particular thought I was ever going to amount to anything very much, but the fact that he and my mum enrolled me in drama college says differently. OK, the Corona Academy in Ravenscourt Park didn't have that great a reputation. It wasn't exactly RADA – although ex-students did include Dennis Waterman – so you didn't really have to do too much to get in: a willingness to keep stumping up that £900 was all it took. But thinking about it now, I can see that my parents were backing me to do something different. And I owe them a lot for having that confidence in me when I might not have had it in myself.

In the long gap between me leaving school prematurely at fifteen and starting at Corona in 1973, they even got a nice Scottish drama teacher to give me some elocution lessons. Mrs McNair's daughter went to my school – I'd done an amateur play in Enfield with her – and she was a really good teacher who helped me build up confidence in my voice before I went to drama school. It was all about being able to speak clearly and with crisp enunciation – qualities for which I am now of course renowned throughout the world (and you should've heard me before I had the elocution lessons!)

CHAPTER 13

THE THEATRE ROYAL, STRATFORD EAST

When I'd left school it had been very much in a fuck-you-I'm-off kind of way, but that probably made starting at Corona more daunting, not less. It felt like a very grown-up place, more of a college than a school. I was walking into this different world without having really done anything to earn the right to be there. It's not like I'd won a scholarship for acting or gone through a gruelling audition process. My mum and dad applied on my behalf and all they had to do for me to get in was come up with £900 three times a year.

I was probably a bit embarrassed about that. I knew I was now growing up to a point where I was going to have to take responsibility for how I was living, and I couldn't rely on my mum and dad to look after me for much longer. I enjoyed my day-to-day existence, but beyond the odd little scam here and there, taking a bird out and saving up for a nice holiday every now and then, I didn't have much idea of what I wanted to do with my life.

None of the experience I'd gained being out in the big wide world – either boxing or working for my dad – seemed to count for very much at Corona. It couldn't have been much further off my usual manor without me needing a passport to get there. I had to catch the train from Lower Edmonton, change at Seven Sisters onto the Victoria Line tube to Victoria and then get the district line to Ravenscourt Park. That was a funny old journey. It took at least an hour even on a good day. On the upside, John Le Mesurier did get on my train once. I still love *Dad's Army* now, but it was a huge show then. He boarded a carriage full of schoolkids and signed autographs for all of them – what a lovely man!

There were other compensations to hold on to in my first few weeks at Corona. All the girls were beautiful and there were probably three other boys in my class who were straight, so I had a field day in that department – it was a bit of a fox-in-the-chicken-coop situation. I also had two really good teachers, Bill Happer and Vernon Morris, who both did their best to encourage me even when I was refusing to play the game.

Vernon Morris was a very good actor in his own right. He'd played the Polish traitor – the one who ends up getting hanged – in *Colditz*. What he did for me was help me get over any problem I might otherwise have had with three quarters of the geezers in the class being gay. His methods were unconventional but effective. First he sat me next to a guy called Paul, who as a child actor had been the kid who offers a cigarette to the parachuted airman in the *Battle of Britain* film, but was now the same age as me and as gay as they come.

I didn't know this at the time, but Mr Morris had told Paul to put his hand on my leg. Now, I'd never been approached like that before, and being a bit of a chap it wasn't really what I was expecting, so I just went really cold on him and said, 'Get your fucking hand off my leg!' At that point I looked up to see the whole class starting to laugh and I realised Mr Morris had set me up. 'That's what it's all about, Raymond,' he said. 'Welcome to the world of theatre.' I knew he'd done it to put me in my place a little bit, and his strategy worked. Mainly because it was for my own benefit – it wasn't like a drama-school version of *Scum* where Mr Morris was trying to break my spirit so I would succumb to the power of musical theatre.

It was actually good for me to have to find a way of fitting into a community of people from different backgrounds, either socially or in other ways, because small-mindedness was only going to hold me back in anything I wanted to do in the future. It's fear that makes you react like that. You're feeling a bit like a fish out of water, anyway, and you try to hide your anxiety about what people might say or think about you by being aggressive or abrupt or a bit of a rebel.

From that point onwards I learnt very quickly that there was no reason for me to be threatened by other people's sexuality. Anything that they wanted to get up to was their own business, and the more of them that were gay, the more girls that left me to choose from. Besides, once I got to know these kids, I found that I actually liked them – even the really posh ones, who I might have considered to be the enemy before. OK, they didn't come from where I came from, but that didn't have to be a bad thing. And if they were willing to tolerate how different my outlook on life was to theirs, then why shouldn't I extend the same courtesy to them?

That's not to say I went along with everything I was asked to do at Corona, because some of it was a bit ridiculous, but I enjoyed going there because every day was a party. And my role in the class I was in was to be the token rebellious working-class kid, so the least I could do was to act up to it.

Ballet was one of the big problem areas. I know this will come as a big surprise to all those expecting me to have a natural gift for the old *pas de deux*, but I lasted about two minutes. I dance like a boxer, anyway, and my insistence that I was going to wear Dr Marten's boots with all the ballet gear probably didn't help. I could be really fucking stubborn – and probably a major pain in the arse – when I wanted to be at that age. (Don't ask my Elaine how much I've changed since.) So everybody else probably breathed a sigh of relief when I decided to skip the ballet lessons and go to the cinema instead. I probably learnt more from the ABC just down the road from Ravenscourt Park, anyway.

Fencing classes didn't go too smoothly either. It wasn't the shouting things in French that I had a problem with – I was fine with all that '*en garde*', '*prêt*' and '*allez*' stuff – it was just a few of the finer points of the etiquette that I struggled to grasp. They had a little demonstration and I thought, 'OK, I can do that.' At first I shaped up like a fighter, but the sword is in the other hand, so you've got to go southpaw because that's the more natural way to go. Next thing I knew, there was a kid coming up to me giving it all that with the swish, swish, swish.

We squared up to each other and then instinct took over. Even years later I still can't believe I did this, but I stepped to one side and clumped him with the cup of the sword handle. At that point he's gone on the penny and while he's down on the ground I've stabbed him a couple of times just to be sure. Obviously I've not really stabbed him because the end of the blade is covered and he's got the wire mask on, but I thought that was what sword-fighting was all about. All the other kids are laughing and the instructor's going, 'No, no, no, that's not how you do it.'

The first few times you get given scripts that you have to learn is even more nerve-racking. Everyone has to work out their own way of doing it. At first I just used to read them over and over, but that wasn't really doing the job, so then I started to write them out. I would read the line and then write it out again for myself – no punctuation, just how I thought the character would say it – and that way I'd find I could really take the words in. I don't have to do that all the time now, but I still will if I've got something really heavy to learn. Generally, the better the script is, the easier it is to get the hang of it. If it's shit you'll just find yourself looking at the page thinking, 'I've got to do something to try and make this better.'

The first play I was in at drama school was called *The Trojan Women*. I'm not sure who it was by – I couldn't even pronounce the name – but I had to wear a little skinny loincloth with nothing covering my chest, and this Greek helmet with all these feathers in it. I've got the spear, the sword, everything – its almost like 'they're taking the piss, now'. As soon as I opened my mouth in that outfit everything I said sounded ridiculously London-y. It turned the whole thing into a comedy, but not necessarily in a good way – it's not a good feeling when you can see everyone laughing but you're not sure if they're laughing with you or at you.

It wasn't the most sympathetic piece of casting – I felt like a total dick. I suppose they just threw me in there thinking they'd test me, and I failed the test miserably. The next play we did was some jolly-hockey-sticks Agatha Christie thing, where I was meant to come through some French doors but one of my mates had tied them together, so I tried to squeeze in through the French windows instead and got stuck. Even though no one was taking the whole thing very seriously, once I finally got onstage it actually felt OK. I couldn't be getting any worse because the only way to go from *The Trojan Women* was up, and at least I wasn't wearing a loincloth.

The third part was the breakthrough. It was in Edward Albee's *The Zoo Story*, which I actually managed to learn properly because it was good and I wanted to do it. The play's about a couple of guys who meet on a bench in Central Park, and Mr Morris directed me and a guy called David Morris (no relation to Vernon) in it. That was where I really started to learn, partly because it was a two-hander and I like small company, and partly because I played the weaker character. I didn't have to be the nutter. I got to play the guy who was scared and had an emotional crisis. This was the first time I'd ever done anything like that, and I was surprised at how comfortable it felt – almost like freeing myself.

I enjoyed the intensity of just having two people in a scene and what happened when they met shaping the direction of the story. David Morris was a terrific actor, far in front of where I or probably anyone else was at that school at the time. With him leading the way I was improving from rehearsal to rehearsal. And by the time we finally put the play on, the audience were quite shocked by how good it was (especially given what a disaster my earlier appearances onstage had been). I could feel myself holding their attention, and when you do that it's like finding your timing as a boxer – you feint and you pull them in, then you jab and get 'em off balance. That was when I started to think, 'Maybe I can do this after all.' It wasn't just that I was taking it seriously, I was really enjoying it.

Needless to say, not every assignment at Corona went so smoothly. Shakespeare was something I thought I'd never be able to do, because it was too wordy for me and I didn't have the necessary command of the English language. As it turned out, not having that received pronunciation they teach you gave me quite a natural way of reading Shakespeare.

I did the thing I normally do, anyway, which is leave all the punctuation out. People stop in the middle of sentences all the time when they're talking, so why shouldn't characters in his plays do that too?

This technique stood me in good stead, and even though I might not have known what all the individual words meant, I seemed to be able to get across the overall meaning pretty well.

We'd have lessons on it where they'd tell us precisely what everything was supposed to mean according to the experts, but my attitude to the Shakespeare scholars was that they could fuck off. It's the same with a play as it is with a book – fair enough, the authors' intentions were important to them at the time, but it's how the whole thing comes alive in your imagination that matters to you.

Sadly, the examiners of my London Academy of Dramatic Arts exam didn't feel the same way. I'm not sure how much use those exams are – they certainly aren't going to get you a job – and they're normally incredibly boring because everyone has to do the same fucking speech. In my case it was the 'Wherefore rejoice what conquest brings' bit from *Julius Caesar*, which I probably know better now than I did then. I decided to make my version a little bit different to liven things up, so I set it in a pub. This was before Steven Berkoff and all that, so it was still quite an original idea (or at least I thought I was).

To me, the way the speech read was that this was a geezer praising the new guy coming in and mugging the old one off – the gangster who used to run that plot has been topped and all his mates are saying, 'Hold up, better get in with Tiberius.' So that's how I did it. I got zero for acting ability, which I can't argue with because it's an opinion. But the one that really got me was zero for imagination. I thought, 'Everyone else has done it exactly the same way except me, so surely I brought something to the table that no one else did?' I wasn't thinking I should've automatically got ten, but I should've certainly got something.

The good thing was that instead of discouraging me the way that it might have, the unfairness of this was actually a bit of a turning point for me. It brought my stubbornness into play by making me think, 'You're having a pop here, and I think I'm right, so I'm going to show you.' I wish I thought someone who wanted the best for me came up with this idea as a deliberate plan to motivate me, but I don't.

One of my first professional engagements was at the Theatre Royal, Stratford East. It was a revival of the Alan Klein musical *What a Crazy World We're Living In*, which Joe Brown had done as a film years before. By the time I got there in the mid-seventies Joan Littlewood (whose name was always associated with that theatre) wasn't so involved with the place any more. Her partner Gerry Raffles, who still ran it, was about to die of diabetes. He'd stood in front of the bulldozers when the Stratford shopping centre redevelopment threatened the theatre building with demolition, but he'd taken his eye off the ball a bit afterwards. I'd never have got cast in a role that required singing and dancing otherwise. It wasn't a very good part, and I wasn't very good in it. 'Dad's gone down the dog track/Mother's playing bingo' is one of the only lines I can remember.

I went to Stratford East with very little idea about the technique of being onstage and all that palaver, but what I learnt there about the reality of life in a professional theatre had much more impact on me than any acting tips I picked up. It turned out that my idea of it was much cleaner and more glamorous than the way things actually went down.

I'd expected almost regimental discipline and a dedication to the craft worthy of Sir Laurence Olivier. Instead, I found a load of fucking hippies smoking fags and drinking beer. I hated all the mess backstage and the whole thing felt a bit studenty for my tastes – it crushed a lot of my illusions about how the acting game was run. Maybe that was no bad thing in the long term, but when you see some actor you know off the telly and they're just like some scunger, you end up thinking, 'I don't wanna be that.' It destroys the fantasy.

As if getting paid £30 a week and a bowl of rice wasn't bad enough, you had to put up with Vanessa Redgrave coming down to tell you how you should give half your wages to the Workers' Revolutionary Party. Now I respect anybody else's opinion, but I've never been into all that commie lark. My thing was always 'you've got to look after your own', which I suppose is kind of what communism is in a way, or at least how it usually seems to turn out when people try to put it into practice. Either way, I ain't giving you £15 a week of my money. 'Sell your house, darlin'', that was how I looked at it.

I didn't say that while Vanessa Redgrave was giving her talk, of course. That would've been rude. I sat and listened to her for a while and then got up quietly to make my exit. She saw me and called out, 'Where are you going?' When I politely called back, 'Thank you, but I'm leaving. I've heard enough', she seemed pretty pissed off, because she shouted, 'But you won't learn anything unless you listen', so I said, 'Well, I won't fucking learn anything from you', and off I went.

I've never met her again since. She's a fantastic actress and she's probably a nice woman as well. I'm sure she did her bit for the party, and good luck to her, but from what I can gather it came out later on that some of the people running her organisation weren't exactly whiter than white in how they conducted themselves. A lot of that kind of sleazy shit was going on in those days, and not just in the *Top of the Pops* dressing room.

There's a Pizza Express alongside the theatre now, where we played football in the builders' sand. Another shopping centre's gone up since – the much flashier Westfield, which was opened just in time for the Olympics – but the Theatre Royal looks pretty much the same as it did forty years ago. I'm not sure it's even had a coat of paint since then. It's still there in all its horrible purple glory.

I guess we're still living in a crazy world too, so no change there either. I'll never forget the opening night of that musical. My parents came down to Stratford to watch it. My dad was all suited up with a silk hankie in his jacket pocket and he had a gin and tonic in his hand. I came off stage and I'd been terrible – danced the wrong way, told jokes no one laughed at, the lot – and he just shook his head and said, 'Give it up while you're in front, son.'

CHAPTER 14

YORK HALL

I've got to tell you about the boxing match I had in Canterbury when the Repton and Fitzroy Lodge clubs went down there together. I'd been out Kent way a couple of times before as a young kid – to the hop farms. Going 'hopping' used to be a bit of a working holiday for East End families who wouldn't have had too many chances to get out of London otherwise, but that particular boxing match was more a gypsy coach-crash than a busman's holiday.

My dad's mate Terry Spinks, who'd won the Olympic gold medal, was there. I'm on the scales weighing in ready to fight. I've got the velvet shorts on, the green-and-gold top – to be honest with you I look a million dollars (if I don't say this, no one else is going to). Then the kid I'm fighting gets up there. He's got a pair of old pumps, baggy shorts, no front teeth and a broken hooter. So straight away I'm thinking, 'He's been hit a few times, this is gonna be easy.'

Right from the start of the fight, I'm just going ping! Picking him off nicely. Can't miss – he's walking into 'em. Then at the end of the first round, I hit him square on the chin and he's straight down on the canvas – wallop! He came out for the second like a fucking lunatic – bit me, elbowed me, kneed me in the groin, stood on my feet, hit me with everything. He just lost the plot completely. I probably won the fight easier than I would've done otherwise, but he did make me pay for it. I don't think I got out of bed for a day and a half afterwards.

He was a little rat, but he had some heart. My career record as an amateur boxer was eighty wins out of eighty-eight fights, and in all that time I met one opponent I disliked as a person. It wasn't this kid with the broken hooter, it was another guy who I could tell was a nasty fucker from the moment we shook hands.

Even while I was boxing him, I was thinking, 'You are not a nice fella.' He had all the technical knowledge to be a good fighter, so why was he trying to head-butt me in the clinches? He didn't want to know when it was time to shake hands after I'd beaten him, either, and I just thought, 'You can go fuck yourself. You've just had one hiding – do you want another one?'

That fight was one of the very few bad memories I took away from York Hall in Bethnal Green. Obviously there's Wembley and the Albert Hall as well, but as far as grassroots boxing in England goes, York Hall is the home of it. The building is a swimming pool in the daytime, so if you go there at any other time, it doesn't really feel like anything special. But I had some great nights there, and when you step into that ring and the roar goes up, there's an atmosphere like nowhere else – because it's a municipal baths, you can imagine the echo you get.

I had thirteen wins at York Hall, and it's been my lucky number ever since.

A boxing match is nothing like street fighting. First off because you've got a referee to stop it – that's a major difference. Also, street fights (when they're not a formal 'straightener' like that time in Spitalfields Market) are usually over anger, whereas if you let anger come into boxing, you're probably going to lose.

The one time I lost at York Hall, it wasn't me who got angry. The kid I was boxing was good and it was close, but I thought I won it. In fact, it was probably the best I've ever boxed. But the Repton was a big club, and every now and then they used to surrender someone to make it look fair. York Hall was effectively our home venue so they had to show that we weren't in control of the decisions, and that night it was my turn to be sacrificed. Well, that's my story and I'm sticking to it. I know this might sound like I'm making excuses, but as a general rule in boxing you know when you've won and you know when you've lost.

Either way, old Sammy Keyworth who worked with us on Roman Road Market wasn't too happy about the decision. He'd come along to watch me fight, and when the verdict went against me he took umbrage in a major way. The mayor of Tower Hamlets was sitting in front of him, and Sammy was so angry he kicked the guy's chair over. The mayor went flying in all his regalia, chains and ermine everywhere – it was hilarious.

I got a nice little consolation prize at the end of that evening when I won the Fighter of the Night award from the Marksman pub. As you can imagine, it was pretty unusual for that to go to a boxer who'd lost, so I think that showed where their sympathies lay.

Another great night at York Hall was when I won John H. Stracey's trophy as Fighter of the Year for going a whole twelve months undefeated. He's a great mate of mine even now, John. I'll never forget the time he won the world title against José Nápoles. The funny thing about that was that they didn't televise the fight live – it wasn't on till the day after, and the commentator (I can't remember if it was Reg Gutteridge or Harry Carpenter) had to put the voiceover on afterwards, pretending he hadn't already seen it. But he couldn't help himself, so he kept saying things like, 'I definitely feel John H. Stracey is going to win.'

The East End had more than its fair share of world boxing champions in those days. Charlie Magri was another one. He was a great boy, Charlie – I think his dad was a tailor. He boxed at the Arbour youth club in Stepney, which wasn't far from the Repton, and he was about the same age as me, so we all became mates when he was coming up through the ranks. I was there when he won the world title and I had a drink with him after he lost it. You made so many connections in boxing – more than any other business I've ever come across, and they're real friendships as well. Obviously you meet a lot of people in the acting game, but there's more loyalty in boxing.

I had three fights in one night at York Hall once at the London Federation of Boys Clubs championships (which I think I'm still the only person to have won in three different years). That took me right the way through to the NABC's, but it all went wrong with the last punch of the semi-finals. I jabbed the fella and he ducked his head and took my hand under with him, which broke the finger on my jabbing hand. If it had been the right hand I'd have probably got away with it, but as it was I couldn't box in the final. Obviously, I was gutted at the time, but I'd have had to take on a good fighter. His name was George Walker, and he was a big strong kid who might have been too much of a handful for me, anyway, at the time. But we'll never know because he got a bye and became the champion.

Boxing for the Repton does open doors, because it is a big famous club and they do produce some great fighters, but I never looked at myself as being good enough to join them. That's not me being modest, I honestly didn't imagine myself as being that good at anything. I never had that ... inner belief is, I suppose, what you call it. Even now when I watch a sportsman perform really well I always think it's absolutely fantastic, but I never see what they're doing as something I'd be capable of, any more than I did when I saw Bobby Moore lift the World Cup.

I did get to box for England a couple of times. I was still a junior then – maybe sixteen – and I got picked because I'd won the Middlesex and London championships, which automatically gives you the chance to box for your country. I'd have been a light welterweight at that time, and it was a home nations fixture, England versus Wales.

There were two bouts and I boxed a kid called Gary Ace in the first one. They're tough kids from that part of the world and he was a good fighter, but I had the secret weapon that was Repton coach Jackie Bowers in my corner. You never wanted to go back in your corner at the end of the round when Jackie was there because he'd give you a harder time than the other fighter would. He'd tell me, 'You'll never be a fighter', and I'd say, 'I don't want to be a fucking fighter, Jack – do you think I want to get punched in the face all my life?' That's how the conversations between us used to go.

I had a lot of time for Jackie, both as a coach and as a man, and he did me proud that night. Because I was known as a counter-puncher, Gary was expecting me to be on the back foot from the off so Jackie said, 'Just walk straight across and hit him on the chin with a right-hander.' I did, and he went straight through the ropes. That kind of livened him up and from that point on I boxed beautifully – he says modestly – and I won in the end. My other fight was against another little Welsh tough-nut. I did alright in that one as well, but not alright enough to win. I'm not saying I was robbed, but it was a good job Sammy Keyworth wasn't there.

Although I appreciated my dad coming to watch me, I always thought I boxed better when he wasn't there. He used to get rather excited, and I suppose I was more worried about what my dad was thinking than I was about what I was doing. I bear that in mind with my eldest girl Lois these days. She's a singer and I really like what she does, but I don't go to every gig – even though she wants me to – because I like her not to have to worry about what I'm thinking of it.

I had a particular way of being nervous before a fight, which is still how I get to this day when I'm doing a film. Some people would be physically sick with nerves, but I'd get very tired and start falling asleep instead. I'd try to keep myself going but I'd just feel really lethargic – I think it was the loss of all the energy my nerves were burning. I'd get a kind of fear as well. Not a fear of being punched – well, I suppose there might have been a bit of that – but more a general anxiety about not doing what you're supposed to do, just forgetting it all. That's how I'd feel until the bell went at the start of the first round, then I'd wake up – like the drunk guy in the pub who springs to attention when he hears 'last orders'.

I'm more or less the same on a film set, even now. There's always that fear in the time leading up to it. You're thinking, 'Why couldn't I have done this yesterday when I was feeling great, instead of today when I've got no energy and can't remember the words? What are the fucking words again?' Then someone shouts 'Action!' and nine times out of ten – thank God – it's alright. You work the scene out because you've got a fine actor opposite you, the timing's working and bam! some energy floods into you.

That's why I say boxing was probably more of an education for me as an actor than stage school was (apart from the ballet, obvious- ly – that was an essential). Because without the boxing I wouldn't have known what that feeling is where you step through the ropes into the ring thinking, 'Why am I putting myself through this shit?'

Whether you're climbing into the ring or walking onstage there's no fundamental difference, what matters is what you do next.

I remember the first senior fight I had at the age of seventeen. It was at Alan Minter's club in Crawley, and I've got to tell you that when I was seventeen, you'd have looked at me and guessed I was at least fucking twelve. I was reasonably tall – five foot nine or ten – but I looked like I should still be in shorts and plastic sandals. I think I've said before that when you get in the ring you have a little look in the guy's eyes opposite and you know whether you're going to win or not. This time, when the other geezer took his gown off, he was covered in tattoos (and this was when having a tattoo still meant something) and hairy as a fucking gorilla. I don't know what they're putting in the water down Crawley way. He was meant to be my age but he looked about thirty-five.

All of a sudden you're not boxing boys any more, you're boxing men. It's like moving up from borstal into prison. I mean, the geezer had hairy legs – I'd never had a hair on my legs in my life! At this point you either decide you've got no chance and give up, or you approach it like a chess match and try to find a way to win. The first round I went with plan A and I was just totally overwhelmed. But then I went back in my corner and thought, 'Fuck this!' The second round I started boxing differently and it was much more even. Then I pissed the third round and won the fight.

That discipline of standing there thinking, 'I can't do this', and then taking a deep breath and giving it a go really stands you in good stead for the rest of your life. It's not just a matter of digging deep inside yourself, you've also got to clear your mind. The way you calm yourself down and convince yourself that nothing's impossible is almost like meditation – that's what gives you the confidence to keep yourself out of harm's way. If you do it right, you can almost get a feeling that the other geezer can't hurt you (even though obviously they can). It's funny with pain, I find I've got a way of switching it off. I don't know if that's a good thing or not, because sometimes pain is there for a reason.

It's the same with a script where there's something dark or difficult that's going to happen. You've got to close that down a bit so you can go beyond it. And the fear you have when you first pick it up and maybe think you can't do it is the thing which is going to help you do that. It's the equivalent of Jackie Bowers in my corner when I was boxing a kid called Terry Parker at the London Feds Finals. I came back at the end of the first round and got beaten up worse than I had been in the ring. Jackie's slapping me round the head going, 'C'mon, liven up', and I'm thinking, 'Fuck that, I'd rather be out there boxing than in here fighting him.'

Once you're out there, that's when the ringcraft comes in – the stuff that Billy Howick taught me at the Repton. It's all about the positioning of your feet and where you move – all the little tricks of pushing someone's arms down to get them off balance and then getting a jab in. A lot of it is kind of on the borderline of being illegal, but there are ways of being illegal which are still within the spirit of the game. And so long as the head coach Burnsy's matched you up not to get hurt, like he always does, hopefully you'll keep the old face intact.

CHAPTER 15

THE PROSPECT OF WHITBY, WAPPING

It was partly going to Corona that pushed boxing into the wings. But the gloves were also coming off as far as drinking was concerned, and they were already long gone when it came to girls. I didn't give the boxing up for good. I would put the gloves back on and return to the ring for two more fights a couple of years later, but that would be my Elvis in Vegas phase.

In the meantime, the discipline I'd learnt at the Repton helped keep me out of some of the scrapes I'd probably have got into otherwise, but not all of them. One incident which has stuck in my mind, for reasons which will soon become obvious, was when I went away for a few days with a mate from drama college called John Walford. His mum lived with a French Basque geezer in Andorra, this strange little tax haven in the Spanish Alps who are one of the few teams England can usually be expected to beat in the World Cup.

Now, the Spanish and the French Basques don't tend to get on with one another particularly well, but I wasn't too bothered about all that. I was too busy sliding around the place in all this moody ski gear – basically a pair of jeans and a woolly hat. One night we went to a club that was up on the top of this mountain. It was full of Spanish and French, not mixing particularly well. You know that feeling when you walk into a room and you can just smell the trouble that's coming? This was one of those.

The French fella we were with was some kind of karate expert, and when it all eventually went off he started really putting himself about, karate-chopping everyone. If I'd had a choice I probably wouldn't have been on his side, but I didn't have a choice because all these Spanish geezers attacked us. In that kind of mass tear-up you basically just end up hitting anyone who's near you who you didn't come in with. We're dishing out a few good clumps, but we're taking some as well.

What you don't want in that situation is for someone to take things up a level, and John's mum's boyfriend pulling out a gas gun and shooting the geezer next to him in the chest with a flare was never really going to calm things down too much. The other guy went up like a human torch. Although he was alright in the end because everyone jumped on him to put the fire out, I had to get John's mum and throw her under the table to keep her out of the free-for-all that followed. At this point, the Old Bill – or the Vieux Guillaume as the French call them – arrived, and whatever language we were speaking, this was definitely a 'stoppo'.

We all sprinted out the side door, Johnny's mum and the French fella jumped in one car, and me and Johnny got in his little motor which we'd been running around in, and now we're bombing down the mountain. It's about one o'clock in the morning and we're both quite bruised up after taking a few good clumps (as well as having had a fair bit to drink). John sees a bend coming up and puts his foot down hard on the brake – never the best idea when you're driving on black ice. As the car starts to spin, I'm looking out of the window and it's a good thousand feet down the side of the mountain. I'm not exaggerating – the Pyrenees are high. I'm thinking, 'This is it, I'm gonna die.'

The car spun and it spun and all I could see was down. There was no panic – just a total feeling of calm and knowing there was nothing we could do about it. Then we smashed into a wall and came to a dead stop. It was a bit too much like the end of *The Italian Job* for comfort.

We sat there for a minute in silence, probably shaking a bit and just getting used to the fact that we were still alive. Then we started to think, 'What are we gonna do now?' The car was a write-off and no one who came past seemed that into stopping, so we had no choice but to walk down the mountain. It took us about an hour, and when we finally got to the town we went into this little place and ordered some strawberries and cream and a bottle of champagne. It was almost like 'this is the first day of the rest of the life which just nearly ended'.

Brushes with death notwithstanding, I was primed for going abroad by then. I love going to places I've never been to before, and the great thing about the kind of travelling I do now in the film industry is that you don't necessarily go to the same places as normal tourists do. You'll end up in the parts of a country where people actually live. I suppose my lucky escape in Andorra was a foretaste of things to come in that area. These days I try to get into and out of a place without participating in a mass brawl like you'd get in an old-fashioned Western, although I was fine with that back then. I didn't know who or what I was meant to be fighting for, I was just hitting everybody who came near me. I was a mercenary doing it for love – Margaret Thatcher's son Mark had nothing on me.

John Walford changed his surname to Segal later on and became quite a successful actor for a while. There was a David Niven-ish quality about him that the birds liked (and he liked them back), almost a gentleman-fraudster kind of thing. His mum was a survivor as well. She was still a good-looking woman and it turned out she knew the chief of police in the town, so the whole flare-gun thing got nicely smoothed over and I managed to get home to Blighty without having to bring the consulate into it.

Obviously not everyone who went to Corona got the chance to have a career as a professional actor when they left – in fact, if you did you were kind of the exception that proved the rule. Even my old *Zoo Story* sparring partner David Morris never really got a break, which was a shame because he was good enough to make it – he really was.

What tended to happen was that you might get a few little chances as an extra or in small speaking parts and whether or not anything came of it was kind of in the lap of the gods. I could tell you that I was grateful for any opportunities that came my way and did my best to grasp them with both hands in an appropriately appreciative and professional manner, but that would be a complete load of bollocks.

Truth be told, I was a bit of a handful at this stage in my life. I'd found it quite easy to adjust to the kind of discipline boxing required, but knowing how to behave at casting calls was a completely different matter. I wasn't used to people treating me like a piece of shit in normal life, and I wasn't ambitious enough to accept it in the interests of getting a part.

The first audition I ever turned up for was in Reading, and I was late 'cos I had to get the train and I didn't really know what I was doing. It was for something called *The Perils of Pauline*. I'm not sure if it ever even came out because the most recent film with that title which I could find on the internet was made in America in 1967. Anyway, I finally got in there and the casting woman really had the hump. I said, 'I'm really sorry, I got lost. I've never done this before.' She was really short with me and just sort of hissed at me, 'Sit down, you're not in this scene.'

I remember thinking, 'I ain't gonna like this much if that's the way they're gonna talk to me.' But the scene they were filming at the time was some kind of basketball game, and at that point someone blew a whistle and all the girls took their tops off. Turned out it was one of those things they made a lot of in the mid-seventies that are a bit raunchy but not quite raunchy enough to be soft porn. Either way, there were threepennies everywhere, and even though I didn't get the part, I did get the train back to London thinking, 'Maybe there's something to this acting game after all.'

Not long afterwards, I went up for a part in the Ken Russell film *Lisztomania*. We all had to stand in a row and this woman with blue hair came down the line with the great man. It was for a little Hitler scene where you had to have your hair cut like *der Führer* (Adolf, not Ken), so she was going down the line kind of barking at us: 'You, get your hair cut. You, get your hair cut . . .' She wasn't even looking at us properly as she was saying it, and it seemed like she was channelling the spirit of the Nazis a little bit too effectively.

So when she got to me, I just told her: 'I don't want my hair cut.' When she told me I'd have to if I wanted the part, I asked her how much extra you got paid for having your hair cut and she said, 'Nothing.' Then she asked me if I even wanted to be in the film and I said, 'No, because I don't want to fucking look like you.' Part or no part, I wasn't having someone treating me so disrespectfully. And I didn't regret standing up to her, even when I found out she was Ken Russell's wife.

It would be wrong to characterise this as an isolated incident. There was another time when I got sent up for some work as an extra in *Get Some In*. It was an ITV sitcom about National Service which my mate Karl Howman – who I'm going to tell you about in a minute – ended up starring in. He hadn't got there yet, though; I think Robert Lindsay was doing it at the time, maybe before he did *Citizen Smith*. Anyway, all of us extras were standing there in our RAF bits while the actors did their piece. And instead of just asking me to move, the director kind of picked me up and moved me by my shoulder.

I was a skinny little thing in those days, so he probably thought it would be OK. But it wasn't, because I turned round and nutted him. He went sprawling over the chairs and I was obviously asked to leave the premises in no uncertain terms. At that point I was looking around to see if anyone else wanted to have a fight, but no one did, so I was out of there.

After that, Corona became a bit reticent to send me up for things, which I suppose I couldn't really blame them for, as I was a bit of a little fucker and I probably wasn't doing the school's reputation any good either. Maybe I just wasn't quite ready for the film industry, or the film industry wasn't quite ready for me. Either way, to be honest, I'm still a bit the same today. Ask me nicely and I'll do anything for you, but if you're trying to mug me off, sitting in the director's chair (or next to it) won't get you a free pass.

It wasn't that I wasn't willing to learn. I got a part-time job as the token straight man with all the lesbians and gays in the wardrobe department at the National Theatre for a while, when it was still at the Old Vic. You'd get £28 a night or something like that, which wasn't bad compared to what the Theatre Royal Stratford East was paying (and there was the added bonus that you didn't have to give any of it to Vanessa Redgrave). The three plays they were doing at the time – because they revolved them at the National even then – were *Playboy of the Western World, Hamlet* and another one. My job was looking after two actors called Patrick Monckton and Michael Keating, but sometimes a mate of mine (John Walford/Segal again) who was looking after Albert Finney would be off and I'd have to stand in for him.

Finney had been one of my favourite actors ever since I'd seen him in *Saturday Night, Sunday Morning*. It didn't matter that he was playing a Northerner – I recognised that character, and that was the first time I'd ever seen the kind of person I could relate to from my own life up there on the big screen in such a convincing way. I used to love watching him in *Hamlet*, giving it the full Shakespearian thing, but doing it as a man, so I'd go missing during the play to watch him from the seats right upstairs at the back.

Unfortunately I was late getting back once and Albert missed his cue. As I went running round the back to help him, Susan Fleetwood came off the stage after the mad scene. I think she'd got a bit carried away during that one because she picked up my hand and placed it firmly on her left tit saying, 'Feel my heart.' I said, 'It's not your heart I'm feeling, Susan.'

I went in the bar afterwards knowing I'd fucked up, which I felt really bad about, as I had a lot of time for Albert Finney as a person, never mind how great his acting was. I still wasn't quite ready to face the music, though, so when he came in looking for me, I ducked down behind a table. Through the forest of furniture legs I could clearly see Albert's human ones walking across the floor, so I crawled off between the stools in the opposite direction.

When I came up for air, there he was standing right in front of me, like one of the twins in *The Shining*, only with Albert Finney's face. I don't know how he did it; it was like he floated there or something. His first two words were not promising – they were 'You' and 'cunt' – but when I explained, 'Albert, I'm so sorry I fucked up, I was watching you from up the back and I just missed the call', it seemed to do the trick. All he said after that was, 'What do you want to drink?'

Even though I was only in the wardrobe department, I was quite proud of the fact that I was part of the company for the crossover from the Old Vic to the new building on the South Bank, which might have been a bit of a concrete block but it had great theatres inside it. Being out and about doing that was much better than just being stuck in Corona doing little plays. Not only did the wages help pay my tube fare into college in the mornings, I was also getting paid to watch the kind of actors I admired go to work at close quarters. It wasn't just Albert Finney, there were Angela Lansbury, Frank Finlay and Dinsdale Landen as well; all of whom were great technicians, far beyond any level that I could ever aspire to.

Not all of my early brushes with the film and TV industries were quite as disastrous as the Mrs Ken Russell and *Get Some In* incidents. Occasionally my ebullient approach to the kind of small parts I was getting offered at that time paid off. At the age of eighteen, I was cast in an episode of *The Sweeney* called 'Loving Arms'. It was meant to be a non-speaking role where I was at a table in the pub with a guy who was buying a gun, but I couldn't (or wouldn't) stop myself improvising dialogue with him.

The director kept saying, 'Excuse me, quiet, please. You're not meant to talk in this scene.' Now I didn't know they had to pay you an extra £30 for talking – that's why they want you to keep schtum – but John Thaw and Dennis Waterman obviously did, because they were standing at the bar laughing while I was arguing the toss. They weren't being horrible, they could just see how green I was. My point of view was: 'It just seems silly that I'd be sitting here not saying anything when we're doing something as important as buying a gun', but the director still insisted I keep quiet, so I ended up taking the gun off the guy and having a look at it.

The director was climbing the walls at this point, telling me to put the gun down, but I was getting pissed off now. 'Well, what do you want me to do?' I asked him, 'Just sit here and play with my cock?' I suppose it was good of him not to just send me home after that, but this was one of my first-ever paid jobs so I didn't know any better. And I got the last laugh at the end, because for the next scene we had to go out in the street where me and the guy with the gun had to run away. I was supposed to get caught, but instinct took over and I jumped over a fence and escaped. They didn't have time to reshoot the scene so it had to stay in done my way. I've seen the episode quite recently – I think it's out there on the internet somewhere – and it's quite funny. One minute I'm running alongside the other guy, the next I'm gone.

Another of my first paid outings in front of the cameras brought me into contact with someone who's still one of my best friends now. I'd got a day's work as an extra on the David Essex film *Stardust*, down by the Thames at the Prospect of Whitby pub in Wapping. It's one of the oldest – if not the oldest – riverside pubs in London, and Captain Cook lodged just around the corner for a while, so he probably would've had a drink in there at some point.

This was in 1974, so it was still all old warehouses down that way then. The cobbled streets are still the same forty years later, but all the warehouses have been turned into flats now.

Karl was in one of the bands in the film (with Keith Moon, who was his great mate at the time). I'd never met Mr Howman before, and when I got my lunch and went upstairs with it on one of the double-decker buses they do the catering on, I didn't see him sitting up the back. Then he said, 'Alright?' and asked me to join him, which was a nice thing to do because I was only an extra and he had a much bigger part. He's a South London boy, which is unusual for me in friendship terms, but I'm not prejudiced. I think his dad was a colour sergeant in the band at the Woolwich Arsenal.

Anyway, we started talking and became mates – not close mates who keep in touch and everything, but mates. Then a few years later, in the late seventies he played my brother's friend in the ITV series *Fox*, we remembered each other and it went from there. I think Karl was playing the young copper in *The Long Good Friday* around that time, and I was just about to get married. Once our wives palled up too that was it, and we've been going on holiday together with the kids ever since. We've got in a few scrapes together too, over the years, but they might have to wait for volume two.

In the meantime I'd still – as my old mate Bob Hoskins used to say – 'got overheads', and one way of dealing with them was to get a bit of work doing adverts so people could dig them up to put on TV shows and embarrass me years later. My sister Laura did a bit of modelling in her teenage years, and through her I ended up signing with a place called the Norrie Carr Agency.

It was thanks to them that I ended up doing a low-calorie bread commercial where I had a cap on and I followed the Slimcea bird down the road before she went off in a balloon. Then there was one for Pot Noodle where I had to climb up and down some ladders. As you might have noticed, it was only the most high-end products that wanted to use me.

The most painful one of all was the ad for Double Diamond pale ale (apparently it's still Prince Philip's favourite beer, which just goes to show money can't buy you good taste). It had all these old *Carry On* actors and people you knew in it – Liz Fraser, she was one of them – then at the end the camera settled on me and this other kid holding pint glasses, and the slogan said: 'And here's another two mugs you might recognise.' Not only were we nobodies, we were nobodies selling Double Diamond – we had literally mugged ourselves off.

CHAPTER 16

NASHVILLE'S, WHITECHAPEL

I was lucky to be starting out as an actor at a time when people in the TV and film industries had just about got used to the idea of casting real kids from real areas. The BBC's *Play for Today* slot had a lot to do with it — take that out of the equation and it might still all be 'Gorblimey, guv'nor, can I doff my cap for you, sir?' And you'd have probably ended up with Hugh Grant in *Sexy Beast* instead of me. His head would have wobbled a lot in that role. Especially once Gandhi got hold of him.

A few years back when I was doing a film called *Macbeth on the Estate*, I had a conversation with some of the West Indian geezers who were in it about how the black actors they saw on TV didn't seem to represent them. These kids didn't feel like they were allowed in the game. It occurred to me that they were facing exactly the same problems that white working-class actors used to have. It's probably the writers and directors who are the key: the more people who come from where you come from and know what they're talking about start to make inroads into the business, the more chance you've got of telling your own stories.

By the mid-seventies, more than a decade had passed since the kitchen-sink dramas brought Richard Harris and Albert Finney and that whole generation through. When characters that you'd consider to be normal working people turned up on TV or in film roles, you didn't expect them to be some posh bloke putting on an accent any more. It was the time just before punk, and it was almost becoming fashionable to talk like me or the dowager Phyllis Daniels. What opened so many doors for us was the fact that directors like Ken Loach and Alan Clarke and Frank Roddam were starting to have enough clout to get the kind of films made that would need actors like us to be in them.

I was the token working-class kid at Corona, but there were already a couple of others there who were making themselves out to be that too (admittedly on slightly shakier credentials). The school acted as our agency, but without the kind of philanthropic intentions that guided Anna Scher. Basically it was a money-making machine, whereas Anna's was all about encouraging kids who might need a bit of help to come out of their shell. That was a fantastic thing, but I've got no regrets about not going there. I didn't know it existed at that time, anyway, and going to Corona was the kind of chapter in your life that makes you what you are. There I was a minority of one. If I'd gone to Anna Scher's, I'd have been just like everyone else.

Les Blair was another one of those directors who wanted to put actual working-class people on the screen, rather than the cardboard cut-out variety. Another of my first proper pieces of TV work was a thing for him called *Sunshine in Brixton*. It was about a school football team, and doing that was when I met all the boys from Anna Scher: Tony London, who was a really good actor and became a close mate of mine for a while, Ray Burdis and Elvis Payne among others.

I enjoyed meeting them all, but that didn't necessarily mean I wanted to join their gang. It was a funny old film, that. One of the main characters in it was this black guy with dyed blond hair who was called 'The Negative'. For me, the experience was all positives. Although this was my first time being in front of the cameras for extended periods and I could tell that I had a lot to learn, I definitely felt like I was getting somewhere.

I still have much to thank Bill Happer and Vernon Morris for, because I wouldn't have lasted nearly as long as I did at drama college without them nurturing and protecting me a little bit. I think those two must have thought I at least had something – not that they ever told me – because I was such a monumental pain in the arse at the time, why would they have bothered with me otherwise?

To say that other people in the Corona hierarchy viewed me with less enthusiasm would be putting it mildly. By the time I'd been there a couple of years, things were coming to a head. They'd fitted me up for the angry young man role and I was kind of acting up to it. I probably was a bit like that inside, anyway, but when you know that's all people are expecting of you, sometimes you mask your disappointment with an extra layer of bravado. That's probably how the *Get Some In* and *Lizstomania* incidents came about – because I felt like a fish out of water, I was more likely to behave like one.

In the autumn of 1976, which should have been the start of my last year, Corona didn't just stop sending me out for auditions, they started actively trying to keep the other kids away from me. They said it was because I was 'a bad influence, language-wise', which I can understand now, but at the time it made me feel like a nonce. I thought they were being snobby about the way I spoke, and they probably were. I don't think the big news about the increasing fashionability of working-class accents had quite got through to them yet.

Either way, at the end of that term there was a Christmas party at the college which I specifically wasn't invited to. Everyone else was, but not me. When I asked about it they didn't even have the decency to pretend my invitation got lost in the post. I was fuming, and as a result I did something really pathetic which might have been designed to confirm their worse assumptions about me. I got a lolly stick, glued some tacks on it and put it under one of the tyres on the headmistress's car.

Thinking about that now, it was fucking dangerous – she could have been on the motorway or something when the tyre went. Luckily for me, she didn't make it out of her official parking space. One of the other kids was summoned into her office and threatened with expulsion unless they turned in the culprit, so they lollied me right up – which I couldn't really blame them for, as they didn't come from where I came from – and I was expelled on the spot. To be honest, all concerned probably breathed a sigh of relief when that happened, not least my mum and dad, who wouldn't have to find the £900 a term any more.

The day I was expelled, some of the other boys were going out to audition for a BBC TV play called *Scum*. Obviously, I wasn't because I was considered too badly behaved to be trusted as an ambassador for Corona's reputation. But I went along with them, anyway, so we could all go out for a beer together afterwards to say goodbye.

I've told this story a lot of times over the years but I'm not going to add any dramatic embellishments about statues being seen crying in the foyer of the BBC or my mum making me a piece of toast for breakfast in the morning that had John Blundell's face on it. While I was waiting outside for the others to do their auditions I got talking to the receptionist, who was a lovely girl and just the sort of person any red-blooded young man would want to be whiling away the hours with. After I'd been chatting her up for a while she asked me, 'Do you wanna go in and meet the director?' I said, 'No, thanks, not really, darling – that ain't really my scene no more.'

She persisted: 'Go on, he's really nice.' So on her advice I went in and met Alan Clarke, who obviously I'd never heard of at that point, and we had a laugh together. I didn't know what the part was and I didn't really care when he said it was originally written for a Glaswegian. Alan told me afterwards that it was only because I was the last one in that he watched me walk out of the door and down the corridor afterwards. But that was why he gave me the job, because I walked down the corridor like a fighter, which of course is what I was. If that's not fate, I don't know what is. If there'd been one more person coming in after me, you wouldn't be reading this book now, and God knows what I'd be doing.

It wasn't just through divine intervention from a BBC receptionist that the stars had aligned for me to play Carlin in *Scum*. A couple of the kind of incidents which no drama college would workshop had also helped prepare the ground. Both of them involved the iron bar we used to stop the front gate in Enfield hitting the flowers behind it being employed for another purpose.

The first time had been when I was still in my early teens. I was playing football with some of the other local kids in the alleyway that ran up the side of our house in Enfield. We used to put jumpers down to make one goal at our end of the alleyway, and a wall at the far end, which was the back of the maisonettes' garages, served as the other.

In the end house, two along from where I lived, there was a couple who had a great big lump of a son. I suppose he must've been in his mid-thirties. Remember we're just kids, and we're probably making a bit of a noise, but there's no history of that being a problem. I suppose the geezer must've had a bad day or something, because instead of him just coming out and telling us to turn it down a bit, he's come running straight towards me.

In my innocence I thought he was wanting to join in the game and have a bit of a kickabout, so I dropped my shoulder to take the ball around him. The next thing I knew he'd grabbed me by the throat and slammed me up against the fence of the cemetery we used to play about in trying to scare people.

At this moment, it just so happens that my dad is looking out of the window and sees what's going on. So he appears from nowhere, grabs the iron bar from behind the front gate and, in a single graceful movement, vaults over the wall. He's got this move down to a tee. You'd think he'd practised it (and who knows, perhaps he had done). Either way, he runs up to the guy who's got me by the throat and tells him to put me down.

Now this geezer is a big unit and for whatever reason he's pretty angry, so as he puts me down he steps towards my dad, which is a big mistake. Because my dad leaps up in the air and hits him straight across the top of the head with the iron bar. He could've killed him, and to be honest at that moment I think he might've meant to, because he'd seen what the guy was doing to me, and my dad's instinct to protect his family was very strong.

I'll never forget what happened in the next few seconds. The fella did the splits as the weight of the bar forced him to the ground. Then he was instantly, violently sick from the clump on the head, before going out like a light – sparko – on the pavement. It scared the life out of me, but the additional anxiety that my dad might go to prison for what he'd just done didn't come to me till a bit later on.

It didn't seem to bother my dad, though. He just turned round, put the iron bar back in the flowerbed, and went back to whatever he was doing. I'd like to say that we went back to our game of football as well, but of course we didn't. And not long after we'd all melted away a bit lively an ambulance came, and my dad was charged with causing grievous bodily harm. He was lucky they didn't try to do him for attempted murder, to be honest.

We always say don't get the police involved, but if someone else does and you've got an out, then it's best to counter-nick 'em. This was a lesson that would come in handy for me later in life, and it was exactly what my dad did – he counter-nicked the other guy for assaulting me. Not only was this an effective tactic, it was also fair enough, because the geezer did have me round the Gregory, and I was only a kid. In the end they both went to court, although I don't remember having to give evidence, and the judge bound the two of them over to keep the peace for a year.

They managed it for longer than that, because we never saw the other guy again. Apparently he did recover from the attack physically, but if he ever came round to see his mum and dad after that, he did so at night. Even I'm a bit shocked by how brutal that looks written down, but in this book violent incidents are like London buses – you wait sixteen chapters for them and then two come along at once.

The iron bar's second appearance was on the night of the ABA finals. These always used to take place on the eve of the Cup Final at the old Empire Pool, Wembley (now spruced up a bit as the Wembley Arena). There must've been a kid from the Repton on the bill that night as our seats were more or less ringside, and there was an East End fight promoter sitting in front of us who my dad hated for some reason. He was bald on top with ginger hair at the sides and I'm sure his name will come to me in a moment . . . Mickey Duff, that was him, though I don't think that was his real name as he was from Polish stock originally.

Anyway, Duff was talking to a black boxer called Billy Knight and another promoter we didn't know, and he was 'giving it the big I am' in the way some promoters will. Then my dad overheard him saying, 'My meat will fight your body any time' – meaning that some bout or other was on. Now my dad loved boxers, really respected them, and he wasn't going to have them talked about in such a disrespectful way. So he piped up from the row behind: 'What did you say? What did you just fucking say? Is that how you talk about the fighters who get you a living?'

At that point my dad completely lost the plot and really gave it to this guy with both barrels while Billy Knight stood there listening, open-mouthed. By the end of the exchange it was clear that someone was going to have to move. We stayed, they went . . . but don't worry, the iron bar isn't coming into this for a while yet. I'm just establishing the atmosphere of the evening.

All the way home in the car, my dad was still bubbling with anger: 'That's the kind of slags fight promoters are,' he kept saying, 'that's how they use people.' I don't know if he'd had bad experiences with them himself when he was younger, because it's not the kind of thing we would have talked about, but I don't suppose you can rule out that possibility.

When we got back from Wembley to Church Street – and this was bad timing on everyone's part – there were a group of bikers blocking the entrance to the same alley where the first incident with the iron bar had taken place. I don't know what they were doing there as none of our neighbours were bikers as far as we knew, but there were about fifteen of them, with ages ranging from twenty going up to about forty.

The Old Man pulls round into the alley to park, and at first he doesn't see them. But as we get out of the car to go into the house, one of the bikers blocks his way and says, 'You nearly fucking knocked me over.'

I'm shitting myself a bit now thinking, 'Don't just wade in, Dad, we're on a hiding to nothing here.' But never mind the odds not being exactly in our favour, after the night my dad's had, I already know it's gonna go off. 'No, son,' he says to this biker. 'I didn't nearly knock you over. If I'd have wanted to knock you over, I'd have fucking knocked you over, so get out of the fucking way.'

The guy does what he's told, but as we walk on towards the house, the biggest of the bikers gets off his bike and says, 'Who are you fucking talking to?' By this time I'm already moving towards the gate where the iron bar is, because I've seen how it's done and they're more than mob-handed. At this point, the biker's gone to throw a punch at my dad, and my Old Man's hit him with a left hook of such force that the biker's just gone down where he stood.

The geezer hits the ground so hard that you could see the dust come up in the glare of the streetlight. I know that sounds like something from a film, but I swear on my life it's what I saw. I think Scorsese's *Raging Bull* is the only movie that's ever got the impact of that kind of punch right, and De Niro didn't have an iron bar to hand either.

Before the biker's even finishing bouncing up off the ground, my dad's taken the iron bar off me. This other guy's already coming at him – a black fella as it happened, which was unusual for a biker – and my dad's knocked the teeth out of his head with the bar. Next thing I know he's got the fella on the floor beating him round the ribs saying, 'If you ever come back, I'll fucking kill you.' Needless to say, the lot of 'em fucked off – I've never seen a crowd disperse so quickly – and we never saw their leather jackets in that alley ever again.

That iron bar could do a lot of damage to people, and my dad knew how to go to work with it. I'm not saying this because I want to glorify these actions, but because that was the atmosphere I was brought up in. For a particular generation which came out of post-war England, that's what was handed down to us. You had to get on with people working on the markets, but if someone came down and wanted it then you had to be able to dish some out, otherwise people would walk all over you. My dad wasn't a gangster, but you don't fuck with family people either.

I suppose by telling these stories I am condoning them in a way. I do regret my dad being in a position where he felt he had to do those things to protect me, but I understand where the impulse to do them came from. I'm not being PC about this because fuck it, that was our way of life, and the idea that these people got what they fucking deserved is embedded quite deep within me. I know that's not necessarily the right way to think, and it's something I've tried to change over the years – not so that your family doesn't come first, but just because you don't want the aggravation.

Some of the success I've had as an actor has probably been down to the fact that when people see me in those kinds of situations in films, they believe I've been in them in real life, which I have been. The sequence in *Scum* where I have to hit Baldy with the iron bar was one of the easiest I've ever had to do, because I'd seen it happen, and not too long before either. A lot of people might've been shocked by what went on in that film, but I certainly wasn't.

I was nineteen going on twenty when we made the TV version of *Scum* in early 1977, and twenty-one going on twenty-two by the time we remade it for the cinema in 1979 after the first one was banned from being shown on the BBC. Although the second film is basically the same script as the first but with some extra violence and swearing added, the first is by far the scarier of the two in my opinion.

We're all just babies really at that stage, so you get more of a sense of the terrible things kids will do to other kids, and the ways grown men will manipulate them. By the time we got to do the film, which was cobbled together on more of a money basis, we were young men instead of boys, and it was a stretch to imagine that we were in borstal rather than an adult prison.

A lot of water, and other drinks, would pass under the bridge in my life between the two *Scums*. A fair proportion of those fluids would be taken in establishments run by a mate of mine called Neville Cole. His brother Eamon was Tony Yeates's godfather (in the being-there-at-your-christening sense, not in the mafia sense) and they were a couple of really good boxers who ran pubs and clubs. They used to have a big black fella who knocked about with them, a really nice bloke whose name was Tiny. Well, I don't suppose that was what it said on his birth certificate, but that was what we all called him.

Neville's original place was the Salmon and Ball. It was, and is, just down the road from the Repton, on the corner of Cambridge Heath and Bethnal Green Road – by the tube station where the terrible disaster happened in the Blitz. Neville changed the name to Tipples for a while. Locals would pronounce that in the proper East End style with a hard 'p' that was more like a 'b', so it sounded more like you were saying a cat's name than somewhere you'd want to go to have a pint.

Me and Tony Yeates saw a geezer put a gun to someone's head in there, once. We were only young fellas at the time – seventeen or eighteen at most – and we were in there having a Sunday lunchtime drink when we noticed two smart old boys and a couple of young 'uns sitting together. There was some uneasy laughter and then it all kind of went quiet. We looked round and saw that one of the young fellas had pulled out a gun and put it to the old boy's head. I say the old boy, but he was probably in his fifties – the same age as me now.

The young guy never swore at him, he just said, 'If you dig me out, I'll blow your head off.' The old guy replied, 'Come on, son, there's no need for that – we was just having a laugh.' A silence followed that seemed to last quite a long time, then the kid put his gun away and got up and left. There was no shouting and screaming or calling the police. Everyone just went back to their drinks.

After a while Neville opened up another place down on the Mile End Road, near Trinity Green. He set it up with a geezer called Martin Nash, and I only realised recently that this was probably where they got the name Nashville's from. My mind must have been on higher things at the time. There was certainly no one in there wearing rhinestones, although the odd cowboy might have put in an appearance.

For my money, quite a lot of which I spent in there, Nashville's was the best club in London. The vibe of it was somewhere between an East End disco and a piano lounge. Me and Tony Yeates were in there on the opening night and we were in there when it closed, and we had a lot of good times in between. The only note of sadness in these memories is that we lost Neville Cole a couple of years ago. He was a good man, and him dying would've been sad enough even if he hadn't won the fucking Lottery a while before he died. The truth of the old phrase 'You can't take it with you' was never more starkly or harshly demonstrated.

CHAPTER 17

BENJY'S NIGHTCLUB, MILE END

Neville and Martin really used to look after us. They were running things, and we were the kids on the firm. Being in that role in a group always tends to get you a fair bit of piss-taking, and we were no exception. One day they took me and Tony aside and told us they'd booked a champagne table for us down at Benjy's nightclub in Mile End as a 'little treat from the boys'. They said there were a couple of nice girls who wanted to meet us. Obviously, we knew how to pull a bird, but we weren't the type of kids to look a gift horse (or a gift bird) in the mouth, so we were there on time with bells on. Of course the two girls who turned up were both geezers – how were we to know Thursday was gay night?

That kind of thing is part of growing up, and Neville and Martin didn't mean it cruelly – either to us or the two gay guys. As it turns out, Tony and his mate have been very happy together. (Only joking, Tony, I know the cracks are starting to show.) Benjy's has had more name changes than West Ham have had away kits in the thirty-five years since, but last time I looked it was still hanging on, despite the council's best attempts to relieve it of its licence.

If Neville and Martin were ideal mentors when it came to East London nightlife, which they were, I was going to need someone to do the same job for me when it came to acting on film. And I couldn't have asked for anyone better than Alan Clarke. OK, I'd got the part in *Scum* because I had a boxer's walk, but I had no agent and no idea of what I was getting into.

The original TV version was a two-bob fucking BBC production where you had to get down to London Bridge under your own steam and then get the train down to Redhill. There was some messing about on that train which I can't even tell you about, but let's just say if the kids from *Scum* got in your carriage, you probably knew they were there. I think they based the kids from *Fame* on us, only we never wore the leg-warmers (though we could have done with them in a way, because it was freezing fucking cold on that set). Once we got there, we didn't really have too much idea of the kind of thing we were making, as Clarkey was keeping it all together in quite a secretive way to get what he wanted out of us.

I felt comfortable being around the Anna Scher boys, but they were their own gang and I wasn't part of it, which suited how I was and was also good for the film. We became mates over the years, but they were from North London. Now, Islington might not look a long way from the East End on the map, but the possibility that they might be Arsenal or Spurs supporters did not sit comfortably with me (Phil Daniels even supported Chelsea, for some reason which he was never able to adequately explain). It probably made it easier for me to be around a load of guys who never really acted like they were actors. I can't speak on their behalf, but I don't think most of us even booked that as our job description.

The performance I gave in *Scum* (and the later film version which more people have seen and is basically a cinematic Xerox of the first one) was purely down to Clarkey. He got the anger out of me, and I suppose the cunning, but what was really clever was the way he made it look like I was aware of what I was doing technically, even though I wasn't. I was on the screen a long time in those films for an actor with so little experience, and left to my own devices I would have had no idea of how to pace what I was doing. It was Alan who made sure I did what I did in the right places so the whole thing hung together properly.

Alan Clarke was an Evertonian, a tall, skinny guy with a scar on one side of his face, which I think he got from falling on a step outside a pub drunk, but that's his story, not mine. The best introduction to his character would be a tale he told me about him and Roy Minton (the writer of *Scum*). They were both quite fiery individuals, to put it mildly, and once they were coming down in a lift at the BBC when an argument came to blows. Basically, they're having a fight in this lift – eyes wide, nostrils flaring – then when it reaches the ground floor and the doors open, who should be outside but Moshe Dayan? The Israeli military leader and foreign minister – who was famous for the eye patch he had to wear after a sniper's bullet smashed some binoculars he was using – had obviously seen some brutal conflicts in his time, but Alan never told me if he tried to intervene in this one.

The most important thing I learned from Alan was that putting a performance together in a film is all about the moments where you demonstrate your power as a character. You're telling a story that might stretch over a year of someone's life or even longer, and you've got to compress a man's whole emotional appearance changing into an hour and a half. I wasn't capable of structuring that believably on my own because no one had ever taught me how to do it. Of course, I didn't see how much Alan was shaping what I was doing at the time. It took me a long while to actually develop some discipline about acting, and only once I'd done that did I realise the extent of Alan's influence. That's the mark of a clever teacher, when you are learning things without realising it.

I never forgot the way he went to work with me. There were moments when he'd just whisper in my ear and make me very calm and relaxed by saying, 'Don't worry about them, just concentrate on what you're doing.' Then there were other times when he'd say, 'You're fucking me about here', and that would upset me, because I had a lot of respect for him. Obviously, he was just saying that to wind me up, but it worked because I'd get really fucking mad.

I've learnt to use that technique on myself over the years. Sometimes on a set even now I'll call myself a cunt or whatever to liven myself up. It's the acting equivalent of having Jackie Bowers in your corner. The director might think I'm angry with him when he hears me grumbling away to myself, so I'll have to explain that I'm not being horrible, I just talk to myself a lot before a scene. It's funny sometimes when I come out of it to see other actors looking at me as if to say, 'Well, what's the matter with you?'

Most of what you're taught at drama college relates to the theatre rather than cinema, so you have to kind of start from scratch once you make that shift. Being in front of a camera never worried me in itself. Of course, the first thing people will tell you is: 'Forget about the camera. Don't even think about it, just do what you do.' I actually found that advice very easy to follow at first. 'I'm not going to worry about the camera, let the camera worry about me' was the way I approached it.

Ignorance is bliss on a film set, because when you've got no idea of what's happening, you can just get on with it. Things only start to get complicated once you learn more about the technical side – what the different lenses are and how close the shots are going to be. That's when you start to second-guess yourself. One minute you feel perfectly at home, and then you know too much. Suddenly your only option is to relearn how not to be aware of the camera by making the knowledge you've picked up work for you on a technical level without it looking like that's a conscious process. That's when acting becomes a whole different game.

One thing I would say is that the old saying that the camera never lies is bullshit, because it does. I've done things I thought were blinding and when I've seen them played back they were shit. It works the other way too, but when you watch something you thought was going to be terrible and it actually works, that's normally because the director, for whatever reason, didn't let you in on what they were trying to get.

The most important thing when you're shooting out of sequence – which is how it's normally done – is learning to sort the script out in your head as you're going along. People often think it must be difficult to do things in a different order to how they're seen, but it can actually work out better that way. For example, if you do the end before anything else, you understand where you've got to get to and you can start to think about all the different shapes you can put in along the road. In other films – *Nil by Mouth* would be a good example – you don't need to have so much of a journey through it so you can just play each moment and not worry about the next one.

Alan Clarke was well known for having a clear political agenda, and as my little disagreement with Vanessa Redgrave showed, I wasn't always in tune with left-wing opinions. If anything, my family background pushed me more to the right. Even though he's working-class, my dad would always vote Tory.

Some people find that difficult to understand, but there's a long tradition of grafters who run their own businesses being quite right-wing – Margaret Thatcher's dad was a grocer after all. You've worked hard to get what you've got and you don't like the idea of other people getting something for nothing. I can appreciate and even agree with that opinion, but my political views have never been quite as fixed as my dad's were.

Sometimes I'll watch documentaries about working-class people fighting for their rights and see the kind of conditions they lived in and think, 'Dad, what were you talking about?' I'm not saying I've got more left-wing as I've got older, but maybe I've moved a bit closer to the middle of the road. Socialism doesn't add up in my mind, but it wouldn't make sense for me to be a Tory either. After all, both sides of my family came out of the workhouse, and the Conservatives are the kind of fuckers who put us in there. You can't say that's not a conflict of interest, so why should I fucking vote for them now?

As a rule I try to judge individual issues and political personalities on their merits. What I look for is that quite rare brand of politician who makes an honest attempt to do what he or she has said they're gonna do. They don't necessarily have to succeed, they just have to give it a go. The other mob – the ones who promise one thing and then do something totally different the minute they get in power – are much more numerous. But as far as I'm concerned they should be held to account under the Trades Descriptions Act, the same way a butcher who sold you venison which was actually horse would be.

All of this is a roundabout way of saying that I didn't really have a problem with the underlying politics of *Scum*, which were what a lot of the controversy surrounding the film was about. I didn't view it so much as a political thing of left versus right. For me it was a simple matter of people who were in authority – whether that was the warders or the other boys – treating the kids who were under them like shit.

We bang kids up in these fucking conditions, but at the end of the day whatever you've done you're supposed to go into the system to be rehabilitated, and that just wasn't the way it worked at the time. What you see happening in *Scum* is more about punishment, and while I do think there are certain people who need to be punished, it's not a good principle to run the whole system on.

Because of the *Scum* connection I was invited to Rodney Wing at HM Prison Portland a few years after the film came out to see the work they were doing there trying to rehabilitate people. The idea was to come in and have a chat with the kids and try to do a theatre group with them – just to give them the idea that if I can do it, maybe you can too. I must admit I was very apprehensive about doing this at first. I just thought, 'Fuck me, some of these kids are probably in here for murder. How am I going to help them become better people just by doing a bit of acting?'

In a way, I still think that. But when I saw what those warders were trying to do by sitting the kids around and talking about their problems, I started to see the potential of it. They were trying to do something really proper but – and sadly this is how it always works with human beings – the screws in the grown-up nick next door didn't want anything to do with it. Their mentality was: 'We're here to punish these people, and that's what we're gonna do.' Never mind how many statistics might show them that these kids are much less likely to be a danger to others when they go back out on the street if someone's actually given them a chance.

Wherever you stand on this, there's no denying that the reason the criminal justice system should exist in the first place – which is to rehabilitate people so they won't commit any more crimes – has kind of got lost as more and more of the system's energies go towards defending its own status quo. You could see that very clearly in the way the political establishment clamped down on *Scum*. It was like the film itself was the rebel character Archer – played by David Threlfall in the first version and Mick Ford in the second – and Parliament and the BBC were the screws.

Of course, I wasn't overly bothered about all this at the time. I had enough going on in my life not to be too invested in it. So, in the autumn of 1977, when the original TV *Scum* actually got banned – which for all I knew meant my first leading role was going to go forever unseen – I just thought, 'Well, there you go', and effectively retired from the acting business for eighteen months.

I'll get onto how I made ends meet in the next few chapters, but obviously there was a fair amount of rebellion in the air in that particular Jubilee year. I didn't dress like a punk – the safety-pin gear wasn't for me, although the drainpipe trousers were alright – but I liked the Sex Pistols' music. Live gigs still didn't really interest me though. I went up the Marquee Club once and got in a big row with some pogo-ers, and that was about the end of it. If you'd told me that within two or three years, not only would Sid Vicious be dead but I'd have acted with all three of his surviving bandmates, I would probably have been a bit surprised.

One musical opportunity I wasn't going to pass up in the meantime was the chance to DJ for nurses' parties. They love a dance, don't they, nurses? And everyone knows that it's any patriotic Englishmen's duty to try to bring happiness to as many nurses as possible.

How this important landmark in DJing history came about was that Tony Yeates was working as a photographer at St Thomas' Hospital by this time – taking photos of all the operations for their records. He was, and is, a really good smudger (as photographers were always called on my plot), and it was an interesting job, if a bit gory. He took some amazing pictures of surgeons' hands as well, and when someone offered him the chance to fake a different kind of dexterity by DJing for a nurses' party, Tony was hardly going to say no.

'Don't worry, I'll do it,' he'd told them. 'Me and my mate Ray have got all the equipment.' Of course we ain't got any of the equipment, and we ain't got any DJing experience either, but if Tony Blackburn can do this, how hard can it be?

Luckily, Tony's younger brother Steve had some turntables we could borrow for the night, and we also borrowed Steve, who came along to show us how to use them. We set off for deepest darkest South London in an optimistic frame of mind, blissfully ignorant of the fact that there's a mob out of Brixton who had the job before us and got sacked, who are not best pleased about losing their gig to a couple of East London pumpkins. So we're in there on the night, making it up as we go along with all the nurses having a great time dancing to our random selection of old singles. (I remember Rod Stewart's 'Maggie May' going down particularly well. 'Mr Blue Sky' by ELO was another winner – that was about as up to the minute as we got.) Then we look over to see this angry-looking black guy with a big velvet pimp hat on standing at the back with all his cronies.

The message somehow gets through to us that this used to be their gig. Tony goes, 'It's on us,' and I'm thinking, 'Uh-oh. We've nicked their gig, on their manor – we're in trouble here.' It seems like whatever's gonna happen is probably gonna happen, so I go for the 'in for a penny, in for a pound' strategy, and put on that song 'Kung Fu Fighting' – Carl Douglas, I think it was – with a special dedication: 'And this is for the pimp and his mates at the back.'

They're all getting a bit lively at this point but nothing actually happens, so I'm thinking, 'We might have fronted 'em here.' It's only me, Tony and his kid brother with all this expensive DJ equipment which we've got to get back in the motor, because if things had gone off that would've probably been the first casualty of war. So, at the end of the night we pile it all into this green Triumph Herald estate we'd picked up from somewhere which you could only start with a screwdriver.

As we pull away, we look round and see three car-loads of this mob following us. A car chase ensues, only it's more like *Steptoe and Son* than *Smokey and the Bandit* (which was on at the pictures that year) because we're staggering along in this knackered old Triumph throwing records out of the window at them for a laugh – only the pony ones, not The Jam or anything like that. They finally catch up with us around the back of the Italia Conti stage school in Farringdon.

At this point we'd be very happy to discover that the whole thing is some kind of on-location improvisation workshop, but sadly that doesn't look likely. I ask Tony if he's ready, he nods, and we get out of the car. These geezers are all around us and they're more than mob-handed, so I go up to the guy in the pimp hat and say, 'Alright, mate. There's obviously enough of you to do us, but are we men? Put up your two best, me and him [I'm pointing at Tony now because Stephen was only a little fella and we wanted to keep him out of it] will fight them, and whoever wins, wins.'

Now I'm clutching at straws here, but we ain't got no chance otherwise, and the tactic seems to be working because they're back-tracking a bit – it's like they're not sure about us. Taking advantage of their moment of hesitation, I go round to the back of the car, because I know I've got an iron bar in my bag and they're not gonna want to fight one-on-one with that. The minute I reach in the car to pull it out, they think I've got a shooter. One of them shouts, 'He's got a gun', and it's just starting to feel like we might get out of this alive when another car pulls up and another big black guy gets out.

This geezer's a mountain and we're thinking, 'Oh fuck! We're for it now.' He comes up to us asking, 'What's the trouble, boys?' So, trying to keep calm because I don't know who this guy is or what his connection is to the other mob, I go, 'Nothing, mate – the boys are just putting it on us a bit.' At that point he turns round to them and goes, 'You fucking lot, get outta here.' He's literally the biggest black man in the world and he's telling them to fuck off, which they promptly do.

It turned out not to be a black and white thing to him on any level. They were a gang who were picking on us, and he was just a nice guy passing through who saw three kids in trouble and decided to help us out. We shook his hand with a big sigh of relief, in fact I gave him a grateful cuddle, then off we all went into the Clerkenwell night. Result! In fact, a Triumph, although strangely enough Stephen never offered to lend us his DJ equipment again . . .

CHAPTER 18

THE 277 BUS UP
BURDETT ROAD

I had some funny old motors in my first few years of driving round London. I knew nothing about cars whatsoever, but I did have a happy knack for getting hold of dodgy MOTs, which wasn't just useful but vital given the state of some of the heaps I was at the wheel of.

I'd done most of my learning to drive in a knackered Ford Anglia van with a big long gear-stick. I used to have a problem going round corners in it because there was something about the layout of the pedals which encouraged you to put your foot on the accelerator rather than the brake. That's never a good idea, especially when it nearly turns the whole thing on its side, and even more so when that happens on the rare occasion when you've persuaded your dad to take you for a driving lesson (admittedly I had already driven the car around on my own or with mates a fair bit before it was strictly legal). This mistake got me thrown out of the driver's seat with a clump round the side of the head as a bonus and my dad drove home saying, 'I ain't getting in a bloody car with you again.'

On the set of *That Summer!* in 1978.

Shadow-boxing with my mate Tony London on the beach at Torquay – Elaine made the right choice.

They called Esther Williams 'A Goddess when wet'...

In *Quadrophenia* with my leathers and my
Liberace haircut.

On honeymoon in the Canary Islands with
Elaine and a camel.

We got straight off the plane home and went to the premiere of *Scum*
– note the suitcases and my *Quadrophenia* badge.

The concluding riot in *Scum* – no need for Phil Daniels to help me out here.
I was the Daddy by this time . . .

Luckily make-up doesn't sting like a real shiner.

My dad at the bar in Church Street, Enfield – no sign of the Bobby Moore World Cup ice bucket for some reason.

'Black Magic, Raymond?' – 'Don't mind if I do'.

This is the outfit I wore on that plane trip to Cannes with Alan Clarke – not sure if the 'foot up' thing is quite working for me, though.

At the Edinburgh Film Festival with *Scum* in 1979.

In Canada in 1980 filming *Ladies And Gentlemen, the Fabulous Stains*. Clockwise from top left: a) With Paul Simonon b) A beery leer c) With Steve Jones d) Elaine offers me a lesson in microphone technique e) Onstage as lead singer of 'The Looters' f) Elaine is the meat in a Laura Dern/Marin Kanter sandwich g) Paul Cook shows how a Sex Pistol occupies a chair.

Me with Alex Steene, John Conteh
and Perry Fenwick, who plays Billy
Mitchell in *EastEnders*. He's a great
mate of mine who comes from
my manor. Well, close enough . . .
Canning Town/Custom House.

Even Will Scarlet needs a fag break.

The face that launched a thousand arrows . . .

Lois with me, mum and Toffy, and then getting christened with me and Elaine.

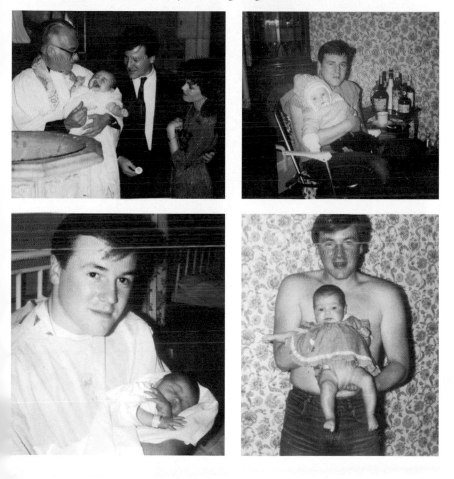

Matthew McConaughey struggles not to look intimidated by my manly physique.

The leafy suburbs of Winchmore Hill was where I took my driving tests. One of the times I failed, the examiner did me on driving too close to parked vehicles. I asked him, 'Did I hit any?' He answered, 'No', so I said, 'Well, how can I have been too fucking close then?' And yet still I failed – where was the justice? There might have been a bit of an altercation after that – I was going through a bit of a hot-headed phase – and I eventually passed at the third time of asking. I don't know how because that was probably the worst I'd ever driven in my life. Maybe the examiners just wanted to get rid of me.

Their plan worked, because as soon as I could get out of Enfield under my own steam, that place didn't see me for dust. I'd had a few trial runs down to Whitechapel and Stratford on my dad's moped. He was in the process of giving up on the fruit and veg game by that point because the big supermarket chains had killed it, and was doing the Knowledge to become a black-cab driver.

He already knew London like the back of his hand, so he passed the test really quickly, but while he was going round studying his little clipboard with a map on it in the daylight hours, I used to sneak into the garden of an evening and borrow his bike to head off to the East End. It was best not to get caught, because he still wasn't the biggest fan of two-wheeled transportation, but he couldn't really say too much about it now he was off out on a bike all day himself.

Once I started to get my hands on vehicles of my own, I loved the sense of freedom I felt bombing back home through Hackney and then up the A10. I had an old claret Cortina for a while (all it needed was some blue trim and the colour scheme would've been perfect). There was a side-window missing which I'd had to replace with some plastic, and one wing was all bent back where I'd hit something. Overall that car was a total rust-bucket, but it did used to go. Then there was the Triumph Herald estate which got us out of the sticky DJing situation, and last but not least was a black Triumph Herald convertible which I borrowed for a long time. That one only started with a screwdriver as well, but it was so worn you had to physically turn the whole ignition. I think in the end only the wires were left.

The places I'd be going to would be Moro's or the Two Puddings in Stratford, or a pub called the Charleston further over towards Maryland Point. Obviously it was the height of the disco era, but although I'd loved Motown and early seventies soul, I wasn't so into disco. I still learnt how to use the music to my advantage. If John Travolta and The Bee Gees could, then why shouldn't I? But I wasn't having the fashion. When the big round collars and the stack-heeled shoes came in I wore them once. That night I slipped on some ice on the platform of Bruce Grove station and to my embarrassment fell down onto the track – fucking stack-heels! No, thank you very much – it was back to the old straight jeans and winkle-pickers for me.

Our status as nightlife apprentices on Martin Nash and Neville Cole's firm broadened our range of places to go out as well. I re-member hearing an enormous crash outside Tipples once. We ran into the street to see a car more or less cut in half and Neville getting out of it with one of the Hariths, who were a big family from another area. They were both all bruised and cut up, but they just walked into the pub and said, 'Come on, we're going to Beirut.'

That's what we called the Old Kent Road in South London, because when you went down there at the weekend, all you'd hear was sirens. On the night in question we got in another motor and drove to Le Connoisseur, which was a Greek restaurant but with a club above it. I remember going to use the toilet in this bar and looking up to see a camera pointing at me. I suppose it was there to stop people snorting Charlie, but that wasn't the purpose of my visit. I went back out there and told everyone, 'There's a camera in the khazi', and they all went, 'No!'

The number of stabbings on the Old Kent Road was outrageous in those days. Someone would say, 'We're going over Beirut on Saturday', and you'd just think, 'Oh for fuck's sake!' You'd want to come back to Bethnal Green for a bit of peace and quiet . . . yeah, right.

It was buzzing on the weekends in E2 at that time too. There were a lot of good pubs, and if you'd pulled and you wanted to take a bird out on your own, the place me and Tony Yeates would always go to was the Venus steakhouse in Bethnal Green Road. I'd always have the same meal in there: start with a prawn cocktail (it was the seventies after all), then T-bone steak, obviously, and a bottle of that Portuguese fizzy rosé to help it go down.

I know what you're thinking – 'That's a well-oiled seduction machine' – and, to be honest, it was. But things didn't always go to plan in that department, especially when you went off your usual manor. And even more so if you couldn't get hold of a car, so public transport had to be factored in.

The incident I'm about to describe definitely took place between the two *Scums*, because I was going to a party with Ray Burdis and some of the other Anna Scher guys I'd got to know on the first one, and by the time the second one came out I'd met my Elaine and was safely off the market. At this particular point in time I'd just split up with a bird, so I wasn't going out with anyone, but I'd met this beautiful-looking girl through a family connection with my auntie Jeanie.

I'm not going to say what her name was, because she's a married woman now and it'll be embarrassing for her, but she lived in the flats round the back of the Londoner pub in Limehouse. I went round there to pick her up and knocked on her parents' door: 'Hello, Mr and Mrs —, I'm Raymond' – all very polite and wanting to make a good impression.

They were the same way: 'Hello, Raymond, come in.' Unfortunately, there was a telephone on the floor of the hallway which I didn't see, and as I walked towards the front room I accidentally kicked it – still on its cord – straight through the plate-glass door to the lounge.

At this point, obviously, I'm mortified. The door is smashed to smithereens, there's little bits of glass everywhere, and I'm saying, 'I'm so sorry, I didn't see the phone', and trying to help them clear up the mess. The girl I'm waiting to go out with is still upstairs getting ready, but her mum and dad are being really nice about it: 'Don't worry, Raymond. Sit yourself down and we'll make you up a nice cup of tea.' They show me to a seat and go off to the kitchen to put the kettle on, but as I lean back on the sofa, the arm splits and falls off. I'm desperately trying to get it back on while they're still out of the room but it just won't hold, so when they come back I just have to say, 'I'm sorry, I've broken your settee.'

Of course, by this time they're looking at me like I'm some sort of nutter. Fucking hell, it's embarrassing. Luckily, at that point their daughter's finally got herself ready, and we set off to get a bus up to the tube at Mile End (normally I'd have got a cab, so I must have been skint). We get on the old 277 and go upstairs, and now the pain of what's happened is starting to fade a bit – I'm not completely over it, but we're having a nice chat.

At this point a Russian sailor comes up the stairs – in full uniform, that's how I can see he's a Ruskie. He walks over and starts talking to us in broken English, but it's clear enough that his intentions aren't honourable.

'You and your girlfriend come with me and we'll have a good night,' he says. I go, 'We'll have a what?' There's no other way this is going to go after that than with the two of us having a fight, and I end up giving the Russian a good fucking hiding right there, on the top deck.

The bus driver's going potty, so we have to get off the bus and walk the rest of the way up to Mile End. Now that's three really bad things that have happened in the space of twenty minutes. We should have quit while we were behind, but we didn't, and for a little while things started to run a bit more smoothly again. We got the tube over to where the party was – in one of those big three-storey houses in Cloudesley Square, on the posh side of Islington.

I've bought a bottle of something. They've let us in fine and we've gone straight upstairs to the front room. I'm having a quick word with my mates. My date doesn't know anyone, but she's having a nice chat with the girls, and I'm keeping half an eye on her the whole time to make sure she's doing alright. Then I look up to see her walking towards me and everything goes into slow motion – always a bad sign with me.

The reason everything goes into slow motion on this occasion is because she's tripped on the carpet, and I can see she's falling towards the marble fireplace. I stick my arm out to grab her, and in that fraction of a second, just as I'm sighing with relief because I've saved the day, my elbow knocks into this huge cut-glass chandelier which for some reason is sitting on the table. First, it rocks – but I can't catch it because I've still got Lucky in my arms – then it falls. And then it hits the marble fireplace and shatters into even more pieces than the door into her lounge did about an hour before.

The host of the party is screaming at me, understandably enough, and I'm trying to explain that I'm very, very sorry, but my friend was falling and I couldn't let her hit her head. We've only been there ten minutes and we've hardly had a drink, but I'm telling her I'll pay for the damage – even though I don't know how, 'cos I've not got more than a tenner on me. By this time the lady of the house is right up in my face shouting, 'Son, if you work from now till Doomsday, you won't be able to afford that fucking light', and I'm saying, 'I think we'd better leave', because now I'm starting to get angry.

Me and the Typhoid Mary of Limehouse had quite a good chat on the tube home, but we never went out together again. She was a lovely girl and everything, but I think on balance we realised that it probably wasn't meant to be.

Not all of my misadventures when it came to girls were quite so much like something out of a romantic comedy. Once we had wheels Tony Yeates and I would go all over East London and Essex in pursuit of a bird, and there was one time in Southend when we both caught crabs at the seaside. We'd nicked the bouncers' girlfriends at a club called the Zero 6, which got its name from the runway at Southend airport that it was sitting right at the end of. They used to play Donald Byrd and the Blackbyrds' 'Flight Time' as their theme song at that place, because it had some great plane noise sound-effects in it. They should've handed out some peanuts and a face towel as you came in to complete the effect, really.

Naturally, the bouncers weren't too happy about what we were up to, and they had a little go at us outside, but we had it away a bit lively and everything was sweet. The two girls took us back to their place and we did what we done – boom boom boom boom. The next day they cooked us Sunday dinner. The two bob went in the gas, then it went off again after we'd eaten and we had a swoppo – which is the opposite of a stoppo.

A week after returning home, we'd both got crabs. There was no way of knowing which of the girls had given them to us – it could've been both of them. Either way, we had no idea what to fucking do about it.

I shaved all the hair off my bollocks, but that didn't do any good and the stubble growing back is the worse thing in the world – worse even than the crabs themselves. Then Tony did some research and got us some blue ointment – 'unction' I think it was called – and they all jumped off, pyong . . . job done.

One night not long after that we were standing in a club at the Seven Kings. It was one of those places where the UV lights give everyone a blue tinge, and this geezer we were talking to had a crab crawling across his eyebrows. They've got a kind of black dot in them – almost like a pin head – and once you've had a visitation you're not going to have any trouble recognising one, especially when it's floodlit by ultra-violet. We both looked at this geezer with his un-wanted guest on his face and we both looked at each other and we were out of there before he'd finished his sentence.

Although I was out and about a lot at this time, I'd still usually be back in Enfield for Sunday dinner (unless I had a better offer on the Essex Riviera, of course). Even now I like to get the family together for a big meal at least once a week if everyone's about. If we've got guests I have to warn them that we don't stand on ceremony. Don't blink at the wrong moment or everyone else will have had all the best roast potatoes.

Of course, bringing people together to eat can cause friction as well as harmony, especially when you're dealing with a family who all have quick tempers. We did have our moments around that Church Street dinner table. Mum and Dad would be sat at either end with me and Laura bickering across the table. Once she got the hump so badly over something I'd said that she threw her knife at me across the table. It stuck right in my sternum and kind of wobbled a bit like a knife-thrower's in a cartoon would. I remember looking down in disbelief to see it fall to the table and a little trickle of blood flowing down my white shirt.

I went garrity and dived at her across the table, then she dived back at me and we're strangling each other, and by the time my mum and dad have got their arms round our necks trying to stop us, we look like one of those Tasmanian Devil cartoons where a fight almost becomes a cloud. Even the dog's going mental. Brandy's gone to the big kennel in the sky by that point, so it's a little Jack Russell called Ben who's barking his head off. In the ensuing melee one of my legs goes through the French windows and gets quite badly cut, but there's no sulking in my house. Something happens and then it's over – done. Twenty minutes later, we're all sitting on the sofa holding hands and watching the Sunday film together.

I clearly remember that film as being *The Champ* because I've got a mental picture of us all holding hands and crying at the scene near the end where Jon Voight's boxer dies (an event which was always going to tug at the heart-strings of the Winstone household). The little kid's going, 'Champ, wake up! Wake up!' My mum's crying, my dad's crying, I'm crying, Laura's crying – even the dog's crying. But that film didn't come out until 1979 and I'd left home by the time it could've been on TV, so maybe I'd just come back for Sunday lunch a bit later on to reconnect with my family. It's good to stay in touch with your family, but not necessarily via a knife stuck in your chest.

I should say at this point that my sister Laura tells this story differently to the way I do. She insists she stabbed me with a fork, not a knife, but I think she's getting mixed up with another earlier occasion, when I'd showed her up in front of her mate and she went for me on the staircase. The only thing that comes back to me from that one is the excruciating pain of the fork she'd stuck in the back of my hand. All in all, there's a lot to be said for plastic cutlery.

There's also a lot to be said for kids who are ready to spread their wings getting the chance to do that, and I finally got my marching orders from the family home after an incident with a party which got a bit out of control. My mum and dad had gone on holiday, leaving strict instructions for me not to have a party. So, of course, I had to have one. It was the classic scenario of loads more people turning up than I'd expected, and by the end it did get a bit outrageous. There was talcum powder and baby oil everywhere – they trashed the gaff.

When I woke up in the morning and surveyed the devastation all around me through the fog of my brutal hangover, it was just like that old Yellow Pages advert where the kid goes, 'French polisher? It's just possible you could save my life . . .' Except there was no French polisher around to do the honours.

I did everything I could to tidy the place up, but it just wasn't within my power to put everything right. When my mum and dad came back and saw what had happened, that was me gone. I was angry with them for throwing me out at the time, but looking back it all worked out OK.

After a few nights of sleeping on different people's settees, I thought, 'Bollocks to this, I'm going to see Granddad', and went and moved in with Toffy, who was on his own by then and didn't mind the company. My mum and dad wanted him to kick me out so I'd have no choice but to come home, but he wouldn't do it. I think he could see that living with him was good for me – it gave me a bit more independence without leaving me completely on my own.

I might've been twenty by this time but I was still a bit wayward, and having a much older role model I loved and respected around wasn't going to do me any harm. Another upside was I got to live in Hackney for the next year or so – just over the road from the house I'd spent the first twelve months of my life in.

There's a postscript to the story which shows how much things have changed these days in terms of everyone knowing what everyone else is up to. On the night of my party a couple of mates who I'd gone to school with took two girls home with them and had a really bad car crash on the way out to Ware. Everyone survived but they all had to be cut out of the vehicle, and the two guys were in hospital in traction for months on end. But because my mum and dad kicked me out the next day and I went off to live with my granddad, I didn't find out what had happened till a year or so later.

I suppose as much as anything this tells you how happy I was to be back in the East End – it turned out that if you took the man out of Enfield you actually could take the Enfield out of the man (well, this one, anyway). But still, no one thought to ring and tell me. Obviously mobiles weren't in use yet – not even the giant ones we had in the eighties – so the next time I saw my mates a year or so later they were really angry with me. 'You fucker,' they said, 'we had a terrible car crash and you didn't even come and visit us.'

CHAPTER 19

GATSBY HOUSE

It's true what they say about your grandparents – sometimes you can talk to them in a way that you can't talk to your mum and dad. I've spoken to a lot of my mates who've said they were always drawn to their granddads, partly because they aren't there all the time, whereas your dad is so close to you that there will often be some kind of trouble either bubbling under or boiling over. It's unfair on dads in a way, but as you get older that competitive element about who is the guv'nor is always going to creep in.

There was none of that with my granddad Toffy. He still lived in the same two-bedroom council flat where he'd been on his own since Nanny Maud died a few years before. It was in an old-fashioned brick block called Gatsby House on the Frampton Park Estate, just east of Mare Street in Hackney. The name Gatsby tends to be associated with good living, and even though his circumstances were obviously less luxurious than Robert Redford's or Leonardo DiCaprio's in the films, Toffy always maintained his own elegant personal style.

This wasn't just about looking immaculate or lifting his hat to the ladies as he walked down the road – it went deeper. He was an absolute gent and living with him for a year was a great education in little things you shouldn't even have to think or talk about. As a result I will still open the door for a woman or stand up on a train to let her sit down, even now. Of course, nine times out of ten women are so independent that they'll just say, 'I'm alright, thank you', but that's no reason for me to stop making the effort.

Because I'd been so stubborn about not going back to my parents', I hadn't just lost my home, I'd got the sack from my job as well. Although I couldn't work with my dad on the markets any more, I didn't want to sign on and all that shit, so I ended up getting a job with Fred, a friend of his who ran a grocer's called Oliver Marcus in Muswell Hill. He was a good man, big Freddie. Even though he was my dad's mate, he wouldn't be pressured into giving me the old heave-ho so I'd have to go home like my dad wanted. Looking back, I put both Freddie and my granddad in a bit of a situation as far as my dad was concerned, but I was grateful that they both stuck up for me, and I suppose this made me feel like more of my own man in a way, which was probably what refusing to come back home was all about in the first place.

Every working day for about a year I travelled from Hackney to Muswell Hill to do my shift in that shop. I was happy to work there because I knew the fruit and veg game inside out by then. I didn't know the area, though. It was very . . . bohemian would be a good word. TV faces would come in all the time – Wilfred Pickles, he was a regular – and there were loads of poets and people like that as well. I know what you're thinking: 'Just Ray's home turf.'

I've always had an affinity with people from earlier generations, and I suppose going off to work in the shop all day, then coming home and maybe going to the pub with my granddad and his mates, I was living the life of someone much older than I actually was. Even when Tony Yeates and I were out and about in the clubs at that time, the older guys would be looking out for us. They certainly knew how to enjoy themselves, and that was true of my granddad as well. Neither of the two main pubs he used to go to is there any more, but one was called The North and the other was The Frampton Park Arms. I remember coming home late one night after I'd been to a party – creeping into the flat as quietly as I could so as not to wake him up at about three o'clock in the morning. Two hours later I heard the front door shutting quietly as Granddad came back from a lock-in.

As far as Granddad's work as a tic-tac man went, I never really got involved with it. That was his business and he just got on with it. He was still going all over the country when I lived with him – not just to Kempton and Sandown, but as far as York, Dublin, even Paris. Tic-tacking is another game which is pretty much over now. Mobile phones killed it. That's a shame because it was a big part of the excitement of going to the races, but I suppose the whole online betting thing has kind of expanded to fill the space.

The idea of having a flutter on your computer at home would've seemed like science fiction to us when we saw Lester time Roberto's run perfectly to win the Derby in 1972. And nothing had changed when I went to Epsom for the big race again in 1978. Lester had won on The Minstrel the year before, but he didn't win this time. Greville Starkey did. Six years on from the day-trip that ended my school career, I wasn't selling umbrellas any more, but my granddad was still tic-tacking, and Billy Brown and his firm who I knew from Chrisp Street Market were still down there too.

Granddad got mugged one day coming home from the races. He was a shrewd old boy in that he'd keep a couple of quid in his pocket and the rest he'd have tucked away. So when two guys followed him on the way back to the flats, he turned round and said, 'What do you want, son? Do you want a few quid off me? Well, that's all I've got. Rather than you give me a bashing, why not just take that?' And they did, so he came home unscathed with his wad of notes in his sock. All we could find out about the main mugger was that he had blond hair, so anyone we bumped into with blond hair was potentially in strife for a while from that point on.

My granddad had been no pushover as a younger man. Obviously he'd done his bit of boxing, and there was a story – which I know is true because the guy who ran the newsagent's confirmed it – about him going to the shop opposite the Frampton Park estate with one of my cousin's kids when they were still a baby. Someone barged to the front past a woman in the queue so Granddad called them on it: 'Mind out, son, you're pushing the lady there.' But the guy didn't apologise, so Granddad handed the baby to the woman and knocked him to the ground, then took the baby back, finished queuing for his paper and justice was done.

On a scale of general belligerence from one to ten, he'd have come a lot lower down than my dad, though. My dad, I'd say, was an eight (although some people might call him an eleven), but my granddad was no more than a three or four. His was the example that made me aspire to be a gentleman, not so much in the way you talk, but in the way you are with people and how you deal with them. I've changed my outlook on a lot of things over the years, but even now I'm still drawn to that idea of an unspoken moral code. It's not necessarily the strictness of it that I like, so much as the sense of everyone having respect for each other.

The atmosphere in that flat wasn't all uptight and old-fashioned. He was a very kind man, my granddad. The whole time we lived together, he did all the cooking. Once I'd made the mistake of telling him a particular meal was my favourite, I used to get it three times a week. The meal in question was a pork chop with some apple sauce, a grilled tomato, chips, baked beans and peas. I did like it at the time, but I ate a lifetime's supply of it in that year.

As well as having a generous spirit, Toffy was also an absolute character. He used to love talking to his goldfish. He'd say, 'That goldfish understands every word I say', and you'd be fairly sure he was joking, but not quite certain. He was also one of those people it's really good fun to play a prank on, and I used to wind him up something terrible.

One time, I was sitting up in the flat with my two cousins Melanie and Tracy. Mel was sitting on the floor and she had these big boots on, so while Granddad was out of the front room for a minute I said, 'Take your boots off and bend your legs back, then we'll put the boots up against your knees so it looks like your legs are stretching straight out.'

Granddad came back in, sat down in his armchair and started talking about his goldfish and the big fights the chivvy men – the men who carried chivs (razors or knives) – used to have at the races. All of a sudden, I just went mad. I threw myself at Mel and ripped one of the boots away so it looked like I'd pulled her leg off. Granddad went fucking apeshit. He was screaming, 'What have you done?' He was so relieved when we showed him her leg was still there that he actually forgot to be angry.

Another memorable occasion was the time Granddad and I went to visit my cousin Charlie in prison. The bright bubbly boy I used to knock about with at the Lansdowne Club had taken a few wrong turnings in the intervening years and got himself banged up for armed robbery. He got himself done for what's called a 'ready-eyed job' in Hatton Garden, which was an insurance caper where a guy on the inside actually wants it doing. Charlie went in when there was supposed to be no one about, but someone had made a boo-boo, and as it turned out there was a meeting going on, so they had to tie everyone up and take a bit of tom away. (Tomfoolery/jewellery – keep up.)

Instead of simply burying the stuff till the heat was off like any sensible person would, Charlie-boy put it on top of the wardrobe in his bedroom and bought himself a Mercedes. There weren't too many of them on the street in Hackney where he lived – just down the road from my granddad's flat, on the way to Victoria Park – so it attracted a bit of attention. In the end the Old Bill came round, and he got captured and sent down for a few years. He got it wrong, old Charlie-boy, and he paid a heavy price in the long run.

The day we went down to visit him in Maidstone prison, there was no sign of how sadly this story was going to pan out. Me and Granddad made it down to the station, probably London Bridge, to get the train to Maidstone, and on the platform there was a bloke done up as a cowboy, with the hat and the six-guns and everything. He had two birds in hot-pants with him, one on each arm. They were good sorts as well, which attracted my interest. I said to Granddad, 'Look at that, I wonder where they're going.'

Eventually the train pulls into Maidstone, we get off and of course the geezer and the two birds do too. You have to walk up the hill a bit to get to the prison, which is like an old castle. The bloke and the two birds are walking in front of us the whole way. When we all get there they take you into a little room at the side, where the guy takes out his six-guns – which I presume were toys, because real six-shooters wouldn't go down too well in a prison – twirls them in the old Western style and hands them over.

Granddad and me are laughing as we follow them into the nick because we can see what the geezer's up to. Visiting time at Maidstone is set up almost like a stage, with all the cons sitting there as the audience. You can imagine the reaction when he walks in there to visit his mate or his brother or whatever with the two birds in hot-pants – the whole place stands up and starts clapping, even the screws.

The other funny thing about prison visiting for me is that I'll always see someone else I know in there. This time it was Sammy McCarthy, the old boxer who used to spar with me when I first used to go to Spitalfields Market. It turned out he'd got done for bank robbery. I had a lot of time for this man – he was one of those guys you could talk to all day long – and I've seen Sammy since at dos for old boxers (he's retired from the robbery business too now).

It was only when I was writing this book that I found out he'd been both British Flyweight and Lightweight champion in the fifties. In those days he was known as 'Smilin' Sammy' aka 'The Stepney Feather'. He was also the first boxer ever to appear on *This Is Your Life*. You don't want Eamonn Andrews or Michael Aspel bringing you the big red book when you're banged up, do you?

On the day of the hot-pants girls' visit, I said hello to Sammy then waited for the place to quieten down a bit before slipping Charlie-boy a tenner, which was still worth having in the seventies. You folded it up and gave it to them and then the con who does the teas comes along and collects it on the tea-tray. I think they did this on the great old Ronnie Barker show *Porridge* once, so someone must've done their research. I suppose he'd pass it on to Charlie later on, so as to avoid it being found in the search at the end of visiting. I don't know, I ain't been in prison.

The tactic backfired this time, though, because when Granddad saw me do it he got up and said, 'I didn't know you could hand over money here, son.' Then he got out his money to give Charlie-boy a score and the whole place fell about – even the screws were laughing.

The sad end to the Charlie-boy story was that years later he got heavily into drugs and they gave him a life sentence in Mauritius for smuggling heroin, even though I know for a fact it was only for personal use. The British government got him sent back home, so he was a lucky boy really to get banged up here rather than out there. After about five years he was released and started trying to get his life together, but by that time the heroin had got to him to the extent where there was no way back. The heroin had done his lungs, and his other internal organs weren't shaping up too well either. That fucking drug doesn't just mess your brain up, it kills your body as well. We lost Charlie-boy a few years ago, which was a great shame when I think about what a lovely kid he was.

One thing I've noticed while visiting mates who've been banged up over the years is how much the vibe in prisons has changed. On that trip to Maidstone and other visits in the late seventies I always registered how many of the cons would get themselves all smartened up – partly out of pride and partly because you've got your family or friends visiting and you want to look good so people don't worry about you – but as time went on you didn't see that nearly so much. More and more of the prisoners would come slouching in looking like shit, not caring what anyone else thought about them. It was definitely the drug culture that did that. Whether people are just smoking a lot of dope or they're actual skag-heads, that basic pride in yourself seems to be one of the first things to go.

The way my granddad lived his life was the opposite of that. He'd had really bad bronchial problems all his life, and in his later years he had no option but to connect himself up to this great big pump inhaler with a bowl at the bottom – almost like a hubbly-bubbly or some kind of giant home-made bong, only he was using it to stay alive, not to get out of his head. And if you saw him out and about he always looked dapper, however bad he might've been feeling.

You'd never hear him complain. Even the prospect of his own death was contemplated with good-humoured resignation: 'I'm up, son, I'm up' – that was his favourite saying. I really loved my grand-dad, and when he passed on a few years later it was one of the biggest losses I've had in my life. The doctors had told him he was going to die way back when he was just twenty-eight, so he did pretty well to live as long as he did. When he was on his death bed he looked up at me with a broad smile and said, 'I'm eighty-two. They got the numbers the wrong way round.'

CHAPTER 20

THE ALEXANDRA
TAVERN

I'll tell you a good trick for getting the best seat on a plane if you can only afford economy class. Get yourself a cast made and strap it on under your trousers like you've got a broken leg – I was lucky, I had a mate whose mum worked in a hospital so I got her to make it up for me. Then borrow a couple of crutches to hobble onto the plane with, and they'll have to upgrade you somewhere with a bit more legroom. Obviously, your leg's got to be straight, so if there's any seats free in business class they'll put you in there. Otherwise it'll be an aisle or (before they stopped allowing you to sit there) somewhere by the emergency exit.

This might seem like a lot of trouble to go to, not least because you've got to lug the cast around with you for the whole holiday if you want to do the same thing again on the way home, but there was a phase in my life when I did it three or four times in quick succession. OK, so you'll get funny looks if anyone who was on the same flight as you (never mind if it's one of the cabin crew) happens to catch you water-skiing, but that didn't bother me at the time.

The flipside of the masterclass in morality and general manners I was getting from my granddad was an overlapping period of several years – probably from the time I left school onwards – when I was a bit of a scammer. I can see the contradiction between those two things now, but again, at the time it never really bothered me. I suppose in my own mind I was keeping alive the heritage of East End fell-off-the-back-of-a-lorry culture. The docks might've been shutting up shop, but that was no reason the proud tradition of spill-age had to die.

You never looked at yourself as doing anything criminal – at least, I didn't. But from stolen tax discs that would come to you through a dodgy postman, to starting a motor with a screwdriver when it wasn't even technically ours, to the odd bit of sleight of hand with a credit card, there was a fair amount of low-level illegality going on. When you're a teenager who ain't got much money the prospect of living like a king in a hotel for the weekend at someone else's expense can look quite tempting, especially once you're caught up in the dubious mystique of the gentleman conman.

Looking back on all this now, my reaction is, 'Fucking hell, what was I thinking?' Not so much in a moralistic way, although that is part of it, but more in terms of my misplaced confidence that if I got caught I wouldn't go to prison. I did some stupid things at that time which I was lucky not to get done for. OK, I enjoyed some of them, but they were still stupid.

There were a couple of pubs down near where my dad went to school – just north of Victoria Park – where I got away with murders. Not literally murders, but certainly stuff that crossed the thin line that separates a misdemeanour from a felony. It's all getting a bit chi-chi in those parts these days, but both the pubs concerned – the Empress and the Alexandra Tavern – are actually still there (albeit under new management), which is quite unusual given how many East End boozers have gone under over the last few decades. Having so many people coming into the area who are Muslims certainly hasn't helped the area's pub trade, and that's before you even factor in the invasion of the white middle classes.

Now, I don't smoke spliff, and I've never really been able to – it just helicopters me, and I don't really like that feeling. But the air was so thick with it in the Alex in the late seventies that walking in there was like opening curtains. One time we decided we could make the heady atmosphere work for us. I had a mate in those days who had access to a big colour photocopier at his place of work, and I got him to take photographs of a ten-pound note and copy them onto both sides of a piece of paper. They came out a bit grey at first but we fucked about with them for a while and got it as close as it was ever gonna get. In normal daylight you could see the colour wasn't right, but in the kind of brothel-red glow they had at the Alex, with a cloud of marijuana smoke to help you, they could just about pass muster. Bosh! Two drinks and we'll keep the change, thanks – no bother.

We absolutely caned it that night. Obviously, we should've just done it once and moved on somewhere else, but I'm not a great one for relocating. If I'm in a pub I like, I prefer to stay there for the duration. How we avoided getting caught and being sentenced to transportation to Australia for forging the tenners of the realm I will never know, but it must've been a bit of a sickener for the poor sod who had to cash up. And the fact that we never did it again suggested that we knew a destiny as Britain's greatest counterfeiters did not lie ahead of us.

Another time in the Empress we had a load of dodgy lighters that were meant to be Ronsons that we were knocking out for fivers or two quid. I remember a funny little geezer who bought one tried to use it straight away and it set his hair alight. We moved so fast to put him out it must've been like watching Red Adair. Luckily he was OK, but it was another deathblow to the idea of a victimless crime.

I mentioned earlier in this book that there was sometimes an element of hypocrisy about the moral environment I grew up in. This was particularly true when it came to fraud. If you get away with it, you're a lovable rogue, but if someone else does it to you, they're a wanker. The same applies when you get a bit higher up the criminal scale to proper white-collar scams.

People who earn their living on the wrong side of the law tend to see those as their equivalent of getting promoted at work, but the idea that 'it only affects the banks and insurance companies' is total bollocks. I've got as much dislike for the banks and insurance companies as the next man – probably more than most – but anyone can see that's just an excuse, because fraud affects everyone. And when it's focused on an individual victim it can be a terrible thing which absolutely destroys people's lives.

Of course, I didn't see things that way then. In my late teens and early twenties I wouldn't have thought of fraud as something that was really hurting anyone. But luckily before my career as a fraudster could really get off the ground, the movie remake of *Scum* came along to save me from myself. Mary Whitehouse might not have thought that film was a good influence on impressionable young minds, but it certainly worked that way for me. Once you become an actor who might be recognised at any time, you can't really afford to get involved in fraud any more (unless people want to look at your acting and say that it's fraudulent – there's nothing you can do to stop that). So being in a successful film changes your life in that way if no other.

There was no road-to-Damascus moment where someone sold me a dodgy timeshare and I realised it was wrong – apart from anything else, there was no way I would ever buy a timeshare in Damascus. But I do understand the implications of fraud now in a way I didn't as a kid. Everyone seemed to be at it in one form or another when I was growing up. From little things like working cash in hand or dodgy tax discs to the boxes of booze or clothes that would mysteriously appear in people's front rooms around Christmas. This was the grease that made the wheels move. But you only need to go up a gear or two and suddenly those wheels are taking you somewhere you don't really want to go.

If you ask me now if I have any regrets about this, in a way I don't because I learnt from it – as well as earning from it – but on the other hand it's a time in your life that you look back on and think, 'I wasn't a very nice person.' You tell yourself you're not hurting anyone, but you know you are really. I don't know if my parents knew what was going on. I don't suppose my dad would've been too bothered, but then again maybe that was what the whole drama school thing was about. They might've been trying to give me something else to focus on.

I'd like to get one more story from the Empress in before I get onto how the second *Scum* put me back on the straight and narrow. We had some great nights in those pubs, and this one was from a few years earlier – a more innocent time, when I was maybe sixteen or seventeen.

I was seeing a barmaid at the time, and her brother was a big lump who came out of the house once when I'd walked her home. 'What are you doing with my sister?' he demanded, before chasing me off down the road. A few years later I saw him on the TV and recognised him immediately. He wasn't on *Crimewatch*; he was

Tommy, the geezer from *Ground Force* (not Alan Titchmarsh – I don't think I'd have run away if he'd chased me). I met him again a short while after and said, 'You probably won't remember me', to which he replied, 'Oh yes, I do.'

When I was stacking up the fruit and veg for that year in Muswell Hill, I never saw myself being a greengrocer for the rest of my life. Not because there was anything wrong with it as a job, just because the example of what had happened to my dad's shop in Watford had showed me how hard it was getting to compete with the supermarkets. I had no idea what else I'd end up doing. I wasn't really thinking about being an actor any more after *Scum* got banned. So I was lucky to get a break out of the blue which led me down a career path I really enjoyed. I do believe there probably is something like that out there for everyone, but a lot of people just never get the chance to find it.

I was at home at my granddad's one day and happened to answer the phone.

'Hello.'

'Is that Ray?'

'Yeah.'

'We're thinking of making the film *Scum* again.'

'Oh, are you? Well done.'

They asked me if I'd like to do it and told me the fee would be £1,800, so I thought about it for a minute and said, 'OK, alright.' In my mind I still didn't particularly want to be an actor, I just thought of it as work. Then they offered me another film for the same money, which they were going to shoot just before. It was called *That Summer!*, and doing it would mean going down to Torquay and living in a hotel for eight weeks over the summer of 1978. I didn't hesitate so long over that one. I thought, 'Blinding, I can have some mates down – it'll be like a holiday.'

It was like that too, and without me coming home empty-handed and with a sore head like I normally would, either. Not only did I have a great time down there, I also met my wife-to-be Elaine, and before I'd even come back to London, she'd already helped me start to heal the breach with my parents.

That Summer! was a film for young teenagers. You can guess the kind of thing it was from the title. I was in some kind of round-the-bay swimming competition and these three Glasgow sweaties kept having a pop at me so I had to sort them out. The same people who did *Scum* produced it – Davina Belling and Clive Parsons – but I wasn't actually meant to be playing the same character again. I've heard this suggested a few times, but the film certainly wasn't scripted that way. I probably just acted like that because I didn't know how to do anything else. I didn't have the ability to find another character yet, so I just played me every time.

This film is rarely seen these days, although it was shown on TV late at night in the Granada region once, when someone was kind enough to make me a copy of it on video. For some reason I got a BAFTA best newcomer nomination for it, even though I didn't deserve it because I didn't really have the first idea of what I was doing. Julie Shipley, who played the girl in it, was good, though.

When I eventually went to the BAFTAs, eighteen months or so later, I knew I wasn't going to be in luck from the moment I got there. We were sitting way back in the cheap seats, and the iron rule of award ceremonies is: 'If you ain't down the front, you ain't gonna win.' Even if you are down the front, you still probably won't win – they might just have got you there so the cameras can catch the pissed-off look on your face.

That Summer! didn't win me my first piece of acting silverware, but it did bring me the ultimate prize, which was my Elaine. She lived in Manchester at the time, but she was down in Torquay on holiday with her mum and dad and a mate called Carol, who we still see sometimes to this day.

My mate – the actor Tony London, who was in the film with me – went after Elaine at first, but she didn't want to know. I've never really got into competition with friends over women – if that's the way it is, that's the way it is – but I couldn't help holding Elaine's gaze and doing the old puppy-eye thing every now and again. I'd been going out with Julie Shipley for a while, but even though she was a good girl, we weren't really getting along. So me and Elaine met up again on our own the next day and that was that. Tally-ho, chaps, bandits at three o'clock.

Brandy's legacy had served me well. To be honest, I think Elaine had also tapped into it, because she did me with the eye thing too. All of which goes to show that there is such a thing as eyes meeting across a room, and the buzz is even better when you both catch each other looking away and then back at the same time.

Before we met, Elaine had gone to college doing art and design and then got jobs window-dressing for a chain of department stores. But by the time we got together she was working as a Bunny Girl at the Playboy Club in Manchester, although she wasn't wearing her costume when we first met. I soon put paid to that once we got together – I told that bunny costume to hop it.

It's not like Elaine was short of rivals for my attention in Torquay that summer – and the same applied the other way round. All of which made the strength of the instant bond between us even more obvious.

I was certainly a bit of a handful in those days. It was my first time away from home working with a film crew, and it wasn't so much the other actors who were the problem, it was the sparks. This mob were murder – their motto when they went away was 'Drink, fight and fuck' – although obviously they weren't all like that, and I don't want to get anyone in trouble, so if you're still married to one of them, it wasn't him. But the fact that when the film was finally finished I would drive back to London with the electricians rather than my fellow performers shows you who I felt most at home with.

At the end of her holiday Elaine went home with her parents, but pretty much as soon as she got to Manchester I was asking her to come and see me again. She borrowed a car to drive back to Torquay, but she turned the wrong way onto the motorway and headed north instead of south. A psychologist might see this as evidence of her subconscious mind trying to protect her by taking her as far away from me as possible, but really it was the opposite. What made this mistake a good omen was the fact that she carried on driving until she got to Gretna Green, which was where couples used to run off to if they eloped.

When she got there, she asked a policeman if she was 'anywhere near Torquay', and he told her (and feel free to read this in your worst *Braveheart* accent), 'Sorry, love, you're in Gretna Green.' So she turned around and drove all the way back to Devon.

Elaine made it down to Torquay eventually, but obviously her mum was worried as to why it had taken her a whole day. 'Don't you know where the sun goes down?' I enquired respectfully when she finally turned up at my hotel. 'It goes down in the west, babe. So all you've got to do is look at the sun and you might have some idea of where you are.'

A sense of direction has never been my Elaine's strongest suit, but she knows how to put people on the right road when it comes to the things that matter. She was showing this quality already in the first weeks we were together in Torquay. My parents had wanted to make peace for ages but my dad's as stubborn as I am – we were like two rams butting their heads together (and we still are). He wouldn't just say, 'Come home,' he wanted me to ask, but I wasn't having it. So when the two of them made the gesture of bringing my granddad down to Torquay on holiday at the same time as I was working there, that was quite a major concession on their part. I don't think my dad would have come up with that on his own – Mum probably nagged him.

They stayed in a suite at the Imperial Hotel, so they must've been doing alright for money at the time. And Elaine was with me when I got the call to tell me that they were there, so she came along too to have dinner at the hotel. Things could still have gone either way at that stage, as I hadn't seen much of them over the last eighteen months or so, and there were still issues that needed to be sorted out. But it was all kind of cool – Elaine met 'em and then she danced with my granddad, and by the time we parted company at the end of the night, we were all on friendly terms and she'd made a really good impression on them.

It went so well that before *That Summer!* was even finished I'd hired a car to drive her back to London to see them all again. There's a big street in Winchmore Hill near where our house was that all the rich people used to live on. It was sort of like a lower-key version of Bishop's Avenue, just off the North Circular, where all the millionaires have mansions that are going to rack and ruin because they never get around to actually living in them.

I turned down this road saying, 'Nearly there, babe', and I could see the pound-note signs lighting up in Elaine's eyes. Once I'd taken it that far I thought, 'I've got to follow through with this', so I pulled into one of the driveways and went up and knocked on the door. An old boy came out who she probably thought was the butler, so

I spun him a line about being lost or some other bollocks and went back to the car. She'd got out of the passenger seat by that time and was looking a bit confused. Luckily I was able to put her mind at rest by telling her, 'I fucking had you there, didn't I? You thought we were cake-o bake-o!'

She still married me within about a year of seeing where I actually lived, though. So she can't have been in it for the money, which subsequent events would confirm was definitely for the best.

CHAPTER 21

THE TATE & LYLE SUGAR FACTORY, SILVERTOWN

There was one thing I came back from Torquay with that I could've done without, and that was a charge of marijuana possession for a bit of wacky baccy that wasn't even mine. One night I had a party in my room in the Grand Hotel — just for a few of the boys in the crew. Unfortunately, there were two of the make-up women staying downstairs who were not very nice. I usually get on really well with the make-up girls, but I didn't with these two – not in a nasty way, I just didn't have 'em in the company because they were horrible gossips.

Anyway, I had this party, and they complained about the noise. Maybe they were just pissed off that they hadn't been invited, I don't know. Either way, that was fair enough. The bad part was that they told the concierge I had drugs in the room – which I didn't because that's not my game. So I came back from the set the next day to be met by a police detective who had already been in there (which I thought was a fucking liberty, but obviously I don't own the room, the hotel does).

He told me they'd found a small quantity of marijuana. I said, 'It ain't mine – you can give me a drugs test if you like', but that didn't stop them taking me down the station. I knew who it belonged to – a mate of mine who did like a smoke – but just because he'd dropped me in it with some grass didn't mean I had to become one. Maybe he should've come forward and held his hands up, but he didn't. The whole thing was a bigger deal then legally than it would be now, but my main concern was that I didn't want my dad thinking I was on drugs – especially when I wasn't. Relations with my parents were just starting to get back on track, and this was the first time I'd been away working on a film, so I didn't want them thinking I was on the slippery slope to reefer madness.

When I went back to Torquay to appear in court in December of 1978 I decided to plead guilty. I'd been brought up never to do that, but in this case there was fuck all else I could do. I just wanted this one out of the way with nothing in the papers to upset the family.

Not long before my court appearance, the producers Davina and Clive phoned me up and said, 'Since you're going back, anyway, could we do some pick-up shots?' They'd been really good about sorting out the legal side of things, so I couldn't say no. Next thing I knew I had to swim out into Torquay bay in the middle of winter, which was a bonus – especially when my ankle got snagged by a fishing hook that dragged me under the sea. I just about managed to pull the hook out of my leg and get home in one piece. Then I got found guilty and paid the fine without my Old Man finding out, so that was more good news.

Fast-forward thirty-five years, and having this conviction on my record still causes me problems getting into America. Every time I go there, which I do a lot, I get pulled out of the line and have to sit in a room and be investigated (not intimately, but it's still a pain in the arse). When you get off a plane after an eleven-hour flight the last thing you want to do is spend another four hours being asked pointless questions in a brightly lit room, especially when you're a smoker like I am. And all because someone who was a mate of yours – bless him – smoked a joint in your hotel room and left a bit of gear there. The worst thing is that at the end of the interrogation they always say, 'You shouldn't have to come here any more, this will clear off your record now', but it never does. I always tell them, 'You say that every time.'

I often see Frank Roddam when I'm on those flights back and forth to LA, either that or hanging about in the Chateau Marmont. He's the guy who got me to be a rocker in *Quadrophenia* between the two films for Belling and Parsons, and he's still got those little-boy looks he always had – I suppose the millions he must've earned for inventing *Masterchef* can't have done any harm in that area.

I wish he'd let me have a haircut like his in *Quadrophenia*, instead of sending round Danny La Rue to give me Liberace's old barnet. I was happy to pay tribute to my childhood memories of mods and rockers roaring through Plaistow, and I didn't even mind sharing a bath with the lovely Phil Daniels, although I'd have rather not done it with hair that looked like it'd just got back from a three-month residency in Vegas.

The funny thing about my performances in the two films I did with Phil at that time – *Quadrophenia* and *Scum* – is that I wasn't either capable or interested enough to have a say in how I looked on the screen yet. I didn't realise I could have a say in the development of the character – I just turned up, listened to what the director had to say and did the lines as best I could. If I'd played those parts a few years later I would have done them very differently, but they might not have turned out nearly so well, because how little I knew about what I was doing probably fed into the rawness of the characters.

A lot of the Anna Scher boys were in both films too, and they knew the ropes a lot better than I did. They were winding me up a bit on *Quadrophenia*. One of them (not Phil) came up behind me in a dressing room and said, "Ere, Ray, I'm doing your part in *Scum*." I just held his gaze in the mirror and said, 'Oh, are you mate? Well, good luck to ya.' I knew he was digging me out. You do get tested in those situations, especially when you've got a load of young fellas together.

When the time came to do the scene in the alley at Shepherd's Bush Market where they're chasing me on the bikes, the guy who was needling me about *Scum* was meant to be the first one off and at me. Peter Brayham, who was the stuntman and a great mate of mine, told me what I had to do, which was basically crash into the boxes. I'm not that great on a bike, but all I had in my head was 'he's the first one off'.

After I'd crashed the bike, I was supposed to stay there while they all piled into me. Instead, I jumped up and chinned him. All the stunties were going, 'Stop! Stop!' but they couldn't get there in time to stop me giving him a good larrapping. The geezer didn't bear a grudge afterwards. I think he respected me for it, because he knew he'd been out of order. Either way, we're still mates a quarter of a century later.

When you're doing these films – the second *Scum* was the same – you don't know whether they're going to end up being any good or not. One of the things I was beginning to learn at this time was that the scenes which work the best tend to be the ones that are done in a very simple way. The billiard-balls scene in *Scum* was a good example.

Phil Mayhew, who was on the camera, did hand-held all the way while I walked down the stairs, took a sock out of my pocket to put the billiard balls in and then hit poor old Phyllis over the head with 'em. Because subconsciously you know there's not been a cut, even people watching with no interest in how films are made think, 'How the fuck did he hit Phil over the head and not kill him?' I think Phil was thinking that too.

Here's how we did it: there was a geezer lying on the floor by the door who swapped the sock with the balls for another one – containing ping pong balls in *papier-mâché* – as I walk in. We still have to have some weight in it so you can see I ain't giving Phil a chance when he turns round and I go whack. It's the shock of it that makes it effective.

I've not said too much about the technical side of things in this book, because I've found that the more I've learnt about those aspects of film-making, the less I enjoy actually watching a movie. And I don't want to put you lot through the same pain I've suffered. One thing I do think is that we don't give audiences enough credit for being willing to be challenged by something real. I remember when Hollywood made a more commercial version of *Scum* called *Bad Boys* – with Sean Penn in it – they swapped the billiard balls in a sock for a pillow-case full of Coca-Cola cans. I suppose there might've been a bit of product placement going on there, but I don't think it was very credible.

By the time we got to the second *Scum*, Alan Clarke was manipulating us quite mercilessly to get the level of realism he wanted. When it came to the race riot in the borstal hall he went up to all the black kids and said, 'Listen, all the white guys are going to have a go at you here.' Then he told the rest of us to 'watch the black kids – they might be gonna stick it on ya'. They were alright that lot – I think they'd come out of a youth club in Leytonstone – but they were definitely there to do a job, and there was never much doubt about what was going to happen as soon as someone said, 'Action!'

I remember saying to Francis – who played Baldy, the black guy I use the tool on in the film – 'Are you with them or with us?' When he said the latter I thought, 'Thank God for that! He's a second dan karate expert.' It was actually Phil Daniels who saved me from getting a belting in that scene. One fella came at me and as I chinned him he grabbed my legs and pulled me down on the floor. They were all piling in on top when Phil pulled me up and got me out of there, laying about him all the while. That's one of the things I love about Phil – he's a game little fucker who takes no prisoners, especially when he's got some red wine inside him.

I'd had my last little go at the boxing by then. After a couple of years away I'd found that I missed it and wanted to get back in the ring. As comebacks go, mine went better than Ricky Hatton's but not as well as George Foreman's. Having left the Repton I trained at the Black Lion in West Ham, an excellent boxing gym with a blinding pub attached. My first fight was in the old Territorial Army place on the side of West Ham Park. I got off to a good start but I wasn't fully fit yet, so I ran out of steam halfway through the second round. I tried to batten down the hatches as I was probably ahead at that stage, but it was too long to last and I lost on points.

You think you'll be a bit wiser two years on and your mind will be working better, but I found I'd lost some of that speed I'd had before. There's a natural kind of fitness you have in your late teens – especially if you're not drinking too much yet – which gets much harder to maintain by the time you're in your early twenties, so I wasn't in much better shape by the time I got to the second fight.

That was in the old Tate & Lyle sugar factory, the big white building in Silvertown. I think they were renting it out for events to try and make a bit of money, because the docks had more or less gone by then. The night in question was a West Ham boxing club show and I fought a guy called Chris Christiansen – not Kris Kristofferson, he'd have been singing.

Chris was a pretty solid performer who went on to win the Southern area title, but by now I was a bit less ring-rusty so I just about managed to pull through. I still wasn't fully fit, so I had to hold him a lot in the last round – I needed something to lean on by then, anyway. I know Chris didn't think I'd won it, but he had a head as big as Bournemouth and I couldn't miss it. Either way, once I'd staggered out of the ring at the end of that fight I knew the game was up. As soon as I won, I retired.

Stanley Kubrick used some of the old warehouses up that way to film his Vietnam movie *Full Metal Jacket* a few years later. The funny thing about that was that we always used to know Dagenham as 'The 'Nam', anyway, so a war story about a bad night down there – which there were plenty of, as that place was almost as bad as Beirut – was always a 'Nam flashback.

That last fight was it for me as far as boxing was concerned. Although I still enjoyed socialising with people from the fight game, the only time I put my gloves on again was for a long boxing sequence in the ITV series *Fox*, which I'll come back to a bit later on. Once I was with Elaine I didn't need to get in the ring to take a bit of punishment any more, anyway. All I had to do was come home late. And when she'd come for me with those verbal volleys, there was no time to put my head-guard on.

Not long after *Scum* was finished, I got a last-minute call from the producers saying the film was being shown in Cannes and they needed me and Alan out there quick. They couldn't get us on a normal flight, so they'd chartered a little three-seater to get us from Gatwick to Nice.

We must've looked a right odd couple on that runway. I know what I was wearing, because I recently found a photo taken just before I left. I was modelling a smart college-boy look with a crisp pair of cream Sta-Prest, brown brogues, a pale green linen shirt and a Pringle-type jumper, topped off with some nice blond highlights in my hair (well, it was nearly the eighties). By way of contrast, Alan was probably the unsmartest man in the world. I had a great time with him, but he wouldn't know how to put a bit of clobber on if you paid him.

On that occasion he was wearing cowboy boots and three-quarter-length flared jeans with a crusty roll-neck jumper, and a velvet jacket with a little tear at the back. His hair was all curly and it didn't look like it'd seen a comb in a while, never mind a blond highlight. Factor in our very different accents – his Scouse and my London – and it was obvious we weren't brothers.

Alan never gave a fuck about money or success. After *Scum* he got offered six movies out in LA, including *The Omen II*. He was sitting in a shed down the bottom of someone's garden out there, trying to work out what to do, then he just said, 'I can't have this', and came home. He shunned Hollywood to make the documentary-type films that he really believed in back in the UK instead. All power to the man – he was another Ken Loach as far as I was concerned.

Alan was ill at the time of that Cannes trip. He had yellow jaundice, and probably shouldn't have been leaving the house, let alone getting in a very small plane. I love flying now and I've been up in Spitfires and Mosquitoes since, but at that stage the idea of strapping myself into a metal coffin was quite new to me, and it was hard not to be struck by how fucking tiny that plane was.

The weather wasn't looking too clever either. And as we were standing around waiting to get introduced to the pilot in the VIP bit of Gatwick, it was all starting to feel a little bit Buddy Holly. I remember thinking, 'I don't want this plane to go down now I've just cracked it.' Living fast and dying young worked alright for James Dean, but that's no reason for me to be doing it.

At that point the captain came out to meet us and I was reassured by the fact that he had the biggest moustache I'd ever seen – a proper old RAF handlebar, like a rear-gunner in a Lancaster would've had. So we got on the plane, with me and Clarkey in the two seats at the back and him at the controls in the front. The take-off was OK, but once you're properly flying in one of those little planes you feel yourself dropping out of the sky every time you hit an air pocket.

It was a three-and-a-half-hour flight. At times it felt like it would've been quicker to go by car as the pilot negotiated his way around a series of storms. About halfway through, Clarkey leant forward – don't forget he's got yellow jaundice – and said to the captain (and you've got to read this to yourself in a really strong Scouse accent to get the full picture), 'Eh, Captain, you know, could you drop down a couple of thousand feet so I can have a piss out of the window?' Understandably, the captain's not having that, so I give Clarkey the sick bag and say, 'Do it in that, Al.'

Now he's got to stand up to take a piss, but the problem is the plane is too cramped for him to do that, so he ends up all bent over. He whacks his cock out into the sick bag and pees into it. I've got to say that the smell from the yellow jaundice is diabolical. I'm gagging, the captain's moustache has drooped, but Clarkey's feeling very relieved. Finally we come into Nice airport and the captain taxis the plane round the runway. At this point he's supposed to see us off and show us where to go, but instead he just opens the door and runs away. He's had enough of us, so he's just fucked off.

Me and Clarkey haven't got a clue what to do, so we're just wandering around on the runway – if that happened now you'd probably get shot. Eventually we find our way into the terminal, and at this point it suddenly dawns on me that we've left Alan's piss in the sick bag on the floor of the plane. When that pilot gets back onboard for the return flight, he's in for a nasty surprise.

Once we finally made it to Cannes, our accommodation went up a couple of notches. We were staying on Don Boyd's boat. Don was the overall producer of the film – who'd just got Clive and Davina in to do the donkey work – and this was the first of several great trips abroad he took me on. Don was someone I had a lot of time for. He's one of those big figures in the British film industry – like Jeremy Thomas who I ended up doing *Sexy Beast* with – without whom very little would ever actually happen.

It was very exciting being at Cannes for the first time. After what happened with the TV version being banned, the idea of the second *Scum* even being shown in a cinema seemed very unlikely to me. Now all of a sudden I was in this mad glamorous world with the Palme d'Or and all that stuff going on. There were film stars everywhere – I was the only one I didn't know.

Alan Clarke was the perfect person to share that experience with, because however much of an outsider I thought I was, I could never be as much of one as him. That didn't stop him making the most of his opportunities, though. Fuck me, that man loved a bird, and they were still attracted to him, despite what he looked like.

Clarkey could talk to anyone, he just had that way about him. I remember the film I really loved which was out at the time was a vampire comedy called *Love at First Bite*. The first time I saw it (in Margate with Elaine when I was filming *Fox*) I was laughing so much it made me cry. So you can imagine how excited I was when

I saw the star of it, George Hamilton, standing outside the Carlton Hotel in all his Transylvanian gear and the make-up and everything. I pointed him out to Alan, who must've smiled at him as he walked up the steps, because George Hamilton – thinking that he knew him, even though they'd never met before – said, 'Hello, how are you?'

Actors in those situations usually pretend they know everyone, because otherwise they get too stressed out trying to remember whether they actually do or not. Alan would've known this and was happy to take advantage of it, so he was standing there with George Hamilton going, ''Ow's the kids?' And then they got into some big debate about something. That was what the whole week was like, and even though I've been back to Cannes on a bigger budget a few times since, you never forget your first time. Especially not if Clarkey's involved.

CHAPTER 22

HACKNEY MARSHES

In between my first brushes with the international jet set, I was still doing the same kind of things I'd always done, like trying to stay out of strife at the Charleston or the Two Puddings in Stratford, or playing Sunday football on Hackney Marshes. As a consequence of going to school in Enfield, I'd had to play a lot of my football in alien territory, where people's skill and understanding of the game were frankly not up to the level I had been raised to expect. But once I was a bit older and back in East London, I was finally in a position to put that right.

Hackney Marshes was the place I liked to play best. It's amazing the way the pitches stretch out into the distance, and if you're one of those East Enders who doesn't leave your manor too much, that might be one of the biggest open spaces you ever get to know. You can't let the sense of freedom go to your head, though – you have to keep your wits about you. I remember playing there once when a car drove onto the pitch next to us and tried to run one of the players over. Maybe England might have more of a chance at the World Cup if we were allowed to do that. Either way, there were a few shooters flying about that day on the Marshes. A couple of the games stopped to watch, but it was the ones which carried on as if this was a perfectly normal everyday occurrence that made the biggest impression.

I'd like to be able to say that at the time I was taking a similarly level-headed approach to how well things seemed to be going with what was now officially my acting career. Unfortunately, that wouldn't be true. I didn't carry on being the same no-nonsense down-to-earth geezer I'd always been. When I saw myself in the finished version of *Scum* – more or less holding my own with a lot of much more experienced and technically gifted actors – I didn't think about how much I still had to learn, I decided I was Jack the fucking Biscuit.

Going to America with Don Boyd probably didn't help in that regard. Because *Scum* was kind of the big underground film at the time, my first trip to New York found me moving in very different circles to the ones I was used to. Don took me to the Mudd Club, which was full of all these fucking strange people. Siouxsie from Siouxsie and the Banshees was there being 'punk' – which seemed to be a bit of a pose where everyone had to look really solemn and try to fuck everyone else off. She seemed like a bit of a prat to me at the time but I'm sure she was just doing her thing.

Siouxsie's wasn't the only famous face to come looming up out of the dry ice in that place. Yoko Ono was floating about too, as was Andy Warhol . . . hole . . . hole. I didn't know too much about all these arty types, but I went up to him and said, 'Alright, how are you going?' He said hello back politely enough, so as far as I was concerned he was one of the good ones.

It's at about this time that I take a hit on something that is probably angel dust and start to notice that the waitresses are all the most beautiful women you'd ever see. But after a few 'Hello, darlin''s my eyes start to adjust to the light properly, and now I'm thinking,

'Woah, fuck me! Something ain't right here – the old Adam's apples are a bit prominent. These birds are all geezers. You could make a mistake here!'

By now the angel dust is properly taking hold and I'm not used to this kind of feeling. To be honest, I'm properly shitting myself, so I'm working my way around the outside wall like a kid who can't swim hanging onto the edge of the pool. Eventually I get to the exit and promptly fall all the way down the stairs. So I get in a cab and ask the guy to take me to the Gramercy Park Hotel and he goes, 'Well, I ain't gonna take you to California am I, bud?' When I finally get back to the hotel, Don Boyd's standing there looking at his watch going, 'Raymond, you were twenty-five minutes longer than I expected you to be.'

It was a great way to see New York for the first time because I was going in through the underbelly – not the gangsters but the artists and bohemians. I still had a massive chip on my shoulder, though, so I probably didn't make the best impression.

Before one screening I remember being introduced to Richard Gere, who was one of the biggest stars in the world at the time, and he totally blanked me. I can understand why now – after all, he didn't know me from Adam Ant – but at the time I remember thinking, 'Fuck you, that ain't very nice, is it?'

After we'd all sat there and watched the film, Richard came up to us again. I think Don Boyd probably knew him because he said, 'Ray, invite Richard to the party after.' But I said, 'No, Richard's very busy. Ain't you, Richard? He's definitely too busy to come to the party.' Richard Gere's probably a nice guy who has to talk to a million people a day – why should he have any idea who I am? – but that was my attitude at the time. I was quite fuck-you about everything. So maybe I had a bit more in common with Siouxsie than I thought I did.

When I eventually got to the party, they fitted me up with this starlet who became quite a famous actress later on. I'm just talking normally to this reporter from *Hollywood Tonight* and all of a sudden this bird has been slipped onto my arm. It ain't her fault they're trying to pair us up like Beauty and the Beast – she's been told to do it, which they used to do years ago, and I suppose they still do today. It's good for you to be seen with a starlet, and good for them to get their face out there, but all the time I'm thinking, 'My fiancée's at home – how's she gonna react if she sees this?'

I'd rather not say who the unlucky lady was – not because she had anything to be embarrassed about, but because I did, as she was a lovely girl and under other circumstances, yeah . . . Oh, alright then, it was Jane Seymour, and I ended up being quite rude to her. I've done enough things I've had to apologise for over the years not to have to make up imaginary misdeeds. So I don't see why I'd have a painful memory of telling the future *Dr Quinn Medicine Woman*, 'This is my film – it's nothing to do with you, love', if I hadn't actually done it. That's just one step away from 'Don't you know who I am?' really, though, isn't it?

The problem with thinking you've cracked it is it's all too easy to get complacent and piss the whole thing up the wall. I'd come out of shooting *Scum* and gone straight into *Fox*. It was a thirteen-part ITV drama series about a big South London family. They weren't so much gangsters, more a strong, old-fashioned family who looked after each other in a way that was becoming less and less common then, but which I still believe in today. Maybe that was why it struck quite a chord with people at the time, even though not many people remember it now.

It was while I was doing *Fox* that the hype really started for the cinema release of *Scum*. I remember watching it come on Barry

Norman's *Film 79* with some of the other actors in *Fox* – Peter Vaughan from *Citizen Smith* and Larry Lamb, who was on *EastEnders* for a long time years later, were definitely there. You could tell something big was happening, but I ended up being quite distanced from it all, because I'd chosen the two weeks leading up to the London opening to get married to Elaine and go on our honeymoon in Lanzarote.

Once we landed back in London, we got off the plane and straight into a cab to the premiere at the Prince Charles just off Leicester Square. There was quite a lot of hysteria and people fainting in the cinema (which I'm sure was a rent-a-crowd Don Boyd had paid for. Why not? They'd do it in America. That's why I love Don to death, because he'd set that kind of thing up – even though he never admitted to me that he had). I remember thinking, 'Fucking hell! I had no idea this was going to be such a big deal.' It was probably a good thing I didn't, because I'd already lost enough of whatever discipline I'd managed to accumulate as an actor.

I remember one of the producers of *Fox* telling me something that got me quite annoyed at the time. 'You're doing alright, Ray,' he said. 'But there's nothing going on in your eyes.' Looking back now, I can see that what made me angry about this remark was the fact that it was absolutely bang on. It took me a couple of years to get over the initial shock of someone digging me out like that, but as time went on I began to realise that just because you were saying the right words and making the right movements, that didn't mean there was anything actually behind them.

I'm not sure exactly how I eventually managed to make a deeper connection between who I was and what I was doing as an actor. Maybe it was getting a bit more life experience. Maybe it was having a few disappointments. Maybe it was losing some people who

I loved. But I don't think I'd ever have been able to do it without Elaine at my side.

People have sometimes said to me that it was a strange time to get married – just as my career was taking off. But it's not a choice I've ever regretted, in fact quite the reverse. I wasn't one of those people who needed showbiz to get a bird. I'd done all that by then, and I needed someone around who was a strong enough character to stand up to me when I was getting a bit full of myself. My Elaine didn't just do personal guidance. On the next job I got after *Scum*, she gave me the most important bit of professional advice I've ever received.

If the people making the film had got their way, Elaine wouldn't even have been around to save the day. We'd only just got married when I was offered the lead role in an American film called *Ladies and Gentlemen, The Fabulous Stains*. Well, that wasn't the original title. At first it was called *All Washed Up*, but I think they changed that title because they were worried it was going to become a self-fulfilling prophecy (which, in a way, it did).

It was a funny old script about a load of punk rockers on a tour bus, which was going to be directed by an old hippie and self-confessed mate of Roman Polanski's called Lou Adler. They'd cast some big old characters to be in such a confined space, but we'll come to them in a minute.

When they asked me to do it off the back of *Scum* I said, 'OK, fine', but only if I could bring my wife with me. They didn't fancy that too much but I said, 'Listen, I've just got married and I want to stay that way, so either my wife comes with me, or I don't come at all.' Neither Elaine nor I have ever been the jealous type – that's part of the reason we've stuck together so long – and these days when I go away for work she's probably glad to get rid of me. But at the time we'd only just got hitched, and I didn't want to be out in Vancouver for a big chunk of 1980 without her.

It was a good job I felt that way. Because when I was trying to get my head around the idea of playing a character who was the lead singer in a band, I didn't have the first fucking clue of how I was going to do it. Singing a song I could do, but the idea of me becoming a rock star and putting on some kind of performance just seemed completely impossible.

It was Elaine who told me something which now looks embarrassingly obvious written down, but that was all the more reason why I needed to hear it. She said, 'But you're not a singer, are you? You're an actor . . . so act it!' I realise how ridiculous this sounds, but that's when the penny dropped for me. 'Oh, so you've got to make out to be something else other than what you are, and make it look real. I get it now.' I must have been driving her mad. When it comes to how I'd managed to get through a couple of years of drama college and lead roles in two versions of *Scum* without somehow waking up and smelling that particular cup of coffee, your guess is as good as mine.

The message had got through just in time, because when it came to looking comfortable onstage, I was about to face a pretty searching examination. The other three members of my band were going to be Steve Jones and Paul Cook of the Sex Pistols and Paul Simonon of The Clash, all of whom had a certain amount of experience in that area.

There was a fair bit of tension around our first meeting. As I've said before, I'd enjoyed the Sex Pistols' music, but a bunch of fucking geezers who picked their nose and spat at people? I ain't gonna like them very much, am I? What made it worse was I'd had a couple of run-ins with Johnny Rotten at the auditions for *Quadrophenia*, where he was up for Phil's role as Jimmy (Jimmy Pursey had a go at that one too – I think Frank Roddam was aiming for the punk audience at that point). He's funny, John, and he's a bit of an intellectual on the quiet, but he's one of those people that if you ask him a question, he'll answer it with another one.

That type is all very well in real life, so long as you don't have to live with them, but they're a nightmare to do acting improvisations with. John's probably grown up a bit now – or maybe he hasn't, it's hard to tell from the butter adverts – but the concept of two people working together for the benefit of the piece was not something he could really get his head round at the time. It was all about him being Johnny Rotten.

To be honest I thought he was a bit of a cunt, and when I got the hump with him, he didn't like it. But if I was expecting things to go the same way when I met Jonesy and the two Pauls, I'd got it completely wrong. I actually loved them, and we're all still mates to this day. Jonesy's still a live wire now. I was on his radio show in LA a while back, and we kept talking in rude cockney rhyming slang that no one else in the studio understood, so you can see how much we've matured.

Looking back at that film now, I'm quite happy with the singing, and the bits where I beat up a couple of rock stars – Fee Waybill of The Tubes and a new-wave guy called Black Randy (who wasn't actually black) – it's the stuff in between that's the problem. I was making progress, but the odd line is still a bit slow and some of my acting's a bit naff.

Diane Lane played the girl who ends up turning into a kind of prototype Lady Gaga in the film. She was only fifteen or sixteen at the time, but she ran rings round me, which worked well on screen as the story needed her to be fucking me over left, right and centre, anyway. I didn't mind playing second fiddle to her because she was a tremendous actress then and she still is.

The same is true of Laura Dern, who plays her sister in it. They were both a bit young to be in a film where there was an element of nudity involved, to be honest, and there was something a bit sleazy about the way it was being directed. Diane had her version of my dad's 'Give up while you're in front' moment at the premiere, when someone in her family asked her, 'What about that film was worth your arse?'

I kind of agreed with that verdict, to be honest. But after Paramount effectively shelved the movie for some complicated tax reason that I didn't understand, its reputation started to grow, to the point where it's now considered a 'cult classic' by a lot of people who haven't actually seen it. The saying 'absence makes the heart grow fonder' is as true in the cinema as it is anywhere else. As my experiences with the first *Scum* and now *Ladies And Gentlemen, The Fabulous Stains* proved, sometimes the best thing that can happen to you as an actor is to be quite shit in a film and then have it not come out.

Getting no work and having to receive secret food parcels off your mother-in-law is not quite such a good look. But that's how things worked out for me in the first couple of years after Elaine and I got married. After the success of *Scum* and *Quadrophenia* I'd thought, 'This acting lark's a doddle.' But once we got back from America, the phone suddenly stopped ringing.

I probably didn't do myself any favours by moving up north and buying a house in Stockport, but that was where Elaine's family lived, and it's important for a woman to be near her mother after she's got married. Well, maybe not for all women, but certainly for this one.

We'd tried living in London together for a while before we got married. My mum wouldn't let Elaine stay overnight in Church

Street until we were officially man and wife, so we moved out into a flat above a launderette in White Hart Lane. You didn't need any heaters in the winter because of the warmth from the machines, but in the summer it was unbearable. I was trying to do the place up a bit to make it nicer for her, so I got my cousin Charlie-boy round to help. Let's just say the two of us going into business together as handymen if and when the acting work dried up was probably not an option.

Charlie was in between prison sentences at the time and he brought over this nail-gun he had to help me put up a curtain rail. We should've been drilling holes and putting rawlplugs in, but instead we were just nailing this fucking thing into the concrete walls. At one point the gun jammed, and he was bracing it against the floor to free it when it shot a nail down through the launderette's ceiling. It was like a cartoon – this round hole appeared in the floor and we were stood above it doing a double take. Then we looked down through the hole and saw a woman sitting there with a laundry bag.

We ran down the stairs and to the front of the shop to check she was alright. There was the woman sitting perfectly contentedly reading a magazine, and there was her laundry bag next to her – nailed to the fucking floor. It frightened the life out of us because that nail could've gone straight through her head.

I was working on *Fox* at this time, so we were doing OK for money, but I was away on set a lot and probably not quite adjusted to the discipline of paying rent yet, so I must've missed the odd week here and there. One day, the big burly geezer who owned the launderette came round when I was out. He said, 'Tell your Old Man to sort this out', but Elaine ain't telling me because she knows there'll be murders. So, a few days later he comes back, and this time he's really pushing his luck.

While he's popped into the shop downstairs, Elaine phones up my dad and says, 'This fella keeps coming round.' Within ten minutes he's down the A10. All she's heard is his car pull up and the next thing she knows my dad's dragged the guy out of the launderette and is smashing his head against his car door. We lived there for another six months without paying rent after that, which seems a bit wrong of us in hindsight, but needs must when you're young and making your way. And on Elaine's part you'd probably have to classify this incident under 'Welcome to the family'.

CHAPTER 23

THE CORNER OF
WELL STREET AND
MARE STREET

Elaine and I had our wedding reception in the Belgrave Hotel in Reddish, near Stockport. Her family are Irish, and I was a bit worried about bringing the London mob, the Manchester mob and the Irish mob together. Especially as Mountbatten had just got blown up on his fishing boat. I remember thinking, 'It'll be just my luck if one of those that've come from over the water decides to make a joke about Lord Louis' plimsolls floating past and the whole place goes up like a tinderbox.'

Luckily, on the day it all went off surprisingly smoothly, in fact it was a fantastic occasion. The mums got on well – I think that was the key to it. There had been a bit of an incident the night before when the guy running the hotel got the hump about the noise in the early hours and shut the bar. I was safely tucked up in bed by then to be at my best for the big op in the morning, but by all accounts my cousin Charlie-boy got a jemmy out of his car and cleared the optics, so there were murders over that the next day. They didn't know how lucky they were though – at least he hadn't brought his nail-gun and tried to do some DIY for 'em.

We didn't have a lot of money to spend on it, but that night was one of the best parties I've ever been to. We had about 250 people and not a black eye or a freshly broken nose between them. When it was over, Elaine and I fucked off on honeymoon and came back to *Scum*. Then by the time we were in Canada for *Ladies and Gentlemen, The Fabulous Stains* a few months later – watching Roberto Durán beat Sugar Ray Leonard on TV, live from Montreal – we'd bought a house in Bredbury, Stockport, for twenty-eight grand.

This was where the food parcels from Elaine's mum came in. When we'd got married, I'd been quite old-fashioned about it, saying, 'You don't need to work no more, I'll look after you.' But it turned out that promise was much easier to make than it was to keep. The buzz around *Scum* having evaporated so quickly, and all of a sudden being 200 miles from home meant that there was very little prospect of getting any work.

I had no choice but to sign on, which I didn't like doing, but fuck me it was hard up there at that time. The mills had all just shut down and the unemployment was unbelievable – way worse than down south. If I'd been a Mancunian I could maybe have got more acting work, but they didn't need another Londoner in *Coronation Street*, because they already had Mike Baldwin aka Johnny Briggs.

The one positive thing about the whole situation for me – and I did have some great times up there – was in terms of my understanding of people. Without even realising it I had probably been raised to believe in a clear dividing line at Watford Gap services, where the Northerners started, but all I could see when I lived up there in the early eighties was a lot of really hard-working people who were having the choice to go to work taken away from them.

Everyone wanted to be a cab driver, because if you're a normal guy who is lucky enough to still have a car, that is the one job you can give yourself without anyone else's say-so. The only problem was how many cabbies could Manchester sustain? Especially when there was hardly any trade because no one could afford to get a cab.

In professional terms at that time in my life I couldn't get arrested. But off-screen it seemed I got arrested all too easily. For someone with a quick temper like mine, the possibility that someone might recognise you – which had become a fact of life after the second *Scum* came out – can make day-to-day life a lot more complicated. I was walking through the West End down in London one day, when I saw a security guy I knew outside Bobby's Bar at the back of the Café Royal. I asked him what he was doing there and he said, 'I'm looking after James Cagney – he's inside talking to someone.'

Cagney was one of my all-time favourite actors, so I decided to hang about for a while in the hope of saying hello to him when he came out of the bar. After about half an hour I had to go, so as not to be late for a meeting with an agent, but the bodyguard said he was going to be a while yet, so I decided to come back later. If I hadn't made that decision I'd have been on the tube and gone in forty minutes' time, instead of stepping off the kerb to cross Piccadilly on the way back to the Café Royal at the exact moment one of those motorcycle despatch riders decided to run a red light.

He sees me step out, but instead of braking he revs up and comes at me even faster. I have to step back quickly to stop myself getting run over. Obviously I've called him a cunt or whatever under my breath and he's heard me – I don't know how through his helmet – and stopped his bike to have a row. But where he's slammed on the brakes too suddenly he's turned the front wheel and fallen off his bike onto the bonnet of a parked car. It's not just me laughing at him now, it's everyone at the crossing, and this doesn't seem to have improved his mood, because now he's charging at me like a lunatic.

I'm all done up smart for my meeting in a new cream Mac and I'm on my way to meet Jimmy Cagney, so I am not interested in this geezer. But he's still tearing towards me with his head down and his crash-helmet on, so I give him a bit of a barrage – bang, bang, bang – on the visor, but it's still hurt him, and as I've upped him for what I thought was going to be the last time, his crash-helmet's come off. At this point I'm seeing his biker's earring with a cross in it and thinking, 'Now you're in trouble, mate', so I give him a proper larrapping.

I don't want to get nicked, so I've got to have it away sharpish, which should be easy enough because there are thousands of people around. Unfortunately, a high proportion of those people suddenly seem to be wearing police uniforms. I don't know how or why this has happened, but the Old Bill are coming at me from all sides. It's as if a gate has opened in the Statue of Eros's arsehole and they've all piled out, waving their truncheons like the *Keystone Cops*.

At this crucial moment, some brain surgeon standing by the railings shouts out, 'It's the fella off of *Scum*!' I give him a look as if to say, 'Much obliged, mate – thank you very much.' The police have got me in the long run now even if I do get away, which I don't, because I am thoroughly nicked.

The Old Bill take me away to the station round the back of Savile Row, and by the time I get there I can hear the other geezer shouting and screaming. They've pulled him 'cos I've said that he attacked me – counter-charge, and in any case it's true. Once the police have got you for something, it's best not to make a fuss – there's no point turning them any further against you.

Me and the biker had to go to court together at Bow Street magistrates court, which used to be just off Covent Garden, which isn't there any more. We both said our piece and I ended up getting found guilty, which wasn't really fair because he did attack me first, but because the police dragged me away I didn't get a chance to find myself any witnesses.

I was fined £120, which normally I'd delay paying as long as possible – 'I'd like time, please, your honour', that's how you put it off – but on this occasion I just said, 'I'll give you a cheque now.' The despatch rider – horrible geezer he was, totally in the wrong – was there too, so as I walked past him I said, 'It was worth every fucking tenner, and if you want to come outside now, I'll gladly have another hundred and twenty quid's worth.'

He didn't accept my offer, which was probably good news for both of us. The whole day had been such a downer. I lost the chance to meet the great Jimmy Cagney and gained a big dent in my wallet, all because of this wanker on a motorbike – and me to a certain extent, because I could've avoided it if I hadn't said anything when he nearly ran me over. As I've got older, I've learnt to avoid these kinds of situations much more effectively. It wasn't so much that I used to start trouble – in fact I don't think I've ever actively started a fight in my whole life – just that I wouldn't make that leap to trying to keep myself out of it.

'Attack is the best form of defence' – that's what I was taught – but really the best form of defence is not getting yourself in that position in the first place. Looking back on that incident with the biker now, I still think my dad and my granddad and his granddad before him (although then the messenger would've been riding a horse, not a motorbike) would have probably got in that fight, as well as all my mates and probably most of their wives.

When I look at my two older daughters I think, 'Yeah, probably them too.' But then I was still doing all this stuff when they were kids growing up, and it couldn't help but rub off on them. And hopefully now they're all out in the big wide world they're learning to do things differently. I've cleaned up my act a bit with my youngest, Ellie-Rae, so maybe she'll be the start of a new way of doing things.

Don't get me wrong, I still think you've got to stand up for what you believe in. I got in some funny situations when things weren't going too well as far as getting work was concerned and I certainly never regretted standing my ground in any of those.

Mike Leigh has never really been my cup of tea as a director. I like some of the stuff he's done, but it's the actors that make it – I just think he's a lucky fucker.

I went up for one of his things quite early on in my career and he was bombarding me with all these really strange questions. I wasn't ready for that because I didn't know him yet. I thought it was too early to be getting into such personal areas. I remember he asked me something about my dad and I said, 'What's my dad got to do with it? My dad ain't here.' Mike Leigh said, 'I'm just asking,' and I got a bit narky with him: 'Well, I don't want to answer that, alright?'

Then he told me he wanted me to 'find a character'. I said 'What character?' And he said, 'Make him up.'

At that point I got to my feet and walked out. I said I had to go to the toilet, but in fact I just fucked off home. They sent a message back later asking what had happened and I said, 'Ray's character wanted to go to the toilet, and then he wanted to fuck off home.'

The next person in after me that day was Mark Wingate who was in *Quadrophenia* with me. The story as I heard it was that Mike Leigh said, 'Shock me!' So Mark picked up the table in the room they were in and threw it out of the window. There was a rumour that the BBC made him pay for the damages, and if that was true then it was very wrong. If you're going to play that game, then you've got to follow through with it. You wanted to be shocked, and he fucking shocked you, so no one except you should be paying for any windows that got broken.

The Northern Irish actor Stephen Rea had a great victory over Mike Leigh by all accounts. Mike Leigh was following him down the road like he does when he's getting you to do things and Stephen went into a pub. Mike Leigh crept in after him and hid under a table – all the usual bollocks was going on. But then Stephen came on the screen in a film that was showing on the pub TV. So he looked across at where Mike Leigh was hiding and called out, 'Look, Mike, I'm on the telly!' I don't think he got the job either.

Another meeting I didn't get any work out of was with Steven Berkoff. It was for his play *West*, which he'd already done once and it was apparently quite famous, although I didn't know too much about it at the time. The idea was for it to be a kind of tongue-in-cheek cockney Shakespeare, but quite surreal, and our first meeting was certainly surreal enough. I know Steven now and I like him, but it would be true to say we didn't quite hit it off at first.

He's standing there with some kind of jump-suit on, all zipped up to the top and his big dot in the middle of his forehead, rolling his Rs when he talks to me and going, 'Rrrraymond-ah . . . I loved the way you walked across the room.' So I go, 'What do you want me to do then, mate?' And he says, 'I want you to walk in the bar and you're looking for someone.'

It's all that kind of broad caricature stuff he wants me to do, but I don't know that at the time. So I walk into this pub in my normal unobtrusive kind of way and just stand at the bar very quiet and not looking at anyone. Steven bellows, 'Stop! What are you doing?' and I say, 'I'm looking for someone.'

Steven says, 'But you haven't looked,' and I say, 'Exactly. When you're looking for someone, Steven, you don't look for someone. If I come in a pub and start looking around, they'll all know what I'm doing.' He's getting exasperated now: 'But I want you to look!'

So that was another job I didn't get. A fella I knew at the time called Ken did it in the end, and when I went to see the play the penny finally dropped. 'Oh, fuck me,' I thought to myself. 'That's what it's all about.' It was good, it was funny, but I'd thought it was a drama when it was actually more like a panto. Over time I've had to learn when to use what I got from Clarkey in terms of always trying to make things as real as possible, and when not to use it. Sometimes you might be doing something that's in a completely different genre where playing it for real is not the best way to go. Asking yourself, 'But how would I feel about this?' isn't something you necessarily need to do if you're in a musical.

It took me a few years to learn that, and it took me a few years to learn some other things as well. Drink-driving was another old habit that died hard. One time when I was still living up North I came home for the weekend and borrowed my sister's car to go out for the evening with my mate Tony Yeates. That car had holes in the floor – it was like something Fred Flintstone would drive.

We'd had a few drinks on Mare Street and when I stopped at the lights, a cop car pulled up alongside. What I tended to do in that situation – especially if I didn't have a seatbelt on – would be look the policeman straight in the eye as if to say, 'Hello, how are you?' So they don't think you're hiding something.

This time it was an old sergeant with a younger cop alongside him. I was a bit pissed and we didn't have seatbelts on, so I did the old 'hello' stare and the older copper kind of nodded, so that was going OK. Unfortunately, as I went to pull away, I stalled the car and by the time I'd got the engine started, they'd slowed down. I went up the side of them and fronted 'em out, but the damage was done. They pulled us over round the corner of Well Street – right outside Granddad's flat – and wallop, they were on us.

Me and Tony had this ploy where if we were ever going to get arrested, we'd always give each other's name. I'd be Tony Yeates and he'd be Ray Winstone – we'd swap birthdays and everything. Then if they get me to court as Tony Yeates, I can just say, 'No, that's not me.'

We're doing that when they get us out of the car. The young constable is about our age – early twenties – and he badly wants to nick us. I blow in the breathalyser bag as Tony Yeates and he's going, 'Blow in it properly.' When it makes the noise that means you're nicked, I can almost hear Tony going, 'Oh thank you very fucking much', under his breath.

Because I can see we're not going to get any joy out of the kid, I start talking to the old sergeant. I say 'old' but he's not walking with a stick, in fact he's probably in his thirties. His name is Alan, and as I'm explaining what's happened, I can already see he's a blinding fella. My story's basically true, which always helps. I'm telling him, 'Look, Sergeant, I don't live here at the moment, because I've moved to Manchester. But I've come down for the weekend and I've borrowed my sister's car to visit a mate I've not seen in years.' That was where the only slight element of exaggeration came in. 'We got on it and we've taken a bit of a liberty but we're home now – I'm staying up in those flats with my granddad – and we certainly won't be driving again tonight.'

Anyway, we have a good old chat, and because his mate is so hell-bent on nicking us, Alan decides to show him that there's a different way of doing things. So he deliberately breaks the breathalyser bag and says, 'If I ever fucking catch you boozed up round here again . . .' I say, 'Oh thank you very much, Sergeant', and off we went.

Cut to about three years later. Me and Phil Daniels – who is a terrible goalhanger by the way – are playing charity football against the Old Bill at a police ground up on the North Circular, near where Walthamstow dog track used to be. I think Tony Yeates has come up to watch, just to complete the circle, and as I'm sitting there having a fag as part of my half-time fitness regime, this copper comes up and says, 'I know you, don't I?'

'Not me, mate' is the standard answer to give a policeman in that situation, but Sergeant Alan isn't having it. He says, 'I breathalysed you in Well Street, and your name ain't Yeates, is it?' From that point on, we became really good mates. I used to do a lot of charity football for him out by Chadwell Heath. Alan ended up going into the special armed services and he does security now. His boy joined the force as well and he used to play against us. He was a lovely kid who sadly got cancer and passed away, but not before we did a few charity things for him as well.

When you look at how this whole situation developed, Alan gave me a chance, so I gave him one too. If you'd asked me if I'd ever liked a copper before I met him, the answer would be no. But what he did for me changed my whole perception of the Old Bill. I wish I could say it rehabilitated me on the drink-driving front too, but there were a couple more incidents later on before I threw in the towel as far as that was concerned.

The first one I was unlucky on. It was another charity football match, this time out at Hungerford in Berkshire. Terry Marsh, the former welterweight world champion, was meant to be driving us. Now Terry is a great guy to drive you because he doesn't drink. That whole thing where he was accused of shooting the promoter Frankie

Warren is something I would never ask him about. I don't want to know and it's not my business, but all I would say is that Terry had been a marine and I don't think someone with that training would have used a .22 to try and kill someone from that distance.

Anyway, I got a bit pissed at the do after the game, and suddenly started to worry that Terry had gone without me, so I jumped in another car to catch him up and tell him, 'You're meant to be taking us home.' Obviously, that wasn't the smartest or most logical decision I've ever made in my life, especially as I came round a corner and nearly hit a police car. In a country lane – what were the chances? By the time one of the coppers had opened the door and I'd fallen out onto the road, it's fair to say my fate was sealed. To make matters worse I found out afterwards that Terry was at the do all along and when the time came to leave he'd been wandering around looking for me.

You'd think this embarrassing incident would've done it for me, but no, I needed one more lucky escape. The day after I got my driving licence back, I was out at Worley Park playing golf when I got the hump at someone and stormed off home pissed. Then I took the wrong turn and ended up going down the M11. I was lucky I didn't have time to kill someone before I got collared and banged up in Epping police station. Talk about three strikes and you're out! It took me two convictions and someone giving me a chance before I finally got the message, but I've never done it since.

You couldn't drink and drive these days, anyway. There are too many idiots on the road.

CHAPTER 24

TROSSACHS,
BARKING ROAD

It wasn't just my grasp of road safety that left a lot to be desired in the early eighties, I had plenty to learn about married life as well. I thought holy matrimony just meant the woman staying at home to cook the dinner while the man goes out to meet his mates. In my defence, all that New Man bollocks was still a long way off yet.

To be honest, I probably wasn't the greatest husband in the world. I was away a lot – not always getting arrested, only sometimes – and we both took a while to find our feet. It was tough. But Elaine never moaned about it when the money ran out. She's not one of those wives who'd say, 'It's all gone pear-shaped – you need to go out and get a normal job.' We never had that conversation.

She's always been very supportive when it's come to my acting. Her approach was: 'Whatever you wanna do, babe, however you wanna go about it.' Not that she was a soft touch – far from it – but I think because I was already doing what I was doing when she first met me, she understood that this was the way things were gonna be.

She's quite arty herself, and I think she knew she'd got herself an artful one from the beginning.

Elaine certainly did her bit when we were stuck up in Manchester without a pot to piss in. She'd make curtains for people or do a bit of interior designing for anyone who had the money to pay for it. And the food parcels from her mum down the road came in handy too, although I didn't like to admit that at the time.

By the time we'd had a couple of years of this, I think she was as fed up with it as I was. And the fact that we'd never really got around to keeping up the payments on our mortgage was inevitably going to bite us on the arse at some stage.

At one point we got a very welcome cheque through for some residuals – probably from *Fox*. It was five grand or something like that, which was a lot of money in those days, especially to people in our situation. I looked at Elaine and said, 'We've got two choices here – we can either pay the bills or go on holiday.' She asked me what I wanted to do and I said, 'Let's go on holiday.'

So we went away for a few weeks – I can't actually even remember where to, that's how much we enjoyed ourselves. By the time we got back we'd knocked out the five grand and I knew we were done as far as that house was concerned. The mortgage company said, 'We're gonna take your house from you and we're gonna sell it.' So I replied, 'I'll tell you what we're gonna do. I'm gonna give you the house – you're not gonna take it – and then I'm fucking off. How's that?'

They probably had a nice earner out of it in the end, and we were both ready to give it another go down south. It was either that or starve. Elaine's mum couldn't keep feeding and watering us forever. So we packed up what stuff we had and headed off back down the M6 (the right way this time, because Elaine wasn't driving).

Coming back to London was tricky at first because we had to go back and live at my mum and dad's for a few months to get ourselves sorted. It was really good of them to have us, but it was impossible living there as a married couple. My mum looked after us really well but Elaine wanted to be her own woman and the tension in the kitchen was horrible. I wasn't exactly jumping for joy about getting bossed around by my Old Man again either.

Luckily for everyone's blood pressure, my mum had taken the precaution of putting me on the council housing list in Enfield when I first went up to Manchester. I'd asked her why she'd done that at the time and she said, 'Because I know what you're like.' Maybe that wasn't the greatest vote of confidence, but it turned out Mum knew best, especially as Elaine was pregnant by this time.

There was nothing doing in housing terms at first, but we kept on going up the housing office until finally they gave us a maisonette at a rent we could almost afford. We were lucky to be part of probably the last generation where having a single child could still get you a council house somewhere near your family home – you didn't need to have one-legged triplets and an Arts Council grant yet. Once Maggie Thatcher sold all the council places off, some people made a lot of money, some more people got absolutely stitched up, and the lives of future generations got a lot more difficult.

I didn't see as much of the inside of that maisonette as I might've done in the early years of my lovely little Lois's life, because I was still what you'd call a going-out dad. (What would being a stay-at-home dad even mean? Being indoors all day and doing fuck all?) And the kind of places I used to go out to still weren't exactly domesticated. There was a pub called Trossachs on Barking Road which went through a few name-changes – always a sign of somewhere with a reputation to shake off. A lot of pubs and clubs did as the eighties progressed but there weren't many that could hold their hands up to calling themselves a hat-trick of Raffles, Valentino's and Memory Lane at one time or another.

Now that I think about it, I'm not absolutely certain the following incident did take place in Trossachs, but it's the kind of thing you're generally best advised not to be too specific about, so let's say it did. I was in there or somewhere very like it one night when a fella walked in wearing motorbike leathers and a crash-helmet and carrying a shot-gun. The place was packed, and I guarantee you seventy-five per cent of the geezers drinking in that pub thought he was there for them. People were diving over the bar, under the tables, glasses were going everywhere. Some guys even put their birds in front of them, which probably didn't win them any prizes for chivalry afterwards. Saddam Hussein hadn't pioneered his human shields yet, so maybe this was where he got the idea.

The guy with the shotgun looked all around the gaff and obvi-ously the geezer or bird he wants ain't in there – either that or he can't see them through the helmet. But he still wants to make an impression, so he shoots the carpet – bang! A big hole right there at his feet, and just walks out. At this point everyone slowly comes out from their hiding places, and the only one not joining in the collective sigh of relief is the guv'nor of the pub: 'Look what he's done to my fucking carpet!'

The carpets back at the maisonette in Enfield might not have got bullet holes in them, but the place did need a bit of a touch-up. And before that could happen I had to find a way of putting some food on the table. Luckily, a message that came to me via Don Boyd seemed to offer the prospect of some much-needed acting work. It was a big part, but there were some strings attached, as the phone-call came from a guy called Joey Pyle who was quite a major underworld face (although he denied everything till the day he died).

I ended up becoming a great friend of Joey's, and I still know his son today – little Joey Pyle Jnr – but at the time his was a name that made people (me included) very nervous. And when he told me they wanted me to play Ronnie Kray in a film Don Boyd had more or less ready to go, the stage was set for me to renew acquaintances with the man I had rather tactlessly pissed all over a quarter of a century before.

I didn't know where they'd got the idea of me playing the part from, because the twins certainly hadn't seen my *Trojan Women*. It was possible the idea had come from an old mate of my dad's called Laurie O'Leary, who was the only person I could think of who knew both them and me.

Sure enough, when the meet finally happens, Laurie is one of the men in the car that picks me up. He sits on one side of me in the back, with the intimidating figure of Joey Pile on the other. Talk about a rose between two thorns! In the passenger seat is a guy called Alex Steene, who I've never met before, but I know by his formidable reputation. The car's being driven by an old fighter called Alex Buxton, who'd boxed a world champion called Randolph Turpin years before.

Alex Buxton is a lovely man, and him being at the wheel gives the whole trip an extra layer of grandeur, not that it really needs it. No one really tells me where we're going at first, so I'm thinking, 'Who the fuck have I upset now?' Then as it slowly dawns on me that we're heading out into the country in the general direction of Broadmoor, I get more and more sucked into the drama of the whole thing.

It's almost like we were going to meet folklore – this terrifying character who was one of the great gangsters of all time. That's certainly how I'd have seen it when I was younger, and although I'd developed a bit more of a balanced perspective by the time all this was happening, it wouldn't have been a good idea to let Joey or Alex Steene see me taking the whole thing too lightly.

So even as I'm having a laugh with Laurie O'Leary, I'm being careful not to let anyone think I'm too relaxed. I'm also bearing in mind that it is a nuthouse we're drawing nearer to. And not just any nuthouse, but one that's full of sex offenders and murderers. What do I want to be going there for?

Once we've arrived and are going through all the rigmarole of getting in, I'm thinking, 'In an ideal world we'll be out of here in a few hours, because an overnight stay doesn't really appeal.' In a normal nick you're surrounded by people who've stolen a car or got pissed and hurt someone. In Broadmoor you're in there with people responsible for some of the most heinous crimes in history.

Every now and then you forget where you are, because it feels more like a hospital than a prison, but then you remember again. There's one kid serving the tea who it transpires has murdered his entire family. You're thinking, 'How did he kill his family again? Not that it's any of my business, but, just as a matter of interest, was it poison?' It's all very English in a way – sitting in a public place having a cuppa while trying not to mention the terrible things everyone around you has done.

One of the big questions on my mind when it comes to my re-acquaintance with Ronnie Kray is whether he is going to remember our earlier meeting. He does – either because he's been primed to remember it by Laurie, or because it's stuck in his mind for some other reason. I can't imagine he got pissed on too many times in his life (at least, not in company), and he makes a little joke about it as I arrive, which puts me more at my ease.

Ronnie is very smartly dressed, and looks well in himself, but he's quite a frail man at this stage in his life. He's not the same person you would've met on the outside fifteen years before, and you don't know what medication he's on, but there's still no mistaking the force of his personality. He doesn't just look at you, he looks straight through you to the wall behind, and his eyes have that kind of blankness where you feel you can't lie because he knows everything you're going to say before you actually say it, anyway. The only other time in my life I'd encounter a stare like that would be a few years later at Lewis Collins' house, where I met a few of the real-life SAS boys at a party for the film *Who Dares Wins*.

There are a couple of additional factors Ronnie is bringing to the table in terms of how intimidating a presence he is. First, he hangs on every word you say with an intensity that you never come across in normal people. Second, he sits very close to you so that his leg is rubbing against yours, and his leg does not keep still – it's constantly moving back and forth, almost like there's a twitch in it.

From the moment I've sat down he starts talking to me about Bob Hoskins, who I haven't yet met at the time. Ronnie's telling me about this play he's heard Bob's doing at a pub-theatre somewhere in South London. He says, 'Do you know this fella, Bob Hoskins?' His voice is a little bit nasal – almost like he's got a peg on his nose. I say, 'I know of him, Ron. He's just done the film *The Long Good Friday*.'

Ronnie nods. 'Well, he's been playing me in this play,' he continues. 'And this play implies I have incestuous feelings towards my mother.'

Ronnie doesn't swear very much, if at all, in conversation, because he's old-fashioned like that, so when he pauses for a moment and then asks, 'Is it a fucking crime to love your mother?', it's important to take him very seriously indeed. 'No, Ron,' I reply solemnly. 'It's not a crime to love your mother.'

You can see how angry he is about the whole thing. At this point he starts whispering something to one of the other fellas and I'm getting a bit concerned about the implications for a fellow professional. So I say, 'Let me tell you something, Ron. Bob Hoskins doesn't know you. Bob Hoskins is an actor who plays what's written in the script as close as he can to the way the director wants it. So it's not Bob's fault if there's something in the play that you don't like.' At this point Ronnie goes, 'Right, so who's the writer?' So now I've taken the heat off Bob and put it on a couple of other people without meaning to.

Nothing happened to them in the end, so presumably Ronnie thought better of it, but this wasn't the last time that day I'd inadvertently end up putting someone else in the frame. One of Ron's more upbeat topics of conversation was telling me about how when he got out he was going to go on a round-the-world cruise. Whether he meant that last word in both its usual senses Ronnie didn't make clear, but he did announce – leg twitching particularly forcefully at this point – that he was planning to take me with him.

I didn't think this was too good an idea for obvious reasons, but because I was still excited about the fact that this film seemed to be happening, I did mention a mate of mine who I thought might be good for a part in it: 'You know the family, Ron. It's Terry Murphy's boy, Glenn Murphy.' My old mate Glenn from the Repton was getting started as an actor around that time, and I knew he'd be perfect for the film, but afterwards I realised I had kind of dropped him in it. He's a good-looking man, Murph, and I think he did have a meet with Ronnie in the end which proceeded along very similar lines. There's not too much else to do in Broadmoor, after all, so talking to actors must've been a distraction. Our conversation was reasonably amicable apart from the leg thing and the Bob Hoskins thing (which I enjoyed telling Bob about years later – there was a smile on his face at the time, but you could see the cold air hitting the back of his neck). I was watching and listening to Ronnie very closely to prepare myself for the role, and the thing that most struck me about him was how different he was to the way people normally portray gangsters. His voice had that kind of old London sound to it where you could almost feel his mouth making shapes around the words.

Another person I ended up spending a fair bit of time with who talked like that was Bruce Reynolds, the mastermind behind the Great Train Robbery. He was an absolute gent, but I think I'd better save that story for another time.

As the Krays film got closer to getting the green light – I was gonna play both Ronnie and Reggie by that time, with the whole thing being done in split screen – Don Boyd also put me in touch with the Krays' mum, Violet. She'd moved out of the house on Vallance Road by then and into some flats at the back of the Repton. I had a really good day with her and she gave me some blinding photos, which I sadly can't find, of the twins with Billy Hill, who was an early face from Brighton Races. As far as Violet was concerned, she was just a normal East End mum and they were her boys. She didn't really want to think too much about all the people they'd hurt or killed.

The Krays film didn't happen in the end. Well, it did, but in another form. I think there were some financial complexities of some kind and the project changed hands. Ray Burdis from the Anna Scher mob took it over and he wanted it to go in a more glamorous direction, so he cast the Kemp brothers instead of me. I had no regrets about it – these things happen and I actually thought the two Spandau Ballet boys did a blinding job in the end.

I didn't come out of that Broadmoor trip empty-handed either. I'd hit it off quite well with Alex Steene, and when the film didn't happen he asked me, 'Do you need a few quid, son, because work's not that good at the moment? Come up West and answer the phone for me.' At this point, given that you're talking to someone who's a very well-respected face, you're wondering what the fuck you might be getting yourself into. But it turned out to be a straight business, albeit a straight business that I always thought would make a great sitcom.

Alex's set-up was called The Unobtainables, and they were essentially high-class ticket touts. They traded out of an office in Panton Street, just near Leicester Square, selling city debentures at Wimbledon or the best seats at the rugby.

Anything you wanted The Unobtainables – as the name suggested – could get, and they'd pay a good price to get it as well. The ticket justified the means. Alex gave me a desk and a phone, and I soon found that I was pretty good at it. Basically it was the same thing I'd done on the markets – buying and selling commodities – only this time you were dressed a bit smarter, and there was less chance of being hit on the head with a flying cauliflower.

What I liked about working there was that you weren't hurting anyone. You were giving people something they wanted, and if they could afford to pay the money you were asking, that was up to them. Most of the clients were big companies in the City who were writing it all off, anyway. It was getting towards the mid-eighties by then, and there was a bit more money around.

The really funny thing about the job was the other people who worked there. As well as me, we had a couple of other actors. First there was Patrick Holt, a tall veteran of the Rank era who also played one of the old boys in the Roger Moore film, *The Sea Wolves*. He was a lovely stylish fella, very well spoken – in fact I once remember him telling me, 'You could've been my batman during the war'. He also gave us a fantastic recipe for goulash, which Elaine still cooks to this day.

Then there was Derren Nesbitt, who'd been quite a big star in the sixties and seventies, and played the sadistic SS officer in *Where Eagles Dare*. But the guv'nor when it came to selling tickets was a guy called Michael, who'd never acted in anything. He loved a drink so much that one night he went out for a beer in the West End and woke up on a boat in Norway. We had murders trying to get him back that day because there was a big deal depending on him. It was quite a high-pressure job in a way, because if you fucked up you knew who you had to deal with.

One day, a load of police swarmed the office. They were top-level Old Bill from Scotland Yard, and I assumed it was nothing to do with The Unobtainables because we were all working in the other room and we never got touched. But when I poked my head round the door to see what had happened, I found out that someone had sold two tickets for the Trooping of the Colour that were right next to where John Nott was going to sit. Given that he was Margaret Thatcher's Secretary of State for Defence at the time, this was a major security breach.

All they wanted to know was who had sold the tickets, but no one would admit to it, so I put my hand up and said, 'I did it', even though I didn't know if I had or not. The police said, 'Who are you?' And I said, 'Alex rents me the office next door and I do a bit of buying and selling for him.' When they asked me who I bought them off I just said, 'A couple of geezers came in. I didn't know who they were.' It turned out that it had been a couple of soldiers who'd come in with the tickets hoping to make a few quid, but it wasn't me they'd sold them to.

Alex's other business interests did sometimes make their presence felt in Panton Street. He was a Yorkshireman who was known for his tact and discretion, so that marked him out from the crowd for a start. And he was so good at not so much sitting on the fence as bringing people together that his office functioned almost like a relationship counselling service for London's biggest faces. He'd summon all the different firms to try and stop things getting nasty when there was a difference of opinion. It was fascinating to watch him in action, but sometimes when I'd hear Alex calling 'Ray-mond', because he wanted me to sit in on one of those meetings, I'd think, 'I'd rather not, thanks.' If it all went pear-shaped, I might end up being the patsy.

Sometimes you'd feel like you needed a blue helmet from the UN just to go into work. Notorious adversaries like the Richardsons from South London and Johnny Nash from North London would come in and sit round his table together. The interesting thing was that on the face of it, nobody wanted a row. Everything seemed to get resolved and they'd all shake hands at the end, but you'd never be quite sure if the handshake was proper or not.

These guys were the last of the old guard by that time – a lot of them had done their bit of porridge, and all they were after was a quiet life. It was the younger fellas coming through who'd tend to be more hot-headed and throw threats around, and the carnage you'd hear about in later years suggested that Alex's softly-softly way of reconciling gangland factions might have died with him.

CHAPTER 25

THE APOLLO STEAKHOUSE, STRATFORD

One of the best trips I ever went on for The Unobtainables was to Salzburg in Austria, where they filmed *The Sound of Music*. Alex wanted me to get tickets for a Leonard Bernstein concert for some geezers in the City. So I flew out there all suited up with twenty large distributed in various different pockets and set up a meet with the concierge of one of the best hotels in town. I've always had this feeling that if you really look after a top-notch concierge, he can probably sort you out with pretty much anything you want. So it proved on this occasion, as I gave him his bit of dough and he got me twenty prime tickets for the opening night, all at face value, which was a touch.

It was very *The Third Man* – swapping envelopes on the continent – and I got back to London expecting Alex to be ecstatic, which he was. I was waiting for him to give me my drink, or whatever other kind of bonus he thought was appropriate. It never came and it never came, until eventually he tried to slip me a measly few quid. I said, 'I think you'd better keep that, Alex. You probably need it more than me.' I suppose it was just that old face's mentality of 'Give someone just enough and they need to come back, give them too much and they'll be gone.' But whatever the reason, it was point taken at my end.

As it happened, the dates I'd been given were wrong, and that's why I'd been able to buy the tickets so easily. Luckily, it was the City boys' fault not mine, so there was a bit of a scream-up about that and everyone went potty back at the office. That's not the point of the story, though.

The thing I'll never forget about that Salzburg trip were these Hare Krishna geezers who were talking to me in this park where I was waiting to see the concierge. I'll have a chat with anyone when I'm bored, and they were nice enough people. They were trying to sell me their way of life – saying I'd never want for anything if I joined them – and I was smiling to myself thinking, 'I've got twenty large in my pockets. How much cash can that robe hold?'

I don't know if what they were telling me about reincarnation got in my head – the same way that thing my mate at school told me about the tape rewinding did – but I had a really strange moment of *déja vu* as I walked around the corner out of that park. It was almost like I knew where everything was going to be before I'd even got there . . . This clock on the right, that shop on the left . . . I'd never visited the place, but I knew exactly where everything was. The only rational explanation I could come up with afterwards was that it was a location I remembered from *The Sound of Music*.

When I was a kid watching films like that one or *Lawrence of Arabia* or *Bridge on the River Kwai* on the big screen, I never dreamed I'd be up there myself one day. Sometimes it can be disappointing when you come across the people who've made the movies you've loved in real life. I met the director David Lean (the man behind those last two films) early on in my career when he was gonna do *Mutiny on the Bounty*. I normally get on well with directors, but he was quite a rude man.

You know as soon as you walk into the room whether they want you or not, and it was plain he didn't like the cut of my jib, but I persisted because I was such a fan of the things he'd done in the past. I asked him, 'What's this one all about then, David?' He said, 'Why do you want to know?' So I told him how much I'd loved his work and that I was really interested in what he was going to do this time round, but he just didn't want anything to do with me.

The only thing that made me feel better about it was a few years later when I went to a talk Alec Guinness gave in a small room at the Young Vic. Guinness had been in a lot of Lean's films so I asked him what he thought of him and he said, 'A wonderful film-maker, but what a horrible nasty man!' So it wasn't just me then . . .

If you've grown up watching films starring the Alec Guinnesses and the Richard Burtons and the Peter O Toole's of this world, you can't help seeing that as the gold standard everyone should aim for. But then you look at yourself and you know you can't even speak the Queen's English. So you think, 'Well, how is that gonna work?' In the phase of my life when I was one of The Unobtainables, it still wasn't really working yet. In fact, I don't think I'd look at a performance I'd done and think it was good enough until *Nil by Mouth* more than fifteen years later.

But I was learning, however slowly. I saw a lot of things go down in those two years I worked for Alex Steene. That guy Alan Lake, who used to knock about with Diana Dors – he came in a lot. They really loved each other those two, and Alan was a blinding bloke – a bit of a nut-nut, but I did like him. He used to come in the office and do handstands. Anyway, a terrible thing happened one night when we all went down the Lyceum together. Diana was there – she knew all the chaps and she was good friends with Alex. But when Alan walked in the room, the whole audience booed him. I never knew why – there must have been something in the papers – but those are the kind of things that stay with you.

It's weird the way people think at times. I was indoors at the maisonette in Enfield once (it did happen sometimes) when a policeman came round. He told me that a guy who'd attacked an old car-park attendant on the King's Road in Chelsea had claimed as part of his defence that he wasn't there because he was having a drink with Ray Winstone. I didn't even know the guy – he must've seen me in a film or on TV and thought, 'Oh, he'll vouch for me.' Like you're gonna vouch for a geezer who's beaten up some old car-park attendant, anyway!

It was a fucking joke – even the copper was laughing. I think he knew it was all cobblers. He was a nice copper, actually – I could accept that they existed now, thanks to Sergeant Alan. This was just one of those shock realisations which were dragging me kicking and screaming into the world of the adult. It's hard to look back and pick out one moment when you really started growing up. But I've got to do it, otherwise I can't really justify calling this book *Young Winstone* and finishing it before I become the international Hollywood love god who Matthew McConaughey knows and envies today.

I'm not one of those dads who'll tell you that they suddenly understood everything about the world the moment they had their first child. As I've said already, my approach to parenting as a younger man – certainly with my first daughter Lois, hopefully a bit less with Jaime – was more in line with that of an earlier generation. Mum's job is to be at home with the kids, while geezers go out and get the bread and butter then go to the pub because they've been working all week and they deserve it. The catch is, sometimes even if they haven't been working all week, they still go to the pub anyway.

I was still out and about a lot in East London. My eating place of choice – where I'd now go with Tony Yeates or some of the other boys – had graduated two stops down the Central Line from the Venus steakhouse in Bethnal Green to the Apollo in Stratford. Steakhouses often have classical-sounding names because they're usually run by Greek fellas, and Panny and Gilly, the two geezers who owned the Apollo, kept a blinding gaff. They did great grills and made lovely margaritas. You'd see all the East End glamour in the Venus over the years: Page 3 girls and West Ham's Frank McAvennie – old Mackers – he was a good mate of mine. There was a party atmosphere and the grub was great – we took Phil Daniels in there a few times, and Perry Fenwick who plays Billy Mitchell in *EastEnders*.

Given how keen I always was to be back in the East End as a teenager, I suppose it's strange I wasn't moving heaven and earth to persuade Elaine that we needed to live there. I'm not going to say East London had become a state of mind for me, because that would sound a bit poncey, but the sense of belonging which endured from my childhood there was definitely something I carried with me – off-screen and on: a kind of happiness, in a way.

It was important for me to have that, given that I was working in a business where I didn't always feel I belonged. And the sense of me being someone who knew who they were was probably something casting directors were picking up on once I started to get a bit more work. The ability to fully inhabit a place you don't actually live in is what acting's all about, after all.

I came out of the job with The Unobtainables to another regular gig, this time as Will Scarlett in the ITV series *Robin of Sherwood*. It lasted three years and was a big breakthrough in terms of knowing what I was doing and all-round professionalism. But some very serious things happened while I was going back and forth to Bristol playing one of Robin's Merrie Men, the kind of things that don't really leave you any other option than to grow up.

The first sucker punch was my mum getting cancer. She had it for two years before finally dying when she was fifty-two and I was twenty-eight. The reason cancer is such a very cruel disease is because it leads you down an alley of thinking, 'Oh, you look alright today, you look good – maybe you've turned a corner', but then you go round that corner and there the cancer is waiting for you again. I was looking at all these special diets for her and places she could go to maybe have another chance – even fucking faith-healing starts getting into your head because you will grab at any old twig in the hope that it might turn into an olive branch.

To be honest with you, I don't think I've ever got over my mum's death. You've got your five basic senses in life – smell, taste and the other three – but on top of that there's a more general sense of yourself and the place you occupy in the world. Some people get that from religion, but as far as I'm concerned it comes from the people you love and the people who love you. And that higher sense kind of went from me a bit for a few years after my mum died. I lost it, and I'm not sure I've fully got it back, even now, because the connection a person has with their mum is like no other. You're from your mum, you've come out of her; two thirds of our bodies are water, and it all flows in the same direction.

One thing that did help at the time was a great conversation I was able to have with Mum just before she died. We all hoped she was going to get better, but I think everyone knew deep down how unlikely that was, especially once she'd gone into a coma. I was away in Bristol at the time doing *Robin of Sherwood* and there was a big fight scene with Jason Connery coming up the next day. We'd designed it a bit like the one in *The Quiet Man* with John Wayne, and we were just going through the final preparations the night before when I had the thought that I needed to go home.

The producers were great about it – I'd told them this moment was going to come. So I raced back to London for the next day and found that my mum had come out of her coma. I sat and talked to her all day long. We had a great chat about my dad, about life in general. It was all the conversations you often end up wishing you could have but don't get the chance to.

My mum had always been very proud of me and backed me to do what I wanted in life (as did my dad, who might not have been easily impressed by musical theatre, but only ever wanted the best for me and my sister). She used to sit around with the aunties and watch me in *Scum*, which can't have been an easy thing for a mum in a way, but she always used to say, 'If that's what you want to do with your life, son, you go and do it.' Still, I think she'd realised that we needed to have a talk. It wasn't all in the past tense as if she knew she was about to die. She made the whole thing feel more natural than that, just like a general reassurance that everything was in place: 'Don't worry about your father, he'll be alright.' Lois can't have been more than eighteen months old at the time, so we talked about how much Mum loved her, and Elaine was pregnant with Jaime, so that was another good topic. And shortly after the conversation ended, Mum passed away.

We'd lost another child in between those two happy births, and Mum had still been alive when the baby boy died, so those two deaths came quite close together. Elaine was about seven months pregnant and the baby wasn't right, but she had to give birth, anyway. I was there with her through the delivery, and I can tell you it was hard. Those are the kinds of experiences that can destroy you if you let them.

I think what helped us through the aftermath was knowing that my mum and dad had been through the same experience. Their attitude was: 'It happens. You're not the only people in the world who have had to go through this, so the best thing is just to get on with it.' Now, while that's not necessarily what you want to hear at the time, it does liven you up a bit. It's like having Jackie Bowers in your corner.

We weren't really the sort of people who would sit down and talk to a counsellor or a psychiatrist. In a way, maybe we needed to, but they'd probably have fucked us up even more. So, following my mum and dad's stoic example was probably our best bet in the end, and the fact that Elaine fell pregnant again quite quickly afterwards with Jaime definitely helped.

It was a tough thing, but when a little bit of time has passed you've got to try and take positives out of those situations, and the way I've always looked at it is that if the other child had lived, we might not have had our Jaime, who we love. The upshot of all this is that I'm the last of the male line, as far as the Winstones are concerned. Lois and Jaime tell me they'll go double-barrelled when the time comes for them to get married, which is very decent of them, but they don't have to do it.

It was funny when all my three daughters were born. I was so caught up in the moment that I didn't even know if they were boys or girls for the first half-hour. It didn't worry me. I just had 'em in my arms and that was all that mattered. Of course, I would have liked to have had a boy – a son to carry on the family name. That would've been wonderful, but I suppose I did have one in a way, if only for a small amount of time.

Elaine and I would have loved to have held him in our arms too – just for a moment – but he was taken away before we got the chance. To be honest with you, I think two Young Winstones died that day. I'll never forget the one who didn't make it, and the pain of my son's passing marked the end of the person this book is about, and the beginning of whoever the older and maybe slightly wiser version was going to be.

PICTURE CREDITS

Also available from Canongate . . .

NOT MY FATHER'S SON
ALAN CUMMING

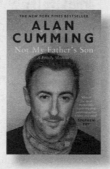

**'One of the most memorable, heart-stopping
autobiographies I have ever read' STEPHEN FRY**

A beloved star of stage and screen, Alan Cumming's life and career
have been shaped by a complex past, troubled by buried memories.
But some secrets don't stay that way. A few years ago, an unexpected
phone call from his long-estranged father brought the pain of the
past hurtling back into the present, and unravelled everything he
thought he knew about himself. *Not My Father's Son* is Alan's journey
of discovery, both a memoir of his childhood in Scotland and an
investigation into family history that would change him for ever.

'Powerful . . . A thoroughly gripping read' *Sunday Times*

'Beautifully written . . . I was completely sucked in' NEIL GAIMAN

'This is a beautiful book   sad, funny, haunting, surprising, suspenseful,
gut-wrenching, endearing' HARLAN COBEN

£8.99

ISBN 978 1 78211 546 5
eBook ISBN 978 1 78211 545 8
Audiobook ISBN 978 1 78211 556 4

www.canongate.tv

JERRY LEE LEWIS
RICK BRAGG

'**Brilliantly funny, moving and exhilarating**' *The Times*

Jerry Lee Lewis has lived an extraordinary life. He gave rock and
roll its devil's edge with hit records like 'Great Balls of Fire'. His
incendiary shows caused riots and boycotts. He ran a decades-long
marathon of drugs, drinking, and women, and married his thirteen-
year-old second cousin, the third of seven wives. He also nearly met
his maker, at least twice. He survived it all to be hailed as one of
the greatest music icons. For the very first time, he reveals the truth
behind the Last Man Standing of the rock-and-roll era.

'I loved every amphetamine-laced, whiskey-soaked, gun-shot page
of it . . . This thing moves. It rocks' ANN PATCHETT

'The best book on rock and roll I have ever read' RON RASH

'There's plenty of richness in Rick Bragg's retelling of
the Killer's life . . . Worth reading'
STEPHEN KING

£10.99

ISBN 978 0 85786 159 7
eBook ISBN 978 0 85786 160 3

www.canongate.tv

GUN BABY GUN
IAIN OVERTON

'A brilliantly researched journey, capturing the gun's strangely accepted place in human life and, far too often, death' JON SNOW

Every minute of every day, somewhere, someone is shot.

There are more guns in the world today than ever before – almost one billion. Despite nukes and ground-to-air missiles, chemical warfare and mortar rounds, it's the still the gun that does the low-level, high-cost damage. Its impact is long-reaching, often hidden, and doesn't just involve the dead, the wounded, the suicidal and the mourning. It involves us all.

Award-winning writer, investigative journalist and filmmaker Iain Overton takes us on a journey to more than 25 countries, from South Africa to Iceland, from Honduras to Cambodia, to deliver an eye-opening investigation into the gun's lifespan, our complex relationship with firearms, and their undeniable impact.

Urgent and hard-hitting, *Gun Baby Gun* reveals that the pain caused by a gunshot does not end with the pulling of the trigger. That is just the beginning.

£18.99

ISBN 978 1 78211 342 3
eBook ISBN 978 1 78211 344 7

www.canongate.tv

Soon to be a major film starring
Johnny Depp, Benedict Cumberbatch,
Sienna Miller and Kevin Bacon

BLACK MASS

DICK LEHR AND
GERARD O'NEILL

The *New York Times* bestseller

One FBI Agent. One Boston Gangster. One Deal.
The greatest and bloodiest story of corruption ever told.

James 'Whitey' Bulger and John Connolly grew up together on
the tough streets of South Boston. Decades later in the mid-1970s,
they met again. By then, Connolly was a major figure in the FBI
and Whitey had become godfather of the Irish Mob. *Black Mass*
is the chilling true story of what happened between them – a
dark deal that spiralled out of control, leading to drug dealing,
racketeering and murder.

From the award-winning journalistic pair Dick Lehr and Gerard
O'Neill comes a true-crime classic which takes the reader deep
undercover, exposing one of the worst scandals in FBI history.

£12.99

ISBN 978 1 78211 623 3
eBook ISBN 978 1 78211 625 7

www.canongate.tv

The bestselling true-crime classic from
the creator of *THE WIRE*

HOMICIDE

DAVID SIMON

'A masterpiece' MARTIN AMIS

Based on a year on the killing streets of Baltimore, David Simon's
true-crime masterpiece reveals a city few will ever experience.
Day in, day out citizens are shot, stabbed or bludgeoned to death.
At the centre of this hurricane of crime is the city's homicide unit,
a small brotherhood of men who fight for whatever justice
is possible in a deadly world.

'An extraordinary book' *Guardian*

'Brilliant . . . desolate, sharp, poetic and passionate' *Financial Times*

'The best book about homicide detectives by an
American writer' NORMAN MAILER

£9.99

ISBN 978 1 78211 630 1
eBook ISBN 978 1 84767 390 9

www.canongate.tv

CANON‖GATE.tv

CHANNELLING GREAT CONTENT

WATCH — INTERVIEWS, TRAILERS, ANIMATIONS, READINGS, GIGS

LISTEN — AUDIO BOOKS, PODCASTS, MUSIC, PLAYLISTS

READ — CHAPTERS, EXCERPTS, SNEAK PEEKS, RECOMMENDATIONS

DISCOVER — BLOGS, EVENTS, NEWS, CREATIVE PARTNERS

SHOP — LIMITED EDITIONS, BUNDLES, SECRET SALES

The story thus far...

Fourth grader Satsuki and her four-year-old sister Mei have recently moved to a house in the country with their father. The healthy environment should be good for their mother, who is in the hospital recovering from an illness. Kanta, a local farm boy, taunts Satsuki, telling her the house is haunted, which upsets her. One day while playing in the fields, Mei encounters a pair of strange creatures. The creatures, who thought they were invisible to humans, suddenly panic and run. Mei chases after them into the forest. She finds another creature, this time much bigger, sleeping. The creature opens its mouth wide and makes a roaring sound that sounds like "Totoro." She decides its name is Totoro!

Japanese Production Credits

Publicity Coordination
Hakuhodo Inc.
Tokuma Shoten
Animage Editorial Dept.

Distribution
Toho

Production
Studio Ghibli

Producer
Toru Hara

Main Cast

Satsuki	Noriko Hidaka
Mei	Chika Sakamoto
Father	Shigesato Itoi
Mother	Sumi Shimamoto
Kanta	Toshiyuki Amagasa
Granny	Tanie Kitabayashi
Big Totoro	Hitoshi Takagi
Mitchan	Chie Kojiro
Teacher	Machiko Washio

Editing
Takeshi Seyama

Titles
Takagu Atelier

Color Design
Michiyo Yasuda

Audio Director
Shigeharu Shiba

Recording and Sound Mixing
Shuji Inoue

Sound Effects
Kazutoshi Sato

Audio Recording
Omnibus Promotion

Production Manager
Eiko Tanaka

Production Desk
Hirokatsu Kihara
Toshiyuki Kawabata

Music Production
Mitsunori Miura
Takashi Watanabe
Tokuma Japan Co., Ltd.

Executive Producer
Yasuyoshi Tokuma

Associate Executive Producers
Tatsumi Yamashita
Hideo Ogata

Original Story and Screenplay
Written and Directed by
Hayao Miyazaki

Supervising Animator
Yoshiharu Sato

Art Direction
Kazuo Oga

Music
Joe Hisaishi

Animation Check
Yasuko Tachiki
Hitomi Tateno

Color Design Assistant
Nobuko Mizuta

Camera Supervisor
Hisao Shirai

Little Totoro
A half-transparent, white Totoro the size of a small raccoon.

Medium Totoro
A blue Totoro who's slightly larger than Little Totoro.

Big Totoro
An owl-like creature from the forest.

Mei
Satsuki's four-year-old sister. She's a little needy.

Satsuki
A sprightly young girl who looks after her younger sister.

Father
Satsuki and Mei's father. An understanding parent.

Mother
Satsuki and Mei's mother is resting at the hospital.

Cat Bus
A giant Cat Bus with headlight eyes.

School Teacher
Class instructor. She is kind.

Friends at School
Satsuki's classmates, including Michiko and Kanta.

BEC

WRITTEN AND DIRECTED BY
HAYAO MIYAZ

3

My Neighbor
TOTORO
C H A R A C T E R
I N T R O D U C T I O N

Granny
Kanta's grandmother.
She looks after Mei.

Kanta's Mother
She's always scold-
ing Kanta.

Kanta
He sometimes ignores
Satsuki, but he's
actually a nice boy.

5

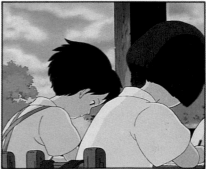

OW.

9

MEI.

GRANNY, WHAT'S WRONG?

14

... AND SEE WHAT WE CAN DO.

I'LL TALK TO MY TEACH- ER ...

HMM ...

16

LET'S MAKE HER FEEL WELCOME.

SATSUKI'S MOM IS IN THE HOSPITAL, SO HER SISTER MEI IS GOING TO STAY WITH US TODAY, OKAY CLASS?

19

20

24

25

26

28

31

DAD LEFT HIS UMBRELLA HERE. I'D BETTER TAKE IT TO HIM.

I WANT TO GO, TOO !!

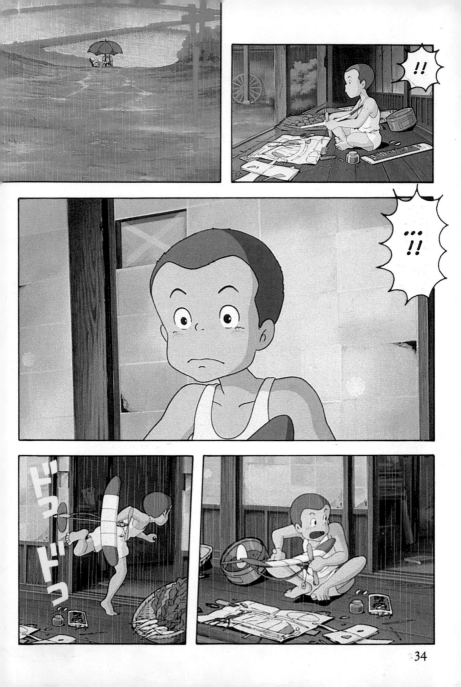

34

35

...HE CAN ALWAYS USE A GOOD DRENCH-ING.

THAT'S OKAY. KANTA IS SUCH A DIRTY KID...

TELL HIM THANK YOU. HE MUST HAVE BEEN DRENCH-ED.

ARE YOU OFF TO MEET YOUR DAD AT THE BUS STOP?

SUCH GOOD KIDS.

YES, HE FORGOT HIS UM-BRELLA.

BYE, MEI.

BYE.

37

38

40

44

45

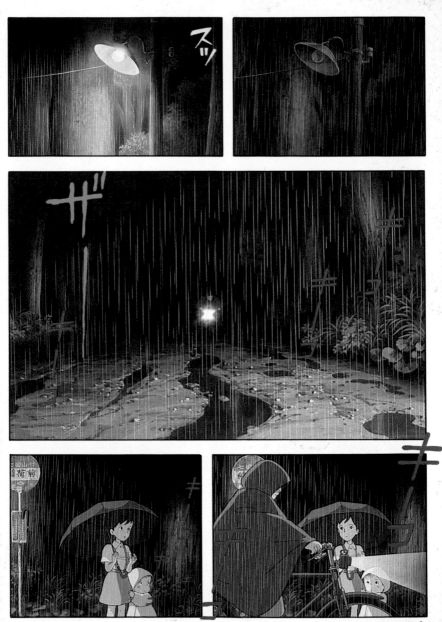

46

49

52

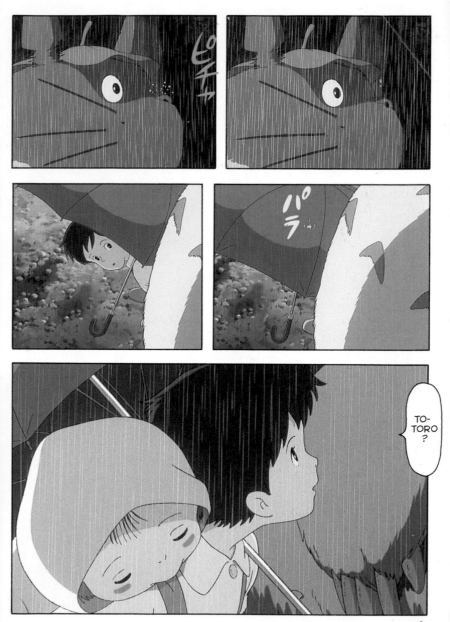

56

57

61

62

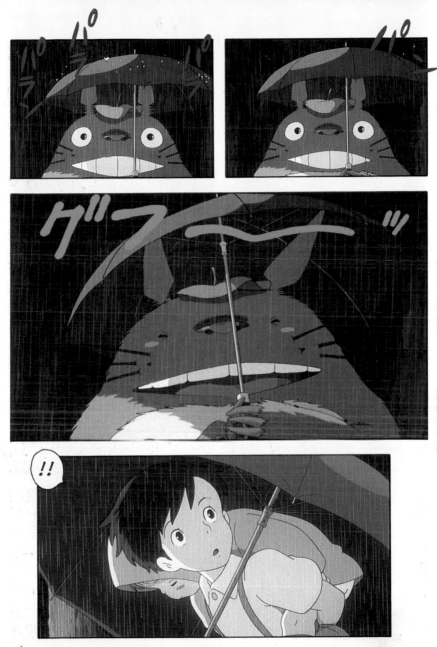

63

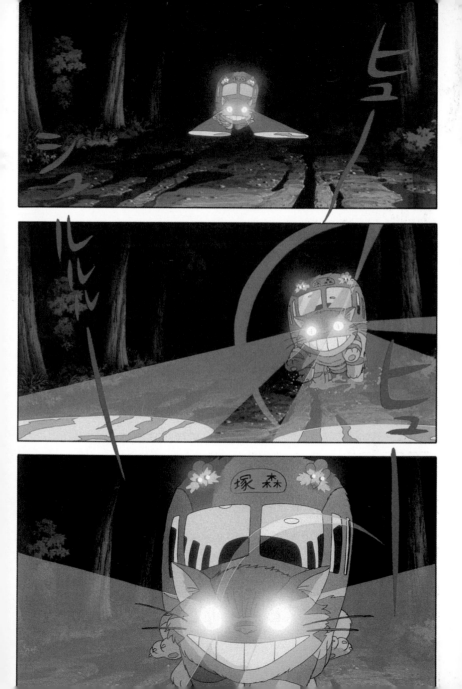

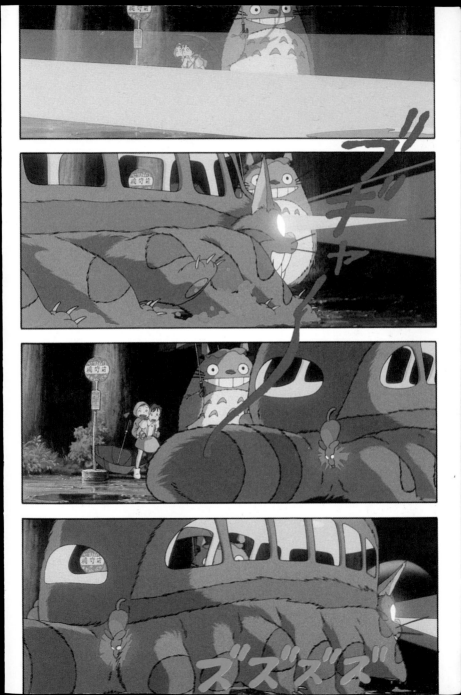

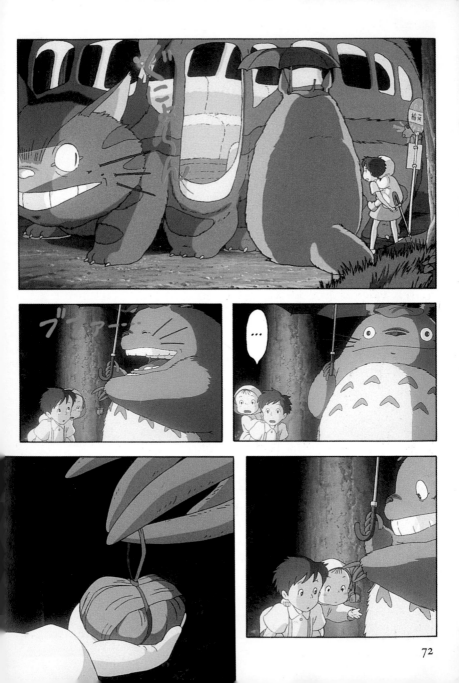

72

75

TOTORO...
HE—
HE JUST
TOOK
DAD'S
UMBRELLA.

77

78

82

...WE OPENED IT.

AS SOON AS WE GOT HOME...

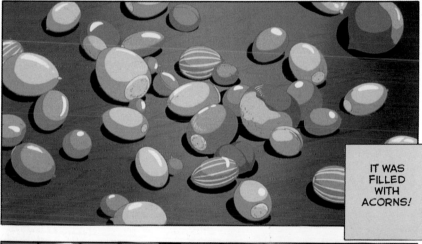

IT WAS FILLED WITH ACORNS!

86

AND IT'S STARTING TO MAKE HER CRABBY. HERE IS A PICTURE OF MEI AS A CRAB.

木の実がたくさん入ってい
いろんな種類のドングリで
れいです。ちょっともった
お家の庭が森になったら
木の実は庭にまくことに
でもなかなか芽が出ませ
日毎日まだ出ないまだ
す。まるで猿カニがっ
カニになったみたい。

HA HA...

メイは毎
いといいま

メイガニ

PLEASE GET WELL SOON. LOVE, SATSUKI.

SUMMER VACATION IS ALMOST HERE AND I CAN'T WAIT TO PLAY OUTSIDE WITH YOU.

87

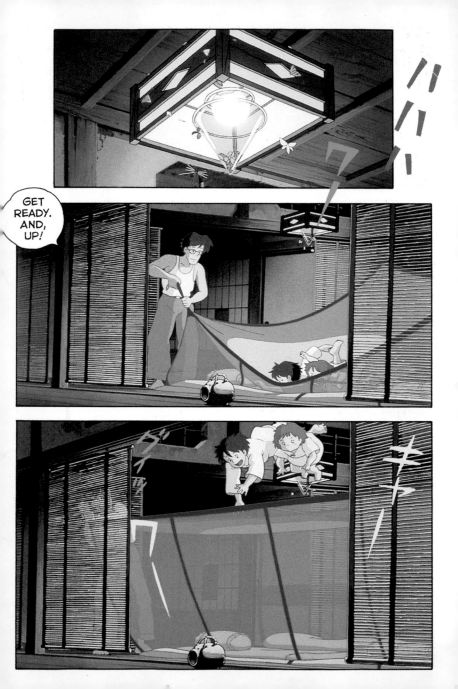

ゲ
ゲ
ゲ

ゲ
ゲ
ロ
ゲ
ロ

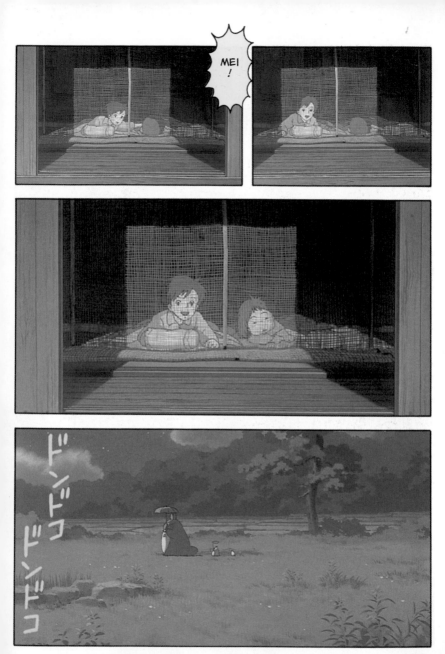

94

98

99

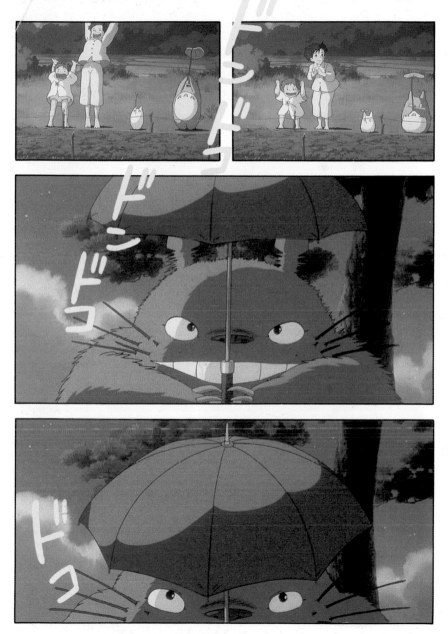

103

104

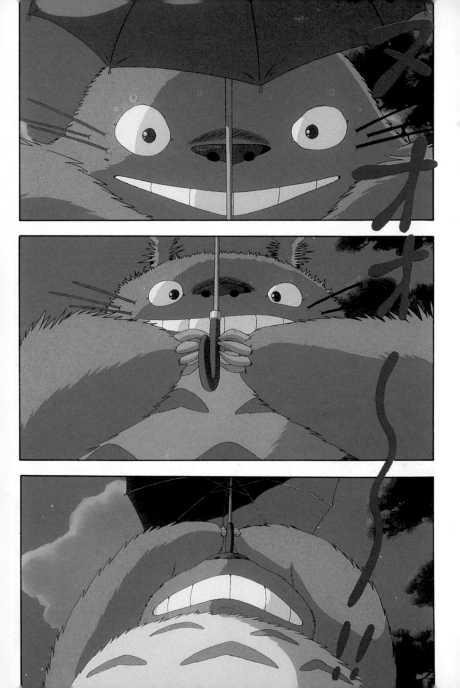

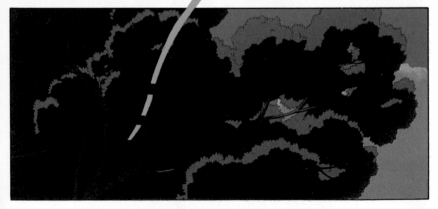

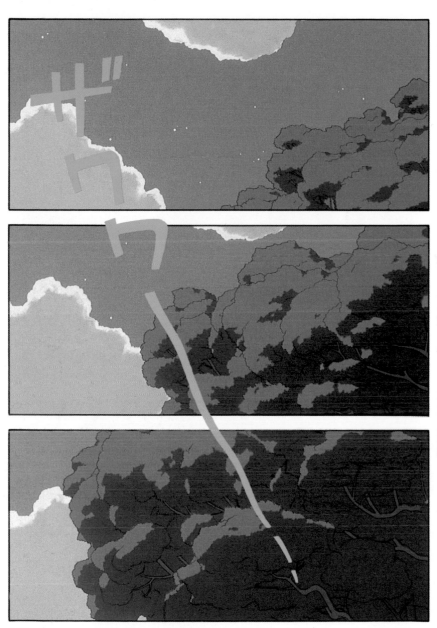

113

ピ
ョ
ン

ス
タ
ッ

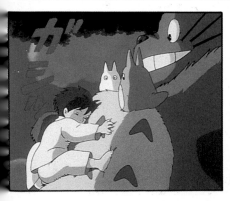

124

126

130

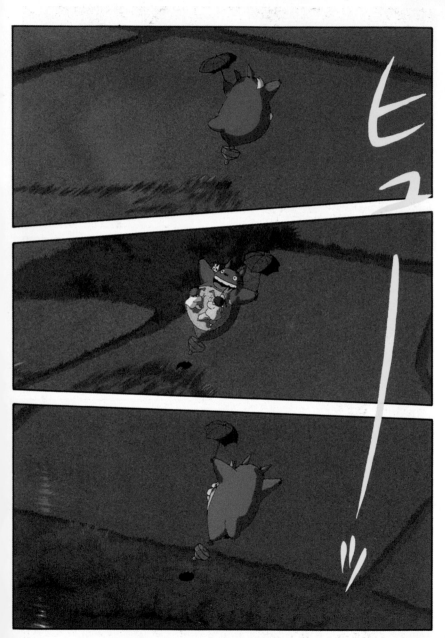

132

138

140

My Neighbor Totoro — Volume 3 — THE END

Your Guide to MY NEIGHBOR TOTORO Sound Effects!

To increase your enjoyment of the distinctive Japanese visual style of MY NEIGHBOR TOTORO we've included a listing of and guide to the sound effects used in this comic adaptation of the movie. In the comic, these sound effects are written in the Japanese phonetic characters called katakana.

In the sound effects glossary for MY NEIGHBOR TOTORO, sound effects are listed by page and panel number, for example, 5.1 means page 5, panel 1 – if there is more than one sound effect in a panel, the sound effects are listed by order (so, 19.2.1 means page 19, panel 2, first sound effect). Remember that all numbers are given in the original Japanese reading order: right-to-left.

After the page and panel numbers, you'll see the literally translated sound spelled out by the katakana, followed by how this sound effect might have been spelled out, or what it stands for, in English – it is interesting to see the different ways Japanese people describe the sounds of things!

You'll sometime see a long dash at the end of a sound effects listing. This is just a way of showing that the sound is the kind that lasts for a while; similarly, sounds that fade-out are indicated by three dots. When a sound effect goes through more than one panel, a hyphen and number indicate the panels affected.

Also, some sound effects are an important part of the dialogue, and these we've translated right on the page on which they appear! You'll see them in square caption boxes on the edges of a panel where the colored sound effects appear, but they are not listed here in the Sound Effects Guide.

Now you are ready to use the MY NEIGHBOR TOTORO Sound Effects Guide!

20.4	FX: SA SA [fp fp]		5.1	FX: KOKKOKEKOKKO– [cock-a-doodle-doo]
			5.2	FX: KOKE KOKKO [cock-cock]
21.1	FX: PARA PARA PARA [plip plip plip]			
21.2.1	FX: TA TA TA [tp tp tp]		8.3	FX: CHIRO ["sound" of glance]
21.2.2	FX: ZAZAAA [fsssh]			
21.3.1	FX: ZAAA FSSSHHH		9.2	FX: POOH [duhh]
			9.3	FX: PASHIIN [wak]
22.1	FX: ZAZAAA [fsssh]			
22.2	FX: BASHA BASHA [plish plish]		12.3	FX: ZAWA ZAWA ZAWA [mrr mrr mrr]
22.3	FX: BASHA [plish]			
22.4	FX: BACHAN [ploosh]		13.1	FX: DADAA [tmp tmp]
23.1	FX: DA [tmp]		15.3	FX: HISHI [thup]
23.2-3	FX: ZAZAAA [fsssh]			
23.4	FX: DA DA [tmp tmp]		19.1	FX: KARAAN KARAAN KARAAN [klang klang klang]
24.1	FX: ZAAA [fssh]		19.2.1	FX: WAAI [yeah]
			19.2.2	FX: GAYA GAYA [yadda yadda]
25.1	FX: ZAAA [fsssh]		19.3.1	FX: WAA [yeah]
25.2-3	FX: ZAZAAA [fsssh]		19.3.2	FX: WAI WAI [yadda yadda]

45.2	FX: BIKU [urk]
45.3	FX: SA [fsh]
45.4	FX: SHIKKA [fup]
46.2	FX: SU [fsh]
46.3.1	FX: KIIKO KIIKO [tweek twook]
46.3.2	FX: ZAAAA [fsssh]
46.3.3	FX: KIIKO [tweek]
46.4	FX: KIIKO KIIKO [tweek twook]
46.5	FX: KIIKO KIIKO KIIKO [tweek twook tweek]
47.1	FX: ZAAA [fsssh]
47.3	FX: SUU [zzz]
47.4	FX: GAKU [lwok]
48.6	FX: HMMM
49.2	FX: GAKU [twok]
50.1	FX: ZAAA [fsssh]
51.1	FX: ZURU [shlip]
51.2	FX: YOISHO [humph]
51.3	FX: PITA PITA [fip fop]
51.4	FX: PITA PITA [fip fop]
51.5	FX: PITA PITA [flp fop]
51.6	FX: PITA [fip]
52.1	FX: PITA PITA [fip fop]
52.4	FX: PORI PORI [skrch skrch]
53.5	FX: SA [fsh]
55.1	FX: ZAAA [fsssh]
56.2	FX: PICHA [plish]
56.3	FX: PARA [plip]
57.1	FX: CHIRA ["sound" of glance]
57.2	FX: BAFUU [FWOO]
58.1.1	FX: DOKI [twump]
58.1.2	FX: BA [fwip]
60.3	FX: ZAAA [fsssh]
61.3	FX: PICHAN [plip]
61.4	FX: DOKI [twump]
62.1	FX: PAN PAN [plop plop]
62.2.1	FX: GUFUU [hmmm]
62.2.2	FX: NIKA ["sound" of smile]
62.4	FX: POCHO [ploch]

26.1-2	FX: ZAZAAA [fsssh]
26.3.1	FX: SAA [fssh]
26.3.2	FX: GATAGOTO GATAGOTO [klaketta klaketta]
27.4	FX: ZAZAZA [fssssh]
27.6	FX: ZAAA [fsssh]
28.1	FX: PITA [fip]
28.2	FX: KURU [fwip]
28.3	FX: ZUI [woom]
29.3	FX: SA [fsh]
29.4.1	FX: TA TA TA [tmp tmp tmp]
29.4.1	FX: PASHA PASHA [plish plish]
30.1.1	FX: ZAZAAA [fsssh]
30.1.2	FX: PASHA PASHA [plish plish]
30.3	FX: BASHA BASHA BASHA [plish plish plish]
31.1	FX: BASHA BASHA [plish plish]
31.1.2	FX: PIYOHN [fwiing]
31.1.3	FX: ZAAA [fsssh]
32.1	FX: ZAAA [fsssh]
32.2	FX: CHIKUTAKU CHIKUTAKU [tiktok tiktok]
33.1	FX: ZAAA [fsssh]
33.3	FX: GOCHIN [tonk]
34.2	FX: SAA [fssh]
34.5	FX: DOKO DOKO [tump tump]
35.3	FX: PACHI [flik]
38.2	FX: BUUN [fwoosh]
38.3	FX: BUUN [fwoosh]
39.1	FX: BUU [vrroom]
39.2	FX: AH! [hey!]
39.4	FX: BURORO— [vrrroom]
40.1	FX: BUOOOOOH— [vrrrooom]
40.2	FX: KIII [kreech]
40.3	FX: BURURU- BURURUUN [vrr vrrr]
41.2	FX: GARAGARA PISHA [zhoop klak]
41.3	FX: VUOOH [vrrrom]
42.3	FX: ZAZAAA [fssssh]
43.1	FX: ZAA [fsssh]
43.2	FX: BASHA BASHA [plish plish]
43.3	FX: BASHA BASHA [plish plish]

78.1	FX: GURUN... [vrr]	62.5	FX: PARAA [plop]
78.3.1	FX: GARAGARA PISHA [zhoop klak]	62.5	FX: PARA PARA [plip plip]
78.3.2	FX: GYU [tugg]		
78.4.	FX: BURORORO— [vrrroom]	63.1	FX: PAN [plop plop]
		63.2	FX: PARA PARA PARAN [plip plip plipp]
80.4	FX: KOWAI! KOWAI! [scary! scary!]	63.3	FX: GUFUU [fwooo]
81.3	FX: KYAHAHAHA— [ha ha ha]	64.2	FX: GYUU [frrr]
		64.3	FX: PYOHN [pwong]
82.1	FX: GUEHH [rrrib]		
82.2.1	FX: GEKO GEKO [ribbit ribbit]	65.1	FX: DENN [foom]
82.2.2	FX: GEKO GEKO [ribbit ribbit]	65.4	FX: DOBABABABABABA [plissssh]
82.3.1	FX: GEKO GEKO [ribbit ribbit]		
82.3.2	FX: GEKO GEKO [ribbit ribbit]	66.1	FX: VURORORORO— [arrrr]
85.4	FX: WAA [wow]	67.3	FX: PYOHN [pwong]
88.1.1	FX: HA HA HA [ha ha ha]	68.1	FX: HYUU [fweee]
88.1.2	FX: WAA [yeah]	68.2	FX: SHURURURU [fwoowoosh]
88.3.1	FX: KYAA [aiee]	68.3	FX: HYUU [fweee]
88.3.2	FX: GUI [tugg]		
88.3.3	FX: WAA [yeah]	69.1.1	FX: HYUU [fweee]
		69.1.2	FX: HYURURURURU— [fwoowoosh]
90.2	FX: KACHI [klik]	69.2	FX: NYAA— [meow]
91.1.1	FX: GERO GERO GERO [ribbit ribbit ribbit]	70.1-3	FX: BUGYAAA [kreeee]
91.1.2	FX: GEH GEH GEH [ribbit ribbit ribbit]	70.4	FX: ZUZUZUZU [krrrch]
93.1	FX: DON DOKO [tump twup]	71.1	FX: NYA— GORO— [meow purrr]
93.2	FX: DON [tump]	71.2	FX: NIKA ["sound" of smile]
93.3	FX: DOKO [twup]		
93.4	FX: DON DOKO [tump twup]	72.1	FX: GUNYOHN [shloom]
		72.3	FX: BUFAA... [yahh]
94.4	FX: DON DOKO DON DOKO [tump twup]		
		73.3.1	FX: GUGU [rrr]
95.1	FX: DON DOKO [tump twup]	73.3.2	FX: SHURURURURU— [vrrrr]
95.2	FX: PYOHN [pwong]		
95.3	FX: DON DOKO [tump twup]	74.1	FX: HYURURURU [fwoooosh]
		74.2.1	FX: PYON [pwong]
96.1	FX: DON DOKO DON DOKO DON DOKO	74.2.2	FX: SHURURU— [fwooosh]
96.1	[tump twup tump twup tump twup]	74.3.1	FX: PYON [pwong]
		74.3.2	FX: HYUU [fwee]
99.1	FX: DON DOKO DON DOKO	74.4.1	FX: PIKA [zing]
	[tump twup tump twup]	74.4.2	FX: SA [fsh]
99.2	FX: DON DOKO [tump twup]		
99.3	FX: DON DOKO [tump twup]	76.2	FX: CHAPOHN [plissh]
100.1	FX: DON DOKO [tump twup]	77.1	FX: BURORORO— [vrrroom]
		77.2	FX: GII [kreek]
102.1	FX: DON DOKO [tump twup]	77.3.1	FX: GACHA [chak]
102.2	FX: DON DOKO [tump twup]	77.3.2	FX: GURUN GURUN [vrr vrr]
102.3	FX: DON DOKO [tump twup]		
102.4	FX: DON DOKO [tump twup]		

123.2	FX: PYON [pwong]
123..1	FX: SUTA [tup]
123.3.2	FX: VWEEEN [zwing]
124.1	FX: KURU [fwip]
124.2	FX: NI ["sound" of grin]
124.4	FX: BA [fwoosh]
124.5	FX: GASHI [tugg]
125.1-3	FX: VWEEEEN [zwiiing]
126.1-4	FX: VWEEEEN [zwiiing]
126.1.2	FX: BA [fup]
127.2-4	FX: VWEEEEN [zwiing]
129.1	FX: VORORORO— [arrrgh]
130.2-3	FX: VOROHH— [arrooh]
131.1-3	FX: HYUUN [fwooom]
132.1-3	FX: HYUUU [fweee]
134.1-3	FX: GOHH [fwoooosh]
135.1	FX: HYUUU [fweee]
135.2	FX: HOOH— [whoo]
135.3	FX: HOOH [whoo]
135.4	FX: HOOH HOOH— [whoo whoo]
136.1	FX: HOOH— [whoo]
136.2	FX: PUPPU— [vwoowoop]
136.3	FX: HOOH HOOH [whoo whoo]
137.1.1	FX: PUPPU— [vwoowoop]
137.1.2	FX: HOOH— [whoo]
137.2.1	FX: HOOH— [whoo]
137.2.2	FX: PUU [vwoop]
137.2.3	FX: HOOH— [whoo]
139.4	FX: DADDA [tmp tmp]
141.1	FX: WAAI!! [hurrah!!]
141.3	FX: GUUN [hmmm]
141.4	FX: AHAHAHA— [ha ha ha]
142.1-2	FX: KYAHAHAHAHA... [ha ha ha ha ha...]

103.1	FX: DON DOKO [tump twup]
103.3	FX: DON DOKO [tump twup]
103.4	FX: DOKO [twup]
104.1	FX: DON DOKO DON DOKO
	[tump twup tump twup]
104.2	FX: VUAAH [arrrr]
105.1	FX: PON [fip]
105.4	FX: WAA [ahhh]
105.5	FX: PON [fip]
106.1-3	FX: ARRRRRGH!!
107.1	FX: POKO POKO [fup fup]
107.2	FX: POKO POKO POKO [fup fup fup]
108.1	FX: UGUGUGU [ummm]
108.2	FX: UH [hmph]
108.3	FX. PA!! [fwoop!!]
109.1	FX. UGUGUGU [ummm]
109.2	FX: PA [fwoop!!]
109.3	FX: DOTEN!! [whud!!]
112.1-3	FX: ZAWAWA— [fwooosh]
113.1-3	FX: ZAWAWA— [fwooosh]
118.1	FX: WAAH WAAH [hurrah hurrah]
118.2.1	FX: SA [fsh]
118.2.2	FX: NI ["sound" of grin]
118.3	FX: BUUN [swissh]
119.1	FX: TO [tup]
119.2	FX: KURU [fwip]
119.3	FX: NI ["sound" of grin]
119.4	FX: UWEEN [zwing]
120.3	FX: MUSHA MUSHA [mnch mnch]
120.4	FX: KURU [fwip]
121.1	FX: PYON [pwong]
121.2	FX: PYON [pwong]
121.4	FX: BESHI [fump]
121.5	FX: PITA [plip]
122.1	FX: WAA!! [ahh!!]
122.2	FX: DA [tmp]
122.3	FX: PYON [pwong]
122.4	FX: BETA [fump]

This book should be read in its original Japanese right-to-left format.
Please turn it around to begin!

MY NEIGHBOR TOTORO
Volume 3 of 4

Original story and screenplay written and directed by Hayao Miyazaki

English Translation/Jim Hubbert
Unedited English-Language Adaptation/Cindy Davis Hewitt & Donald H. Hewitt

Film Comic Adaptation/Yuji Oniki
Lettering/John Clark
Design/Hidemi Sahara
Editor/Megan Bates

Managing Editor/Masumi Washington
Director of Production/Noboru Watanabe
Editorial Director/Alvin Lu
Sr. Director of Licensing & Acquisitions/Rika Inouye
Vice President of Sales & Marketing/Liza Coppola
Executive Vice President/Hyoe Narita
Publisher/Seiji Horibuchi

PARENTAL ADVISORY
MY NEIGHBOR TOTORO is suitable
for all ages.

Printed in Hong Kong.

Published by VIZ LLC
P.O.Box 77010
San Francisco, CA 94107

First Printing, December 2004

www.viz.com

MIYAZAKI'S
SPIRITED AWAY

From the Critically-Acclaimed Cinematic Masterpiece

Full color books from the Oscar-winning* film!

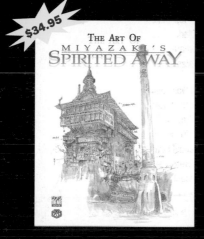

$34.95

The Art of Spirited Away

A hardcover coffee-table book featuring:
- Color illustrations and stills
- Paintings, designs and sketches
- Storyboards and commentary
- Complete English-language movie script

$19.95

Spirited Away Picture Book

Relive Chihiro's magical journey with this hardcover children's storybook, illustrated with color stills from the movie. Complete with character info and theme song lyrics!

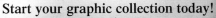

BEAUTIFUL YOU

Beautiful You

CHUCK PALAHNIUK

VINTAGE

1 3 5 7 9 10 8 6 4 2

Vintage
20 Vauxhall Bridge Road,
London SW1V 2SA

Vintage is part of the Penguin Random House group of companies
whose addresses can be found at global.penguinrandomhouse.com

Copyright © Chuck Palahniuk 2014

Chuck Palahniuk has asserted his right to be identified as the author of this
Work in accordance with the Copyright, Designs and Patents Act 1988

First published by Vintage in 2015
(First published in Great Britain by Jonathan Cape in 2014)

www.vintage-books.co.uk

A CIP catalogue record for this book is
available from the British Library

ISBN 9780099587675

Printed and bound by CPI Group (UK) Ltd, Croydon, CR0 4YY

"A Billion Husbands Are About to Be Replaced"

Beautiful You

Even as Penny was attacked, the judge merely stared. The jury recoiled. The journalists cowered in the gallery. No one in the courtroom came to her rescue. The court reporter continued to dutifully keyboard, transcribing Penny's words: "Someone, he's hurting me! Please stop him!" Those efficient fingers typed the word "No!" The stenographer transcribed a long phonetic moan, a groan, a scream. This gave way to a list of Penny's pleas:

His fingers tapped out, "Help!"

They typed, "Stop!"

It would've been different if there had been other women in the courtroom, but there were none. In the past few months all women had disappeared from sight. The public sphere was devoid of women. Those looking on as Penny struggled—the judge, the jurors, the spectators—they were all male. This world was a world of men.

The court reporter typed, "Please!"

He typed, "Please, no! Not here!"

Otherwise, only Penny moved. Her slacks were bunched down rudely around her ankles. Her underthings were ripped away to expose her to everyone who dared look. She swung her elbows and knees, trying to escape. In their front-row seats the sketch artists drew fast lines to capture her grappling with the attacker, her torn clothes flapping, her tangled hair whipping the air. A few tentative hands rose among the spectators, each cupping a cell phone and snapping a surreptitious picture or a few seconds of video. Her outcries seemed to freeze everyone else present, her ragged voice echoing around the otherwise silent space. It was no longer the sound of just one woman being raped; the reverberating, shimmering eddies of sound suggested that a dozen women were under attack. A hundred. The whole world was screaming.

In the witness stand, she fought. She wrestled to bring her legs together and push the pain away. Lifting her head, she tried to make eye contact with someone—with anyone. A man pressed his palms to the sides of his head, covering his ears and squeezing his eyes shut, as red-faced as a frightened little boy. Penny looked to the judge, who sighed piteously at her plight but refused to gavel for order. A bailiff ducked his head and mumbled words into a microphone clipped to his chest. His gun holstered, he nervously shifted his weight, wincing at her outcries.

Others peeked decorously at their watches or text messages as if mortified on Penny's behalf. As if she ought to know better than to scream and bleed in public. As if this attack and her suffering were her own fault.

The lawyers seemed to shrivel inside their expensive pin-striped suits. They busily shuffled their papers. Even her own boyfriend stayed seated, gaping at her brutal assault in utter disbelief. Someone must've called an ambulance, because paramedics were soon rushing down the center aisle.

Sobbing and clawing to protect herself, Penny fought to stay conscious. If she could get to her feet, if she could climb from the stand, she could run. Escape. The courtroom was as densely packed as a city bus at rush hour, but no one seized her attacker or tried to drag him away. Those who were standing took a step or two back. Every observer was edging backward as far as the

walls allowed, leaving Penny and her rapist in a growing emptiness at the front of the room.

The two paramedics pushed through the crowd. When they
first reached her, Penny lashed out, still gasping and struggling,
but they calmed her, telling her to relax. Telling her that she was
safe. The worst was over, leaving her chilled, drenched in sweat,
and shivering with shock. In every direction a wall of faces
looked for blank spots where their eyes wouldn't meet other
eyes filled with their mutual shame.

The paramedics lifted her onto a gurney, and one tucked
a blanket around her trembling body while the other buckled
straps to keep her in place. Finally the judge was gaveling, calling for a recess.

The medic pulling the straps snug asked, "Can you tell me
what year this is?"

Penny's throat burned, raw from shouting. Her voice
sounded hoarse, but she said the correct year.

"Can you tell me the president?" asked the paramedic.

Penny almost said Clarissa Hind, but stopped herself. President Hind was dead. The first and only female president was
dead.

"Can you tell us your name?" Both medics were, of course,
male.

"Penny," she said, "Penny Harrigan."

The two men leaning over her gasped in recognition. Their
professional faces slipped for a moment and became delighted
smiles. "I *thought* you looked familiar," one said brightly.

The other snapped his fingers, exasperated by words that
wouldn't come to mind. He piped in, "You are . . . you're *that one,*
from the *National Enquirer*!"

The first one pointed a finger at Penny, bound and helpless, watched by every masculine eye. "Penny Harrigan," he

shouted like an accusation. "You're Penny Harrigan, 'the Nerd's Cinderella.'"

The pair of men lifted the gurney to waist height. The crowds parted to let them wheel it toward the exit.

The second medic nodded with recognition. "The guy you dumped, wasn't he, like, the richest man in the world?"

"Maxwell," the first declared. "His name was Linus Maxwell." He shook his head in disbelief. Not only had Penny been raped in front of a federal courtroom filled with people, none of whom had lifted a finger to stop the attacker, but now the ambulance attendants thought she was an idiot.

"You should've married him," the first one kept marveling all the way to the ambulance. "Lady, if you'd married that guy you'd be richer than God. . . ."

Cornelius Linus Maxwell. C. Linus Maxwell. Due to his reputation as a playboy the tabloid press often called him "Climax-Well." The world's richest megabillionaire.

Those same tabloids had dubbed her "the Nerd's Cinderella." Penny Harrigan and Corny Maxwell. They'd met a year before. That all seemed like a lifetime ago. A different world entirely.

A better world.

Never in human history had there been a better time to be a woman. Penny knew that.

Growing up, she repeated the fact like a mantra: *Never in human history has there been a better time to be a woman.*

Her world had been perfect, more or less. She'd recently graduated law school in the top third of her class, but failed the bar exam twice. Twice! It wasn't self-doubt, not really, but an idea had begun to haunt her. It bothered Penny that, due to all the hard-won victories of women's liberation, becoming an upbeat, ambitious girl attorney didn't feel like much of a triumph. Not anymore. It didn't seem any bolder than to be a housewife in the 1950s. A couple generations ago, society would've encouraged her to be a stay-at-home mom. Now all the pressure was to become a lawyer. Or a doctor. Or a rocket scientist. Whatever the case, the validity of those roles had more to do with fashion and politics than they did with Penny herself.

As a college undergrad she'd devoted herself to gaining the approval of the professors in her gender studies department at the University of Nebraska. She'd exchanged the dreams of her parents for the dogma of her instructors, but neither of those outlooks was innately her own.

The truth was, Penelope Anne Harrigan was still being a good daughter—obedient, bright, dutiful—who did as she was told. She'd always deferred to the advice of other, older people. Yet she yearned for something beyond earning the approval of her parents and surrogate parents. With apologies to Simone de Beauvoir, Penny didn't want to be a third-wave *anything*. No offense to Bella Abzug, but neither did she want to be a post-*anything*. She didn't want to replicate the victories of Susan B. Anthony and Helen Gurley Brown. She wanted a choice beyond: Housewife versus lawyer. Madonna versus whore. An option not mired in the lingering detritus of some Victorian-era dream. Penny wanted something wildly beyond feminism itself!

Nagging at her was the idea that a deep-seated motive kept her from passing the bar exam. That submerged part of her didn't want to practice law, and she kept hoping that something would happen to rescue her from her own small-scale, predictable dreams. Her goals had been the goals of radical women a century ago: to become a lawyer . . . to compete toe-to-toe with men. But like any second-hand goal, it felt like a burden. It had already been fulfilled ten million times over by other women. Penny wanted a dream of her own, but she had no idea how that dream would look.

She hadn't found her dream as a well-behaved daughter. Nor had she found it by regurgitating the hidebound ideology of her professors. It comforted her to think that every girl of her generation was facing this same crisis. They'd all inherited a legacy of freedom, and they owed it to the future to forge a new frontier for the next generation of young women. To break new ground.

Until a wholly new, novel, original dream reared its lovely head, Penny would doggedly pursue the old one: an entry-level position at a law firm, fetching doughnuts, wrangling chairs, cramming for the next bar exam.

Even now, at the age of twenty-five, she worried that it might already be too late.

She'd never trusted her own natural impulses and instincts. Among her greatest fears was the possibility that she might never discover and develop her deepest talents and intuitions. Her *special* gifts. Her life would be wasted in pursuing the goals set for her by other people. Instead, she wanted to reclaim a power and authority—a primitive, irresistible force—that transcended gender roles. She dreamed of wielding a raw magic that predated civilization itself.

While she mustered her courage for a third attempt at the bar exam, Penny reported to work at Broome, Broome, and Brillstein, the most prestigious firm in Manhattan. To be honest, she wasn't a full associate. But she wasn't an intern, either. Okay, occasionally she ran to the lobby Starbucks for a half dozen last-minute lattes and half-caf soy cappuccinos, but not every day. Other days she'd be dispatched to fetch extra chairs for a big conference meeting. But she wasn't an intern. Penny Harrigan wasn't a lawyer, not yet, but she certainly wasn't a lowly intern.

The days were long here at BB&B, but they could be exciting. Today, for example, she'd heard thunder echoing amid the towers of lower Manhattan. It was the roar of a helicopter landing on the rooftop. Sixty-seven floors up, on the heliport of this very building, someone incredibly important was arriving. Penny had been standing on the first floor, juggling a flimsy cardboard box loaded with a half dozen hot venti mochas. She was waiting for an elevator. Reflected in the polished steel of the elevator doors, there she was. Not a beauty. Not ugly, either. Neither short nor tall. Her hair looked nice, clean and pooling along the shoulders of her simple Brooks Brothers blouse.

Her brown eyes looked wide and honest. In the next instant her clear-skinned, placid face was erased.

The elevator doors slid open, and a scrum of massive men, like a charging football team in identical navy blue suits, emerged from the arriving car. As if running offense for a star quarterback, they shouldered their way out, pressing back the impatient crowd. Forced to step aside, Penny couldn't help but crane her neck to see whom they were protecting. Everyone else with a free hand reached straight up, every hand cupping a camera phone, and began to shoot video and pictures from overhead. Penny couldn't see through the onslaught of blue serge, but she could look up and see the famous face in the screens of the numerous recording devices. The air was loud with electronic clicks. The static and chatter of walkie-talkies. From behind it all came the muffled sound of sobbing.

The woman on the small screens of myriad phones was dabbing at her cheeks with the corner of a handkerchief, the linen and lace already stained with tears and mascara. Even wearing oversize sunglasses, the face was unmistakable. If there was any doubt it was resolved by the dazzling blue sapphire balanced between her perfect breasts. If you could believe what you read in the supermarket checkout line, it was the largest flawless sapphire in history, almost two hundred carats. This stone had graced the necks of ancient Egyptian queens. Roman empresses. Russian czarinas. It was impossible for Penny to imagine what any woman wearing such a jewel would have to cry about.

Suddenly it made sense: The helicopter delivering some megacelebrity to the building's roof while this traumatized beauty scurried out on the street level. The senior partners were taking depositions today. It was the big palimony suit.

A man's voice within the mob shouted, "Alouette! Alouette! Do you still love him?" A female voice shouted, "Would you take him back?" The crowd seemed to draw its collective breath, growing quiet as if waiting for a revelation.

The weeping beauty framed in the small viewfinders of a hundred phones, documented from every direction and angle, lifted her elegant chin and said, "I will not be discarded." Fractured into all of those perspectives, she swallowed. "Maxwell is the greatest lover I have known."

Ignoring a new flurry of questions, the security team forced its way through the curious throng to the street doors, where a motorcade of limousines waited at the curb. In a moment, the spectacle was over.

The woman in the center of all that fuss had been the French actress Alouette D'Ambrosia. She was a six-time Palme d'Or winner. A four-time Oscar winner.

Penny couldn't wait to e-mail her mom and dad and tell them about the scene. That was one of the perks of working at BB&B. Even if she was only fetching coffee, Penny was still glad she'd left home. You never saw movie stars in Nebraska.

The motorcade was gone. Everyone was still looking in the direction it had disappeared when a friendly voice called out, "Omaha girl!"

It was a fellow clerk from the firm, Monique, snapping her fingers and waving to get Penny's attention. Compared to Monique, with her elaborate porcelain fingernails studded with flashy Austrian crystals, and her long weave, braided with beads and feathers, Penny always felt like such a plain, gray sparrow.

"Did you see?" Penny stammered. "It was Alouette D'Ambrosia!"

Monique threaded her way closer, calling, "Omaha girl, you need to be up on sixty-four." She caught Penny by the elbow and towed her toward a waiting elevator. The cups of hot coffee sloshed and threatened to spill. "Old man Brillstein has the entire crew together, and they're screaming for more chairs."

Penny's assumption was correct. It was the deposition. The palimony suit: *D'Ambrosia v. Maxwell*. Everyone knew it was a nuisance lawsuit. A publicity stunt. The world's richest man had dated the world's most beautiful woman for 136 days. Exactly 136. Penny knew the details of the case because of the grocery store checkout lines. In New York the cashiers were so slow and surly that you could read the *National Enquirer* from cover to cover while waiting to pay for your melting pint of Ben & Jerry's butter brickle. According to the tabloids, the billionaire had given the woman the world's largest sapphire. They'd vacationed in Fiji. Glamorous Fiji! Then he'd broken off the affair. If they'd been anybody else that might've been the end of the matter, but this couple had the whole world watching them. Most likely to save face, the jilted girlfriend now demanded fifty million dollars' compensation for emotional distress.

As they stepped into an elevator, a cheerful voice called across the lobby, "Yo, Hillbilly!" The two girls turned to see a smiling, fresh-faced young man in a pin-striped suit sprinting toward them. Dodging between people, he was only a few steps away, shouting, "Hold the elevator!"

Instead, Monique punched the button to shut the doors. She repeatedly stabbed the button with her bejeweled thumb as if she were sending a distress signal in Morse code. Penny had lived in the Big Apple for six months, and she had yet to see anyone press an elevator button fewer than twenty times. The doors thudded together, mere inches in front of the young lawyer's aquiline nose, leaving him behind.

His name was Tad, and he'd flirted with Penny every time they'd met. His pet name for her was "Hillbilly," and Tad represented what Penny's mother would call "a real catch." Penny herself suspected otherwise. Secretly, she sensed that he only paid attention to her because he was trying to endear himself to Monique. It was the way any man might curry favor with a pretty girl by fawning over her fat, stinky dog.

Not that Penny was stinky. Or fat, not really.

Not that Monique cared, either. With her flashy streetwise attitude she was angling for a hedge fund manager or a newly minted Russian oligarch. Unapologetic, she told everyone that her only aspiration was to live in an Upper East Side town house, munching Pop-Tarts and lounging in bed all day. Breathing a huge, fake sigh of relief, she said, "Omaha girl, you should let that poor boy put his slippery little tadpole inside you!"

Penny wasn't flattered by his winks and wolf whistles. She knew she was only the ugly dog. The stepping stone.

Aboard the elevator Monique appraised Penny's workaday outfit. Monique cocked her hip and wagged a finger. There wasn't room left on any of the stylish girl's fingers for even one more glitzy ring. Monique pursed her lips, sporting three distinct shades of purple lip gloss, and said, "G'friend, I love your retro figure!" She tossed her beaded braids. "I love how you're so okay with your big-girl thighs."

Penny hesitantly accepted the compliment. Monique was a work friend, and that wasn't the same as a real friend. Life here was different than in the Midwest. In New York City you had to settle.

In the city every gesture was calculated to dominate. Every detail of a woman's appearance demonstrated status. Penny hugged the cardboard box of warm coffees, holding it like a vanilla-scented teddy bear, suddenly self-conscious.

Monique cut her eyes sideways, recoiling in shock at the sight of something on Penny's face. To judge from Monique's grimace, it couldn't be anything less than a nesting tarantula. "A place in Chinatown . . . ?" Monique began. She took a step away. "They can take care of those crazy werewolf hairs you have sprouting around your mouth." Adding in a stage whisper, "So cheap even you can afford it."

Growing up on her parents' farm in Shippee, Nebraska, Penny had seen cooped-up hens peck one another to bloody death with more subtlety.

It was obvious that some women had never gotten the memo about universal sisterhood.

As they arrived on the sixty-fourth floor the elevator doors opened, and the two young women were greeted by the probing noses of four German shepherds. Bomb-sniffing dogs. A burly uniformed guard stepped forward to wand them with a metal detector.

"We're on lockdown above this level," explained Monique. "Because of you-know-who being in the building, they've evacuated everything between sixty-four and the roof." Sassy as ever, Monique took Penny by the elbow and reiterated, "Chairs, girl. Fetch!"

It was ludicrous. BB&B was the most high-powered firm in the country, but they never had enough seating to go around. Like a game of musical chairs, if you arrived late to any important meeting you had to stand. At least until some underling like Penny was sent to find you a chair.

While Monique ran to the meeting to stall for time, Penny tried door after door and found them all locked. The hallways were strangely deserted, and through the window beside each locked door Penny could see the chairs each associate had safely left behind at his or her desk. Here in the rarified air of the executive floors it was always hushed, but this was spooky. No voices or footsteps echoed off the paneled walls or tasteful landscape paintings of the Hudson River Valley. Open bottles of Evian had been left behind so quickly that they still fizzed.

She'd completed a four-year undergraduate degree in gender politics, and two years of law school, and now she was rounding up chairs for people too lazy or too self-important to take their own to meetings. It was so demeaning. This, no, this was something Penny would definitely not e-mail her parents to boast about.

Her phone began to vibrate. It was Monique texting: "SISTER, WHERE ARE THOSE CHAIRS?!" By now Penny was sprinting down hallways. With the cardboard box of coffees barely balanced in one hand, she was lunging at doors, grabbing knobs only long enough to see whether they'd turn. Frantic, she'd all but given up hope, hurtling breathlessly from one locked office to the next. When one knob actually turned, she wasn't ready. The door swung inward, and she was instantly thrown off balance. Falling through the doorway in a great splash of hot coffee, she landed on something as soft as clover. Sprawled on her stomach, she saw close-up the intertwined greens, reds, and yellows of beautiful flowers. Many flowers. She'd landed in a garden. Exotic birds perched among the roses and lilies. But hovering directly in front of her face was a polished black shoe. A man's shoe, its toe was poised as if ready to kick her in the teeth.

This wasn't a real garden. The birds and flowers were merely patterns in an Oriental rug. Hand-dyed and woven from pure silk, it was the only one of its kind in all of BB&B, and Penny realized exactly whose office this was. She saw herself reflected in the dark shine of the shoe: her coffee-drenched hair swinging in her eyes, her cheeks flushed, and her mouth hanging slack as she panted on the floor, out of breath. Her chest heaving. The fall had lifted her skirt, leaving her bottom stuck up in the air. Thank goodness for old-school opaque cotton panties. Had Penny been wearing a racy thong, she would have died from shame.

Her eyes followed the black shoe up to a strong, sinewy ankle sheathed in an argyle sock. Even the jaunty green-and-gold pattern of the man's sock couldn't disguise the muscles within it. Beyond that was the hem of a trouser cuff. From this low angle, her gaze followed the sharp crease of the gray-flannel pant leg upward to a knee. Meticulous tailoring and cut revealed the contour of a powerful thigh. Long legs. Tennis player legs, Penny thought. From there the trouser inseam led her eyes to a sizable bulge, like a huge fist wrapped in smooth, soft flannel.

She felt the hot wetness between her and the floor. She was wallowing on the squashed cups. A combined gallon of soy latte skinny half-caf mocha chai venti macchiato was soaking into her clothes and ruining the room's priceless floor covering.

Even in the buffed, murky leather of the shoe, Penny could see the blush in her cheeks deepen. She gulped. Only a voice broke the moment's trancelike spell.

A man said something. The tone sounded firm, but as soft as the silk carpet. Pleasant and bemused, it repeated, "Have we been introduced?"

Penny's eyes looked up through the veil of her long, fluttering eyelashes. A face loomed in the distance. At the farthest point of this gray-flannel vista, there were the features she'd seen so often in the supermarket tabloids. His eyes were blue; his forehead was fringed by a boyish ruff of his blond hair. His gentle smile put a dimple into each of his clean-shaved cheeks. His expression was mild, pleasant as a doll's. No wrinkles in his brow or cheeks suggested he'd ever worried or sneered. Penny knew from the tabloids that he was forty-nine years old. Neither did crow's-feet offer any proof that he'd smiled very often.

Still sprawled on the floor, Penny gasped. "It's you!" She squeaked, "You're him! I mean, you're you!" He wasn't a client of the firm. Quite the opposite, he was the defendant in the palimony case. Penny could only assume he was here to be deposed.

He was seated in a guest chair, one of the firm's highly carved Chippendale armchairs upholstered in red leather. The smells of leather and shoe polish were pungent. Framed diplomas and leather-bound sets of law books lined the room's walls.

Behind him was a mahogany desk that glowed crimson from a century of hand rubbing and beeswax. Standing on the far side of the desk was a stooped figure whose bald head glowed almost as red, spotted and blotched with age. In the gaunt face the rheumy eyes blazed with outrage. Thin, palsied lips revealed tobacco-stained dentures. On all of the diplomas and certificates and awards, inked in elaborate gothic calligraphy, was the name Albert Brillstein, Esq.

In polite response to her stammering, the younger man asked, unflustered, "And who might you be?"

"She's no one," snarled the man standing behind the desk, the firm's senior partner. "She shouldn't even *be* here! She's nothing but a girl Friday. She's failed the bar exam *three times*!"

The words stung Penny as if she'd been slapped. In shame she looked away from the blue eyes and once more caught sight of her reflection in the younger man's shoe. Her boss was right.

She was just a gofer. She was nobody. Just some stupid bumpkin who'd moved to New York with dreams of finding some . . . destiny. Something. The brutal truth was that she'd probably never pass the bar. She'd spend her life filing papers and fetching coffee, and nothing wonderful would ever happen to her.

Without waiting for her to get up, Mr. Brillstein snapped, "Out." He pointed a trembling, bony index finger at the open door and shouted, "Remove yourself!"

In the pocket of her skirt, her phone began to vibrate. Penny didn't have to look to know it was Monique, justifiably exasperated.

Brillstein was right. She shouldn't be here. She should be in suburban Omaha. She should be happily married to a pleasant, even-tempered Sigma Chi. They would have two babies and a third on the way. That was her fate. She should be covered in baby spit instead of expensive double-shot espressos.

Reflected in the shoe, there she was, made as tiny as Alouette D'Ambrosia had been shrunken in the screens of so many cell phones. Penny felt tears well up in her eyes and watched one spill down her cheek. Self-loathing flooded her. With her hand, she dashed the wetness away and hoped neither of the men had noticed it. Spreading her fingers against the carpet, she tried to push herself up, but the combination of whipped cream, caramel, and chocolate syrup was gluing her down. Even if she could get to her feet, she worried that the hot liquid would make her blouse transparent.

Despite their cheerful color, the blue eyes watching her were as focused and unblinking as any camera. They were measuring and recording her. He wasn't any more handsome than she was beautiful, but his jaw was firmly set. He oozed confidence.

Mr. Brillstein stammered, "Mr. Maxwell, I can't tell you how sorry I am about this rude interruption." Lifting his telephone and punching a few numbers, he said, "Rest assured that I'll have this young lady evicted from the building immediately." Into the receiver he bellowed, "Security!" Judging from the vehemence in his voice, this would be no simple dismissal. It sounded as if he planned to have her flung from the roof.

"May I offer you a hand?" asked the blond man, reaching down.

A signet ring with a large red stone gleamed on his finger. Later, Penny would discover that it was the third-largest ruby ever mined in Sri Lanka. It had belonged to sultans and maharajas, and here it was coming to her rescue. Its sparkle was blinding. The fingers that closed around her own were surprisingly cold. An equally amazing strength lifted her as the lips, those lips she'd seen kissing movie stars and heiresses, said, "Now that your evening is free . . ." He asked, "Would you grant me the pleasure of your company at dinner tonight?"

The saleslady at Bonwit Teller eyed Penny with a disdainful expression. "May I show you something?" she asked, a sneer in her voice.

Penny had run every step, all eight blocks from the subway to the department store, and hadn't yet caught her breath. "A dress?" she stammered. More resolutely, she added, "An evening gown."

The associate's eyes looked her up and down, not missing a detail. Not Penny's tragic knockoff Jimmy Choos, bought at an Omaha factory-outlet mall. Not her shoulder bag with the fraying shoulder strap and pecan pie stains. Her almost-Burberry trench did little to hide the fact that her clothes were drenched in cold coffee and sticky whipped cream. A few houseflies had found the sweet scent and followed her from the crowded train platform. Penny tried to wave them away with a cavalier gesture.

To a stranger, she must've looked deranged. The saleslady's evaluation felt like an eternity, and Penny fought the urge to turn on her scuffed heel and stalk away from the snobbish woman.

For her part, the sales associate could've been a penthouse socialite slumming from Beekman Place. Chanel everything. Immaculate nails. No pesky black flies hovered around her perfect French braid or roamed the flawless skin of her forehead. After taking cold inventory, the associate's eyes met Penny's. With an aloof tone she asked, "Is it for a special occasion?"

Penny started to explain the situation, but caught herself. The world's richest man had asked her to dinner tonight. He'd suggested eight o'clock at Chez Romaine, the most exclusive eatery in the city. Perhaps in the world. People reserved tables years in advance. Years! He'd even agreed to meet her there. No way did Penny want him to see the sixth-floor-walk-up, one-bedroom she shared with her two roommates. Of course, she was busting, absolutely dying to tell someone. Good news didn't seem real until you'd told at least a dozen friends. But this suspicious stranger in the dress department of Bonwit Teller would never believe her. Such an incredible story would only serve to confirm the impression that Penny was a homeless nut job, here to waste the associate's valuable time.

A fly landed on the tip of her nose, and Penny shooed it off. She willed herself to calm down. She wasn't a lunatic. And she wasn't going to run away. Smoothing the fear from her voice, she said, "I'd like to see this season's Dolce and Gabbana wrap gown, the one with the shirred waist."

As if testing her, the associate narrowed her eyes and asked, "In crepe chiffon?"

"In satin," Penny countered quickly. "With the asymmetrical hemline." All those long waits in the grocery checkout line had paid off yet again. The dress she had in mind was the one Jennifer Lopez had worn on the red carpet at last year's Oscars.

The woman scrutinized her body and asked, "Size fourteen?"

"Size ten," Penny shot back. She knew houseflies were landing in her hair, but she wore them like they were Tahitian black pearls.

The associate disappeared in search of the dress. Penny almost prayed she wouldn't come back. This was crazy. She'd never spent more than fifty dollars on a dress, and the one she'd asked to see couldn't cost less than five thousand bucks. A few keystrokes on her phone showed she had that much available on her credit limit. If she charged the dress, wore it for two hours during dinner, and returned it in the morning, she'd have a story she could tell for the rest of her life. She wouldn't allow herself to imagine anything beyond tonight. Tonight was a gamble. A longshot. Cornelius Maxwell was renowned for his gallant gestures. That was the only way to explain this. He'd seen her humiliated on the carpet in front of her furious boss, and he was trying to salvage her pride. It was chivalrous, really.

From what Penny had read in the tabloids, Cornelius Maxwell was famous for his chivalry.

Their backgrounds weren't all that different. He'd been born in Seattle to a single mother who'd worked as a nurse. His dream had always been to someday support her in high style, but his mom had been killed in the crash of a bus. When it happened Cornelius had been a graduate student at the University of Washington. A year later, he'd founded DataMicroCom in his dorm room. A year after that he'd be among the wealthiest entrepreneurs in the world.

Among the glamorous women first linked with him had been Clarissa Hind, an unlikely candidate for the New York state senate. With his financial backing and political connections, she'd won. Before her first term was complete, she'd set her sights on becoming the youngest senator the state had ever elected to Washington, D.C. It didn't hurt that the media idolized the couple: the statuesque junior senator and the maverick high-tech billionaire. Between his money and her determination, she won by a landslide. Fast-forward to three years ago, when Clarissa Hind had fulfilled not just her own dreams but the dreams of millions of American women. She'd been elected the first female president of the United States.

Throughout it all Corny Maxwell had stumped tirelessly on her behalf, always praising her, always supporting her in public and private. But the two had never married. A miscarriage was rumored. There was even gossip that she'd asked him to be her running mate, but once the election was over, they'd issued a joint press release to announce that they were dissolving their relationship. Sharing the podium at a press conference, the madam president-elect and her dashing consort had affirmed their continued affection and respect for each other, but their romance was complete.

Penny knew that such success involved hard work and sacrifice, but the paparazzi photos made it look seamless and effortless. President Hind had been her inspiration for becoming a lawyer. Dared she dream? What if Corny Maxwell was looking for a new protégée? It wasn't impossible that he saw some innate potential in her. Tonight might be an audition, and if she passed it then Penny Harrigan might find herself being groomed to take a major role on the world stage. She was about to enter the world's most exclusive sorority.

Her reverie was interrupted by a large housefly buzzing into her mouth. There, daydreaming in the dress department of Bonwit Teller, Penny began to cough and hack.

It was just as well. She was getting too carried away with her fantasy, and the future had a way of breaking your heart if you expected too much. Just look at C. Linus Maxwell, who smiled through one failed romance after another. Following Clarissa, he'd been involved with a member of the British royal family. A princess, no less, and not one of the ugly, inbred ones. She was no slouch. Princess Gwendolyn was beautiful. She was third in the line of succession, only two heartbeats away from becoming the queen. Again, it seemed like an ideal match of European aristocracy and Yankee high-tech know-how. The world waited for them to set a date. When the king had been felled by an anarchist's bullet, it was Corny who supported the weeping princess at her father's funeral. And when a freak accident, a plummeting satellite of all things, had killed the heir apparent, Gwendolyn's brother, her coronation was assured.

By all rights Corny Maxwell should be a prince living the high life in Buckingham Palace, but history repeated itself. The tycoon and the aristocrat had parted amicably.

Twice he'd sidestepped marriage to one of the most powerful women in the world.

If you believed rumors, he felt threatened by women whose status began to rival his own. The tabloids despised him. But Penny suspected, as did most people, that C. Linus Maxwell would forever be an orphan still looking for the lost mother on whom he could shower his adoration and riches.

None of Maxwell's ex-flames seemed the worse for their love affair with him. Clarissa Hind had vaulted from shy political neophyte to leader of the free world. Gwendolyn had been something of a heifer, pretty but overweight; during their relationship she'd slimmed down, and the royal had been a fashion plate ever since. Even Alouette had struggled with her own demons. The tabloids were full of her drunken, drug-addled misadventures. Maxwell had gotten her clean. His love had accomplished something that a dozen court-ordered addiction treatment programs had not.

There in Bonwit Teller, Penny's phone began to vibrate. It was Monique. No longer carping about chairs, Monique had texted, "CALL ME!" Everyone at BB&B must've heard the news by now. A part of Penny wished no one had found out. It was going to be embarrassing to be linked in people's minds with President Hind and Queen Gwendolyn and Alouette D'Ambrosia. Penny surfed her memory for the romances that had occurred in the interim. There had been the Nobel Prize–winning poetess. The heiress to a Japanese steel fortune. The newspaper chain baroness. To date, none of their feet had fit the glass slipper. Penny tried not to think about it, but what she did between this moment and midnight might determine the rest of her life.

Before she could respond to Monique's text, the sales associate had returned. A swath of red chiffon was draped over her arm. One penciled eyebrow arched skeptically, she crooned, "Here you are . . . a size ten." She motioned for Penny to follow her toward the dressing room.

President Penny Harrigan. Mrs. C. Linus Maxwell. Her mind reeled. In tomorrow's *Post* her name would be set in boldface among the celebrity names on Page Six. Tomorrow, this snooty woman would know she wasn't a liar. Everyone in the city would know her name.

Whatever the case, she'd wear this dress very, very carefully.

It was three o'clock. Dinner was at eight. There was still time to have her legs waxed, her hair done, and to telephone her parents. Maybe that would help make the situation seem more real.

Scurrying after the saleslady, Penny asked nervously, "You do offer a full money-back return policy, don't you?" And she crossed her fingers that the zipper would go all the way up.

Kwan Qxi and Esperanza were the ideal roommates with whom to share a cramped studio apartment in Jackson Heights.

Months earlier, as Penny's mom had helped her pack for the big cross-country move to New York, the wise older woman had sagely insisted, "Get a Chinese and some kind of Latin to share the lease."

Penelope's folks might sound, at times, like backward, race-baiting monsters, but they really had their daughter's best interests at heart. In a multicultural, racially diverse household, they reasoned, there was less chance of girls poaching one another's makeup. Cosmetics were expensive, and sharing them could spread deadly staph infections. This was sensible advice. Herpes and bedbugs were everywhere. Theirs were salt-of-the-earth words to live by.

Despite her parents' corn-fed good intentions, the three young roomies from a trio of widely divergent cultures had had more in common than they'd ever imagined. In no time they'd been sharing their clothes, their secrets, even their contact lenses. Not much was declared off-limits. So far, this casual familiarity hadn't been a problem.

Esperanza was a fiery high-breasted Latina whose dark eyes sparked with mischief. She often feigned exasperation over the simplest tasks—changing a lightbulb, for instance, or washing a dish—shouting, *"Ay, caramba!"* because such a patently stereotypical outburst never failed to make Penny bray with laughter. Clearly, she wasn't too uptight to poke fun at herself. The fact that Esperanza could toss a gaily embroidered sombrero onto the living room floor and then stomp a lively hat dance around the brim proved that she'd evolved far into the post–politically correct future of personal identity.

Kwan Qxi, so quiet, so implacable, Kwan Qxi was the counterpoint to the hot-tempered señorita. The Asian moved soundlessly about the crowded apartment, dusting the baseboards . . . trimming her bonsai . . . folding the trailing end of the toilet paper roll into origami surprises for the next user, in general always transforming chaos into order. Her placid face and manner acted as a balm on Penny. Her dense curtain of dark hair was a wonder compared with the frizzy, doo-wop ponytail that Penny wore most days.

In the final hours before the dinner at Chez Romaine, Penny begged both girls to contribute their best skills to perfecting her appearance. From Esperanza, she wanted eyelids painted to glow like Havana sunsets. From Kwan Qxi, she wanted hair that hung like great harvest sheaves of heavy silk. Her roommates pitched in tirelessly, coddling her like flower girls attending to an anxious bride. Together, they primped and dressed her.

Resplendent in the gown, Penny was a vision. To complete her look, Kwan Qxi had unearthed an elegant pendant. It was bright green jade carved into the shape of a dragon, with two pearls for its eyes. A true family heirloom. Esperanza dug out her own favorite earrings, each shaped like a tiny, rhinestone-encrusted piñata. Whether or not her roomies accepted her story about dinner with the world's richest man, both girls were teary-eyed at the sight of Penny's stylish transformation.

Someone buzzed from the street door. The taxicab they'd ordered had arrived and was waiting.

At the last moment, Penny held her breath and went to retrieve a small, gray plastic box she'd long ago hidden in the bathroom. The box held her diaphragm. *An ounce of prevention.* She hadn't needed it since the winter formal, her senior year as an undergraduate. Still searching the bathroom cabinets, she wondered whether such a long period of disuse might've damaged the birth control device. Would the latex have dried out and become brittle, like condoms were known to do? Might it have cracked? Or worse, would it have grown furry with mold? She snatched the gray box from the jumble in a drawer and held her breath as she opened it. The box was empty.

Tapping her foot in mock outrage, Penny confronted the

two girls in the kitchen. She held the empty box like an accusation. Printed on its label was her name, Penelope Harrigan, and the name and address of her family practitioner in Omaha. Placing the box on the counter, next to the rusted, cheese-encrusted toaster oven, she announced, "I'm going to shut off the lights and count to ten, okay?" The faces of both girls were unreadable. Neither blushed nor sheepishly evaded her gaze. "No questions asked," she said. A swipe of the wall switch plunged the room into pitch darkness. She began counting.

A faint, wet sound was followed by a gasp. A giggle.

Penny counted, ". . . eight, nine, ten." The lights blazed, revealing the open box, filled with a familiar pink shape. The diaphragm glistened, fresh and dewy, beaded with someone's healthy vaginal moisture. Clinging to it was a single tightly curled pubic hair. Penny made a mental note to rinse the thing off if she'd need to use it later in the evening.

It never failed. The taxi was late getting to Chez Romaine. Traffic had been backed up in the tunnel, and it was impossible to get a cell phone signal. That was just as well. The cabbie kept glancing in the rearview mirror, saying he was sorry. Saying she looked terrific.

Penny knew he was only being nice. For as much money as she'd spent that afternoon, Penny told herself, she'd darn well better look good. To the saleslady's chagrin the dress had fit perfectly, hugging her young body. Her new Prada shoes, another last-minute splurge, also looked amazing. But Penny was sensible enough to realize that she'd never be a ravishing beauty.

At least there were no dirty houseflies buzzing around her. That was an improvement. Anything was an improvement over living in the Midwest.

Nebraska had never been a good fit for Penny. As a young woman in Omaha, or even when she was a small girl growing up in Shippee, Penny had always felt like an outsider. For one thing, she'd looked nothing like her sturdy, pear-shaped, splay-footed mom and dad. Where they were densely freckled and ginger-haired members of the Irish Diaspora, Penny had a peaches-and-cream complexion. As pale as birch bark. They'd both thought she was crazy for kiting off to New York City.

Moments before, when she'd first climbed into the cab, she'd called Omaha to spill the big news. When her mother's voice had answered, Penny had asked, "Are you sitting down, Mom?"

"Arthur!" her mother had shouted away from the receiver. "Your daughter's on the line."

"I've got some pretty exciting news," Penny had said, barely able to contain herself. She looked to see whether the driver was watching her. She wanted him to eavesdrop.

"So do I!" her mother had exclaimed.

There was a click, and her father's voice had joined the conversation. "Your mother grew a tomato that's the spitting image of Danny Thomas."

"I'll send you a picture," her mother had promised. "It's uncanny."

Her father said, "What's your big news, cupcake?"

Penny had hesitated for effect. When she'd spoken, she'd made sure her voice was loud enough for the cabbie to overhear. "I have a date with C. Linus Maxwell."

Her parents hadn't responded, not right away.

To save time, Penny's dad drank his morning coffee while sitting on the toilet. Her mom dreamed of owning a waterbed. Every birthday they sent her a Bible with a twenty-dollar bill tucked inside. That was her parents in a nutshell.

Penny had prompted them, asking, "Do you know who Mr. Maxwell is?"

"Of course we do, sweetheart," her mother had replied flatly. "Your father and I don't live in Shippee anymore!"

Penny had waited for their shouts of joy. For their gasps of disbelief. For anything.

Finally, her father had said, "We love you no matter what, Pen-Pen. You don't have to invent wild stories to impress us." He was calling her a liar.

It was at that point the cab had gone under the river. The connection was broken. Her roommates hadn't believed her either, but they'd fussed over her, helping with her eye shadow and lip liner as if they'd been bridesmaids. Tomorrow they'd all believe her. Normally she'd never take such pains with her appearance. She hadn't primped just because Maxwell would see her. Tonight the whole world was watching. Penny would walk into that restaurant a complete nobody, but by the time dessert was served she'd be a household name. Even her hero, President Hind, would know Penny's name.

Stalled in the traffic beside her, Penny noticed two men seated in a black sedan. Like the bodyguards who had escorted Alouette D'Ambrosia, both wore tailored, navy-blue suits and mirrored sunglasses. Their stern, chiseled features betrayed no emotion. Neither turned his head in Penny's direction, but she knew from long experience that the pair of them were covertly watching her.

From her earliest memories, she'd been aware of similar strange men following her. Sometimes they'd trailed behind her in slowly moving cars or sat parked at the curb outside her grade school. Other times, they'd strolled purposefully in her wake, always at a discreet distance. There were always two, sometimes three men, each dressed in a plain dark suit and wearing mirrored sunglasses. Their hair was clipped short and neatly combed. Their wingtip shoes were highly polished, even as they'd trailed her like two-legged bloodhounds across rain-wet Cornhusker football fields and the sandy beaches of Lake Manawa.

Many a winter afternoon as the twilight faded, these chaperones would shadow her steps over lonely farm fields, weaving between the dead, wind-blasted stalks of corn as she trudged home from school. One man might lift his lapel and whisper into a microphone pinned there. Another sentinel would raise his arm and appear to signal to a helicopter that was also tracking Penny's every step. Sometimes a great slow-moving blimp would hover above her, day after day.

Ever since Penny could recall, these chaperones had haunted the edges of her life. Always in her peripheral vision. They were always in the background. Chances were excellent that tonight, they'd be among the diners at Chez Romaine, albeit seated at inferior tables, ever watchful.

She'd never felt in the least bit threatened. If anything, she felt coddled and safe. From her first inkling that she was being followed, Penny assumed the men were agents of Homeland Security. All Americans, she told herself, enjoyed this same brand of diligent supervision. So enamored was she of her bodyguards that she'd come to accept them as guardian angels. A role they'd fulfilled more than once.

One grim winter's eve she'd been picking her way homeward through acres of rotting silage. The eventide sky was dark as a bruise. The chill air smelled heavy and ominous with decay. In a twinkling, a killer funnel cloud descended, churning the landscape into a dirty froth of fertile topsoil and airborne dairy cattle. Razor-sharp farm implements clattered around her on all sides. Fist-size chunks of hail pelted her young scalp.

Just as Penny thought she'd be killed, some force had knocked her facedown in the furrows and a gentle, insistent weight pressed itself upon her body. The tornado spent its fury in a moment. The weight lifted, and she could recognize it as one of the anonymous watchers. His pin-striped suit soiled with mud, he removed himself from her backside and walked away without accepting a word of thanks. More than just a passive guardian, he had been a hero. This stranger had saved her life.

Years later, when Penny was in college, a beer-saturated Zeta Delt had dragged her down some stairs into a dirt-floored cellar. It was during a high-spirited Pledge Week mixer. In retrospect, she recognized that she might've promised the young man more than she was willing to deliver. Frustrated, he had thrown her to the ground and straddled her, a knee planted on either side of her struggling torso. His muscular hands began the savage task of shredding her brightly flowered afternoon frock. He fumbled with the zipper of his chinos, producing an angry red erection. Dire as this situation seemed, Penny remained a lucky girl.

Thank goodness for the agents of Homeland Security, Penny thought, as a gray flannel–suited stranger stepped from the shadows near the cellar walls. He delivered her attacker a violent karate chop to the windpipe. With the would-be rapist gasping, Penny had raced away to safety.

Even after she'd said good-bye to her home state, the guardian angels had kept tabs on her. In the Big Apple, she saw them, the neon lights glinting off their sunglasses as they watched over her from a discreet distance. At Bonwit Teller. Even at BB&B they wore their sunglasses indoors, and still they guarded her. As the agents of Homeland Security, she assumed, they guarded all Americans. All of the time.

———

While she'd been lost in thought, traffic had begun to thaw. Even now her cab was pulling to the curb in front of the Chez Romaine canopy. A valet stepped forward to open her door. Penny paid the cabbie and took a deep breath. She checked the time on her phone. Fifteen minutes late.

She did a last-second check of her dress and arms. No flies.

In the pages of the *National Enquirer*, Jennifer Lopez or Salma Hayek never walked a red carpet without an escort. Penny Harrigan had no choice. There was no sign of Climax-Well. A cadre of photographers was corralled behind a velvet rope, but they didn't give her a second glance. None of them snapped her picture. No one with a microphone stepped up to say how nice she looked and ask about her dress. Another car arrived at the curb, the valet opened another door, and she had no choice except to proceed through the restaurant's gilded entrance, alone.

In the foyer, she waited for the maître d' to notice her. He did not. No one noticed her. Elegantly dressed men and women lingered, waiting for their cars to arrive or to be seated. The din of laughter and conversation made her feel even more invisible, if that was possible. Here, her dress was barely good enough. Her jewelry drew bemused stares. The same way she'd wanted to run from the haughty saleslady at Bonwit Teller, Penny again longed to turn and flee. She'd wrap the gorgeous red gown in its original tissue paper and take it back tomorrow. Men like Maxwell didn't date girls like her.

Still, something nagged at her. She wished she'd never bragged about this date. Her roommates . . . her parents . . . even the taxi driver had thought she was a liar. She had to prove she wasn't. Even if one gossip columnist saw her with Corny Maxwell or a shutterbug snapped their picture together, she'd be vindicated. This thought pushed her the length of the foyer, toward the door to the main dining room. There, a flight of carpeted steps led downward. Whoever entered would draw every eye in the vast, crowded space.

Standing on the top step Penny felt as if she were on the edge of a high cliff. Ahead of her beckoned the future. Behind her, the rich and powerful were already bottlenecked, backing up like gridlocked traffic in the streets. Someone cleared his throat loudly. Below her, the room was packed. Every table was occupied. A mezzanine held even more watchful diners. Where Penny found herself, on the stairs, was like a stage, visible from every seat.

In the center of the room, one man sat alone. His blond hair caught the light from the chandelier. Open on his table was a small notebook, and he was studiously jotting notes in it with a silver pen.

A stranger's breath touched Penny's ear. An officious voice behind her whispered, "Pardon me. Young lady?" The speaker sniffed loudly.

Everyone in the restaurant was watching the lone man scribbling, but watching in that discreet New Yorker way: ogling him over the tops of their menus. Spying on his reflection in the silver blades of their butter knives.

More insistently, the officious voice at Penny's shoulder whispered, "We must keep this space open." He said, "I must ask you to step aside."

Frozen, Penny willed the solitary diner to look up and see her. To see how pretty she looked. The crowd forming behind her grumbled, restless. She couldn't move. The doorman, the parking valet, someone would have to lift her and carry her out like a sack of potatoes.

At last, the man writing in his notebook looked up. His eyes met Penny's. Every head in the cavernous room turned to follow his gaze. The man stood, and the noise of so many people dwindled. As if a curtain were rising at the opera, every voice fell silent.

Without breaking eye contact, the man crossed to the bottom of the stairs and began to climb toward her. Still two steps down, he stopped and offered his hand. As she had once been below him on the office carpet, reaching up, now he was beneath her.

She reached out. His fingers felt as cold as she remembered.

Just as she'd seen in the *National Enquirer,* C. Linus Maxwell escorted her. Just as he'd escorted so many exquisite women. Down the remaining steps. Across the hushed room. He pulled out her chair and seated her. He took his own seat and closed his notebook. Only then did the voices that surrounded them begin to rise.

"Thank you for joining me," he said. "You look lovely."

And for once Penny actually believed she might.

In the next instant, his hand lashed out. As if to slap her face, he leaned forward, swinging his arm so fast it blurred. She winced.

When she opened her eyes, his fist filled her vision, huge, hanging there, his knuckles so close they almost touched the tip of her nose.

"I'm sorry if I scared you," he said, "but I think I caught him." Opening his fingers, Corny Maxwell showed her the crushed little corpse of a black housefly.

The next morning, Penny was standing outside the locked doors of Bonwit Teller for a half hour before they opened. She couldn't afford even a day's credit card interest on what the evening gown had cost. Even if this made her late for work, she had to return the dress right away.

The fairy tales never showed Cinderella getting up at dawn to return her gown and her shoes, terrified that some wary salesclerk would notice a flaw and refuse to credit her account with a full refund.

Despite the extraordinary food and wine, dinner had been less than magical. The stares had never let up. It was impossible to relax and have fun in a fishbowl. Maxwell wasn't the problem. He'd been attentive, almost too attentive, hanging on her every word. Several times, he'd even opened his notebook and written a few words in a quick, spidery shorthand, as if he were taking dictation. It felt less like a romantic tryst than a pleasant job interview. He'd volunteered almost no information about himself, nothing she didn't already know from gossip columns. In her nervousness, Penny had chattered without taking a breath. Desperate to fill any possible silence, she'd told him about her parents, Myrtle and Arthur, and their suburban life. She'd reminisced about the long hours in law school. She'd rambled on about the love of her life, her Scotch terrier, Dimples, and how he'd died the year previous.

Throughout her monologue, Maxwell had smiled calmly. Thank goodness the waiters had occasionally arrived, giving her a moment to shut up and catch her breath.

"If madam will allow . . . ," a waiter said with a white-gloved flourish of his hand, "the kobashira sushi is a house specialty."

Penny smiled winningly. "That sounds delish."

Max shot her a questioning look. "You do know that's raw aoyagi scallops, don't you?"

She didn't. In fact, Maxwell might well have just saved her life. Unknown to him she had a severe shellfish allergy. One succulent bite and she would've slumped to the floor, swollen and lifeless. Penny's alarm must've shown on her face, because he'd immediately revised her order, saying, "The lady will have the Chicken Divan."

Thank God that someone was paying attention. Her runaway mouth resumed its nervous monologue.

She knew she sounded pathetic. Still, Penny couldn't stop herself. No one here had ever expressed any interest in her, not in New York City. She'd gone from being her parents' little miracle to being miserable and invisible. Most nights she'd force herself to walk around the streets until the neighborhood fell quiet and she felt exhausted enough to go to bed. She'd wander around the Upper East Side, alone except for the doormen who stood behind glass in the elegant lobby of each building and watched her pass. These stately town houses and sumptuous co-op apartments, these were what everyone aspired to. In some way she was trying to train herself to want them also. The truth was: She didn't. Penny only pretended to want the jewelry in the windows at Cartier and the furs at Bloomingdale's.

She didn't want merely the trappings of success. Penny craved actual power. Even to her own ears she sounded *crazy* ambitious.

Above all, Penny didn't want what other women professed to want. They seemed possessed, the way they swarmed to the same mundane things. And that worried her; she felt shut out of some hive. If she didn't crave the correct movie heartthrobs and scented candles, she worried that something was horribly wrong with her.

Daily, she caught sight of lady attorneys and execs furiously crunching numbers and barking demands into phones. None seemed to possess some progressive enlightenment. Theirs no longer seemed like the road less taken. Penny sought a career path beyond the knee-jerk strictures of gender identity politics.

Over the dessert course, Penny Harrigan admitted that she didn't know what she wanted.

Becoming a lawyer wasn't her life's dream. As a teenager in high school she'd been told by everyone—her parents, her teachers, her minister—that a person needed a long-term goal and a plan for achieving it. Everyone said she needed to devote her life to something. She'd chosen a career in law as blithely as if she'd plucked the vocation, unseen, from a hat. President Hind notwithstanding, being an attorney was no more appealing to Penny than wearing a sable coat and walking two afghan hounds in diamond collars to hear Verdi at the Met. No, to be honest Penny said she didn't know what she wanted, but she knew something . . . soon, some glorious destiny would reveal itself to her.

Maxwell hadn't asked about any of this, but he listened intently. He watched as if he were memorizing her. At one point, between the appetizers and the salad, he took out the small notebook in which he'd been jotting notes when she arrived. He opened it to a blank page. He removed the cap from a silver fountain pen and began to write, seemingly transcribing her fears. Penny couldn't tell for certain, because his handwriting was cramped, almost microscopic. Scribbling continuously, he was either remarkably rude, or Maxwell was enormously empathetic and caring.

Having her words recorded made her feel self-conscious, but it couldn't silence the overflow of her pent-up anxiety. She'd never expressed this to anyone, but her life seemed to have stalled. After twenty-five years of getting good grades and behaving politely, she'd reached a terrifying dead end. The full extent of her potential. Even as she talked Penny was aware that she'd most likely never see this man again. That made him a safe confessor.

Her relief was evident. Under his rapt gaze Penny glowed. She preened. Emboldened by his attention, she shook her head to make the piñata-shaped earrings dance. She lifted one hand to her bosom, trailing her fingertips over the sinuous curves of the jade dragon. Both accessories reminded her how blessed she was with girlfriends.

Max's blue eyes seemed fascinated by her every gesture. He

smiled but didn't interrupt. His eyes never left hers, but his hand continued to write.

He almost looked in love. This was more than infatuation. More than love at first sight. Maxwell seemed enchanted by the sound of her voice. With his entire body, he seemed to lean forward with yearning. Something in his expression said that he'd been searching for her his entire life.

Penny wanted this kind of attention from the world. She wanted people everywhere to know her name and to love her. There, she'd admitted it aloud. But she couldn't do anything that would justify such massive public acclaim. She just needed a mentor, a teacher, someone to discover her.

Standing outside the locked department store doors, Penny held the garment bag high, lest it drag on the sidewalk. She recalled each delicious course of the meal she hadn't enjoyed. She'd been too afraid of dropping food into her lap. One itty-bitty stain, and she'd spend the next five years paying for her own sloppiness. When the store's doorman turned the locks she rushed straight to the department where she'd bought the gown.

Waiting at the register was the saleslady who'd helped her less than twenty-four hours before.

Offering the garment bag, her voice as firm as she could make it, Penny said, "I'd like to return this."

The saleslady took the bag by the hanger. Laying it on the counter, she unzipped it and inspected the red satin folds.

"When I got home I tried it on," Penny said. With one hand she made what she hoped was a dismissive gesture. "It isn't at all what I had in mind."

The saleslady tossed and smoothed the skirt, peering at the seams, the hem. She asked, "So you didn't actually wear it?"

"No," Penny replied. She held her breath, terrified that a snagged stitch or perspiration stain would expose her as a liar.

The unsmiling woman pressed, "Not even for a quick dinner?"

Penny was certain the woman had found a wine stain. A smudge of chocolate mousse. Or she'd smelled perfume or cigarette smoke in the fabric. It might've been Penny's imagination, but suddenly the sales floor seemed crowded with shoppers, sales associates, even a security guard, all of them eavesdropping on her interaction. "No," Penny insisted. Now she was sweating.

"Not at Chez Romaine?"

"No," Penny squeaked.

The saleslady fixed her with a stern look and said, "I need to show you something." Tucking the dress back inside its garment bag, she reached below the counter and brought out something. It was a newspaper: today's *New York Post*. There on the front page was the headline: "Nerd Prince Plucks New Cinderella from Obscurity."

And next to those huge words was a color picture of Penny sitting elbow-to-elbow with Maxwell. There was no denying it: She was wearing the dress.

"If you don't mind me saying so, miss," the saleslady said, her expression damning, "this is unacceptable!"

Penny was so, so busted. In her head she did a quick calculation. Based on the price and her current credit card interest rate, she'd have the dress paid for sometime around her fortieth birthday.

"For this kind of publicity," the woman admonished, "the people at Dolce and Gabbana ought to be *paying you* to wear their clothes." Leaning forward like a conspirator, she said, "Prada. Fendi. Hermès. They'd die for this much ink." She winked. "Let me contact a few people on your behalf. If you're going to be accompanying Mr. Maxwell, you could earn a fortune by promoting certain designers."

That might be a problem. Maxwell had asked whether he could call her, but in Penny's experience that was strictly a courtesy. It never guaranteed a second date. They hadn't made definite plans. She didn't say it now, but she might never see him again.

Looking around the dress department, Penny saw that strangers were gravitating toward them. Men. Women. Some wearing uniforms. Some in fur coats. Everyone was clutching the same morning edition of the *Post*. And they were all beaming at her.

This saleslady who'd been so unfriendly only the day before, now her face broke into a shy smile. Her eyes sparkling and alive, she sighed. Placing one hand flat against her chest as if to calm a rapidly beating heart, she said, "Please forgive my unprofessional behavior, but . . ."

Even under the woman's heavy makeup, Penny could see that she was blushing.

Offering the day's *Post*, she asked, "Would you autograph your picture for my daughter?"

C. Linus Maxwell didn't call. Not the next day. Nor the day after. A week went by.

Penny went to work and shrugged off Monique's excited interrogation about Chez Romaine.

After work, Penny went to the Jackson Heights branch of Chase Manhattan and rented a safe-deposit box. It required two keys to open. She watched as the bank clerk inserted his key and turned it. She used her own key, and he left her to open the metal box in the privacy of a small room. Once he'd taken leave, Penny picked something small and pink from her handbag and placed it in the box. Quickly, she locked it and summoned the clerk. Her share-and-share-alike roommates wouldn't get another chance to borrow her diaphragm.

Back at the apartment, she returned the earrings and necklace. Every time her phone chimed with a call or text, she caught Kwan Qxi and Esperanza watching her expectantly. But every time the message was from her mom or dad. Or it was the sales associate at Bonwit Teller announcing that she'd scored some dazzling Alexander McQueen gown or pair of Stella McCartney heels for Penny's next night as Cinderella.

In the checkout line at the grocery store, she stood waiting to buy her ice cream, trying to ignore the tabloid headlines that glared out at her. "Cinderella Gets the Brush-Off!" Another front page showed a huge picture of her buying ice cream, under the headline, "Rejected Cinderella Stuffing Herself!" It was surreal. Here she was buying butter brickle ice cream while she looked at a photo of herself, taken the day before, buying ice cream. To make matters worse, in the more recent photos she already looked fatter! Everyone in the store recognized her and stood ready to pat her on the shoulder and console her. The cashier waved her through without paying, telling her, "No charge, honey." To be an object of pity in New York—the city without pity—that's how far she had fallen.

A few days later she could barely get her pants to button. Too much free comfort food. That's why she was taken aback when Tad asked her to lunch at the Russian Tea Room. There, seated at an intimate corner booth in that swank setting, he made her laugh with his rollicking stories about Yale panty raids. Tad recited his curriculum vitae in its entirety, obviously insecure about how he'd compare with her recent billionaire beau. He boasted about rowing as captain for the Yale team. As proof, he wore a bright green Yale sweatshirt. Boring as he was, Penny was still pathetically grateful. Tad's prattle and bluster distracted her from her current public humiliation and crushing woes. Tad was passably handsome—better looking than bland, blond Max—and there was the possibility that a roving *Post* photojournalist would snap a pic of the pair of them and run it under the heading, "Cinderella Bounces Back!"

To her own surprise, Penny found herself holding Tad's hand across the white linen tablecloth. She'd only wanted to give onlookers the impression that she and Tad were canoodling, but . . . something magical was happening. Vibes. Mojo. Juju. Her fingers and his were already entwined, deeply. She wondered whether she could get to the bank, to access her safety-deposit box before closing time.

Penny wasn't a prude. She wasn't some prim, tongue-clucking schoolmarm type. To her, intimacy outside of marriage wasn't sinful . . . she'd simply never seen the margin in casual sex. During her coursework in gender studies she'd learned that roughly 30 percent of women are entirely nonorgasmic, and that seemed to be the case with her. Fortunately, there were other pleasures in life. Salsa music, for example. Ice cream. Tom Berenger movies. It made little sense to court herpes, venereal warts, viral hepatitis, HIV, and unwanted pregnancy in pursuit of unattainable sexual fulfillment.

Nonetheless, Tad's fingers smelled so good. She'd been wrong about him. So wrong. The ambitious young lawyer had wanted her, not Monique. His eyes said as much. Maybe she was also wrong about sex. With the right guy, maybe she could find pulse-pounding release.

"Penny," he stammered.

"Yes." She swallowed. To calm herself, she rested her gaze demurely on the basket of cheesy bread sticks. When she dared look back at him, she repeated, "Yes, Tad?"

His grip tightened. *The Tadpole.* Their simple lunch was becoming everything that her fabled dinner at Chez Romaine had not been: passionate . . . sultry . . . freighted with erotic suggestion.

Stashed deep in her handbag, Penny's phone chimed. The sound caught her off guard.

"Penny," Tad continued, "I've always loved . . ."

Her phone chimed again. Penny tried to ignore it. Her whole body stiffened.

Tad rallied his courage. "If you're no longer dating . . ." His lips puckered and he leaned close. Closer. She could smell the delicious Veal Prince Orloff on his breath.

Penny dodged the kiss. The incoming call was impossible to ignore. "Sorry," she quipped as she retrieved the phone.

According to the ringtone it was Max.

It was unfair. As Penny tried to tell people, C. Linus Maxwell was more than an Internet whiz kid. So much more! He ran a multinational group of corporations that led the world in computer networking, satellite communications, and banking. Adamantly, she would describe to Monique how Maxwell's enterprises employed more than a million people and served hundreds of millions. Every year his charitable foundation alone poured a billion dollars into each of a dozen high-profile causes, fighting hunger, curing disease, promoting women's rights. As President Hind could attest, gender equality was a dream close to Maxwell's heart. He ran schools in Pakistan and Afghanistan, where young girls could strive toward a brighter future. He financed the political campaigns that brought female leaders into the highest positions of every nation.

That, Penny told everyone, all of that pride and altruism made Maxwell so much more than a wealthy nerd.

What she told herself was that she enjoyed being with him.

It was a hard sell. Especially to herself.

At the office, Monique asked, "Omaha girl, are you wearing a diaphragm?" She gave her head a sassy swivel, making her beaded braids rattle. Without waiting for an answer, she said, "Because if you are—take it out! Burn it! Flush your birth control down the toilet and *let that man knock you up!*"

It was none of Monique's business, but after a month of dating, Penny still hadn't gone to bed with him. Late at night, her parents would call. Penny suspected that they were hoping to catch her in flagrante with Maxwell. Sleepily, she'd answer, "What time is it?"

On the telephone, long-distance, her mother shouted, "How can you not love him? He's so rich!"

On the extension, her father added, "*Pretend to love him!*"

"Your dad and I have never met Maxwell," her mother gushed, "but we already think of him as family."

Penny hung up. She unplugged the phone and went back to sleep. She didn't want to be a pushover. She'd seen too many of her sorority sisters walk down the aisle. Too many of those marriages had devolved into a grim lifetime of mandatory "date nights." Like life sentences in a prison where the conjugal visits were few and far between. Rich or poor, she and Maxwell were still two people who needed the mutual passion to share a lifetime together.

The fact never left her mind: None of his famous romances had lasted longer than 136 days. That couldn't be by accident. They had all lasted exactly 136 days.

And it wasn't as if Maxwell had pressured her for sex, either. He was so detached, so pleasant, but he was so distant that Penny wondered whether Alouette D'Ambrosia had been lying when she'd claimed he was the greatest lover she had ever known. The French beauty must've been with better men, hotly passionate men. Maxwell wasn't exactly aggressive. He did little more than watch and listen and jot notes in his little book. At yachting parties, women whom Penny didn't even know glared at her. Pencil-thin supermodels sneered at Penny's normal hips. They wagged their high-cheekboned heads in disbelief. The men leered at her. They assumed she had some erotic skill that bewitched Maxwell. Their lecherous stares suggested the scenes of unbridled sodomy and expert fellatio they envisioned. How funny it would be to tell them all that the world's richest man had taken her skiing in Bern and to bullfights in Madrid, but he'd never taken her to bed.

Penny wasn't a virgin, not when she and Maxwell had first met. She'd had sex with boys in college, a few. But only one at a time. *Only* boys. And *never* from behind! She wasn't a pervert, and she wasn't a slut. Her boyfriends were mostly Sigma Chis who played at being gentlemen by opening car doors for her. They'd brought icy orchid corsages and had pinned them to her dress with nervous fingers. In her experience every man thought he was a natural dancer, and every one thought he was good in bed. The truth was that most men only knew one dance step—usually the pogo—and between the sheets they were like a monkey in a nature film poking at an anthill with a stick.

She'd had intercourse, but she'd never had an orgasm. Not an *orgasm*-orgasm, not the kind of earth-moving orgasm that made your teeth go numb, the kind she'd always read about in *Cosmopolitan*.

No, when Penny graduated from law school she wasn't a virgin, but neither was she looking to settle down.

———————

In Paris, at an exclusive dinner party on the top deck of the Eiffel Tower, Penny had her chance to meet Alouette D'Ambrosia in person. With a private supersonic jet at their constant disposal, Paris seemed no farther away than midtown Manhattan. Maxwell could zip her almost anywhere in the world for a quiet supper, then return her to her squalid apartment in Jackson Heights by midnight. Seeing the same troop of resentful and lustful faces of the international jet set night after night, at parties and movie premieres, made the world seem even smaller. Even at the top of the Eiffel Tower, with glittering Paris at her feet, Penny sipped a glass of champagne, too timid to engage with other movers and shakers. The night air was warm, but Penny felt a chill down her spine, exposed by the plunging back of her Vera Wang gown. Maxwell, usually so attentive, had been called away, and she sensed hostile eyes upon her. Looking around, she wasn't wrong. Like twin lasers, they flashed from across the tower's open terrace. It was the movie star, the winner of four Academy Awards. She'd been nominated this year, and she was the front-runner to win a fifth Oscar in a few weeks. Here was the woman Penny had seen fractured in the tiny screens of countless cell phones. Now there was only one of her, and she loomed huge.

A confrontation was imminent and every guest was gleefully watching as Alouette strode closer. Circling, she was clearly stalking her prey. The actress moved like a panther in a curve-hugging black leather catsuit. Her lovely nostrils flared. Teeth bared, she was seething.

The Bonwit Teller saleslady had done as she promised and introduced Penny to haute couture designers who dressed her to look fabulous, but compared to this approaching man-eating predator she felt like a bag lady. As always, she fought the urge to flee the battlefield. If only Maxwell would return. Monique would know how to fight off a furious Amazon. Jennifer Lopez or Penelope Cruz would be ready to kick some French ass. All Penny could think to do was turn her back and brace herself for the impending impact.

"Little mouse," a voice said. The heavily accented voice, recognizable from so many films.

The sharp points of long fingernails clutched Penny's shoulder and slowly pulled, turning her to face the speaker. Those impossibly soigné features were now distorted with hatred.

"Are you frightened, little mouse?" Alouette D'Ambrosia thrust her chin forward. "You should be very frightened. You are in grave danger."

Penny tightened her grip on her glass of champagne. If push came to shove, she'd throw the sweet, sparkling wine in the actress's eyes. Then run like heck.

"Whatever you do . . . ," Alouette said. As she wagged a long manicured finger in Penny's face, she warned, "Do not sleep with Max. You must *never* have sex with Maxwell."

The crowd was visibly disappointed as the film star turned away. As she slinked across the room people stepped aside. Before anyone spoke, she'd stridden into an elevator and disappeared.

It was clear to Penny that Alouette was wildly jealous. This French goddess was still very much in love. Penny laughed to herself. She, plain Penny Harrigan, was the envy of the world's most enticing sex symbol. In another minute Maxwell was back and standing beside her. As usual, he was scrawling notes in his little book. He could be such a space cadet.

When Penny didn't speak, he asked her, "Are you okay?"

She described the scene he'd missed. How Alouette had approached her. How the actress had threatened her.

A strange look crossed Maxwell's bland face. It was something Penny had never seen, anger mixed with another emotion. Possibly love. The warm wind tousled his blond hair.

Whatever it was, she couldn't resist. Whether it was physical attraction or the prospect of enraging Alouette, Penny couldn't resist the idea of sleeping with Max. She took his hand in hers. "Let's not fly back tonight." She brought the cold hand to her lips and kissed it, adding, "Let's stay over and go back to New York in the morning."

In bed, Maxwell's touch was so exact it was almost clinical. The way he used his fingers, they were almost calipers, there only to measure her. Like a doctor or a scientist, his fingertips gripped her as if he was testing her blood pressure. Often he'd pause midcaress, lean over to reach the bedside table, and scribble a note in his mysterious, spidery shorthand.

That first night in Paris, Penny found herself slightly drunk, naked in his bed while he knelt between her spread legs.

The bedside table held a strange combination of objects. There were faceted crystal bottles, like perfume bottles, each holding a different vivid color of liquid. They looked like massive rubies, topaz, and emeralds. They reminded Penny of the huge sapphire she'd seen on the neck of Alouette D'Ambrosia. Among these colorful bottles were plain glass beakers and test tubes of the same sort Penny had always associated with high school chemistry classes. There was a small cardboard box, like for facial tissues, but it appeared to be full of latex gloves, and one sprouted from the top, ready for the plucking. One flask held an assortment of wrapped condoms. Maxwell's notebook was tucked among these items. Of course it was. That notebook was almost an appendage. The final object Penny could identify was a small digital recording device, something a busy executive might dictate his thoughts into. The nearest item was a bottle of champagne.

Maxwell was already erect, but he hardly seemed aware of his aroused state. Only inches away from Penny's nakedness, he was leaning half off the bed. First he uncorked the bottle of champagne and poured some into a beaker. It fizzed pink. Pink champagne. He handed the beaker to Penny. Lifting the bottle, he made a toast: "To innovation and progress." They each drank from their respective bubbly.

"Don't guzzle all of it, my dear." Maxwell snapped his fingers to indicate he wanted the beaker back. He poured in a smidgen more champagne and set the bottle aside. With great deliberation, he picked among the crystal flasks. From some he poured dribs and drabs of richly colored syrup into the beaker of pink wine. He paged forward and back in his notebook as if consulting a coded recipe.

As he worked intently, Maxwell mused, "People are so misguided. They will devote themselves to the study of everything except what is of most importance." His lips curled into a wry grin. "I have studied the infinitely finer points of the sensual realm. I've learned from physicians and anatomists. I've dissected many cadavers, both male and female, to understand the mechanics of pleasure."

Sloshing the beaker to thoroughly mix its contents, Maxwell gave Penny a frowning look and asked, "Have you ever enjoyed an orgasm?"

"Of course," Penny answered quickly. Too quickly. It was a lie, and it sounded like a lie.

Maxwell smirked. He continued, "I've apprenticed myself to the world's most accomplished sex experts." There was no boasting in his words, just a determined resoluteness. "I've studied with tantric shamans in Morocco. I devoted myself to mastering the kundalini energy. To understand the coefficient of friction between different types of skin, I consulted the world's leading organic chemists."

Penny let her eyes roam over his naked body. She knew from the *National Enquirer* that he was forty-nine years old. He was old enough to be her father, but his lean frame looked almost insectlike. Each limb was as defined and well proportioned as that of an ant or a hornet. His pale, hairless skin was as perfectly tailored as his clothing, without a wrinkle or sag visible. She searched his shoulders and hands for freckles or moles but found none. The way he talked about his sexual quest, she expected to find his nipples pierced. His torso busy with tattoos or the scars of consensual torture games. But there was no such evidence. This was a child's pristine skin stretched to cover the musculature of a man's body.

"My own secret recipe," he said, offering the beaker for Penny to sniff. The wine, mixed with mysterious extras.

It bubbled less, but it still looked like pink champagne. It smelled sweetly delicious. Like strawberries. Penny peered doubtfully at the full beaker and said, "You want me to drink this?"

"Not exactly," Maxwell said. From a drawer in the table he produced something that looked like a squeeze toy. It was an ovoid ball made of soft red rubber, roughly the size of a grapefruit. One end of the ball sprouted a long, white nozzle of some sort. "A vaginal syringe," Maxwell said, holding it up for her inspection. He demonstrated how the nozzle unscrewed from the ball, revealing a threaded hole in the rubber. Into this hole he poured the pink champagne concoction. As he screwed the nozzle back into place, Penny realized what he had in mind.

"It's a douche?" she asked nervously.

Max nodded.

Penny squirmed uneasily. "You don't think I'm clean?"

Maxwell stretched his hands into latex gloves, saying, "You don't want to get this stuff on your skin."

She didn't like the sound of that. Wasn't he planning to squirt this pink stuff inside of her?

"Don't worry." He chuckled softly. "It's just a very mild neural stimulant and euphoric. You'll love it." He rubbed the thin nozzle between her legs.

The nozzle slipped deep into her. "Enjoy yourself," he said, and began to compress the rubber ball. The syringe.

Penny could feel the cold, effervescent bubbly filling her.

With his free hand, Maxwell held her in place, stroking her belly in slow circles. His entire body was as chilled and hard as his fingers.

When the bulb was empty Maxwell withdrew it. He used a soft, clean towel to wipe away the pink trickle that escaped her. "Good girl," he told her. "Just hold it inside for a minute." He was biting the plastic wrapper off a condom and rolling it down his erection. "You're doing very well."

Penny tried not to imagine dignified President Hind subjecting herself to a similar magic champagne cleansing.

Still kneeling between her spread knees, he said, "I love you because you're so average."

If that was a compliment, Penny had heard better.

"Please don't be hurt," he said softly. "Look at yourself. You have a textbook vagina. Your labia majora are exactly symmetrical. Your perianal ridge is magnificent. Your frenulum clitoridis and fourchette . . ." He seemed at a loss for words, pressing a hand to his heart and sighing deeply. "Biologically speaking, men treasure such uniformity. The proportions of your genitalia are ideal."

Under his gaze, Penny felt less like a woman than like a science experiment. A guinea pig or laboratory rat.

It didn't help that Maxwell added, "Women in your age

group and economic stratum are the target consumers for most of the world's manufactured goods."

Something, perhaps the douche, made Penny's teeth feel as if they were dissolving in her mouth. The bones in her legs were melting.

"This will heighten your amusement." He spread his knees, forcing her legs farther apart. His erection reared over her, already sleeved in one condom. Rolling a second condom over the first, Maxwell spoke idly.

As he spoke, he again eyed the array of sparkling bottles on the bedside table. Selecting one, he put a few drops of something clear into the palm of his hand. To this he added a few drops from a second and third bottle. "The pH of your skin is slightly acid. I'm mixing exactly the right lubricant for your erotic needs."

He slowly wiped the oily handful around her vulva, careful not to dip his fingers too far inside. The last of it he spread on his erect sex organ.

Penny giggled, limp as a rag doll.

From the table he plucked something. It was the mini digital recorder. Pressing a button, he said, "If you don't mind, I'd like to record our session for my research." A tiny red light glowed on the device. Dictating into it, Maxwell said, "Based on the test subject's somewhat *playful* behavior, it's safe to say the vaginal wash is having its full effect."

And now he mounted her, thrusting his hardness against the pressure of the fluid. He was driving it higher into her. Stirring and churning the mixture.

Penny gasped. She cried out, as much from discomfort as pleasure. She felt wetness escape her and soak into the bedclothes. She felt the liquid expanding inside her. In vain she squirmed, trying to escape the sensation. As the pleasure grew, seizing control of her, Penny understood why Alouette had

49

been so bitter and enraged. Whatever the pink fluid consisted of, Maxwell's pumping buttocks and probing cock seemed to force it into her bloodstream. Gradually her legs felt so relaxed she would swear they were floating. The feeling spread to her arms. Her breasts seemed to swell. Her mind stretched to accommodate a joy she'd never known existed.

She was only vaguely aware of Maxwell. While his hips bucked slowly into her, his bland stare observed the reactions on her face. He licked his fingers and softly tweaked her nipples, as focused as a safecracker. Without missing a thrust, he lifted the pen and scribbled a note in his book.

He petted her inner thighs and clitoris. With his hips, he made infinitesimal adjustments in the angle and speed of his thrusts. Gauging her reaction, he calibrated the depth of each stroke. Addressing the recorder, he said, "The test subject's pelvic floor has relaxed in extremis." He reached one latex-gloved hand around to the small of her back, brailling her spine until he found what he was seeking. On that one small spot, his fingertips intensified their massaging.

"Just so you understand what's happening," Maxwell explained, "I'm using two fingers to compress your anterior Hibbert artery. It's a simple tantric technique a yogi in Sri Lanka was kind enough to teach me." He talked like a tour guide, chatty and slightly patronizing. "By restricting the deeper blood flow to your groin, I'm numbing your clitoris." Whatever he was doing, he didn't need to look. His fingers knew their task. His eyes continued to hold hers.

"Your feedback is very important to this process," Maxwell said. His voice sounded fuzzy, but Penny tried to concentrate. "Do you understand?" he asked. "Nod your head if you understand."

Penny nodded.

"You must ready yourself. Do not be frightened." He said,

"Do not be afraid of crying out. You must let the pleasure pass through you." He leveled his eyes gravely. "If you hinder the flow of satisfaction, it could kill you."

Penny nodded. She was barely in the world. As pleasure drowned her, there was no past and no future. Nothing existed outside of this moment of peaking sensations. There was no world other than the energy surging in her body.

"In a moment, when I release the pressure, the blood will rush to your uris major, and you'll experience more satisfaction than you ever dreamed was possible." With that warning, Penny felt the fingertips retreat from her spine. Something, something bright and enormous flared within her.

"Cry out!" commanded Maxwell. "Don't contain your ecstasy. Don't be a prudish fool, Penny. Cry out!"

But Penny could not. A long scream of obscenities built in her throat, but she kept her teeth clenched. Her limbs thrashed and twitched beyond her control. A torrent of animal gibberish and profanities threatened to boil out of her mouth, and the digital recorder was running. She choked back the howls. A cold hand touched the side of her neck and lingered there.

Maxwell announced, "For the record, the subject's pulse is rapid and irregular." He was speaking for the recorder. "Her respiration is extremely shallow, and all signs would indicate that she is entering an erotically induced coma."

Penny sensed that she was dying. Her view of him frosted and grew dark around the edges.

Maxwell reached for something on the bedside table. With the latex-gloved pad of his thumb he lifted one of her drooping eyelids and shined a bright penlight into her iris. "Pupil dilation is sluggish," he announced. Throughout this entire ordeal his hips continued to pump, steadily planting and withdrawing his steely erection.

"Why should sex be any different?" ranted Max. "Everything—

films, music, painting—is calculated to manipulate and excite us."
He licked two fingers and scissored them against Penny, flickering fast touches against her engorged lady-parts. Such small tricks flooded Penny with more pleasure, wiping her mind clean. Whatever she'd been thinking, it was instantly forgotten. "Drugs are designed to be as effective as possible," he said. "Why shouldn't we devote the same attention to the details of sex?"

Penny shook like a criminal being electrocuted. Her limbs jangled, and her flesh jiggled like a nervous puppet. Her tongue jutted from her mouth and lapped at the air.

"Stay with me," he coached sternly. "You're going into shock."

Penny felt something rest against her forehead.

"The subject's temperature is falling . . . ninety-eight-point-five degrees. Ninety-seven-point-five . . ." It was a temporal thermometer. A cold mouth pressed itself over hers. These were Maxwell's lips. His lukewarm breath filled her throat and inflated her lungs. "The subject has stopped breathing," he announced. His lungs once more filled her lungs. Just as his penis was filling her. "I am attempting to resuscitate the test subject." Throughout all of this, Penny was dimly aware that he was still fucking her with the same cadence of long, smooth strokes. He was monitoring the pulse in her neck. "Use my breath," he demanded. "Use the breath I'm putting inside you to cry out. Express your exaltation." In a flat, expressionless voice he said, "Do not die while you have so much pleasure still awaiting you. . . ."

Now Penny knew why the tabloids called him "Climax-Well."

That would be the first and final time Penny would see him naked. There was plenty of sex to come, too much perhaps, but none of it would involve Maxwell's sexual organs.

Once Maxwell had excused himself to use the bathroom, Penny rewound the recorder and tried to find her outcry. To erase it. The filth that had poured from her mouth was totally degrading. To her own ears she sounded like someone possessed by a demon. Out of her mind. The voice was less hers than it was the howl of some animal in heat baying at a primordial moon.

If Climax-Well could be believed, it was that beastly outburst that had saved her life. With it, she had allowed the tension of a life-threatening orgasm to pass through her without lasting damage. A woman's purpose, he claimed, was not to be a vessel, but to be a conduit. For her to survive, all things must pass through her.

Between marathon sessions of arousal culminating in mind-shattering orgasms, Maxwell lectured Penny. He slipped a wet finger into her, matter-of-factly saying, "This is your urethra." Rotating the finger, he said, "And this . . . this is your urethral sponge, often called the 'G-spot.'"

The walking tour his fingers took sent shivers through her body.

He oiled his hands with a pink, rose-scented gel and slipped two fingers into her. "When I massage the rear wall of your vaginal vault . . ."

Unseen, he must've done so, because Penny twitched and shivered with uncontrolled joy. Whatever Max was doing, she drove her hips against his hand, wanting more.

"That," he explained, "is your perineal sponge, a mass of erectile tissue that connects through the pudendal nerve to your clitoris."

Penny didn't need to look to know that her clit was stiffening. Untouched, it was achingly engorged and throbbing.

Massaging whatever he'd found, Max was stimulating her clitoris by remote control. "The perineal sponge is the reason women can achieve orgasms while having anal sex." He slipped a third and a fourth finger inside. "Good girl, your vagina is 'ballooning.'" During arousal, he explained, the inner vagina expands, lengthening to create a dead end beyond the cervix. Now his entire hand was inside.

Penny looked down to see only his smooth, pale wrist disappearing into her. At the sight of it, she moaned.

Maxwell's eyes had a glazed, faraway look, not focused on anything. Through his hand, he was clearly exploring a hidden world. "This, I believe, is your cervix," he said. "If I apply a steady pressure . . ."

Penny's fingers went involuntarily to her mouth, and she bit down on a knuckle, whimpering. She closed her eyes, embarrassed by the mewling that rose from deep in her throat. It was terrifying being coaxed this far beyond her own rational control. It was as frightening as she'd always imagined a heart attack would feel, but she never wanted it to stop.

His voice muted with admiration and wonder, Maxwell said, "This is exceptional. Do you always ejaculate this much?"

Penny opened her eyes and peeked. A rivulet of shimmering juice was erupting from near the top of her pussy. It flowed down Maxwell's arm until it dripped from his elbow. "Sorry," she whispered, instantly ashamed.

"But why?" asked Maxwell, twisting his hand deep inside her.

"I'm peeing on you."

He laughed. With his free hand he collected a smidgen of the liquid. He rubbed it between two fingers, brought the fingers to his nose and smelled it, tasted it with the tip of his tongue. "Enzymes," he pronounced, "from your Skene's glands. That's why it vents from your urethra instead of your vulva." He brought the wet fingers near her mouth and asked, "Would you like to taste yourself?"

Excited as she was, purring and thrashing like an animal,

Penny couldn't bring herself to lick his fingers. She didn't have to.

He shoved them into her mouth. Gagging her. Choking her. The taste of her own sensual emissions was metallic and salty. For a short eternity she couldn't speak or breathe.

Maxwell's voice was reproachful. "I thought you said you were wearing a diaphragm."

She wasn't. Her diaphragm was in Jackson Heights—securely locked in a safe-deposit box at Chase Manhattan. Penny wasn't trying to get pregnant. She just hadn't planned to have sex tonight.

The fingers withdrew from her mouth, allowing her to draw a new breath.

"Don't think you can trick me, Miss Harrigan." The fingers within her were still roving, mapping that hidden world. "When and if I ever marry anyone it will be for love. I had a vasectomy many years ago."

Penny wanted to explain, but she was exhausted. Instead, she lay back, sinking deeper into pleasure as he petted the glans of her clitoris. He described how the short clitoral shaft descended into her skin. Using gentle pressure, he traced the shaft to where it divided into two legs which he called "crura." These legs, Maxwell explained, wrapped around the vaginal cavity.

He said more, a long, rambling travelogue about a land Penny had never visited. A history lesson about the world contained inside her.

Maxwell explained how physicians from the time of Hippocrates until the 1920s had always been formally trained in how to bring their female patients to "paroxysm." Using fingers and oil, it was standard practice for doctors and midwives to treat hysteria, insomnia, depression, and a host of conditions common to women. *Praefocatio matricis* it was called. Or "suffocation of the mother." And even the great Galen recommended that the vagina must be vigorously manipulated until it readily expressed the accumulation of fluid.

Vibrators, he claimed, were among the first household appliances to be powered with electricity. In 1893, a man named Mortimer Granville built a huge fortune when he invented a battery-driven vibrator. A full range of such sex toys were commonly sold through national mass-circulation magazines and the Sears, Roebuck catalog. It wasn't until they appeared in the crude pornographic films of the 1920s that vibrating dildos became shameful.

Galen. Hippocrates. Ambroise Paré. Penny couldn't keep the names and dates straight in her mind. After the sixteenth century, she fell asleep. She dreamed of plummeting from the top of the Eiffel Tower. She was falling because Maxwell had pushed her.

When she woke, Maxwell's side of the bed was empty. The bathroom door was closed, and from the far side of it came the sound of running water.

Was it Betty Friedan or Gloria Steinem? Penny couldn't remember, but she thought one of them had written about the "zipless fuck," an ideal kind of physically satisfying sex that left no emotional obligations. Sex with Maxwell might very well be what the author had in mind. It left Penny weak, feeling as if she'd suffered the flu. That was only for a few minutes; beyond that she was ravenous. They ate and fucked and ate and fucked. Endlessly. Ziplessly.

It was official. Until now, Penny Harrigan had never experienced an actual orgasm. Not like the thrilling sensations that Maxwell coaxed from her eager body. For once, the descriptions of fireworks and convulsions she'd read so often in *Cosmo,* they seemed like understatements instead of exaggerations.

Stroking her pubis, Maxwell said, "I would like to shave you. It would make the testing more accurate." She'd acquiesced. No biggie. She'd been shaved before, and waxed, to be bikini-ready for spring break. "This time," he warned her, "it will never grow back." He used a special formula passed down through millennia of Uzbek tribesmen, a lotion of aloe vera and pureed pine nuts that would forever leave her as smooth as a child.

Penny looked forlornly at her shorn curls lying among the bedsheets. She told herself she'd never liked being bushy.

The aspect of sex that Maxwell seemed to enjoy most was finding ways to coerce her to greater satisfaction. That seemed his sole source of pleasure. Whenever Penny asked whether he wanted to come, he'd simply shrug and say, "Maybe next go-round." Beyond their first encounter he never so much as removed his shirt. Soon he came to don a white lab coat to protect his clothing.

For a beauty like Alouette, a woman accustomed to driving men to fits of lust, Maxwell's failure to come must've been maddening. Penny tried not to think of the French beauty who'd threatened her life, but that wasn't easy. Alouette had enjoyed 136 days of intimacy with Maxwell. Gwendolyn had enjoyed 136 days. The *National Enquirer* never lied. Unless she'd miscounted, Penny figured she had 103 days to go. If the sex kept up like this, she doubted whether she could live that long. But what a great way to die!

If she could just find the recording of her howling, find and erase it, Penny's happiness would be complete. The bathroom door remained shut. Behind it the water continued to run.

Retrieving his recorder from the bedside table, she rewound the memory. Hitting Play, she heard, ". . . don't be a prudish fool." Penny felt like a hypocrite, but she never wanted another human being to hear the insane gibberish that had spilled from her mouth. Again, she hit Play. This time she heard a scream.

With the shower running full-blast, she hoped Maxwell hadn't heard it in the bathroom.

Someone was screaming in French. Not that Penny could understand French, but she could guess based on her own experience. It was Alouette under the influence of pink champagne and secret ingredients. She fast-forwarded and hit Play. "Stay with me, Penny," the recording said.

Even as she listened, spellbound, the device in her hands issued a shrill ringtone. It wasn't only a recorder; it was a telephone! Penny was so startled she almost dropped it; instead she tossed the phone back onto the table, where it continued to ring and ring. When she checked the caller ID it said, "Private."

Penny leaped from the bed. She knocked at the bathroom door. "Max, it's your phone!" She tried the knob, but it was locked. She could hear the shower, his voice singing a song she couldn't identify. After a couple more rings, curiosity got the better of her. She put the phone to her ear and said, "Hello?"

Silence.

The bathroom door opened and Maxwell stepped out with a towel wrapped around his waist. Water dripped from his hair. At the sight of her answering his phone, his eyebrows drew together in fury, and he snapped his fingers, gesturing for her to hang up.

"Hello? Corny?" asked a voice. It was a familiar voice. A woman. "Max," she said. "This isn't my fault." She pleaded, "Please don't hurt me."

Penny handed the phone to Maxwell. She could still hear the voice on the line talking excitedly, loudly. Begging. He put it to his ear and listened. Gradually his eyes wandered to the floor. The longer the caller talked, the more his angry expression changed to one of brooding concern.

"That shouldn't be an issue," he said. "The active ingredients don't fall within any of the federal schedules for controlled or hazardous substances." He listened, shaking his head. "Well, then appoint a new chairman to the FDA. Give that job to someone who *will* fast-track the products."

The caller was someone Penny had seen on television. It was a voice that brought to mind a sensible, shoulder-length haircut. A blue suit. A pearl necklace. A woman speaking behind a forest of microphones.

Talking into the phone, but eyeing Penny, Maxwell said, "I'm in the final testing phase right now. We're timing mass production for a summer rollout. By next month we'll be in a half million retail outlets." He turned his back to Penny and stepped through the bathroom door. "You know what's at stake here. Don't make me take any actions you'll regret." The door shut. Possibly to mask the conversation, the shower came back on at full blast.

Unless Penny missed her guess, the voice, the woman calling, she was the president of the United States. President Clarissa Hind.

Penny wondered what brilliant new invention they were almost done testing.

This constant sexual cavorting, this would be the pattern of their days and nights. Max always had some toy, some potion, some glorious lubricant he wanted to introduce her to.

He'd drive her to climax until her back ached and her legs wouldn't work, and he'd gently bully her, saying, "We're almost done. Just one more adjustment." Saying, "We've got to stay on a schedule here. . . ."

He'd probe with one hand buried inside her. "I'm searching for your pudendal plexus. It should be right *here*."

On other occasions, totally stymied, he'd use his free hand to shake open a folded anatomical chart, like a road map, on the bed beside her. He was a southpaw and kept those fingers planted in her vagina as if marking his place in a book. *You Are Here.* One hand inside her, he'd use the other to smooth the creased paper and trace one finger along some route while muttering to himself, "The *nervi pelvici splanchnici* branches *here* near your *nervi erigentes.* . . ." Discovering his destination, he'd wiggle something deep within her, exclaiming triumphantly, "Penny? Did you know your coccygeal plexus is displaced two centimeters to the anterior?" Feeling along blindly, he'd add, "Don't worry. It seems to be within normal variable parameters."

Every so often he'd withdraw whatever pleasure instrument he was testing. He'd lay its length against a corner of the night table and bend the metal or plastic slightly. Or he might use a pair of pliers or vise grips he kept in the bedside drawer. Worse was when he'd just swing the instrument a mighty whack against the table, whack after whack, marring the elegant furniture until he'd achieved the desired curve.

When that happened the bedroom seemed like those sepia-toned photographs Penny had seen of Thomas Edison's Menlo Park laboratory. Or Henry Ford's workshop. For her part, Penny felt less like a girlfriend than a lab assistant. Like Dr. Watson or Igor. Or Pavlov's dog. As Max tinkered away, bringing her to new convulsions and seizures of pleasure, despite her moods, despite her growing detachment and resentment, Penny half expected him to shout, "Eureka!"

Maxwell would hover over his task, as focused as a Swiss watchmaker or brain surgeon. Often he'd request his valet or butler to wheel a tray of sterile instruments up bedside so Max need not look away from the procedure at hand. "Calipers!" he'd bark, extending one hand, and the attendant servant would slap the tool into his open palm. "Blot me!" Max would command, and the underling would use a fold of paper towel to swab the beads of perspiration from Max's forehead.

At times Max crouched between her knees, a penlight clenched between his teeth, a jeweler's loupe squeezed in one eye, tinkering. His face slack with concentration. "I chose you," Max explained, "because you have never experienced an orgasm. A man can tell. You remain asleep, and no one has yet to awaken you. You are so typical of the women I am trying to help."

"'For too many years,'" Max recited, "'women have been excluded from the full pleasure available to them in their bodies.'" He was reading from a printed sheet of paper. A press release. "'I believe, as do many medical professionals, that a large proportion of chronic mental and physical ailments beset women because they accumulate stress that might otherwise be easily and quickly released with the right tools. . . .'"

Even to Penny's unsophisticated ear, the speech sounded like a string of euphemisms. According to Maxwell, it had to. It was selling sex. Even more controversially, it was selling women the means to better sex than they had ever enjoyed with any man. To some listeners, this announcement would sound like gobbledygook, like an outdated advertisement for a feminine hygiene spray. But to other listeners, namely men who valued only their own greedy sexual needs, this speech would sound like the end of the world.

The two of them were sitting in bed. Lately, they were always in bed. Penny never donned more than a bathrobe, and that was only to accept a gourmet meal brought by the majordomo.

"'That's the reason,'" Maxwell continued, "'we're proud to introduce the Beautiful You line of personal care products. . . .'"

C. Linus Maxwell was preparing to expand his vast corporation and enter the field of empty vaginas in a big way. All of the jewel-toned gels and liquids on his bedside table. The magic pink champagne douche. The fluids engineered to modulate the coefficient of friction. He would be bringing them all to the lonely female consumer.

The packaging would be pink, but not obnoxiously. The whole line would be marketed under the umbrella name Beautiful You. Thumbing the buttons on his smart phone, Maxwell showed Penny a prototype of the advertising, the words *Beautiful You* curved in curlicue white letters. A tagline along the bottom of each ad read, "Better Than Love." The douche, Maxwell explained, would ultimately be sold as a dissolvable powder in a small envelope, which could be mixed with water or champagne. It was only one of several shockingly innovative personal care products. Soon every woman would be able to enjoy mind-bending orgasms at a moderate price.

All of the research and erotic training Maxwell had done with swamis and witch doctors and courtesans—all the sex secrets of the ancient world—he was about to market them to the modern woman. Every gal from Omaha to Oslo would soon be savoring the pounding cut-loose orgasms Penny had only recently discovered. It was stunning to imagine how this might change the world. As Maxwell's former loves had demonstrated, given the right sexual satisfaction women could flower, lose weight, kick drugs. Every woman's personal fulfillment was only weeks away.

Just in the past few days, sequestered in Maxwell's Parisian penthouse, Penny had dropped eight pounds. She slept like a baby. She'd never felt more relaxed and at ease.

In secret, she was a little proud that she'd made her own contribution to the project. Max was still tweaking some recipes. Polishing off any rough edges. In the near future, girls just like her, average girls without stellar bodies and luscious faces, they would have access to the kind of bone-melting pleasure that only movie stars currently enjoyed.

As she scrolled through photos of prototype sex toys, lubricants, and nightgowns, Penny asked, "Why 'Beautiful You'?"

Maxwell shrugged. "The publicity wonks said it tested the best. Plus, it translates into any language."

Young or old. Fat or short. Billions of women would learn to love the bodies in which they were alive. Beautiful You would be a blessing to all womankind. Penny knew that if the mass-marketed products worked half as well as the prototypes he'd been demonstrating on her, C. Linus Maxwell would quickly double his fortune. Kidding him, she asked, "Don't you have enough money?"

There it was again. That sad smile flitted across his lips. "It's not about the profits," he told her. "Not at the price point I have in mind."

It was about his mother, Penny guessed. Wasn't it every boy's dream to fete his long-suffering mom? Maxwell's had slaved away to give her boy a head start in the world, and then she'd died before he could show his gratitude. It was a little creepy: the idea that he was honoring his mother by showering women with great sex . . . but his motives were noble and touching.

A thought struck her. It was none of her business, but she asked, "Do you still miss her? Your mom?"

He didn't answer. He went back to silently reading his press release.

Impulsively, she leaned over and pecked him on the cheek.

"What's that for?" he asked.

"For being such a loving son."

And there it was again. The wan, furtive smile of a lonely little orphan.

———

"It's not like Spanish fly. There's no comparison," he insisted.

The two of them were making a rare public appearance. They were dining in a chic restaurant in the St.-Germain neighborhood of the sixth arrondissement. As usual their candlelit table was the center of attention. Even the aloof Parisians were shamelessly eyeballing them.

The fabled aphrodisiac known as Spanish fly, Maxwell explained, was the emerald-green blister beetle, *Lytta vesicatoria*. When the dead insects were dried and ground to a fine powder, they could be mixed into a beverage. The tainted drink would cause severe urinary tract inflammation. That was the legendary effect that supposedly prompted women to beg for intercourse. In actuality, the effect was about as exciting as an internal case of poison oak.

"This," Maxwell said, rolling a pink capsule between his fingers, "this is different."

He'd removed the new invention from his pocket only a moment earlier. Like all his other toys, the pink pill was a product from the new Beautiful You line. About the size of a robin's egg, it looked like a piece of candy. Like something that should be nestled in an Easter basket. It was the color of bubble gum.

Penny took it from his hand. "So I'm supposed to swallow this?"

Maxwell laughed at her innocence. He shook his head, saying, "No, my dear, it's a vaginal suppository perfectly formulated to heighten female desire."

He observed Penny rolling the pink bead between her fingers. "Note the slight stickiness of the outer coating." He said, "It's a layer of silicone impregnated with a mild herbal stimulant. If a penis were to enter the vaginal cavity and encounter the bead, both partners would share the pleasure of the effect."

Penny squeezed it between her fingers. It felt soft. In the

palm of her hand it was surprisingly heavy. She smiled slyly, lifted the napkin from her lap, and daubed daintily at the corners of her mouth. She asked a passing waiter, "*Excusez moi,* where is your *toilette?*"

On her return from the bathroom, Penny saw her nemesis: Alouette. She was seated at a discreet corner banquette, tucked away where she'd draw no public notice. Alouette's face looked gaunt, her cheeks more hollowed than Penny recalled. The actress's eyes looked sunken.

Somehow the week's bedroom ordeals had calmed Penny and filled her with a quiet confidence. She strode brazenly to her rival's table. The pink bead was inside her, working whatever magic Maxwell had designed into it. Penny regarded the haggard woman and said, "Alouette, you're looking well."

"No, I'm not," the actress shot back. "I look like shit, and it's all Max's fault."

Penny narrowed her eyes. "Are you following me?"

Alouette sighed. She drew the fingers of one hand through her long, rich hair.

Penny couldn't help but notice that strands came off between those fingers. Already, a scattering of fallen hair dusted the table and the booth's upholstery.

"My impulse had been to save you, little mouse," Alouette began. "But now I see that you've let him reduce you to a stupid slut."

Penny winced at the harsh word.

"Despite my warning, you've allowed Maxwell to bewitch you." Alouette's eyes filled with pity. She spoke without rancor in her voice. "You were someone, before. How quickly you've thrown your dreams away and become just your hungry *conass.*"

Penny turned to leave, but Alouette asked, "Tell me. Has he given you the black bead yet?"

"What black bead?" Penny asked warily.

But the actress merely smiled. "This should be amusing," she sneered.

Back at her own table Maxwell didn't rise to seat her. Instead he gestured for her to come to him and hold out her hand. He took it and held it warmly for a moment. He kissed the back, placing something in her palm, and when Penny opened her fingers, there it was: a black bead. It looked identical in size and shape to the first bead. Only the color was different.

"Pink for the vagina," Max announced. "Black for your lovely anus. It's best to keep things simple; the entire Beautiful You line of products will use that same color-coding system."

Dutifully, Penny made a second trip to the toilets.

Before she'd returned to the table the beads were already having their effect. Maxwell seated her, and then returned to his chair opposite. They perused their menus.

The sensation began like a sweet burning within her groin. Then a delicious cramping. This increased until it felt as if something ravenous, with wonderfully soft teeth, were gnawing on her insides, devouring her from within.

She gasped with a sound that caught people's attention. Coiffed heads turned to stare. To save face she put her napkin to her mouth and faked a cough. It was better that people think she had tuberculosis than know she was enduring a string of multiple orgasms.

"Don't worry," Maxwell said, "there will be no permanent damage. The silicone coating is very soft."

Something twisted and wrestled, embedded far beneath her skin.

"Both of the beads are earth magnets," Max explained. "I could not give them to you at the same time because the attraction between them is so strong." He lifted his pen and made ready to jot notes. "The ancient Peruvian tribe the Chichlachies called them 'married stones,' because once they find each other they're almost impossible to separate."

As he described it, the black bead was planted against the anterior wall of her rectum. The pink one was lodged against the posterior wall of her vagina. The stones, even coated in silicone and inserted in her two very different orifices, the stones had found each other. Even now, the thin muscular wall between her two cavities, with all its rich network of nerve endings, it was being crushed and kneaded by the two strong magnets. They ground that most sensitive spot between them.

Savoring her reaction, the gloating genius waved to flag a waiter. "Only your sensitive perineal sponge separates them. You are helpless. Your entire erogenous nervous system is under assault."

To keep from crying out, Penny bit down on her meticulously manicured finger. Her nipples grew so erect that her breasts seemed ready to levitate from the cups of her push-up bra.

"You are still a young girl," Maxwell said. He studied her reaction intently. "If you can't cope with the full potential of a woman's body, I understand." He was mocking her, daring her to endure this trial in public. As elegant twosomes dined and chatted near them, orgasmic waves of sexual energy swept over Penny.

A waiter stepped up to their table and asked, "Would you care to order, madam?"

Her pelvis felt as if planets were colliding, milling together inside of her. Great seas were heaving, eroding her sanity. She crossed her legs tightly, in a vain attempt to clamp down the rising gusher.

A bemused tone in his voice, Maxwell told the waiter, "Tonight the lady would love to indulge in a thick steak." Addressing her, he added, "Or would a helping of juicy tongue be more to your liking?"

Even with shuddering full-body spasms of ecstasy coursing through her, Penny felt the toe of Maxwell's shoe slide up the inside of her leg. From her ankle to her knee, its smooth hardness traveled until it was prodding her crotch. It reminded her of the moment they'd first met: her sprawled on the carpet, seeing her own disheveled face reflected in the polished toe of his handmade footwear. She couldn't speak. With shaking hands she touched the skirt of her gown and found it soaked. The napkin in her lap was likewise drenched. Mindless of the waiter, she shoved Max's foot away and struggled to stand. Clutching the backs of chairs, disturbing their moneyed occupants, she stumbled back toward the toilets. Her legs shook, weakened by spasms of pleasure. When she was almost to the door, Penny's knees buckled, and she fell. She was so exhausted. Her hair hanging in her face, she crawled the final steps and took refuge in the tiled sanctuary. Safely hidden in a cubicle, she hiked up her damp skirt and plunged two fingers into herself. She could feel the pink bead but couldn't capture it. The silicone was too slick.

Arching her back, Penny slid two fingers into her anus and tried in vain to find the black bead.

A voice behind her said, "You cannot extract them by yourself." It was Alouette. The cinema star had followed her into the toilet cubicle. She stood, coolly assessing Penny's erotic dilemma. "Last year," Alouette confessed, "I was caught in this very same toilet. It was a busboy who saved my sanity. That brave teenage boy. As if it were a snake's venom, he sucked the black bead from my derriere."

Thrusting her exposed pubis forward, Penny begged, "Please," her voice nothing more than a whimper.

Alouette appraised the bared vulva and whistled softly. "So this is Maxwell's attraction to you, little mouse. Your pussy is the most beautiful I've ever laid eyes on." She wet her lips. "Glorious."

Penny's secretions dripped to the floor, where they'd begun to pool.

"Let yourself go," Alouette advised. "Only the intense flow of your feminine juices can flush the love stone from its seat!" Alouette knelt on the tiled floor and gripped Penny's hips in her hands. Planting her movie star mouth tightly over the younger woman's dripping vagina, she began to suck. Penny bore down, riding that lovely face as if it were a saddle. She could feel Alouette's fingers exploring inside her rectum.

Gradually the flood of stimulation receded. Alouette lifted her mouth from Penny's groin and spit the pink bead into the toilet bowl. Deprived of its partner, the black bead slipped out easily, pinched between the actress's fingers, and she held it for Penny's inspection before letting it plunk into the water. The two magnets clicked together with a frightening force, and Alouette flushed them away. Appraising the damage done to Penny's *masque,* she said, "Do not thank me, little mouse. One day you will wish I had let you die from the pleasure." As she went to a mirror and began to repair her own smeared lipstick, she said, "It is already too late for you. Soon you will be like the rest of us, his slave."

When they weren't banqueting on delectable food among illustrious people, they were being chauffeured back and forth between Maxwell's penthouse in Paris and his château in the Loire Valley. There she wandered the echoing salons, examining the priceless antiquities that had belonged to so many celebrities before Max. There was something so isolating about being famous. She wandered the château's formal parterre gardens while security patrols armed with machine guns watched her from the roof, and closed-circuit cameras documented her every step.

Penny had chewed her knuckles raw to stifle her shrieks of ecstasy. She thought that if she overindulged for a few months, an overdose of pleasure would leave her satisfied for life. She might momentarily reflect on some larger issue, like famine in the Sudan, but then Max would covertly slip some thrilling new product into her and her mind would become a blank. Euphoria erased everything. She had no energy left over to fret about her stalled legal career or the ominous future of her aging parents in Nebraska. Or global climate change. She was grounded entirely in her body, in the present moment of glorious sensation. No past or future existed, and Max could keep her there. Under his touch the world collapsed. Nothing existed beyond Paris, beyond his bed, beyond her own pulsating clitoris.

She was getting everything she'd ever been taught would make her happy—Gucci clothes, great sex, her name a household word—and every day she felt more miserable. It didn't help that people expected her to be ecstatic. No one wanted to hear the problems of a disappointed Cinderella; she was supposed to live happily ever after. But this . . . none of this was the great life's mission she'd been hoping to find.

Almost eagerly, she counted down. Only eighty-seven days left.

At her age Penny knew she ought to be living large, making herself available to people, and having misadventures. She longed to get smashed at one of the noisy blowout parties that her friend Monique was probably throwing at right this very moment. She would even settle for a Sigma Chi mixer with beer kegs and frat boys using their permanent erections to menace coeds.

In the penthouse or château, when they were alone together, Max never wanted to talk. He only wanted to test his tantric thingamajigs on her. She told herself he was under pressure.

With Beautiful You only a month away from rollout, everything had to be perfect. Still, she tried to leaven his mood. She told him jokes. She complimented him on his cars, his hair, his clothes, but he shrugged off the flattery.

Even the fabled shopping of the French capital wasn't much fun. Not after she'd been in and out of the elegant boutiques for weeks. Top designers vied for Penny to wear their clothes. No matter what she tried on they told her she looked fantastic. They even offered her kickbacks to wear their labels at high profile events. It was all so phony. She knew she looked awful, and that they only wanted the publicity. Her neck was too short and thick. Her breasts were too small. Her breasts weren't even the same size. Her hips were too wide. The mirrors in the ateliers didn't lie.

Before she'd gotten famous, people in New York had openly insulted her body, but at least they'd been telling her the truth.

The only part of her anatomy that was beautiful was her privates. And Penny could hardly ask Christian Lacroix to design a gown that would highlight those.

Out shopping, she looked for gifts that might amuse Max, but that was a steep order. What did you give the man who had everything? Who'd *had everyone*? The only thing that seemed to please Maxwell was when a prototype or a new formula brought her to higher crescendos of pleasure. The greater her excitement, the greater his. Realizing that, Penny resolved to give him a gift in the only way possible.

One night, when a particular device—a toy like a pinecone engineered to expand inside her, based on some pre-Columbian doohickey—when it failed, Penny didn't let on. It felt nice, but that was all. Penny worried that she might be getting jaded. Perhaps she was suffering some sort of pleasure-center fatigue. When she sensed Max's disappointment, she couldn't help but amp up her performance. She flopped around the bed like a sea lion and flapped her arms. She barked like a dog and crowed like a rooster.

At the height of her well-intentioned albeit faked orgasm, Maxwell told her, "Stop."

He looked at her, his jaw set. He tugged the silken cord that tethered the toy and it slipped from between Penny's legs. Like a sulking child, he wrapped the cord around the device, saying, "Don't imagine that you can ever lie to me. A scientist is first and foremost a keen observer. Your heart rate never rose above a hundred and five beats per minute. Your blood pressure hasn't budged since we started."

Clearly disappointed, he set the failed device on the bedside table. "What I treasure most about you is your honest, unfiltered feedback." He pressed a button to summon the butler. "Let's forget tonight. Tonight is wasted."

Maxwell retrieved the remote control and brought the television to life. The noise of gunfire and squealing tires filled the spacious bedroom. Not taking his eyes off the screen, he said, "You must never, ever again fake it with me."

His eyes never leaving the TV screen, he said, "If I wanted fake results I'd still be testing on prostitutes."

Later that night, something snapped Penny awake. A muffled noise. She held her breath, listening to the silence of the penthouse bedroom. The air-conditioning stirred the drapes in the window. Max stretched beside her, asleep against the satin sheets, his bedside clock reading three eighteen a.m. Before she could drift back to dreamland, the sound came again: a male voice, mumbling.

Maxwell was talking in his sleep. In words that were hardly

more than groans, he said, "Maybe." Perhaps it was two words: "Feed me." Penny couldn't be certain. She raised herself onto one elbow and leaned closer. He mumbled again. "Need me," he said.

She leaned closer. Too close. As if in warning, his voice hoarse with panic, now he cried, "Phoebe!" And the force of his frantic outburst stunned Penny. The word rang in her mind. *Phoebe*. After that he was silent.

It would appear that the still waters of C. Linus Maxwell ran deep. Within the pale skinny chest of that scientist beat a real heart. If he could only share his secrets, Penny thought wistfully, maybe then their relationship could rise above fantastic sex and blossom to become a true romance.

It never ceased to amaze her how Maxwell could act so petty. Outwardly, he remained a geeky, science-obsessed boy of a man. A distant tyrant, withholding his heartfelt emotions and affections. His skin was odorless and as cold as metal, like a robot from some science fiction movie. But when he stimulated her . . .

When Max stimulated her, the feeling was like hearing a big-name tenor at the Paris Opera House, or like dining alfresco on some scrumptious Italian thing. Even if Max didn't love her, when he stimulated her glands Penny couldn't help herself. Despite his coldness and cruelty, she felt herself fall temporarily in love with him. When his Beautiful You tools stirred the passion within her, Penny gazed into his remote blue eyes and desired nothing in the world but him. It was as if he'd cast a spell over her.

Penny wanted to believe that making love was more than just fiddling with nerve endings until harum-scarum chemicals squirted around limbic systems. Real love, she knew, was something lasting and soulful. It sustained and nourished a person. The "love" that Max engendered seemed to evaporate as her orgasms petered out. Despite their delightful effects, the Beautiful You products generated merely a powerful love substitute.

Her darkest fear was that the world's women wouldn't know the difference.

The next day, inspiration hit. She phoned her mother in Omaha.

"How's Paris?" Her mother asked this teasingly. "Please tell me you've missed your period!"

"How do you know I'm in Paris?" Penny challenged.

Long-distance, her mother clucked her tongue. "Honey, you're on the front page of the *National Enquirer* every day with the Eiffel Tower behind you!"

Penny shuddered. For weeks she'd been phoning into work sick. She'd told Brillstein she had hepatitis C. Unless everyone at BB&B lived under rocks, they had to know she was lying.

"They're calling you 'the Nerd's Cinderella,'" her mother shouted. She always shouted on long-distance calls.

"Mom?"

"Did you see that picture they ran last week of President Hind?" her mother shouted. "She looks terrible!"

Penny ventured, "Maybe she has hepatitis."

"And that Alouette D'Ambrosia looks even worse." Penny's mother cautioned, "Don't let Maxwell get away. The ladies who break off with him all go to hell."

Penny tried to steer the conversation. "That's the reason I'm calling, Mom. Do you have any back issues of the *Enquirer*?"

"Name a date," her mother said proudly. "I have every issue going back as far as 1972."

"You're kidding."

"It's my life's work," her mother boasted.

"I'd like to surprise Max," Penny said, "but I don't know much about him—you know, his childhood, his likes and dislikes."

"Why don't you just use the Wiki-thing?"

"Wikipedia, Mom. That's no good, either." Her voice heavy with resignation, Penny explained that "Climax-Well" employed teams of hackers who did nothing but comb the Internet and manage his public image. He controlled every detail that could be found. "I'm looking for little anecdotes from before the Internet age."

Her mother sounded doubtful. "It's the *Enquirer,* honey, not *The New York Times.*"

"Please, Mom."

"What did you have in mind?"

Penny thought a moment. "The names of his childhood pets. Old hobbies. Maybe something sweet about his mother; was her name 'Phoebe'?"

"She's dead."

Penny insisted, "I know, but it would be sweet to find an old nickname. A favorite flavor of ice cream. A lullaby. Something along those lines."

Penny's mother sounded energized, thrilled to be recruited on such a project. "I'll head down into the basement right now."

"Thank you, Mom."

The truth was, once Penny had faked one orgasm she found herself questioning all of them. She'd stopped trusting her own physical reactions. With every nightly session, she worried that she was under- or overreacting to his ministrations. She'd never loved Maxwell, but she'd loved what he could generate in her body. Now even the orgasms were losing their hold over her.

She wondered whether this was how his affair with Clarissa Hind had ended. And Princess Gwen. And Alouette.

Only sixty-seven days were left.

Whether or not she did it intentionally, Penny continued to fake it occasionally. On those nights not even the steamy memory of Alouette's hot mouth clamped between her legs could bring on a climax. A few times, she convinced him. More often, she couldn't. He knew more about her body than she did.

The times she was caught—betrayed by her baseline heart rate, the pH of her sweat excretion, her skin lividity—Maxwell would summarily extract the prototype. He'd rip the applicable pages out of his notes and make a big show of tearing them into bits and sprinkling them into the trash can beside the bed. He'd open his laptop and begin reviewing the first generation of marketing materials for Beautiful You.

Once, to defuse his silent anger, Penny looked pointedly at his notebook and asked, "Are they all in there?"

"Who?" Max asked, not looking up from a screening copy of a television commercial. To Penny, these videos all looked the same: manically smiling women, their eyes gleaming, running home from the store or the post office carrying the same bright pink box printed with the curlicue Beautiful You logo. The voice-over tagline at the end of each commercial was a dulcet female purr saying, "A billion husbands are about to be replaced!"

"All of your former lovers," Penny clarified. "Are they all in there?" She nodded at the notebook filled with his spidery shorthand. "The president, the princess, the steel heiress?"

She knew they were. Maxwell collected data like a magpie.

"That's only the latest of many notebooks," said the man who was scrolling down through mock-ups of print ads that would run in every women's magazine in the world. The Beautiful You logo in Basque, French, Hindi, Afrikaans, Mandarin Chinese. "Are you certain you want to hear this?" he asked coldly.

She wasn't sure, but she nodded.

"I have, indexed and cross-indexed, the forensic specifications of seven thousand, eight hundred, and twenty-four females, ages six through two hundred seven." Turning to meet her gaze, he added, "Before you phone the child welfare authorities, my encounter with the six-year-old occurred when we were both that age and playing 'doctor' in the basement of her family home in Ballard." The centuries-old subject was a mystic who lived high on Mount Everest.

He smiled. "I've trained myself with the abilities to please any woman," Max said flatly. He wasn't bragging, not in his own mind. "Young or old. Fat or thin. Any race. From any culture. I can quickly and efficiently bring any woman to greater levels of orgasm than she has ever dreamed possible."

Turning back to his computer screen, he continued. "I've collected data about the sexual responsiveness of high school girls, college coeds, young professionals. I have studied the erotic tricks of Tajikistan temple prostitutes . . . German sex therapists . . . Sufi belly dancers. The women you know of, the rich and powerful, are only the tip of my sexual iceberg. By the time I bedded them I was already very well rehearsed in a thousand ways of providing pleasure."

Penny realized that with numbers like that, very few of his partners had gotten more than a few minutes of Max's attention. "Is that why you pursued Clarissa Hind?"

"No, the purpose of women such as Clarissa and Alouette was not research. It was testing. Testing and connections. Not to mention advertising. I've found it very useful to know the president and the queen of England on such an intimate level. And the prestige of knowing them has lured many more test subjects into my grasp."

"Subjects like me?" Penny asked, at once honored and revolted by the idea.

Maxwell looked at her kindly. He was sitting cross-legged on the bed, the laptop open in front of him. "No, my good girl. You were my victory lap."

He'd pioneered the most extraordinary collection of erotic tools in the history of the world. He knew they worked. In fact, some worked too well. The pleasure they generated might kill an average Jane Doe. This final round of trials was intended to blunt the power of the most dangerous toys. Now the Beautiful You collection could enter the world without fear of lawsuits.

"Before you feel yourself ill-used," he continued, "please remember that you've gotten great enjoyment from our time together. You've been feted by the world press. And your wardrobe has grown to become quite impressive."

Penny couldn't deny any of his statements, but she could understand why a woman like Alouette would file for fifty million dollars in compensation for emotional distress.

"If it helps your pride, my girl," Maxwell said, "you should know that you've saved innocent lives." He pecked away at a few keys, bringing up a new selection of adverts. "However," he added, "I do use the term 'innocent' loosely."

Within hours of each marathon session of erotic bliss, Penny felt her muscles tighten and flare with soreness. It felt as if she'd climbed to the peak of Mount Everest or swum the English Channel. Some episodes, the more extreme, left her feeling as if she'd rebounded from polio. More sex was out of the question until she'd recuperated; Maxwell knew that. He didn't push. Some of the positions they achieved required her legs to be as limber as a circus contortionist's. A pulled muscle or ruptured tendon would delay further testing for weeks.

A battalion of physical therapists streamed through the

penthouse. To aid in her rapid recovery, masseurs stroked her for hours with scented oils, working their muscular, intuitive hands deep into her. Acupuncture specialists performed miracles by pricking her with their thin needles. Only when she was fully revitalized did Maxwell approach her with the next piece of equipment or aphrodisiac. He inflicted his sweet, consensual torture and left her gasping and aching, and once again the recovery team would nurse Penny back to health in time for another round of crippling pleasure.

"I do not want fatigue to dim your senses," Max told her. As a burly Turkish brute fingered the inside of her aching thighs, Max stood by fully dressed in a twelve-thousand-dollar bespoke suit and examined her nude body for bruises. "It is of the utmost importance that you be fully rested and responsive when we engage in our experiments."

He stepped closer to the massage table, where she lay faceup, glistening with oil. Her labia were ruddy and distended from the sensual abuse they'd taken the previous night. Bowing low over her body, he placed his lips against her inflamed clitoris.

Penny winced.

"The lactic acid must dissipate. You are still too tender," Max declared. "We will postpone further trials for two days."

Over the past few weeks, Penny had lost track of how many Beautiful You products he'd tested on her body. A few had proved mediocre, lackluster, unremarkable. But most had left her drained and limp with satisfaction. Fearful for her own safety, she'd even asked Max to dial back the effects of some. She was young, a fit, healthy girl just out of law school. On an older woman or someone with a preexisting health condition, those most effective products could prove fatal.

On the evenings when recent erotic play had left her too damaged for more, Penny lay in bed and asked Max to read to her from his notebook of test results. Freshly massaged and sipping a glass of Côtes du Rhône, she'd curl in her nest of satin sheets. Max would sit on a straight-backed chair beside the bed. Attired in a tuxedo and white bow tie, he'd lick a fingertip and page forward and back in his book until he found just the right test subject.

"'Date: June seventeenth, the year 20—,'" he read. "'Test site: the Mall of America in Minneapolis, Minnesota. Product: Beautiful You item number two sixteen, the Veggie Play Shaper, a food processor that quickly turns any raw vegetable into an erotic tool.'" In his flat, robotic voice, Maxwell described standing at a folding table as a stream of shoppers moved past. A few lingered, watching as he inserted uncooked carrots and zucchini squash into a plastic housing. With a single deft movement, he pressed a lever. Unseen blades within the device shaped the vegetable and out popped a phallus engineered for maximum fulfillment. As curious shoppers coalesced into a crowd, Maxwell demonstrated how the internal blades could be adjusted to make the resulting sex toy longer or shorter, thicker or thinner. Other blades carved channels and ridges that would excite the vaginal opening. His audience giggled and gasped with amusement, but they didn't leave. A voice near the back of the crowd called out, "Will it work on eggplants?"

Maxwell assured them it would.

"How about potatoes?" asked another shopper.

Max asked for a volunteer.

Reading to Penny, seated on a straight-backed chair beside her bed, his legs crossed primly at the knee and his notebook balanced atop them, he said, "The test subject, number seventeen sixty-nine, gave her name as Tiffany Jennifer Spalding, a twenty-five-year-old mother of three and homemaker. Height: a hundred and seventy centimeters. Weight: sixty-one kilos."

There in the Mall of America, he dialed the adjustment

knobs. "How thick do you like it?" He grinned lecherously. "Your potatoes, I mean."

She blushed. "Not too big around. Medium."

"Smooth or textured?"

Tiffany Jennifer tapped a finger against her temple and thought for a moment. "Textured."

"Ridges or nubs?"

She asked, "Can you do both?"

The crowd held its collective breath as he lifted the device's top and wedged the tuberous vegetable into the chopping chute. Like a magician performing a trick onstage, he ceremonially asked his volunteer to press the blade-activation lever. "Is this your first time?" he asked.

She nodded, trembling. Reality slowed to sex time.

To steady her, he slipped an arm around Tiffany Spalding's waist. He placed both her hands on the lever, then laid his own atop them. "You must shove it quickly and smoothly." On the count of three, they pressed together and the onlookers gasped.

Maxwell lifted the safety panel to reveal a perfect phallus. Sleek and slightly curved, it didn't suggest the rude Idaho spud that had gone into the top of the device. With sufficient sanitary precautions and a thorough cooking, he assured the onlookers there was no reason it couldn't go from the farm field to the bedroom to the family dinner table. For a young mother on a tight food budget it would pay for itself in a matter of weeks.

"Now," he boasted, "you can have your good times and eat them, too!"

Several people laughed. Everyone applauded. Money in hand, they surged forward to buy. No one recognized him. They never did. The disguise he donned for such occasions was simple and effective. Even when his false mustache fell off during cunnilingus, as it often did, test subjects never realized whom they were cavorting with. It was too impossible that C. Linus Maxwell, the richest man in the world, was the stranger fishing his prosthetic facial hair from their bedclothes.

Still reading in his Paris penthouse, Maxwell edged his chair closer to the bed. Holding the open notebook with one hand, he reached between the sheets with his other until his fingers found Penny's weary groin.

"The Veggie Play Shaper sold briskly. Even when the stock was gone, one shopper lingered." Test subject number 1769 had asked, "What about me?" Her voice descended to a sex-drenched murmur.

In the penthouse bedroom, Maxwell's fingertips carefully traced the soft contours of Penny's overtaxed pussy. With small circling motions, he provoked moisture to rise from deep within her.

Test subject 1769 still clutched her sculpted potato. Eyeing him from beneath her fluttering lashes, she said, "You're quite the pitchman." She wore Avon Pink Palace lipstick and held the potato suggestively near her mouth. From her skin tone, Maxwell estimated she was seventeen days from estrus. According to his notes, she asked, "Do you have anything else I might be interested in? Another labor-saving device?"

His voice still droning on, even and monotone, Max dipped his fingers, milking at Penny's hot wetness. Unlike earlier in the day, she didn't wince. In fact, she groaned and rolled her battered pelvis against the weight of his hand.

"'Test subject seventeen sixty-nine,'" Max read aloud, "'proved to be a willing and eager participant in preliminary evaluation of the champagne douche product. . . .'"

There was more. Maxwell kept reading for hours. But as his hand worked its customary magic Penny was no longer listening.

On another night of recovery, Maxwell pulled a chair to the side of the bed where Penny lay. That night, from among the recollections of geishas and singsong girls and courtesans, he read to her about a nondescript homebody recruited almost at random. "'Test subject thirty-eight ninety-one,'" he read. "'Place: Bakersfield, California, the auditorium of Hillshire Elementary School. Time: seven p.m., October second, 20—.'"

To prove product number 241, he was on the prowl for a larger woman. Vaginal tissue was wonderfully absorbent, and to exploit that aspect of it, Maxwell had invented the Burst Blaster, a vibrator containing as many as four internal cavities. Each functioned as a reservoir which could be filled with fluid, and the operator could program the device to release measured amounts during use, be it coffee for a quick pick-me-up, or cough syrup for something more euphoric. Even antibiotics. Or an essential oil for extra lubrication as needed. The tip of the vibrator would spout at the desired time. To prove its efficacy, he approached a lone mother and initiated small talk. To cut her from the pack of other mothers, he complimented her appearance. The strategy proved successful, and soon he'd sequestered her in an otherwise unoccupied kindergarten classroom.

"'There among the caged gerbils,'" he read, "'I wooed the test subject.'"

Her eyes closed, listening, Penny sighed. She knew product number 241 very well. Its caffeinated secretions had helped her stay present on many long nights of endurance testing.

"'Despite her body mass index, the test subject had exhibited an enthusiastic response to the device.'" As usual, Maxwell's voice was monotone. His delivery deadpan. "'Once application of the appliance began, the subject inexplicably shouted the name Fabio at regular intervals.'"

Penny smiled at his apparent failure to grasp the cultural reference.

"'The test subject's heart rate accelerated rapidly to a hundred and fifty-seven bpm,'" Max read. "'Her skin conductivity increased dramatically.'" He paused to turn a notebook page. "'It must be noted here that the scientist conducting this experiment had great difficulty in maintaining full possession of the product. Test subject thirty-eight ninety-one displayed enormous pelvic strength and was determined to usurp the device and complete the procedure on her own.'"

Penny pictured this. Some lonely woman wrestling with pale, scrawny Maxwell over control of a squirting sex toy. A caged gallery of hamsters and rabbits docilely witnessing these antics.

"'It was at the zenith of her climax—respiration twenty-five breaths per minute, blood pressure one seventy-five over one-oh-two—that test conditions were radically altered.'" Deciphering his own faded shorthand, Maxwell read, "'While application of the product was an unqualified success, the testing location failed to provide adequate privacy.'"

Someone had walked in on them.

"'The elders of the church school,'" Max affirmed, "'entered unannounced. Apparently alerted by the din of our procedure.'"

In a scientific aside, he noted, "'For the record, the test subject must've boasted an exceptionally large *corpus spongiosum*. Upon the entrance of additional parties to the scene, she expelled a copious stream of ejaculate from her urethra, thoroughly drenching them.'"

He briskly rapped his hairless knuckles against Penny's hypersensitive clitoris, a technique that drove her near to madness. Penny giggled softly. The poor test subject in Bakersfield, she'd spewed fluids all over the leaders of her religious charter school. Penny hoped it was worth the short-lived pleasure Maxwell's toy had provided. But knowing firsthand the power of the Burst Blaster, Penny suspected the woman had never regretted her furtive encounter.

The majordomo entered the penthouse bedroom carrying a silver tray. Lolling among the satin pillows and soft folds of the sheets, Penny accepted a flute of champagne. Taking a sip of the icy, thrilling wine, she tossed her head and gestured toward the book that lay open across his knee. "Read me another," she begged.

Injury and exhaustion weren't the only factors that impeded Maxwell's testing. When Penny's monthly period arrived, he took it in stride. Seeing her shake with cramps, her stomach bloating, Maxwell came to her aid with tablets of morphine and tiny cordial glasses of sweet sherry. She dozed in a twilight half-sleep, unaware of anything except him sitting near her, reading aloud from his notebook.

"'Test subject number thirty-eight twenty-eight,'" he announced. "'Location: Lower Manhattan, Zuccotti Park. Date: September seventeenth, 20—.'" He described seducing a young idealist who'd arrived only days before from Oklahoma to participate in the Occupy Wall Street event.

"'She gave her age as nineteen,'" he continued, "'a fact I asked that she confirm with her driver's license, as I had no desire to skew any statistical patterns with data garnered from not fully formed, preadult genitalia.'"

The scene had been late at night. While the majority of protesters slept, Maxwell had introduced the test subject to Beautiful You product number 223, the Love Lizard. It was a simple but brilliant telescoping tongue extender. A silicone tongue prosthesis calibrated to augment reach during oral coitus and engage vigorous contact with the cervix.

Even now, her mind drifting in drugged torpor, Penny recalled the clever novelty device and how it enabled Maxwell's relatively stunted oral appendage to access her to an astounding depth. At the memory of his attentions, she writhed with unfettered lust.

"'In a symbolic act of political street theater,'" Maxwell read, "'the test subject requested that the scientist conducting the experiment chain her spread-eagled to the security gates of the Bank of America Building.'"

The image played vividly in Penny's drugged imagination. The girl was nude in the moonlight, her smooth limbs bound wide apart. Test subject 3828 offered herself as this youthful sacrifice on the altar of capitalism. Maxwell knelt at her feet and adjusted the tongue extender to its full functional length. He cupped his gaping mouth over her pubis.

"'The trick was to wag the tongue,'" he read, "'as if singing. To avoid tiring the muscles of the mandible, don't hold the jaw rigid. After only a brief application of the product, the test subject expressed her approval by shouting, "I'm giving my body to you, the ninety-nine percent!"'"

Maxwell recounted how such outcries had lured a throng of bearded radicals, all eager to participate in the test. "'With only a brief tutorial,'" Maxwell recited from his notes, "'all present were able to successfully operate product number two twenty-three.'"

To Penny the boundaries between fantasy and reality evaporated. Awash in morphine dreams, she felt herself tongued by legions of hirsute political activists. Maxwell's voice threaded through a hallucination where a team of New York riot police arrived on the scene. Faceless behind the Kevlar shields of their helmets, they unsheathed their batons and menaced the test subject's nude, shameless form.

"'Once testing was complete,'" Maxwell concluded, "'the subject appeared self-conscious and professed to having ingested an unspecified amount of the drug commonly known as LSD. She requested the shackles be unlocked and asked for a sum of money sufficient to cover one-way airfare to Tulsa. . . .'"

Olympic training camps. Unsuspecting book clubs. Quilting circles. It was in all of these places Max found test subjects, and it was into this elite sisterhood that Penny had entered.

After Maxwell's umpteenth reprimand for faking an orgasm, Penny found herself doing the opposite. She held back her reaction to his efforts. No matter how Maxwell labored to please her, she began to withhold her usual squealing confirmation of his genius. Clearly she was punishing him, but Penny didn't care. She'd grown resentful. In Max's world she felt like nothing more than an instrument whose only purpose was to register the degree of his success.

One night he was testing a pair of nipple clamps on her, subjecting her to low-voltage fluctuations that shot sine waves of excitement up and down her spine, branching out along her arms and legs. Sparks of electric ecstasy shot out the ends of her fingers and glowed from the crown of her head like a halo. Throughout the entire pleasing ordeal, Penny willed herself to remain quiet. She tried to distract her own attention with thoughts about the few bar exam questions she could still recall. She willed herself to silently recite the Gettysburg Address, word for word.

Without a warning, he deactivated the batteries and made a point of unceremoniously removing the clips from her nipples. Before he spoke, Maxwell wrapped the wires in a tidy bundle and set the apparatus aside. Only then did he confront her. "You're angry at me, aren't you?"

"Don't blame me," Penny replied. "This gadget of yours must be a dud."

"A dud?" He snorted a laugh. Squinting at the notes he'd jotted in his book, he said, "Miss Harrigan, your pulse was a hundred and eighty beats per minute. Your anal temperature was a hundred and three degrees Fahrenheit. If this 'gadget' were any more effective, it would give you a coronary or a fatal brain embolism."

The last time Penny saw Alouette D'Ambrosia in person was at a cocktail party in the Rue St. Germaine. The actress had been escorted by a handsome novelist, Pierre Le Courgette, the winner of that year's Nobel Prize for literature. They made a striking couple. She lost track of them, but near the end of the get-together Alouette approached her. Glancing around nervously the French beauty asked, "Where is Max?" Without waiting for an answer, she whispered, "I was wrong not to confide in you. We must be allies, you and I. If we are not, we are both in gravest danger."

This was the first time the two women had met since the incident with the married stones. The Frenchwoman looked starved, like a leathery husk of her former self. There wasn't a whiff of booze on her breath, but she was obviously agitated. The heavy sapphire that hung around her neck glowed against her flushed cleavage. "He will spoil you for other men." Maxwell had entered from a door at the far end of the salon. As usual, his head was bowed as he took notes in his book. He'd yet to catch sight of Alouette as she insisted, "The sisterhood of us, all his castoff lovers, we are his harem around the world."

Tensing as Maxwell grew nearer, she said, "I am nominated for a new Oscar, so I must be there, but next month we will talk more deeply, no?"

Penny stammered, "I'd like that." The sensation of Alouette's lovely mouth against her came to mind unbidden.

"You will not like what I have to say," warned the actress. Nevertheless, the look she gave Penny was warm. "We will be bosom friends, no?" As Maxwell wandered closer, she kissed Penny on both cheeks and hurriedly returned to her own escort.

Without taking his eyes off her undulating body, Maxwell pulled open a drawer of the bedside table. He lifted out something and held it to one eye like a mask. It was a video camera, and he panned slowly up and down her nakedness.

Penny wasn't afraid. On some level she knew she was safe. If these images were ever made public Maxwell stood to suffer more embarrassment than she did. Many mornings she would wake to find him preparing a new device for her enjoyment. While softly twisting a new toy into her, he'd explain the ancient sex magic rituals of the Sudanese tribesmen. There were more basic tools. Soft pink versions of medical clamps that would spread her buttocks and hold them apart for his leisured convenience.

Scanning her through the lens, he said, "Good girl, don't struggle. There is no film in the camera." He assured her, "I merely want you to feel as if you're under observation." Whether or not he was actually documenting her, Penny savored the fact that someone was paying her so much regard. She wondered whether all of his test subjects had loved the attention as much as (or even more than?) the physical sensations he prompted.

During the day sunlight fell on the bed from tall windows, and Penny snuggled under the smooth sheets, naked, nibbling on a brioche, sipping a latte, and studying her old textbooks on tort law. These days the fashion houses brought their clothes to her. The designers themselves fitted her. If she insisted, Maxwell took her out to the symphony or the theater; otherwise she seldom left the penthouse.

Beautiful You would launch in another month, and she wondered whether Max would have further need for her. She didn't delude herself. As demonstrated by his elaborate coldness he'd never loved her. It had been sufficient to have someone who could read her needs so intuitively. Often Max dismissed the team of massage therapists and treated her himself. He could stroke her tense muscles and know exactly her mood. He listened as closely to her breathing as he did to the words she spoke.

Maxwell had come to know her so well that Penny seldom needed to speak.

Here was a man who found her intensely fascinating, and who delighted in guiding her to peaks of aliveness she had never dreamed existed. He savored and appreciated her.

Billions of people were watching him—the wealthiest, arguably the most powerful man in the world—and he was watching Penny. The gaze of his camera, the scratched shorthand of his notes, they imbued her life with even more value. Under his watchful eye she felt secure. Cherished. But, no, not loved.

Two weeks before the rollout of the Beautiful You product line, Max abruptly froze in the middle of lovemaking. With a resigned slowness he carefully withdrew the current apparatus from her and laid it on the bedside table. Pulling off his latex gloves, he said, "You're of no further use to me." He lifted his notebook. "The integrity . . . the authenticity . . . the *truth* of your reactions have become too compromised."

As he made his notes, he checked the time on his wristwatch. "My jet is already prepped. You'll find that your clothes and personal items have all been packed, and your luggage is already aboard, waiting for you."

Maxwell turned to her, her head still cradled in the white satin pillow. He pressed two fingers to the side of her neck and timed her pulse. "The pilot is instructed to take you anywhere in the world you desire." Penny had no chance to protest. She had yet to even close her legs.

He wrote down the last statistics of her heart rate and temperature. "I've deposited fifty million dollars in a numbered Swiss bank account for you. I will wire you the details for accessing it, if you agree to never contact me again." To underscore his commands he looked at her. "You must never speak of our experience together or I will block your access to those funds."

A forever of silence passed. Despite his icy demeanor she sensed Max's little-boy heart was breaking.

"Do you understand?" he asked finally.

Blinking back tears, pulling her knees together, Penny didn't answer. She was surprised by the suddenness of the rejection.

"Do! You! Understand?" he shouted. The fury of his words broke her shock and she nodded her head.

"Test subject unresponsive," he muttered over his work. There was no mistaking it. His voice sounded choked with grief.

Penny curled onto her side, facing away from him. It was over. It had been a dream to be Cinderella, but now it was time to wake up.

"Please know that you've made a significant contribution to the development of the Beautiful You line," his voice continued, a droning. "As a token of my appreciation I've placed a small gift aboard the jet. I hope it will meet with your approval."

Penny felt the bed shift. His weight left the mattress. She listened as his bare feet crossed the carpeted floor. "You will leave my house within the hour." The bathroom door closed.

It had been exactly 136 days.

Aboard the Gulfstream, Penny found a small ribbon-wrapped box in the only seat that wasn't heaped with heavy suitcases and garment bags. She'd been hustled from the penthouse so quickly that she wore nothing except a floor-length chinchilla coat and a pair of Prada high heels. Alone in the quiet cabin, she lifted the gift and held it in her lap as she fastened her seat belt and the pilot announced takeoff.

After they were airborne, she slipped the ribbons from the box and lifted the lid. Inside was a thin gold chain. When she lifted it out, a ruby swung from the lowest point. It was the ruby that Maxwell had always worn in a ring, reset as a pendant, the third-largest Sri Lankan ruby ever mined. Sharing the box was a bright pink plastic dragonfly. Its wings were thick and soft, printed with the curlicue Beautiful You logo. Penny inspected its antennae and the underside of its plastic body.

The dragonfly-shaped souvenir was a sex toy. The mass-produced version of a prototype Max had tested on her several times. She'd never grown tired of the effects the little flapping wings had generated. Those unfettered sessions were among her most intense memories, and the sight of the device made a blush rise in her cheeks.

A trust fund of fifty million dollars. Enough clothes to fill a department store. No, Penny told herself, she hadn't been too mistreated. As she fastened the chain around her neck and felt the weight of the frigid ruby between her warm breasts, she slipped the plastic dragonfly into the pocket of her coat and began to plan the first day of her new life. Within reach, an open bottle of champagne bubbled in an ice bucket. The flight attendant poured her a glass and turned off the cabin lights at Penny's request.

As she sipped the dry sparkling wine, she felt a twinge of sadness in remembering how, just months before, the taste had been a special treat. Between the multiple pounding orgasms and the champagne, life with Max had spoiled her rotten.

She was spoiled but not despairing. If anything, she felt excited about the future. Tonight she'd need something more than champagne to help her fall asleep.

Once she was sure the flight crew wouldn't see, she opened the front of her coat and slipped the dragonfly between her legs, settling it snugly in place. She'd watched Max do this dozens of times. As a special selling feature, he'd designed the toy to automatically warm itself to the perfect temperature. Even without looking she felt the button that activated it.

She wondered how he would fill his time once Beautiful You was launched. Maybe he was already planning new additions to the product line. Maybe he'd find another girlfriend with "ideal" genitals on which to test his prototypes. Someone who didn't hesitate in expressing her arousal.

Girlfriend was the wrong word. More like *guinea pig*.

In the inky blackness high above the Atlantic, Penny poured herself a second glass and lay back to enjoy the delicious pulsations between her thighs.

Her first weeks back in New York were a blur.

The money Maxwell bestowed on her came in the form of an annuity. She couldn't withdraw the entire lump sum, but she could live very well off the accruing dividends for the rest of her life. Prudently, she invested in a small town house on the Upper East Side. When the realtor had shown her the sunny tiled kitchen, the elaborate scrolled-ironwork elevator, and the carved marble fireplaces, Penny had written a check for the full asking price. It had plenty of closet space, which Penny's burgeoning wardrobe almost filled to capacity.

On her first day back at BB&B, she found someone to share the house.

Despite her self-professed identity as a crunchy bohemian, Monique was thrilled to give up the squalid studio she shared with two ethnic roommates under the Kosciuszko Bridge. Before Penny could entertain any second thoughts, Monique was dragging cardboard boxes from a taxi into the town house's elegant foyer. The smell of sandalwood was inescapable, but Monique's weird sitar music helped to fill the emptiness. To celebrate their first night together the transplanted neohippie cooked a curried tofu feast. Afterward, the two young women flopped on the sofa in the media room. Each with a bowl of popcorn in her lap, they watched the Academy Awards ceremony being broadcast live.

As the camera in the Kodak Theatre panned the crowded audience, Penny couldn't help herself. She searched for Maxwell's pale boyish face and limp blond hair. There, seated on an aisle, was Pierre Le Courgette, Alouette's boyfriend. Of course he would attend; she was a shoo-in to win best actress. Other faces Penny recognized, powerful people who had snubbed her or leered at her. It was hard to believe she'd rubbed elbows with them. That part of her life was fading like a sexually charged dream. She'd allowed Maxwell to isolate her in a fantasy of addictive pleasure and no emotional attachment, but now she was free.

Between being constantly examined by Maxwell and judged

by the thoroughbred jet-setters they met in public, Penny had shed any sensitivity she'd had about getting ogled. She might occasionally hear it, the clicking of paparazzi camera shutters, but she no longer reacted. She'd come to assume that every eye was always on her, and she carried herself with a new relaxed poise.

Whether it was this new self-confidence or the new clothes, she often caught men staring. Whenever she walked down Lexington Avenue, she almost didn't recognize her own reflection in the windows of Bloomingdale's. Striding along was a leggy Amazon. Gone was the layer of baby fat. Her hair swung in a shining wave.

In retrospect, Penny was glad the City of Light had never heard of butter brickle ice cream.

In the media room, she and Monique fought good-naturedly over the remote control. Both shouted jibes at the screen, where lesser-known cinematographers and producers expressed their verbose gratitude. The winner of best documentary was ushered offstage, and the network cut to a commercial.

The television showed a group of delighted, smiling young women gathered around a table. In the center of the shot the prettiest of them blew out the candles on a birthday cake as her friends pressed gifts upon her. To comic effect, every gift turned out to be a bright pink box emblazoned with a very curlicued white logo. *Beautiful You.* The girls rolled their shoulders and giggled. As if sharing some glorious secret, they pursed their lips and leaned to whisper in one another's ears. The birthday girl squealed as if the pink boxes contained nirvana.

To Penny, it was unlikely that girls like these—thin, doe-eyed, clear-skinned—would have any problem finding men who'd romance them. They were the last women who'd need to buy Maxwell's throbbing whatchamacallits.

Suddenly Penny envisioned a billion lonely wives or single

women abusing themselves in isolated resignation. In ghetto tenements or tumbledown farmhouses. Not bothering to meet potential partners. Living and dying with no intimate companions beyond their Beautiful You gadgetry. Instead of being either whores or Madonnas, they'd become celibates who diddled a lot. To Penny that didn't seem like social progress.

The television commercial ended with the familiar tagline; a dulcet female voice intoned, "A billion husbands are about to be replaced . . ."

"They have a store on Fifth," Monique said through a mouthful of popcorn. "I can't wait until it opens tomorrow."

Penny thought of the flagship outlet. Already a line of women was forming and it snaked for two blocks, down almost all the way to Fifty-fifth Street. The building's facade was skinned in pink mirror, so anyone trying to peek inside saw only a flattering rose-colored reflection of herself.

Penny hoped the eventual products were better made than the one Maxwell had left for her aboard the Gulfstream. She'd fallen asleep to its soothing pulsations, but as they'd been descending into LaGuardia she'd blinked awake to find it broken. The two wings of the plastic dragonfly had fallen off, and the pink-silicone body had split down the middle. It was almost as if the thing had hatched. Metamorphosed, she'd thought. But it was caterpillars that turned into butterflies. Butterflies just died. They laid their eggs on cabbage leaves and died. As the pilot had prepared for landing, Penny had discreetly picked the shattered scraps of silicone out of herself and stuffed them into her coat pocket.

Resolutely, she decided to find a real, live, flesh-and-blood lover before she'd resort to standing in line on Fifth Avenue.

Monique called, "Pay attention, Omaha girl!" and began to pelt Penny with salty, buttery kernels of popcorn.

On television, Alouette sauntered across the stage to accept her award as best actress. Her floor-length gown swirled around her toned legs. Her shoulders bare and thrown back, her breasts held high in her strapless bodice, she was the perfect image of self-assurance and accomplishment. It was thrilling to watch.

"God, I love her," Monique sighed. "Is that bling for real?"

Glowing in the center of the actress's cleavage was the huge sapphire.

The camera zoomed in on Maxwell seated ten rows back, on the aisle. The lovable dork, he appeared to be playing a hand-held electronic game. As his thumbs danced over the keys on a little black box, he seemed to be ignoring Alouette's triumph onstage.

In vivid contrast, the audience of big names applauded with genuine admiration. Standing behind the clear Plexiglas podium, the French beauty beamed, graciously accepting their accolades. A few people stood. Then everyone was standing. A tidal wave of adoration. As the applause subsided, leaving room for her to speak, a shadow of pain seemed to drift across Alou-ette's delicate features. Her lips and brow tightened almost imperceptibly. It passed, and her smile returned. Even under her makeup her face looked flushed, and rivulets of sweat flat-tened strands of hair to her cheeks.

She looked a little dazed, Penny thought, but who wouldn't be?

The actress began to say, *"Merci,"* but winced again. *"Alors,"* she cried out. She gasped for breath. Hugging the golden award to her chest, she took a step toward the wings, but looked uncharacteristically wobbly in her stiletto heels.

Taking a second step, she stumbled and fell. The golden Oscar landed with a clunk and rolled a few feet. A murmur of concern rippled through the auditorium.

"Somebody help the lady!" Monique shouted at the televi-sion screen.

As she lay on the stage, trying to raise herself onto her elbows, Alouette's legs began to tremble. A palsy began at her feet, but quickly traveled upward to her knees until both legs were shaking from the waist down. Her ankles moved slowly apart. Positioned toward the audience, her legs gradually spread, stretching her skirt taut between them. Even as Alouette reached down, gripping the hem and trying to keep it at a modest level, the tension on the fabric was too great. It sprang up, collecting above her crotch. She wasn't wearing underthings, Penny realized. You never did with a gown that clingy and formfitting.

"Are you seeing this?" asked Monique in a whisper. One hand hung frozen in the air, midway between the bowl of popcorn and her gaping mouth.

To Penny, the five-time Oscar winner clearly looked deranged. She twisted her head violently from side to side, lashing the stage with her long hair. Her eyes rolled up until only the whites showed. Her chest heaved, and her back arched, thrusting her hips into the air as if to meet a phantom lover.

In heavily accented English, she was screaming, "No!" Shrieking, "Please, no! Not here!" It seemed as if the suffering movie star was staring directly at C. Linus Maxwell.

None too soon, the network cut to a commercial.

Instantly, the panting woman lying on her back, shoving her bare pubis at an audience of millions, was replaced by a new bevy of giggling twenty-somethings brandishing bright pink shopping bags.

Everyone at BB&B was talking about it. Alouette D'Ambrosia was dead. According to the front page of the *Post,* she'd suffered a brain aneurysm onstage and died before an ambulance had arrived.

The rumor was that after the broadcast had cut away to an emergency break, the cameras had kept rolling. In front of that vast audience of industry swells, Alouette had acted like an animal in heat, going so far as to violently abuse herself with the gold-plated statuette. Penny couldn't believe that. Or she didn't want to. The extra footage was reportedly on the Web, but she couldn't bring herself to view it. If anything, the shocking episode only reinforced her impression that Alouette had been seriously mentally ill. It was a sad idea, but she'd likely relapsed into abusing drugs and alcohol.

Whatever the case, it was tragic. In more ways than one. Brillstein had hoped to make Penny an associate. He'd planned to appoint her as lead counsel to represent the plaintiff in the palimony lawsuit filed on behalf of their client, Alouette. It would've looked great: the defendant's most recent lover championing his jilted lover on the witness stand. Such a strategy would've made Alouette look injured and deserving. BB&B would've won the case, but not before the firm had oodles of billable hours to their credit. With the actress dead, her lawsuit was dead. BB&B would have to find a new rainmaker, and Brillstein would need to find a new shop window in which to showcase Penny's lawyering talents.

Brillstein wasn't the only person watching out for her at BB&B. Tad was back in the picture. Tad Smith, who'd always called her "Hillbilly." He was the young fresh-faced patent law specialist whose private man-parts Monique referred to as "the tadpole." After Penny's Beautiful You transformation in Paris, Tad hardly seemed to recognize her. Now a boldly beautiful eyeful, utterly unashamed to be seen by all, she was no longer anyone's fat, stinky dog. If he still had a hankering for Monique, he never asked about her. Instead, he invited Penny to lunch.

He escorted her to La Grenouille and regaled her with anecdotes about his days editing the *Yale Law Review*. After lunch they'd hired a carriage and ridden through the park. He bought her a handful of helium balloons from a street vendor, a simple romantic gesture that Maxwell—despite all his brainpower—would never think to do.

Tad didn't even tease her about being "the Nerd's Cinderella." The *New York Post* had long since moved on to other stories. Alouette's death, for instance. A forest fire in Florida. The queen of England had collapsed in convulsions during a meeting to negotiate duties on consumer goods manufactured in China. As their carriage clip-clopped down Fifth Avenue, Penny tried to ignore the pink-mirrored building that loomed ahead at Fifty-seventh Street. A line of shoppers waited to enter. The line trailed into the distance as far as she could see.

"Look," Tad said. "Is that Monique?"

Penny followed his gaze to a girl cooling her heels on the sidewalk, her arms folded across her chest. All of the people waiting in line were women. In the carriage seat she slumped her shoulders and slid down. She cringed with disappointment and resignation, pulling the balloons low to hide herself.

Tad shouted, "Mo!" He waved until the girl's eyes found them.

"Can you believe this?" Monique yelled. "This is worse than when I bought my BlackBerry!" The midday sun sparkled on her rhinestone-studded fingernails and the bright tribal beads braided into her hair.

Tad asked the driver to halt at the curb.

As before, Penny felt ignored, relegated to being her glitzy friend's stinky mutt. She looked up, pretending to only now notice her housemate. She knew Monique had a list of Beautiful You products that she was anxious to cart home and try. The online buzz posted by early adopters was positive. Beyond positive—it was raves. Despite the fact that a huge inventory had been stockpiled before the launch, the offshore factories were having trouble keeping up with orders. The praise spread like wildfire. Media wags speculated that so many women were calling in "sick" and staying home to indulge themselves that the gross national output would take a short-term dip.

Penny resented how male newscasters treated the story like a dirty joke, reporting it with winks and an implied "hubba hubba" in every pause.

"Save yourself the money," Tad shouted to Monique. "Jerald in copyright law has a crush on you." The horse shifted, restless. A taxi behind them honked.

"Haven't you heard?" Monique shouted in response. "Men are obsolete!"

The declaration drew a small cheer from the assembled women.

Monique played to the crowd. "Anything a man can do to me, I can do better!" She snapped her fingers dismissively, making the crystals glued to each nail flash in the sunlight.

This evoked a louder cheer. Jeers and whistles sounded in her support.

The taxi honked again. The line of shoppers began to move.

"Can a sex toy buy you dinner?" challenged Tad, clearly flirting.

"I can buy my own dinner!" With another step, Monique and the women nearest her were swallowed up by the big pink store.

As if she needed proof that she was back in wild-and-woolly New York City, Penny was attacked her first month there. Standing on an otherwise deserted subway platform, she was headed uptown after a late night at work. She was idly musing whether to order Thai food or pizza when two arms grabbed her from behind. They crushed the breath from her, squeezing at her chest and throat, and her vision pinholed to a narrow awareness of the fluorescent lights overhead.

She was on her back, her Donna Karan slacks stomped down around her Jimmy Choos. Later, what she'd remember most about her attacker was his stench of stale urine and peach wine coolers. What she'd never understand was how quickly it had happened. One moment she'd been deciding on lemongrass chicken, and in the next she'd felt the stranger's erection ramming to enter her.

Maxwell flashed into her mind. Not that the attacker was either curious or clinical, but how the assault was so impersonal.

Even as Penny felt herself yielding, felt the angry hardness rip into her, she also heard the man scream.

Faster than he had fallen on her, he jumped to his feet, his hands cradling the filthy penis that hung from the open front of his ragged trousers. He kept on yelping, tears streaming from his eyes as he looked down and examined himself.

Her first impression was that the man's fly zipper had snagged some tender fold of skin. Before she could rally her strength to scream or run away, she saw a large bead of blood swell from a puncture wound in the glans of his penis.

The stranger's attention shifted from his bleeding self, his eyes rising to glare at her. His voice timorous, he whined, "What have you got in your snatch, lady? A Bengal tiger?"

Penny watched as the drop of blood grew to a steady stream. She edged backward, sliding herself away from where the blood dribbled to form a growing pool on the subway platform. She saw that he'd been wearing a condom, and the latex of it had also been torn.

In another beat, a train arrived, and the man was gone. That was all she could tell the policeman who responded to her 911 call.

The doctor she'd gone to for the necessary STD tests said

she showed no signs of infection but insisted she come back for further tests in six weeks. The doctor, a sympathetic older woman with frizzy, graying red hair, insisted on giving her a pelvic exam and swabbing for DNA evidence. While she told Penny to place her feet in the stirrups of the examining room table, the woman donned a pair of latex gloves. She said to exhale while she inserted a speculum.

While the doctor clicked a penlight and began her careful inspection, Penny asked for a pelvic X-ray.

"That's usually not necessary," the doctor assured her.

"Please," Penny insisted. A wave of dread was fueling her request.

"What are you worried about?" asked the doctor, still squinting through the speculum, rotating the beam of the penlight.

Penny explained about the man's lanced penis. The hole torn in his condom.

"Well, there's nothing here that might account for a puncture wound," said the doctor. "Your first impression was probably correct: He got it caught in his trouser fly." She began to slowly withdraw the speculum. "Serves the bastard right."

They ordered the X-ray.

The X ray came back showing nothing.

Penny told herself it was nothing. Probably just the sharp metal teeth of the man's own zipper. It was only after that fact that Penny realized the worst part. Her guardian angels, in their tailored suits and mirrored sunglasses . . . for the first time in her life, they hadn't come to her rescue.

At work, Penny was cramming like crazy to pass the bar. Brillstein was still searching for the perfect class-action case for her to helm, but that wouldn't happen unless she was an attorney.

Until then, she still had to juggle the occasional coffee run and wrangle extra chairs for big meetings.

It didn't help that Monique kept calling in sick. Since the day she'd lugged home two bright pink shopping bags, the girl had been barricaded behind her locked bedroom door. From what Penny could tell, she didn't even emerge to eat. Day and night, a faint buzzing came from behind the door. When Penny knocked the buzzing stopped.

"Mo?" Penny waited. The buzzing was all too familiar. She knocked again.

"Go away, Omaha girl."

"Brillstein asked about you today."

"Go away." The buzzing restarted.

Penny went away.

Around Wednesday, Monique stumbled into the kitchen, squinting against the sunlight as if she'd been trapped for months in a collapsed coal mine. Fumbling in the fridge for a carton of milk, she grumbled. "Damn cheap piece of junk." She drank from the carton. Gasping before another swig, she added, "I can't wait to buy a replacement."

Penny looked up from the textbook she was highlighting. "It broke?"

"I guess," Monique said. "At least, the wings came off."

Penny stiffened. She was sitting, the breakfast table in front of her covered with books and legal pads. "Was it the dragonfly?"

Guzzling milk, Monique grunted in the affirmative. All the bright Austrian crystals had been chipped off of her fingernails. Her braids were kinked and tangled in disarray.

Warily, Penny asked, "Did it split down the middle?"

Monique nodded. "I was asleep."

Penny made a note to talk to Brillstein. This might be just the high-profile case she needed. With the land-office way Beautiful You was selling, if even a small percentage of the products were defective it might warrant a recall. If she could prove real damages and assemble a pool of plaintiffs, women from around the world who'd been hurt in any way by the shattered dragonflies, she might have an enormous class-action lawsuit. The idea wasn't without precedent; it seemed that every time a new tampon or form of birth control came to market women died. Toxic shock. Ruptures of the vaginal wall. Men engineered these innovations, but it was always women who paid the price.

Alouette, for example. She'd been among Maxwell's stable of lab rats. What was to say her embolism wasn't the long-term result of some stimulant-infused silicone coating? It wasn't impossible that the queen of England and the president of the United States might be compelled to testify. Penny could see herself as another bold Erin Brockovich. This was a case that would make her career.

Sure, Maxwell would be furious. He might cut off the payouts from her trust fund, but the income and prestige from winning a huge settlement might yield more than that loss.

Highlighting passages in a text about patent law, Penny said, "I was afraid you'd died in your bed."

"Only about three thousand times," Monique quipped.

"Have you used the douche?" asked Penny.

Monique was peeling the top off a cup of yogurt and stirring it with a spoon.

"When you do," Penny continued, "read the directions. Make sure you use imported champagne, not domestic sparkling wine. Definitely do not use brut. And the temperature must be between forty and fifty degrees Fahrenheit." She wondered whether this was how Max had felt when he was coaching her.

Jotting a citation in the margin of a page, she felt like Maxwell. Without meeting Monique's curious gaze she said, "When you use product number thirty-nine, start with the oscillations at fifteen bpm and slowly dial them up to forty-five bpm. After that, you'll maintain the best effects by alternating between twenty-seven-point-five and thirty-five-point-five."

Monique was impressed. She'd yet to eat a spoonful. She kicked a chair back from the table and lowered herself into the seat. "What's product number . . . ?"

Penny completed the sentence. "The Happy Honey Ball." She asked, "Do you know where your urethral sponge is?"

"In the bathroom?" Monique ventured. "On the shelf next to the tub?"

Penny gave her a wilting glance. "Did you buy a pair of those awful Peruvian married stones?"

"Of what?"

"Good," Penny confirmed, remembering the miserable scene where Alouette had come to her rescue in the restaurant. "Don't."

Monique set her yogurt on the table, careful not to cover any of Penny's study materials. "You sound as if you designed this stuff."

Penny thought, but didn't say, *I sort of did invent them*. Her resentment toward her housemate dwindled. Life was too short. A few days of physical indulgence wouldn't kill Monique. It was pleasure without affection; she'd recognize that and outgrow it. "Listen up," Penny said. "When you use the Daisy Love Wand, keep in mind the coefficient of friction and only use it with the Glassy Glide Cream."

The expression on Monique's face was one of complete bewilderment. "This shit," she marveled, "is going to change the fabric of society."

Tearing a blank page from her legal pad, Penny went to work with a pen. "Don't worry," she said. "I'm writing this all down."

That same day she went to Tad's office and asked him to lunch. As boyfriend material Tad had more moxie than skill. He was fun and spontaneous, often sneaking a quick kiss and trying to slip his finger inside her while they rode crowded subway cars. Over hot dogs on a park bench she broached the subject. Maybe she was hypersensitive to it, but it seemed like half the women on the street were toting the bright pink shopping bags of Beautiful You. Even if half those bags were just being reused to carry sack lunches, they'd become the new status symbol for liberated, take-charge females in Union Square.

Penny mused that Max's greatest accomplishment wasn't the toys themselves. It was the idea of combining ladies' two greatest pleasures: shopping and sex. It was like *Sex and the City,* but the four playgirls didn't need Gucci belts or troublesome boy toys. They didn't even need to sip cosmos or share girl talk.

"Theoretically speaking," she began gradually, evading Tad's gaze, "what if there was a fantastically successful new consumer product? It was making its inventor a fortune."

Tad listened attentively, his thigh almost touching hers.

She tried not to think about what went into making hot dogs.

Since Maxwell's toys had gone on sale, New Yorkers seemed so laid-back. At least the half who'd made the trip to the big pink store and forked over their cash. The only tension seemed to be in the grinding teeth and toe tapping of the shoppers who were waiting. The line was longer every day. Today the *Post* carried a front-page article about a woman who'd tried to cut into the front of the queue. The frustrated shoppers already waiting there had beaten the interloper almost to death.

"Just suppose," Penny ventured, "a potential client had been crucial in the testing and development of these successful new products."

The pink bags really were ubiquitous. A city bus drove by,

the side covered with the slogan "A Billion Husbands Are About to Be Replaced."

Penny didn't especially want to tell Tad the gory details about what she'd done with Maxwell, but there were larger principles at stake.

"Let's say the person in question is a woman," she proposed, "a young innocent woman, and she allows a man to experiment on her with a number of sex-toy prototypes?"

"Hypothetically speaking," Tad confirmed, a burr in his voice. His eyebrow arched quizzically. "That sounds hot."

"Hypothetically speaking," Penny redirected, "do you think the test subject might have a claim to part ownership of the subsequent patents?"

Tad licked a dab of mustard that threatened to drip from his dog onto the pant leg of his Armani trousers. "Is the plaintiff over the age of twenty-one?"

Penny discreetly picked at the chopped onions on her own wiener. "A couple years."

"Is she someone you know personally?"

Penny nodded glumly.

"Is she very pretty?" he teased. "With flawless skin and a brilliant legal mind?"

Penny protested, "Don't be patronizing. She's not a slut. This girl could really use some sound legal advice." It might've been her imagination, but some of the ladies with bright pink bags appeared to be limping. She worried that demanding partial credit for the Beautiful You products meant she'd be culpable if they—the Dragonfly in particular—were found to be faulty and dangerous. A cut of the profits might also mean a share of the actionable blame.

Tad looked at her. His features darkened with concern. "Is the client ready to go into court and publicly describe the testing process?"

Penny swallowed. "Would that be absolutely necessary?"

"'Fraid so." He asked, "Are there any corroborating witnesses?"

Penny thought. There had been the flight crew of Max's private jet. The household staffs at his château and penthouse. And his various chauffeurs and admin assistants who at times, when she lost all control of her flailing, had been drafted to hold her spread-eagled on the bed. None of them could be subpoenaed as anything but hostile witnesses. Brightening, she said, "But there are handwritten records that we can subpoena."

"What kind of records?"

Penny considered all the names that might be in Max's notebooks. The anonymous women as well as the sex workers and the world leaders. "Would it complicate the process if those notes might be considered a threat to national security?"

"You mean," Tad asked ruefully, "if they depict the president of the United States in some compromising situations?"

He was way ahead of her. Tad Smith had a sunny, take-charge outlook on life, and Penny found that she enjoyed pulling in harness with this hopeful go-getter.

When she didn't speak, he did. "If the plaintiff will make a deposition, we can file it and begin the discovery process." He took a sip of soda. "If we get the defendant's written records and they match the deposition, your theoretical client would have a very winnable case."

Penny didn't ponder her reaction. She didn't need to. "What's our first step?"

It wasn't two days before Penny was summoned to Mr. Brillstein's office. BB&B, it seemed, had a leak. Some insider had tipped off higher-ups to the possibility of a pending lawsuit, and her boss wasn't happy. To make everything worse, the president was in town to address the United Nations, and that meant traffic in the city was gridlocked. Armed squads of antiterrorism guards were patrolling the subways with bomb-sniffing dogs. The few citizens whose tempers weren't on edge were the placid, relaxed ladies with their bright pink bags. Watching them stride, calm and unfazed, down the streets made even Penny want to get in line on Fifth Avenue.

Conversely, the male residents of the city—more specifically the hetero ones—were grouchier than ever. Not a man could compete with Maxwell's lifetime of erotic training, and the effects of his tantric studies could now be bought with a bright pink Beautiful You credit card.

Tad's idea was to immediately start by fishing for plaintiffs. They'd run a series of television ads to identify consumers who'd bought the faulty Dragonfly device and found that it broke while they were using it. Those numbers poured in by the millions. Around the world, users had fallen asleep while enjoying the deep pulsations, then awakened to find the toy in pieces. In every statement they collected the details were the same: The wings had snapped off; the body had split. Just like what Monique and Penny had experienced.

It would be difficult to prove real damages, because no one was so much as scratched in the process. Many of the women had gone to see their doctors, but no fragments of the toy could be found lodged internally.

In Tad's office, Penny stuffed her case notes into a file folder. The manila folder she stashed in her Fendi tote bag to take home. That done, she hurried to Brillstein's office on the hushed, wood-paneled sixty-fourth floor, the carpeted inter sanctum where she'd first met Max.

Outside his door, she knocked. A familiar voice said, "Come in, please." It was a female voice. Penny turned the knob, stepped through the doorway, and came face-to-face with someone she'd seen on countless newscasts. The woman's cheekbones were high and widely placed. The combination of these and her small, pointed chin gave the impression that she was always smiling. Her golden-brown eyes glowed with a warm compassion.

Penny's cantankerous boss sat behind his polished desk.

President Hind turned her serene smile on Brillstein. "Would you be so kind as to leave Miss Harrigan and me alone for a few minutes?"

"Miss Harrigan," she began.

"Penny," the younger woman prompted.

The president motioned for her to take a seat. She was roughly the same age as Penny's mother, but much more put-together. Her tailored suit fit as snug as a uniform. She wore a silver-filigree brooch on one lapel like a badge. She waited for Penny's boss to leave the room. Shutting the door, she locked it. The president motioned for Penny to sit in a red leather wing chair. She took the chair facing that, and the two sat toe-to-toe like old chums enjoying a chat.

"My dear," she said, her tone placating, "I'm here on a matter of gravest national security." She spoke as if giving a speech in the Oval Office. "Please do not pursue any legal action against C. Linus Maxwell."

Penny listened, dumbfounded. It was impossible to picture this resolute leader subjecting herself to Max's torrid exercises. Penny could scarcely imagine this well-dressed, articulate woman reduced to the chicken scratchings in a notebook. Clarissa Hind had been her role model, but the courageous leader

Penny had always imagined bore no resemblance to the person who now glanced furtively at the locked office door and spoke to her so softly.

"As a fellow attorney," continued the president, "I can empathize with your desire to see justice done, but this showdown must not be undergone in a public forum. Trust me when I say that millions of people, worldwide, will presently be put in danger by the legal actions you're about to embark upon. For you to organize this class action or contest Maxwell's patents would jeopardize their lives as well as yours."

She was no longer the pretty woman smiling on the cover of the *National Enquirer*. Three years in the Oval Office had etched wrinkles across her forehead. The president said, "I understand that you were attacked on a subway platform a few weeks ago." Her tone sounded tentative, hushed with sympathy. "That must've been terrifying, but, my dear, don't assume that it was a random crime. Whoever was hired, Max's motive was not to harm you." The president's eyes were earnest and pleading. "Maxwell was simply demonstrating his own power. For the rest of your life you must always assume that no matter where you are, he can reach out at any time and destroy you."

It struck Penny that the president was seated in the same chair Max had occupied when she had cowered at his feet. Today the carpet showed no stain to bear witness to the flood of coffee drinks. Penny thought back to the last time she'd heard this same subdued voice. Suspicion sharpened her own voice into a dart.

"How much is Max paying you?" Penny spat the accusation. "You helped him. When I answered by mistake in Paris, that was you on his telephone." She waited for a denial that didn't come. "You persuaded the FDA to approve the distribution of his . . . personal care items." Penny was livid. "People are being sold defective, dangerous sex toys, and you're helping."

The older woman continued, unfazed. "In exchange for your cooperation I'm prepared to mentor you as my political protégée."

Penny understood their plan. To avoid being exposed, Max and the president were offering her a slice of the global political pie. They would groom her to inherit their corrupt dynasty. A weaker person might've accepted, but she felt nothing but disgust for their bargain.

"It doesn't matter what office you eventually run for," the president offered. "If you side with us you'll get virtually every vote cast by women between the ages of eighteen and seventy."

Politics aside, Penny knew it was an insane promise. "You can't guarantee that," she said.

"I can't," countered Hind, "but Max can." The president lifted her wrist and slid back the sleeve of her suit jacket to check her watch. "I'm due to speak at the UN. Can we continue this discussion in the car?"

The gray Manhattan streetscape oozed by outside the limousine windows. President Hind shut her eyes for a moment and kneaded her temples with her fingertips, as if she were suffering a migraine.

"First he makes you famous," the president said in a weary voice, "so famous that you can't show your face in public." From that first paparazzi snap, she claimed that Maxwell had hired the press to hound Penny. He'd stoked the public's curiosity. He'd created the circumstances that left her trapped at home. Hind smiled ruefully, knowingly. "Eventually, the only place you feel safe is at his penthouse. He isolates you. He becomes the only person you can trust, and he provides the only comfort you know."

The tabloids that seemed to vilify him? According to President Hind, Max owned them all. He'd acquired them a few years back, when journalists started to dig a little too deep. With this arrangement, as secret owner, he could publish red herrings. He libeled himself with outrageous stories, providing a smoke screen to hide the real truth while undermining the credibility of all news media.

"Even if you discover the truth about Maxwell," the president warned, "you'll never be able to make it public. No one believes anything they read about him, not any longer." Apropos of nothing, Hind muttered as if to herself, "I never wanted to be the president of *anything*."

En route to the United Nations building, the president's cell phone rang. Settled into the leather seat, partitioned from the driver by a soundproof panel, Penny held her tongue and looked out the tinted window.

"I'm trying to reason with her," Hind told the caller. "Please don't take any action." She paused a moment, eyeing Penny. "No, I'd never tell her. And even if I did, she wouldn't believe me."

Without hearing a word on the other end of the discussion, Penny knew the caller was Max.

The motorcade moved through the streets, unhindered by traffic lights or competing vehicles. As they passed Bryant Park, Penny glimpsed a long line of people standing, waiting to enter a shop on Sixth Avenue called Bootsy. For the most part, the same consumer demographic that had gone nuts for Beautiful You was now swarming to buy a new style of shoes. It was a trend Penny couldn't understand. To her, the shoes were clunky and ugly, with wide straps across the arch and thick heels, but some group dynamic had taken hold. The same block of women, nationwide, was making a banal romance novel about vampires into a megabestseller.

The president ended her conversation and pocketed her

phone. Her attention drifted to the crowds of women waiting to buy shoes. "My relationship with Maxwell started like any other addiction," she reflected. "It was fun. I was your age. At the time I thought Max was everything I'd ever need in the world."

There was something tragic in her face as she talked about her younger, naive self. Her voice was heavy with self-disgust. "I trusted him."

Penny shifted uncomfortably in her seat. As the president talked, the younger woman's body was responding to some sexual cue. Whatever the stimulus, her nipples were almost painfully hard, so erect that even her silk lace bra felt like sandpaper against them. Perhaps it was the motion of the car, or the smell of the leather seats, but she felt a warm wetness collecting in her crotch.

President Hind asked, "Have you tried to have intercourse with anyone since him?"

Penny thought of the rapist, but shook her head: *No*.

"He thinks he's protecting us, but he's controlling us. To Maxwell it's the same thing."

By Lexington Avenue, Penny's breathing had grown so slow and labored that she had to open her mouth and gulp for air.

President Hind looked at her with sad eyes. "I asked him not to." For an evil conspirator she did something odd. From where she sat facing Penny, she leaned closer and took the trembling woman's feverish hand. "Just breathe. Just keep breathing," she said.

Clarissa Hind's voice was hypnotic. "Pretend it's like the weather, like a sudden storm. You can do nothing about it, so just be with it. Let it pass." She placed two warm fingers against the side of Penny's neck and counted silently. "There," she said. "You're returning to normal."

Cupping Penny's hands in her own, Hind entreated, "Listen!" She said, "Only one person can save the women of the world.

That person lives in a cave, high on the slopes of Mount Everest. Her name is Baba Gray-Beard, and she's the greatest living sex mystic." The president tugged Penny close and wrapped the younger woman in a warm hug. Cheek-to-cheek, Hind whispered in Penny's ear, "Go to her! Learn from her! Then you can fight Maxwell on a level playing field!"

Hind broke the embrace and sat back.

Whatever had come over Penny, the arousal was receding. She was confused, but had fully recovered by the time the car arrived at its destination. Accompanied by President Hind, she breezed through security. To Penny, the secret servicemen at the United Nations were interchangeable with the bodyguards who'd escorted Alouette on the day she'd given her deposition. They took the two women backstage. There, a makeup artist sat Hind at a mirrored dressing table and began styling her.

Reflected in the mirror, she addressed Penny. "I've told you everything I dare. If I told you more, he'd kill us both." Her eyes steely, she lifted her Dooney & Bourke purse to the counter and took out a bottle of pills. After she'd swallowed two, she replaced the bottle in the bag and zipped it shut. "Someday you'll understand." Her eyes shifting to see only her reflection, the president said, "You'll understand that what I'm about to do is my best and only option."

Madam President didn't say another word until it was time to take her place in front of delegates from every nation in the world. The chatter of the press corps fell to silence as she was introduced, and she strode confidently out from the wings to take center stage.

Growing up, especially through the arduous years of law school, Penny had all but worshipped this woman. As reported in the tabloids, Clarissa Hind had been the plucky community organizer who'd battled to improve funding for impoverished public schools in Buffalo. She'd spearheaded a drive for corporate sponsorship and gone straight to C. Linus Maxwell for a big-money donation. They'd been an immediate item in gossip columns. He'd recognized some innate quality in her and groomed her for greatness.

As Penny watched, here was the fearless international leader she'd always idolized.

"Citizens of the world . . . citizens of the United States," the president began. "I humbly stand before you. Three years ago I took the oath of office and promised to serve and protect."

Her amplified voice echoed around the vast council chamber. "I have failed."

The reaction to her words was a shocked murmur that grew as dozens of simultaneous translators delivered the equivalent message to the earphones of everyone present.

"My failure and cowardice are mine alone." As if facing a firing squad, the leader of the free world held her head high. "I only pray that the disaster I fear will never take place."

She unbuttoned her suit jacket and slid a hand inside, next to her heart. "In closing, I ask God to forgive me." She glanced at Penny standing in the wings, then cast her gaze out over the audience as if looking into eternity.

"The mistakes we make in our youth," she said solemnly, "we pay for with the rest of our lives."

There was no debating what occurred next. With the television cameras delivering the sight to viewers around the globe, Clarissa Hind, the forty-seventh president of the United States, withdrew a .35-caliber pistol from the inside pocket of her jacket. She placed the barrel of the gun to her head. And she pulled the trigger.

In the product liability department of BB&B, a disquieting pattern had begun to take shape. Over late-night cartons of Chinese takeout, Tad described how 70 percent of women who'd originally joined the proposed class-action lawsuit had withdrawn their participation. Of the remaining 30 percent, not a single potential plaintiff had filed a statement. This left them with a pool of zero women seeking damages for pain and suffering. From millions to zero.

In fact, as Tad told it, the situation was just the opposite.

Chopsticking a cold eggroll, Tad said, "It gets even weirder. All of our original respondents have purchased replacement Dragonflies from Beautiful You."

Penny dipped a sliver of barbecued pork in some spicy mustard and nibbled it, listening.

"Their brand loyalty," Tad continued, "crosses all consumer categories. These same ladies now flock to buy the same cologne for their husbands and boyfriends. They all buy the same novels from the same publisher." Microwave ovens, dog food, soap, it didn't matter. As he explained, all the products were manufactured by DataMicroCom.

Penny almost choked. "Maxwell's company!"

Tad nodded. "This tectonic shift in buying habits has made each subsidiary of DataMicroCom the sales leader in its niche."

Now Penny was confused. How did selling personal care products to 150 million women affect whole industries?

"These women in particular," Tad said, "control ninety percent of the consumer spending in the industrialized world." He sipped at his carton of egg drop soup. "The hand that rocks the cradle decides how almost all household income is spent."

Playfully Penny shook a deep-fried prawn in his face. "Oh, whatever work they do, believe me, those gals earn that money."

Tad's teeth snapped, biting the tasty crustacean and plucking it from her fingers. That was just as well, seeing how Penny had a severe shellfish allergy. Chewing, he said, "Wait until you hear *this:* According to our family law department, divorces are up by four hundred percent since Beautiful You launched. Gals are choosing gizmos over men!"

Aghast, Penny laughed, "I'm not!"

"Prove it!" Tad shot back.

Tad wanted to take their relationship to the next level, but Penny couldn't risk it. She'd been rejecting Tad for weeks. After what had happened with the attacker in the subway, she still worried that something inside her pelvis might be amiss. Tad was such a nice guy that he didn't press the issue. He was open and genuinely honest with his feelings for her. The polar opposite of Max. The last thing she wanted to do was to slash the genitals of the only serious boyfriend she'd had since college.

To change the topic of conversation, she asked, "So we have no class-action lawsuit?"

Tad shrugged. "No plaintiffs, no lawsuit."

Penny licked almond gravy off her chopsticks, thinking. "But we could still file my patent-rights brief?"

Tad sighed. He looked at her, his eyebrows arched with concern. "The deposition process might be humiliating for you. Brillstein won't pull any punches. He'll want to know the kinky details of every experiment you submitted to."

Brillstein. Penny hated him. But she knew that he'd argue her case. The firm stood to make a fortune if she won even a fraction of the profits from Maxwell's sex-tool empire.

Tad's eyes drifted to the huge ruby pendant on her chest. That souvenir. To spare his feelings, she could leave it at home. Beautiful or not, Penny resolved to stash the gem in the safety deposit box where her diaphragm resided.

She leaned over the desk and began to gather the statement forms for the product-liability case. "Let's not give up on the class-action case." She wrapped the forms with a rubber band

and headed for the door. "If you'll give me the day off tomorrow, I promise I can get us the plaintiffs we need!"

The next day Penny set off from her town house on foot. Gucci-booted, she cheerfully strutted down Fifth Avenue juggling a clumsy armload of clipboards. The pockets of her short-short Donatella Versace trench coat were stuffed to bursting with ball-point pens. Beneath the coat she wore a fun, rainbow-colored Betsey Johnson microminiskirt.

The birds chirped. The morning sun felt delectable on her smooth, bare legs, as did the appreciative, pop-eyed stares of handsome male strollers. Being at the center of such ego-boosting attention, it was hard to not get sidetracked from her legal fact-finding mission. Inevitably the warm weather lured her to take a detour through Central Park, where changes in the city's social fabric were impossible to overlook.

The usual legions of efficient British nannies and trim Swiss au pairs, those willowy young helpmates who shepherded the privi-leged children of wealthy Manhattanites, those girls were pain-fully absent. In their stead, packs of grimy, sticky-faced urchins roamed Sheep Meadow like feral coyotes. Also missing from the pastoral scene were the steadfast ranks of female third-world economic refugees who normally served as dutiful nurses and caregivers. A few elderly wheelchair-bound patients seemed to have been abandoned on the spot. Clearly these hopeless cases had been left to fend for themselves along the fringes of the park's paved pathways. As Penny sauntered past their slumped, blanket-clad forms, the odor of full diapers and colostomy bags goosed the already brisk pace of her cheerful steps.

It sounded crazy, but the few females around were either unattended prepubescent girls or drooling geriatrics. Aside from the very young and very infirm, the only women seemed to be pictures smiling from countless sheets of paper that, overnight, had been pasted up everywhere Penny looked. Lampposts . . . bus stop shelters . . . plywood construction barricades, every vertical surface in the Big Apple was covered with photocopied posters, each dominated by a photograph of a different woman. Captioning each photo were the words *Missing: Beloved Wife* or *Cherished Daughter* or *Adored Mother. Treasured Sister.* "Have you seen this woman?" the posters asked. "Missing since . . ." followed by a date within the past two weeks. To Penny they suggested tombstones, fields of headstones, as if the city were becoming a vast cemetery of women. It was really depressing. Scary, even.

Dark rumors already circulated that the new Beautiful You devices were somehow responsible. According to whispers, the early adopters had retreated to live like reclusive hermits under bridges or in unused subway tunnels. They'd left behind families and careers. Homeless now, their only allegiance was to their new personal care products.

Penny considered this frightening possibility as two overly groomed fellows jogged past her elbow. The joggers' immediate presence, so close, almost made her drop her load of clipboards. To her Midwestern eye their running shorts fit far too snugly, crassly displaying their hypertrophied buttocks and their constantly shifting, poorly supported man-parts. In the fey up-speak of a ten-year-old girl, one man commented to the other, "Let the gals have their fun!" His hale running partner replied, "I don't care if they never come back!" And the pair trotted away in a cloud of expensive cologne.

Watching them recede into the distance, suddenly Penny found her path blocked. Dead ahead stood a stranger. His short, neatly cut hair was disheveled, and the two ends of an untied necktie flapped down the front of his wrinkled suit coat. His coat, his trousers, and his shirt, they all looked as if he'd worn them to bed. "Can you help me?" he begged. His face was dark with stubble. In one hand he offered a sheet of pale-green paper. In the crook of his other arm he held a ream of the same. "Her name is Brenda," he whined, "and she's my fiancée!"

Balancing her armload of clipboards, Penny accepted the paper. It showed yet another smiling woman, a grainy head-shot enlarged and enlarged on a copy machine until the finer details were lost. She wore a Jil Sander blouse and gave the camera a dazzling grin. Below her picture were the words *CFO Allied Chemical Corp.* There was a phone number and the words *To Report a Sighting, Call Anytime, Day or Night.* Below that, the word *Reward.* Penny quickly stashed the flyer in her coat pocket, deep among her cargo of pens.

This unshaven stranger grabbed her around one wrist. His grip was painfully tight. His fingers sweaty. "You're a female," he marveled. "You've *got to help me!*" He was almost shouting. "As a woman, *you've got to take care of me!*" He barked a quick, hysterical laugh. His gaze swept hungrily up and down her remarkable body. "Oh, I haven't seen a real woman in so long!"

To escape required a swift, well-aimed kick of her Gucci boot. Her pointed toe connected with the man's groin, and Penny was able to pull away. Even before she'd landed her crippling blow, she'd noticed one final detail about the stranger. His face, his cheeks in particular . . . His skin was shining, wet with tears. He was crying.

Terrified, Penny didn't risk a second look. She took off in a mad dash toward the tapering pink tower on Fifth Avenue.

Lately, Beautiful You customers had started to call the mirrored pink building the "Mother Ship." Every dawn, the faithful patrons were out in full force. Although the doors were still locked, a line of antsy women stretched away for two city blocks. Impatiently shifting their weight from foot to foot, they all wore the same ugly, clunky shoes. Just as Penny had once waited outside the locked doors of Bonwit Teller, they waited. To a woman, they carried the same vampire romance novel. Many carried their lunches in bright pink bags to signal that they were repeat customers. Some among them looked exhausted, with lank hair and sallow faces. They made her think how Monique's pretty face had shrunken in recent weeks to a skull-like mask. Oh, and the unwashed smell that wafted from the poor girl's room . . . These days Monique didn't even call in sick, and Penny felt compelled to save her housemate's career by making excuses.

Midway down the line a middle-aged man wearing a Promise Keepers T-shirt was accosting a woman. Penny recognized the T-shirt because her dad had one exactly like it. Like an uncouth caveman the man held the woman by a fistful of hair, trying to drag her toward a taxicab that sat idling at the curb. The woman had lowered herself to a crouch, using her body weight to retain her place in the queue of early morning shoppers.

As Penny neared the struggling couple, she could hear the man saying, "Please just come home!" His words were broken by his sobs. "Johnny and Debbie miss their mommy!"

The woman, Penny guessed, was his spouse. For her part in the marital spat, the wife repeatedly clubbed her husband with something bright pink. Her weapon was floppy, flexible, and very long. On closer inspection Penny realized it was product number 6435, the Honeymoon Romance Prod. Normally it held six D batteries, and Penny could hear the weight of them slamming into the man's ribs like a bludgeon while his wife yelled, "This hunk of plastic is more of a man than you'll *ever* be!"

Gingerly, Penny sidestepped their quarrel and hurried to

the head of the line. In her arms she carried her stack of clip-boards, each already loaded with a registration form and a pen. She started her pitching with the most drained-looking women. These dead-eyed wretches stood at the locked doors as if they'd been waiting here all night. To judge from their body odor and sleepy, slouched postures, Penny thought that perhaps they had.

"Excuse me," she chirped, offering a clipboard form to the first woman. "Have you experienced a catastrophic failure of any Beautiful You product during use?"

She felt like a sex-toy ambulance chaser, but her ends would justify her means.

Shivering despite the morning warmth, the woman's ema-ciated hand accepted the pen. No intelligence shone in the stranger's expression as she turned her glazed eyes to the legal paperwork. Penny could see that she was young, but something had sucked the vitality from her. The bones showed beneath the papery skin of her face.

Penny recognized the look. After grueling rounds of ecstasy she herself would see this ghostly wretch in the mirror. Reduced to this level of exhaustion she'd been massaged and plied with hand-squeezed fruit juices. Max would order acupuncture and aromatherapy to aid in her recovery. These girls had nothing. They were dying from pleasure.

Their eyes glittered, glassy and sunken in deep hollows beneath their brows. Their clothes hung limp and heavy with dried perspiration. Their lips were slack. These had been the confident, relaxed gals who'd been striding around Union Square only a week before. It was obvious to Penny that their new toys had become a dangerous compulsion.

Jumping the gun, she told the woman, "We're organizing a class-action lawsuit to charge Beautiful You with malfeasance."

The woman croaked a response. Here, too, was a condition

Penny recognized. Often, after long bouts of testing, loud moans of ecstasy had left her own throat parched and useless.

Others edged closer, swaying, unsteady, craning their thin necks to see what Penny was up to. These curious zombies, Penny could see that their hair was breaking off at the roots, no doubt from malnutrition. Bald patches shone on their scalps. It wasn't lost on her that an earlier sexual revolution had created walking skeletons so similar to these. Not long ago, these staggering skeletal waifs would've been the victims of AIDS.

To rally them, Penny said, "You don't need another sex toy." Thrusting clipboards into every pair of hands, she said, "We need to make Beautiful You accountable for their crimes against women." By now she was shouting. "We need to shut down their business and demand reparations!"

The cadaverous girl at the head of the line swallowed. Her thin lips moved with the effort to form words. "You . . . want . . . to . . . *close* . . . them?" Her voice was a thin whine of terror. A murderous grumble echoed back along the line.

A voice called, "Wait until after I get my new Dragonfly. *Then* sue them."

Another voice charged, "Whoever she is, she's against a woman's right to own her sexual fulfillment."

A clipboard sailed through the air, barely missing Penny's head. It clattered to the sidewalk. A chorus of catcalls followed:

"She's a self-hating, body-hating antifeminist!"

"Loosen up, sister! And get your fat ass to the back of the line!"

"We've got to protect our right to shop at Beautiful You!"

A painful hail of clipboards came at Penny from every direction. The air was thick with hurled ballpoint pens and vituperative screams of female anger. This army of frustrated women was stoning her with vampire-themed paperbacks. In another minute they'd remove their clunky shoes and beat her to death. Helpless, she called out, "Maxwell is only manipulating you!" Her arms raised to ward off the hurtling books, she yelled, "He's making you into his slaves!"

As the crowd surged at her, countless hands seized Penny's hair and colorful Betsey Johnson micromini. Enraged fingers clutched her around the wrists and ankles, and she felt herself being pulled apart. Subjected to cries of "Oppressor!" and "Prude!" she was being painfully rent limb from limb. Torn to shreds.

A wild voice shrieked, "Beautiful You helped me kick my drug addiction!"

Another shrieked, "Thanks to Beautiful You I've lost seventy-five pounds!"

Almost inaudible against the animal screams of the mob, a lock clicked. A key turned, and a bolt snapped open.

Almost inaudible. "The store," Penny gasped. Faint with the effort to save herself, she gasped, "They've opened the store. . . ."

The announcement rescued her, as thousands of frantic shoppers turned en masse and stormed the big pink building. Dropped to the sidewalk, Penny curled into a protective fetal ball as countless ugly, clunky shoes stampeded past her to embrace their ultimate fate.

That night Penny slipped into a comfy pair of flannel pajamas from L.L.Bean. She went to bed early, nursing a glass of pinot gris and not a small number of clipboard-shaped bruises. After the day's aborted mission to collect plaintiffs, she'd arrived home crestfallen. She ached. Her smart micromini was grubby with handprints, and the crowd had shredded her Versace coat. She'd decided it was beyond repair and had searched the pockets for coins and chewing gum before consigning it to the trash bin. Crumbled in one pocket was the pale-green handout given to her by the frantic man in the park.

"Call anytime, day or night," it read. "Reward."

In bed, Penny smoothed the paper. She set aside her wine and retrieved the phone from her bedside table. A man's voice answered on the first ring. "Brenda?" It was the stranger. Her wrist still tingled from where he'd held her so tightly.

"No," Penny told him sadly. "I met you this morning."

"At the park," he interjected. He said he remembered because she was the only normal woman he'd seen all day. Actually all week.

"Every day," he wailed forlornly, "I pace that waiting line along Fifth Avenue, searching . . . searching . . . but Brenda is never there."

Choosing her words carefully, Penny encouraged him to talk. "Her disappearance, how did it happen?"

The man poured out his anguished tale. Feeding his grief was guilt. He had been the person who'd bought the initial Beautiful You item for her. It was supposed to be a birthday gift: product number 2788, the Instant-Ecstasy Probe. Brenda had blushed with embarrassment when she'd opened his gift in a crowded restaurant, but he'd gently encouraged her to use it. "Not right there in the restaurant," he added, insisting, "Only a tramp would submit to using a sex toy in a public restaurant."

Penny's mind flashed on her own French eatery episode with the Peruvian married stones. She squelched a twinge of embarrassment with a deep swallow of chilled pinot. Lying abed, she watched the fresh bruises on her arms shift in color from pink to red to purple. She reflected on her time in Paris and thought how it seemed as if she'd spent half her life drinking wine in bed and covered with contusions. This, it occurred to her, was how it must feel to be Melanie Griffith.

"One day," continued the man on the phone, "Brenda was the most influential power broker in the chemicals industry, and the next day . . ." His words trickled off in tired resignation. "She was gone." He'd searched her duplex co-op on Park Avenue and found that the only thing missing was the Instant-Ecstasy Probe. That was two weeks ago. Since then people had phoned to report a few sightings. One was under the rotting piers near Hoboken. Another time, security cameras in a bodega caught her shoplifting batteries in Spanish Harlem.

Listening to his account, Penny gulped her wine. She reached to where the bottle stood on the bedside table and poured another glass. She'd finished every drop by the point the lonely man's mood evolved from hopeful to fearful to savage.

His fury was audible over the phone. Even soused as she was, Penny could sense that he was red-faced and that his entire body was trembling. "If I ever meet the person who invented those demonic sex playthings . . ." He paused, choked with rage. "As God is my witness, I'm going to strangle her with my bare hands!"

The ugly shoes and fantasy novels were just the tip of a newly emerging trend. Day by day, Tad tracked the swing in shopping habits. One Monday almost sixteen million housewives abandoned the laundry detergents they'd been buying for decades and switched to Sudso, a brand introduced only the previous week. Likewise, an entire generation of female music lovers flocked to concerts by a new boy band called High Jinx. They fainted. They screamed. Watching these girls on television, Penny observed that they didn't behave very differently from the convulsions that had seized Alouette on the night of the Academy Awards.

Behavior and marketing specialists couldn't make heads or tails of the phenomenon. It was as if vast blocks of female consumers were responding to the same impulses. In the shadow of the president's self-assassination, the stock markets were a roller coaster. Share prices tumbled for almost all publicly traded companies. But, as Tad pointed out, every subsidiary of DataMicroCom was rocketing in value.

"Especially Henhouse Music," he insisted.

When the people around him responded with vacant looks, he added, "That's the record label that represents High Jinx. They've got songs in six slots of the weekly top ten."

Investors with forethought, Tad explained, were flocking to the commodities market. Manganese and potassium, specifically. Zinc, also. All the ingredients that went into the production of alkaline batteries. Speculators were bidding copper through the roof. Battery shortages had sparked riots, and a robust trade on the black market was prompting burglars to swipe half-depleted batteries from flashlights and children's toys. In the same way car break-ins had once prompted drivers to post "No Radio" placards in their windshields, now homeowners tacked highly visible "No Batteries" signs on their front doors in the hope of deterring thieves.

The whole world was struggling to make sense of what popular culture called the "Beautiful You effect." On television, pundits and analysts bantered about something known as arousal addiction. Prior to now, no one paid it heed, because it had hampered only the lives of boys. In recent decades it had been primarily young men who'd fallen victim to the crippling pleasures of sustained arousal. They'd been seduced by the soaring levels of endorphins generated by playing video games and perusing sexy

Web sites. A generation of young men had become entranced by the lure of loveless release and had fallen through the cracks of society. They were hunkered down in basement rooms heavy with the reek of their dissipation, oblivious to maintaining real relationships with actual love mates.

Penny tried to dismiss the reportage as male hysteria, but the concept was hard to ignore. According to experts, the trouble arose when our primal animal impulses were manipulated by breakthroughs in modern technology. Butter brickle ice cream was an excellent example. Its sugary, fatty goodness was exactly what our animal selves craved to survive. That was why Penny could never stop eating until the pint was empty. Her own evolutionary instincts were being used against her by product marketers. To date, arousal addiction had come to men visually, via fast-paced video games and high-speed Internet pornography, but Maxwell's new product line seemed to be having a similar effect on women.

It made perfect sense! The constantly changing stimulation was gradually rewiring their female brains. The limbic portion of the mind was awash in surges of dopamine. The hypothalamic regulation of rewards was foiled, and the prefrontal cortex was no longer in control. Oh, Penny thought as she pored over the medical studies—it was so complicated, yet so obvious!

Once addicted, ladies would binge on pleasure. The Beautiful You effect. Ordinary leisure activities would bore them. Regular pastimes would fail to hold their interest. And without the constant arousal of Maxwell's personal care products, women would lapse into severe depression.

Social commentators were quick to point out how advertising had long ago exploited men's natural sexual impulses. To sell a certain brand of beer, the media needed only to display idealized female bodies, and male buyers were hooked. This age-old tactic looked like it was exploiting women and pandering to men, but savvy observers had recognized how the minds of intelligent men were constantly being erased—their ideas, their ability to concentrate, their ability to comprehend—by each glimpse of enticing breasts and taut, smooth thighs.

It was the same way Max's Beautiful You tests had wiped Penny's mind clean of dreams and aspirations . . . of plans for the future and love for her family. The general culture had been blithely using sex to attack the brains of young males for so long that society had long ago accepted the evil practice.

Perhaps that was why the world was so quick to accept the disappearance of women into the same abyss. Artificial over-stimulation seemed like the perfect way to stifle a generation of young people who wanted more and more from a world where less and less was available. Whether the victims were men or women, arousal addiction seemed to have become the new normal.

On a rare evening outside the office, Penny and Tad had gone to a mixer at the Yale Club. Surrounded by Bucks County blue-bloods, he seemed to be immersed in his element. No, he wasn't ready to drop the class-action lawsuit, despite Penny's bruising failure to rustle up some plaintiffs. He'd adopted a sensible wait-and-see attitude. Given some time, he was certain more women would materialize to file claims. Until then, he was ready to move forward with her suit to contest the ownership of Beautiful You patents.

That was another reason to venture out tonight and have some fun. Tomorrow Penny would be confronted by the senior partners of BB&B and she'd be compelled to give her deposition.

At the Yale Club, Penny admired the casual way Tad wore his tuxedo. He greeted some of the wealthiest people in New York as old friends. He was a keeper for sure. If only he didn't keep pressuring her for vaginal intercourse. They'd done pretty much everything else, but Penny couldn't risk hurting him. Nor did she care to explain her growing fear to him.

Lost in these thoughts, she collided with another guest. A few drops of champagne were spilled, but no permanent damage was done. The tall, bearded man looked familiar.

"You are Penny Harrigan, no?" He offered his hand. "I am Pierre Le Courgette."

It was the prizewinning novelist who'd been dating Alouette at the time of her death.

"It was very sad," he said.

Penny squeezed his arm. "You must miss her very much. She was so lovely."

Wistfully, he replied, "Do not be mistaking me. We were not intimate lovers."

Penny waited for him to say more.

"We tried many times," he admitted, "but I could not know her in that way."

Dread washed over Penny. She pictured the blood gushing from her attacker's erection in the subway.

"Something . . . inside my Alouette," he began, but his voice trailed off in misery.

Penny risked finishing his confession. "Did something jab you?"

"Jabbed?" he asked, confused by the word in English.

"Like a harpoon," she coaxed. "Something impaled your penis."

His eyes flashed with understanding. *"Oui!"* he cried. *"Mon dieu!* It was hidden there, inside her *chatte*. She was convinced that Maxwell had left some tool inside her, although the doctors could find nothing." He reached to grip her by the elbow and steady her, saying, "My dear, what do you know of Alouette's condition?"

Penny reeled. The room spun. Was this the secret Alouette had planned to tell her over lunch?

At this Tad materialized and slipped an arm possessively around her waist. "I think it's bedtime for somebody." He held her so close she could feel his erection through the thin fabric of his tuxedo pant leg.

There it was again. He was pressuring her for sex. Just out of her growing irritation Penny was almost ready to let Tad take that dangerous chance.

The following day, on the sixty-fifth floor, seated in a conference room where she'd delivered so many extra chairs in the past, Penny gave her deposition. The only employee of the firm not present was Monique. Poor Monique was still barricaded behind her bedroom door. Otherwise, Penny faced associates and partners on all sides. Their expectant eyes scoured her for traces of falsehood. Any nervous tic might suggest she was lying. A microphone collected her words as she described the first night Maxwell had filled her with the pink-champagne douche. A stenographer scribbled notes as quickly as Max had.

The majority of her coworkers listened, spellbound. Their jaws hung in disbelief as she haltingly described the process by which Maxwell had battered her cervix to racking spasms of fulfillment.

Periodically, Brillstein fired off questions to challenge her. "Miss Harrigan, you said earlier that Mr. Maxwell placed a hand inside your vaginal orifice. How is that possible?"

The memory shocked and excited Penny. With the entire firm watching, she stammered, "I don't know."

"Take your time, sweetheart," Tad assured her. He gave her a wink and a quick thumbs-up. "You're doing great!"

Relentlessly, ruthlessly, Brillstein continued. "Would you say, Miss Harrigan, that your anatomy was especially suited for such extensive exploration?"

Penny bridled. "Are you asking if I'm a slut?"

"I'm inquiring," Brillstein sneered, "whether you contributed any unique abilities to the research process." He said *unique* as if it were a dirty word.

"There were times I almost *died*," Penny shot back. She tried not to fidget under his penetrating gaze.

"From the pain?" Brillstein hated her.

"Not exactly." With eyes in every direction, the only safe place for Penny to look was the floor.

Brillstein redirected. "You mentioned how Mr. Maxwell had made an exhaustive study of all things erotic. . . ."

In turn Penny told them what she could remember about the various swamis and courtesans Max had mentioned. She described Baba Gray-Beard, Max's primary mentor, and how the great woman lived high in the Himalayas in a hermit's cave, where he had sought her out. Penny related how the ancient teacher had mentored her billionaire student in erotic techniques that dated back to the dawn of human evolution. Penny did not mention Clarissa Hind and how the doomed president had urged Penny to also seek out and study with the fabled crone. Why drag the tormented president's memory through this?

Again, Brillstein interrupted her. "If my questions seem antagonistic, Miss Harrigan, please understand that I'm doing you a great favor. The counsel defending Mr. Maxwell won't be any easier on you."

Penny steeled herself. Shoulders squared, chin held high, she waited.

His eyes leered. "You're saying that you allowed Mr. Maxwell to anally stimulate you in a posh French chow hall?" Brillstein was grilling her with relish. His gaze was dissecting her body the same way so many wealthy strangers had tried to analyze her sensual secrets at Parisian parties. His clear assumption was that she was a deranged nympho in the sack.

In icy tones she replied, "Maxwell and I were coresearchers." She sensed he was preparing to fire his big guns. Despite the steady incoming rush of air-conditioning, the conference room felt like a sauna. Men pulled at their collars and loosened their ties. The few female associates seemed to swoon in empathy with her, fanning themselves with whatever legal documents were at hand.

"Is it true"—Brillstein consulted his notes—"that on the date of April seventeenth, between the hours of seven and eight p.m., you affirmed to Mr. Maxwell that you'd enjoyed forty-seven distinct orgasms brought on by what you now refer to as 'research'?"

Penny stiffened. It was true, but there was no way Brillstein could have those numbers. She hadn't mentioned them. He could only know those details if he'd conferred with Maxwell himself. The realization chilled her: Brillstein was secretly allied with Max.

Emboldened, Brillstein pressed his point. "For one full hour your heart rate averaged a hundred and eighty beats per minute." Referring to his notes, he read, "Your respiration was a hundred and ninety-one breaths per minute." These facts were clearly gleaned from Max's little notebook. "Doesn't that seem like sufficient reward for your participation in this so-called experiment?" He smiled a self-satisfied grin, his beady eyes daring her to deny his implication.

Not waiting for her reply, the senior partner clicked a button that was installed in the conference room tabletop. A projection screen quickly lowered from the ceiling. Another button brought a video projector to life, and screams roared from unseen speakers. Monstrously enlarged, the shape of a nude woman filled the screen. She rolled on her back amid white satin pillows, her fingers clutching white satin bedsheets. The hilt of something bright pink protruded from between her thighs. When her frenzied thrashing threatened to dislodge the pink instrument, the hand of an unseen man entered the shot. It pressed the tool fully into place. One of the fingers wore a ring set with a huge ruby.

It was Max's hand. It was Penny on-screen, heaving like a sexed-up Hottentot.

"Miss Harrigan," asked Brillstein, sneering at the video, shouting to be heard above the torrent of her recorded grunting, "how do you explain *this*?"

Penny looked to Tad for support, but he'd turned away. Resting his elbows on his knees, he was covering his face with his hands, shaking his head in despair.

It was one thing to discuss the testing process using lofty verbal legalese, but to actually see Penny wallowing, near-insane with wild animalistic release . . . spitting vulgar obscenities . . . she didn't look like a dedicated, hardworking scientist. During that scorching moment of humiliation, with scores of legal minds wondering whether she was a wronged coinventor or just a wanton harlot, Penny heard a familiar racket. A loud thrumming rebounded from the office towers around their building. A helicopter was preparing to set down on the roof two floors above them.

Penny didn't need to ask. She knew who was arriving.

The video stopped. The screen disappeared up into the ceiling.

"Gentlemen," Brillstein announced, "should we move on? We've got another lengthy deposition to take this afternoon."

As the weary attorneys rose from their seats and began to vacate the room, Brillstein offered Penny his hand. "If you don't mind a little advice, young lady," he said, "I think you'd be very foolish to pursue this claim."

Penny let him steer her toward the door.

As they parted company in the hallway, he asked whether she'd perform a favor for him.

Stunned, mute, she nodded.

"If you'd be so kind," he asked, his voice dripping with contempt, "please tell your little friend Monique she's fired!"

"Please don't be mad at me, honey." It was Penny's mom calling from Omaha.

Penny had been at the kitchen table, reading the newspaper when the telephone rang. All the day's news was about the late president. Officially the White House wasn't offering any explanation, but a fact-finding commission had issued its report. According to the security protocols the commander in chief was seldom searched or directed through metal detectors. It was always assumed that she would be the target. Not the shooter. Hind had been both. The vice president—a man, of course—had been hastily sworn in. Talk radio's bombastic pundits were blaming the self-assassination on menopause.

With the gun so close to the microphones, the noise had been deafening. Penny's ears were still ringing, and she had to concentrate to hear her mother speaking from Omaha.

Weighing her words carefully, the Nebraska housewife said, "I bought some of those Beautiful You doohickeys."

Penny held her breath.

At that confession, her mother's voice changed pitch, rising to a girlish squeal. "Why didn't you tell me?" she exclaimed. "The feeling is incredible! This is why God made me a woman!"

Penny tried but couldn't get a word in.

"Your father had been sulking in his woodshop all week." More bashfully, she offered, "They're not made to last, are they?"

Penny interrupted: "Which one broke?"

Her mother's blush was audible. "God only knows how those engineers product-test the durability of those things. I really gave it quite a torture test. Worse than John Cameron Swayze used to give to Timex wristwatches."

Vaguely, Penny remembered the watch's advertising slogan: *It takes a licking and keeps on ticking.*

"Until it broke"—her mother gasped—"I was having the time of my life!"

Penny crossed her fingers. "Which appliance was it?" *Please don't be the Dragonfly,* she prayed.

"It was the Dragonfly."

"Mom!" Penny protested.

Oblivious, her mother prattled on. "Have you got a pair of those new shoes everyone is so crazy for?" With the chatty enthusiasm of a teenager she said, "Well, call me crazy, too. Those shoes are so ugly, but the TV commercials give me a little tingle inside. Just seeing those shoes on television, I'm tickled pink."

Earlier that day, Penny had knocked on her housemate's bedroom door. She'd not had the heart to deliver the bad news about Monique being fired for absenteeism. Instead, she'd stood in the hallway and rattled the locked doorknob while repeating, "Open up." She'd put her ear to the wood and listened to the ominous buzzing sound that emanated from within. "Open up," she'd demanded. "We need to get you some help."

Finally, the door had opened a crack. The stench was appalling. The crack was just wide enough for Penny to see a skull-like face framed in untidy braids. "Girlfriend," the skull had said in a rasping voice, "you need to go fetch me some batteries." The door had slammed. The lock had snapped shut. Once more, Penny had heard the muffled sound of humming.

It was maddening that now her own mother was threatened by the same terrifying obsession. Trying to redirect the older woman's attention, Penny asked, "Have you checked out those back issues of the *National Enquirer* like we talked about?"

Automatically, Penny's fingers rose to her own neck. Her pulse was 127. Time with Max had made her compulsively aware of her own vital signs.

Her mother didn't respond, not right away. It might've been Penny's imagination, but she thought she heard a distant humming over the phone. "Mom?" she asked, "is Dad using the chain saw?"

"I keep meaning to tell you," her mother said, "your father might be calling you." Her voice dropped to a whisper. "He wants to put me into a straitjacket and trundle me off to a loony bin." Exasperated, she hissed, "Just because I'm fulfilling myself so much."

"The tabloid research, Mom?" Penny persevered. "You were going to find out about Maxwell's childhood?"

Her mother changed the subject. "What are you up to tonight?"

Penny counted 131 beats per minute. "Tonight?" She needed to test something. "I'm inviting a friend over for the evening."

"Someone special?" her mother asked.

"Yes," Penny replied, without a trace of irony in her tone. "I'm spending the evening with someone very special."

Brillstein must've seen her name on his caller ID, because he answered on the second ring. His voice hushed, husky with desire, he breathed, "Yes?"

In the background, a matronly woman's voice asked, "Honey? Who's calling so late?"

"It's no one," he shouted away from the receiver. "Just work. I might have to run into the office for a few hours."

After she gave her address in a breathless purr, Penny hung up and ran to her wardrobe. She ransacked the enormous closets, looking for the most scandalous negligee. On a shopping spree in Paris she'd collected dozens of lurid teddies and nighties, hoping one would spur lust in Maxwell. None had. But this evening she selected a narrow strip of marabou feathers which had been artfully dyed dark purple. The way it was worn, it trailed down her otherwise nude torso, leaving her breasts exposed and only partially obscuring her vulva.

With moments remaining before Brillstein arrived, she turned on the chandelier in the town house foyer and took a position that would allow its light to throw her shadow against the inside of the frosted-glass front door. Waiting there, she undulated her hips in a way that would make her shadow look enticing from the street.

She stood undulating in ludicrously high heels—another purchase she'd hoped would pique Max's lust. Her trap was set. The doorbell rang: *ding-dong*.

"It's open," Penny called in as sultry a voice as she could muster.

Brillstein shouldered his way inside, panting as if he'd run every step of the way. Catching sight of her in her marabou splendor, he smacked his wrinkled lips with great gusto and said, "Well, just as I suspected . . . It is a spicy little whore, after all."

Penny sidestepped his lunge. Luring him through the spacious rooms, she allowed her hands to roam up and down the silken curves of her body. "Oh, Mr. Brillstein, oh!" She giggled and dodged another grab. "How long I've wanted this to happen!"

The foolish lecher was already discarding his overcoat, his

shirt, his pants. He trailed her around sofas and tables, always a step too late to snatch at her young, supple skin.

Baiting him, Penny asked coyly, "Are you working on behalf of Maxwell?" She giggled and flitted away.

Brillstein smirked. He wiped drool from his lips with the back of one discolored hand. A cat ready to munch on a very sexy canary.

Sulking, pretending to be offended, Penny evaded yet another grab and asked, "How did you know so many details about Max's notes?"

His Brooks Brothers boxer shorts were tented in her direction, and his porcine, hairy hips were already bucking in helpless anticipation. His withered buttocks clenched, thrusting his engorged groin. Frustrated little growls rose from his throat. "Let me catch you," he promised, "and I'll tell you everything."

She led him upstairs to her bedroom. There she feigned arousal, mewing and wriggling in the same counterfeit way that had enraged Maxwell. Brillstein didn't seem to notice that her heart rate remained flat. Neither did she sweat. He climbed atop her on the bed and bullied her legs apart. Shucking his undershorts, he made no pretense of giving her pleasure. A trickle of clear slime dripped from his erection as he stroked it against her. Smearing this discharge against her hairless skin, he crooned, "So smooth! So *smooth*!"

He merely spit on his hand and applied this sickening gob of saliva to her. He was having some difficulty hitting a moving target, so Penny stilled her loins a moment as he entered.

Giving a single shove, he drove his full length into her. She gripped handfuls of his wasted flesh and tightened her hold in preparation for the worst. All this time, she was praying that her theory was correct.

It was. Before he could withdraw for his second thrust, Brillstein began to bellow like a knife-stuck Nebraskan hog. He thrashed to escape, but her strong fingers held his flesh firmly between her legs. Whatever it was, something within her was hurting him, and Brillstein begged to be released. His spotted hands pushed and slapped at her, but Penny held tight.

"Tell me!" she demanded, driving her hips upward to keep him well inside her vaginal torture chamber. "Tell me what Maxwell is doing!"

Brillstein howled. Whatever Max had planted within her, it was doing its guard-dog duty.

"Did he have anything to do with Alouette's death?" she demanded. "Did he kill her because of the palimony suit?"

"Yes," Brillstein screamed. "You're hurting me!"

Shouting directly into his red, straining face, Penny demanded, "Does this have anything to do with Beautiful You?"

"I don't know!" He sobbed, twitching as if swarms of hornets were stinging his buried manhood.

If he was bleeding inside of her, Penny didn't care. Her best friend and her precious mother were in danger. Millions of women were threatened. Continuing her inquisition, grilling him the way he'd grilled her at the deposition, she demanded, "What is Maxwell's evil plan?"

"I don't know!" he wailed piteously.

At this, she released her deathlike grip on his sweat-soaked butt, and the weeping senior partner threw himself from her embrace. Bleeding copiously, through gritted teeth he said, "Maybe your IUD or something's slipped."

Stepping to the bathroom for rubbing alcohol and cotton swabs, Penny couldn't help but feel vindicated. Brillstein's small confession had confirmed her worst suspicions. There actually was a conspiracy. When she doused his damaged privates with the harsh antiseptic, her boss screamed and screamed. His blood still streaming down the insides of her thighs, she yanked a suitcase from her walk-in closet and began packing it with Vera Wang. At the same time she ordered her phone, "Siri, lease me a jet from JFK to Nepal, with one connection through Omaha, Nebraska. For when? For tonight!"

Before fleeing her town house, Penny had shoved her boss out the front door naked and bleeding, his clothes bundled in his arms. She'd also gone to Monique's locked door and knocked, saying, "Mo? Can you hear me?" She began sliding blueberry Pop-Tarts through the crack at the bottom. "Eat something," she urged. "Try to stay hydrated. I'll be back as quick as I can."

Her only answer was the familiar muted buzzing that had resonated from the bedroom for days.

As she raced through the concourse at JFK she noted, distractedly, that she saw no other women. From the ticket agents to the travelers, everyone was male. By all appearances women had ceased to exist in the public sphere.

To avoid drawing the focus of hostile men—New York City was turning into a sexual powder keg!—she'd prudently dressed in a vintage Yves Saint Laurent pantsuit. The look was a touch mannish, especially when paired with a ribbed white turtleneck that minimized the appearance of her stunning bustline. She'd coiled her abundant hair beneath a knitted watch cap, and wore no more than a smudge of sparkling lip gloss. Walking, she rolled her shoulders and affected a brusque swagger. If she caught the eye of a passing stranger she'd look like nothing more than a hip young sailor on shore leave.

Whoever it was at BB&B who had leaked word of the pending lawsuit to President Hind, that same source had apparently slipped the news to the tabloid media. At airport newsstands, the headlines blared: "Cinderella Penny Harrigan Invents Sex

Toys!" Front-page stories detailed her claims that her erogenous zones had perfected the Beautiful You carnal gadgetry. To accompany the story, each newspaper ran a photo of Penny's head sunk into a white satin pillow. Her crossed eyes and the slack tongue hanging out of her mouth confirmed that these photos were screen captures from the video Max had shot in Paris. The images were astoundingly sexy, but they hardly made her look like the ergonomic genius the tabloids claimed her to be.

Seated safely in the plush cabin of a chartered jet, Penny propped open her laptop and began to surf. It took only a few headlines to buttress her worst fears. For the first time in its history the National Organization of Women was canceling its annual conference due to lack of participants. Six weeks ago the roster had been almost filled, but in the days since Beautiful You had launched, all of the delegates had canceled their plans to attend. Some cited more personal interests they wanted to pursue. The rest claimed to be exploring alternative avenues to self-fulfillment. Whatever the case, with no active members and no conference, NOW teetered on the brink of nonexistence. Likewise, when Penny phoned the national office for the League of Women Voters, a recorded message told her that the organization was experiencing a temporary staff shortage and would be closed for an indefinite period of time. The female members of the Senate and House of Representatives had missed roll call for almost a week.

Fear bloomed in Penny's heart, but she kept on surfing.

In a seemingly unrelated story, all of the female members of the U.S. Olympic team had resigned. Every great female athlete—from field hockey players to gymnasts to figure skaters—was choosing to stay home and eschew a chance of winning the gold. Another news feature described how all of the altos and sopranos were AWOL from the Mormon Taber-nacle Choir.

Almost 100 percent absentee rates were being reported among women in all the helping professions.

Meanwhile, according to the Web sites that reported busi-ness, the stock of DataMicroCom was sky-high. All of its sub-sidiaries, Beautiful You in particular, were reporting record sales.

In Omaha, a plain white van waited on the arrivals level of the airport to collect her.

"Penny," a voice called from the driver's seat. It was her father. His expression was puzzled as he asked, "Pen-Pen, why are you dressed like a sailor?"

The door on the side of the van slid open. A stranger crouch-ing within shouted, "Get in, quick." He motioned for her to hand over her suitcase, saying, "We need to go rescue your mother!"

The stranger's name was Milo, and he was the leader of the local chapter of Promise Keepers, the chapter her dad attended. The van was Milo's, and the back was mostly empty except for a first-aid kit, some folded blankets, and an ominous coil of nylon rope. As her father drove them through the silent late-night streets of Omaha, Milo and Penny scanned the sidewalks and alleys for the missing woman. Milo plunged the needle of a syringe through the rubber cap on a bottle and drew it full of some clear liquid. In a seedy neighborhood, they spied some-one wearing a bathrobe and pushing a rattling chrome shopping cart. Her hair hung in her face. Her runny eyes were swollen. The woman's bare legs were streaked with dirt. In the basket of the cart jiggled an assortment of soiled, dulled pink Beautiful You products. A cardboard sign was taped to the side of the cart. Hand-lettered in black felt-tipped pen, it read: "Will Work 4 Batteries."

"Pull up here," Milo whispered. "Don't spook her."

He rolled open the side door before they'd come to a complete stop. The woman standing near the shopping cart hardly had time to register their arrival before Milo was charging toward her with a blanket spread open between his hands. He threw the blanket around her and the pair fell to the ground. The woman was screaming now, fighting Milo as he held her wrapped. He shouted, "The rope! Bring me the roll of duct tape!"

Penny cowered in the van, but her father leaped from behind the steering wheel and grabbed the coil of rope. Together, the two men trussed up the woman in the bathrobe and carried her quickly back to their vehicle. Through all of this, she was screaming, "Not without my playthings! Let me have my toys!"

Milo slid the heavy door shut and Penny's father hit the gas, peeling rubber. Behind them the abandoned shopping cart and its sad cargo receded into the distance.

The entire abduction had taken less than ninety seconds. In the dark back of the van the kidnapped woman continued to shriek until Milo plunged the syringe into her arm.

Still breathing hard, but driving slower, her father said, "I'm sorry you had to see that, sweetheart."

Only now did Penny recognize the sedated wretch wrapped in rope on the floor.

It was her mother.

"Look at her, the poor woman," Milo said compassionately, as he sealed her mouth with duct tape. "We need to deprogram her." They drove through picturesque streets and neighborhoods Penny recalled from childhood.

Her dad described how her mom had quickly spiraled into madness. He and fellow members of their church had staged an intervention and confronted Penny's mom about her Beautiful You compulsion, but she denied she had a problem. Tonight they were taking her home, where they could keep her tranquilized while she'd undergo a series of hypnosis and aversion therapies to help manage her self-destructive behavior.

Penny wasn't surprised that she'd failed to recognize this ranting maniac. Her mother's face was jaundiced and lined with exhaustion. At the family home they carefully carried the trussed body up the porch steps and through the front door. Once the patient was safely stripped of her clothing, and her wrists and ankles were tied to the bedposts of an attic bed for her own protection, Penny ventured to the basement, where her mother's collection of *National Enquirers* filled floor-to-ceiling shelves. Each shelf was labeled with years and months which corresponded with the back issues, but Penny didn't have to look far. Set aside in a stack were issues that contained the facts pertaining to C. Linus Maxwell. Bless her mother, Penny thought. The beleaguered wretch had gotten this far in her research, winnowing out these precious copies from the thousands she'd hoarded over the past half century.

After fixing herself a well-deserved cup of cocoa, Penny carried the tabloid newspapers to a favorite overstuffed chair near the fireplace in the living room and began to read.

There wasn't much new information to be gleaned. Maxwell had been born as Cornelius Linus Maxwell, January 24, 19— at Harborview Medical Center in Seattle. There was no record of his father. His mother had raised him by herself. She'd had no other children.

He'd attended the University of Washington, but dropped out his junior year when his mother had been killed. It was rumored that he'd abandoned his studies in order to apprentice to some mystic in the Himalayas. Less savory gossip placed him in far-flung brothels and covert medical facilities, where anything could be bought. Debauched sex . . . designer drugs . . . whatever the case, Corny Maxwell had disappeared for six years. Within a few months of his reappearance he'd allied himself with the youthful, ambitious Clarissa Hind.

In an issue dated ten years ago the business section of the *Enquirer* contained a ten-part series about DataMicroCom's ongoing research projects. Over the following ten installments, the tabloid detailed how Max had become a pioneer in the field of tiny-robot technology. Called "nanobots" or "nanites," these were robots so small they were measured in millionths of a meter. They were hardly larger than molecules. Science had always bored Penny, but she found the reading fascinating. The primary application for nanobots was in medicine. More correctly referred to as "nanomedibots," these robots were so infinitesimal that they could travel freely through the bloodstream or neural pathways and repair damaged tissue on a molecular level.

An in-depth feature in the science section of the *National Enquirer* filled in the picture. Some nanobots were designed to scour veins and arteries, removing dangerous buildups of plaque. Other swarms of nanobots sought out cancerous tissue and killed it with heat or targeted chemotherapy.

A faint voice in Penny's head whispered, *And some nanobots leak out of personal care products and hijack the crura of your clitoris!*

She searched for more news about nanobot development, but the newspaper articles arrived at a dead end. Following a decade of groundbreaking work in the field of miniature robots, DataMicroCom had apparently dropped the entire matter. A small follow-up article quoted Max as saying that nanobots weren't cost-effective. He'd closed the bot division and redirected those resources toward the development of the more lucrative Beautiful You line of products.

Shocked, Penny remembered the episode in the president's limousine. Without any apparent stimulus she had felt herself becoming aroused. And not merely aroused—she'd been building toward an orgasm. Her entire awareness had been reduced to the tips of her erect nipples and clit. Only the president's gentle assurances had coaxed her through the tidal wave of erotic frenzy.

She thought of Alouette's breakdown onstage at the Kodak Theatre. And of her own bedeviled mother, bound to the bed upstairs. It was the broken item: the Dragonfly. The idea sounded crazy, like some conspiracy that a frothing-at-the-mouth women's libber might propose. But it was possible that the toy hadn't broken so much as it had *hatched*. Its body had split, releasing swarms of microscopic robots small enough to navigate upstream through her cervix into her uterus. Small enough to pass through the blood barrier in her ovaries and travel throughout her nervous system. Even to her brain. Who knew how they might be affecting her behavior and perceptions?

On her flight from New York, Penny had read about a crowd of twenty thousand female shoppers who rioted in Times Square, fighting one another for the chance to buy a new perfume. Likewise, in Rome, female shoppers were battling to lay their hands on a new face cream that was being heavily advertised.

That X-ray Penny had had after her attack on the subway platform, of course it'd shown nothing. Nanomedibots were smaller than anything a diagnostic tool could detect. And now, Penny realized, now they were implanted in tens of millions of women throughout the industrialized world.

If Brillstein was to be believed, and Max had caused Alouette's death, then perhaps the nanobots could do more than bring pleasure. Perhaps they could also kill.

Penny finished her mug of cocoa, then slowly climbed the stairs to the attic. In the darkness her father and Milo stood over the nude form of her mother writhing in bondage, moaning and gagged with duct tape.

"We can't cure her," Milo was saying bravely, "but we can curtail her self-destructive habits." The men knelt on either side of the bed and began to pray quietly into clasped hands. Fresh syringes and bottles of tranquilizer crowded the top of a bedside table.

Looking on, helpless, Penny wondered whether she might be correct. Nanobots might be behind her mother's wild sexual acting-out.

"Dad," she said. "I have to go."

Her father looked up, stricken. "You know, Pen-Pen, back when your mother and I lived in Shippee, the doctors warned us that she could never have children."

Penny listened. She'd never heard this. She checked her watch. The jet was already waiting on the tarmac.

Gazing down on his wife's dazed, helpless form, Penny's dad said, "Every expert we saw said she'd never have a baby. That's why you were such a miracle."

Penny stepped closer and hugged him around the neck.

Still kneeling, he smiled up at her. "You were our little gift from God." In a hopeful tone, he said, "If God can give us a daughter as wonderful as you . . ." He reached up and mussed her hair. "Then maybe God can deliver your mom from this hideous affliction."

Milo looked on, beaming with simple faith. Penny's naked, deranged mother was in good hands. "Stay," Milo insisted brightly. "Stay and bake us something!"

Penny checked her text messages. "The pilot says the weather is getting thick. We'll need to take off within the hour."

"Where to?" her dad asked. The poor man. His whole world was falling apart.

Her voice cold and resolute, in the voice of a stranger, Penny said, "To Nepal." She repeated, "I have to go to Nepal."

The yak would only carry Penny so high up the rocky slopes of the Himalayas. After the remote hamlet of Hop Tsing she was forced to ride the narrow, bony backs of Sherpas the last three almost-vertical miles. And even they would not take Penny the full way. As a distant cave came into view, the Sherpas trembled with fear. Muttering oaths to ward off evil, they lowered her to the sun-baked ground and began to retrace their steps. When she protested, one stout fellow pointed toward the distant cave and babbled in his native talk, hysterical.

Penny had no other choice but to continue on alone.

As she scaled the crumbling stone face of the mountain, she could picture Maxwell making this same pilgrimage as a young man. In Paris, he'd described spending years with this strange, aged mystic. He had presented himself to her as a willing apprentice, and she had agreed to mentor him in the most esoteric ways of the tantric. Despite his youthful vigor, Maxwell said those years practicing sex magic with the crone had almost killed him.

In fact—and this detail frightened Penny—he said the cave where the mystic dwelt was littered with the skeletons of men and women she had sexed to death. Their bones frozen in Kama Sutric positions of unbearable erotic contortion.

With her Louis Vuitton roller bag strapped to her back, she inched higher, clinging to toeholds in the sheer stone wall.

Remembering the tales of orgasmic agony Max had told, she almost hoped the mystic had died. It had been a decade since anyone had seen her. The dry, icy winds threatened to pluck her fingertips from the thin cracks at which she clawed. Native birds dived at her, pecking and scratching to protect their nearby nesting grounds. The stench of guano was overpowering.

What choice did she have? Even the president had sworn this was the only means to counter Maxwell's plot. By murdering Alouette in such a public fashion, he'd proved he could murder anyone, anywhere. He held millions hostage whether they knew it or not. Even if they discovered the nanobots, it was too late.

Only Baba Gray-Beard might offer an antidote . . . a treatment . . . a training that could counteract the legions of implanted microrobots.

A gust of wind tugged at Penny, tearing her grip from the rocks. In desperation, she unbuckled the Prada belt that held the suitcase to her back and watched it plummet into the void below her. It seemed to fall forever, turning in the air slowly before exploding in a burst of vividly colored Anne Klein separates. Unencumbered, she climbed faster. By midday, she felt exhausted as she hauled herself over the lip of the cave. It was unoccupied.

According to Max, Baba Gray-Beard spent most of her lonely days creeping about the steep cliff faces, gathering the lichen and mosses that constituted her meager diet. She subsisted on pillaging the eggs of cliff-nesting birds. Many of her aphrodisiac salves and poultices were formulated from the wild fungi she foraged. Her nights, Max said, she spent alone. For two centuries she'd lived in such solitude, exploring new, ever more powerful ways to pleasure herself. These were the techniques the Baba had schooled into Max and that he was co-opting in the mass-produced products of Beautiful You.

Just as he'd described, the cave was populated by skeletons and desiccated cadavers of people who appeared to have expired in the grip of extreme climaxes. Among the deceased were other items. Man-made items. These were the crude prototypes of what Maxwell had perfected and tested on Penny. Here, crafted from dried reindeer antlers and lashed together with animal sinews, were the erotic inventions of the solitary Baba. To endure innumerable nights of isolation, she had crafted and perfected these many devices for stimulating herself. Her boundless solitude had yielded this treasure trove of sensual tools.

Penny crossed the cave and examined them. Some, carved of living rock and polished to a glassy smoothness, were obviously designed to abrade the perineal sponge. Others were fashioned of bird bones and wrought to excite the clitoral legs that encircled the vagina. Still others had clearly been used rectally.

Evil Maxwell. With a single glimpse of these ingenious sex toys, the inventions of this aged hermit, he must've known that their power would overwhelm and enslave the civilized female. Each was astounding, and Penny marveled over them, not noticing that a stooped figure had climbed into the cave's entrance and was shambling toward her.

A creaking, quavering voice said, "I have a guest."

Penny spun around and caught sight of a hag who strongly resembled the surrounding devices and skeletons. Baba Gray-Beard was herself sculpted of bones and tendons, a knotted tangle of dried muscles and gray hairs. Her eyes shone like two moonstones, entirely white with thick cataracts. Her wasted body was unclothed, and her namesake abundance of ratted, off-white pubic hair had grown so long that it swept the ground between her bare feet.

Maxwell had said she was blind. The Baba, he said, found her way along the cliffs, climbing and hunting entirely by touch and smell. She knew the feel of every cleft and crevice in these mountains. She knew the distinct scent of every dirty crack.

She lifted her nose and sniffed the dank air. In a weathered voice, she said, "Do I detect a young, fresh pussy?"

Penny held stock-still. She quieted her breathing.

"Do not try to hide your smell," the crone chided. "It has been many years since I have had a student." She lowered a ragged pack from her back and began to remove clumps of moss from it. Carefully she lifted out small bird eggs, while saying, "From your odor alone, I know you arrive here from New York City, and that you come by way of Omaha."

Maxwell had warned that the Baba could tell a person's entire sexual history from the taste of his or her genitals.

"Expose yourself," the hag beckoned. "Let your flavor tell me all the truths that you cannot." She took another step closer, but waited.

Penny knew that she had no choice. Her mother and her best friend might be dying. A vast segment of the population was implanted with a power they refused to believe existed. Slowly she slipped off her Christian Louboutin shoes. Followed by her DKNY slacks and blouse. Lastly she lowered her Agent Provocateur panties. Each item she folded and carefully laid over a large rock.

When Penny was nude except for her Victoria Secret Miracle Bra, she stood and waited.

Baba Gray-Beard waddled up to her. The spotted crone petted between Penny's thighs with a trembling hand, croaking, "Ah!" Marveling, she whispered, "You have no hair. Is this Maxwell's malevolent doing?"

It was, but Penny was too frightened to speak. She nodded. It was the Uzbek tribal method with aloe and pine nuts.

The Baba proudly tapped a wizened fingertip on the cracked skin of her own chest. The constant tug of dry, icy winds had stretched her breasts until they flapped like leathery dugs. She nodded and smiled to herself. "It was I who taught him that technique."

Without hesitating in her caresses, the hag lifted the same bent finger toward Penny. Inserting just the gnarled tip of the finger, she said, "Little one, your vagina is so juicy!"

Like a dried twig, knobby and brittle, the rest of the finger slid inside as far as the knuckle. The old woman cackled. "So receptive, too! You will make an excellent student, my dear!"

As the centuries-old recluse probed her, Penny tried to remember all the things she loved in the world. Things like the carriage ride she and Tad had taken through Central Park. And butter brickle ice cream. And Tom Berenger movies. She thought of Fendi purses and summer carnivals with Ferris wheels and cotton candy. Wistfully, she recalled how much she'd admired Clarissa Hind, and how excited she'd been to see the first female president sworn into office.

When she could no longer dredge up pleasant thoughts, Penny squirmed in futile resistance to the old witch's finger. It seemed to be exploring the deepest recesses of her psyche.

After much poking about, the finger withdrew. It glistened in the dim light of the cave for only a moment before it disappeared between the hag's puckered lips. Sucking at it, the Baba groaned with understanding. She pulled the finger from her craw and licked it several times with a gray tongue before she spoke. "C. Linus Maxwell, he is the one who taught you." She was reading everything about Penny from this one sample. "He instructed you in all the arts which I taught him. He was my greatest student. A teacher craves such a student. But modern persons are too impatient; they seek only the fastest route to orgasm. They have no time for an old teacher. Maxwell had time."

The thorough examination sated the old mystic's curiosity. As her coarse red hands continued to stroke Penny, she said, "Yes, I trained Maxwell in the erotic ways of the ancients." Her voice creaked like the rusty hinges of a door opening onto someplace truly awful. "Those practices are almost lost to humanity. No one will devote the copious time and diligence required to acquire the sensual arts." Maxwell did. She was glad to have a student to mentor after all these years. "Before Max, my last apprentice was sixty years ago. His name was Ron Jeremy."

She continued to lick the finger, savoring it as she spoke. "Maxwell learned everything that was mine to teach. Those centuries of self-stimulating my loins, he benefits from all I've discovered." Dismay clouded the hag's expression. Even her blind, pale eyes darkened. "Now Maxwell has used the sexual wisdom of the ages to hurt many women and benefit himself."

Penny was shocked at the mystic's comprehension. When the hag again extended her twig of a finger, Penny gladly mounted it and rode it with excitement.

Tasting this new sample, the Baba intoned, "You feel a great guilt. You betrayed your sister women. You helped him to calibrate his weapons of control. Numerous are Maxwell's slaves due to the work you performed."

Hearing this, Penny wept. It was true. It was horrible, but it was so true that she'd never allowed herself to admit it.

The Baba sucked the finger in her mouth. She pulled it free and smacked her lips. "You, Penny Harrigan, have come to me for training so you can fight against him."

The gray tongue stroked the finger. Savoring whatever truths lingered in its wrinkles.

"You know my *name*?" Penny asked incredulously. It was the first time she had spoken in the cave and her voice echoed shrilly. "Just from the taste of my *juices*?"

Baba Gray-Beard's withered lips smiled. "I know many things." She motioned to a mat woven from dried lichens and her own shed hairs. "Come and sit. You will need strength for your erotic training. I will brew us some tea."

In the same way Penny had submitted to Max's experiments, sequestered in his lofty penthouse, now she gave herself to the Baba in the cloister of the old woman's stony cavern.

Penny had never been with a woman, but this was different. She never felt as desirable as she did when her tender, supple flesh was juxtaposed with the wizened hag-flesh of the ancient. The Baba was teaching her, instructing her in the greatness of sex magic. The crone fingered her relentlessly until Penny cried out, screaming as if these words would be her last on earth. The witch seldom asked her to reciprocate, but when she did Penny went about the task of pleasuring the wrinkled elder with the utmost respect. And when Penny wrested from her teacher even a modest cry of pleasure, it occurred as the greatest triumph.

When she embarked upon her hunts, the ancient teacher encouraged Penny to utilize the many bones and rocks available to build her own pleasure tools. Brandishing an armature of feathers welded to sticks with thongs of stout leather, the Baba boasted, "These may seem like the crippling versions that Maxwell has bastardized. But they are meant to enhance a woman's energies. They will make you stronger, not weaker." With a wink of one cataract-eclipsed eye, she assured the girl, "They will not exhaust you." Leaning closer, she leered. "But you must be *disciplined*!"

The Baba warned, "The erotic wisdom of the ancients is too much for most who seek it." She grinned wistfully. "The students trek here to acquire these skills. Many die from the hardships of the journey, but more die by their own hands." She explained how she would bring them eggs, but they would not eat. She'd invite them to her bed of moss and feathers, but they'd refuse to sleep. "So it goes." She shrugged with resignation. "I introduce them to a few rudimentary sensual practices, but they are soon consumed by self-pleasure."

To her own surprise, one night Penny brought her mentor to prolonged, strenuous release. Dabbling expertly with her lips and tongue, she teased the wily crone to a full-pitched fit of fevered yelping. The scrawny sex witch bounced violently atop their bed of twigs. Her toothless gums yammered incoherently.

Penny sustained the sweet torment to the verge of cruelty before she gradually lessened her campaign on her mistress's private parts. At last Penny lifted her drenched face from its task. She swiped her dripping chin with a clump of absorbent moss. Playfully, she caught the Baba's eye and demanded, "Tell me a secret, old one. Tell me a secret, or I will return to my licking until you go mad."

Penny knew her mistress was well pleased. The old woman looked drunk with pleasure. Breathless, the Baba shook her head to stave off the onslaught of orgasms.

"A secret, then!" Penny demanded.

"A secret," the Baba agreed. Lying on her back, she lifted herself to her elbows. "Did Maxwell tell you why he sought me out?"

Penny shrugged. "For instruction?"

No, the Baba shook her head sadly. "For distraction. To help him forget a great sorrow which had visited him."

"His mother's death," Penny ventured. This was hardly a secret; it had all been well documented in the *National Enquirer*.

Again, the mystic corrected her student. "Max launched his journey for sexual training in order to forget his *wife's* death."

It was Penny's turn to be confounded. Nothing could've surprised her more. "His wife?"

The Baba nodded in silent confirmation. Maxwell had once taken a wife. In college he'd met and courted a wholesome girl who was studying prelaw. The two of them had been deeply in love. This wasn't the cold, clinical Max with whom Penny had dallied. This younger man had been utterly devoted to his new bride. They were two lovers on the threshold of a blissful life together.

The sex witch sighed. "The details of the girl's death are unimportant. A severe allergic reaction. Without her, Max's life was also ended."

He'd arrived at the Baba's cave a recent widower. Embittered, his only goal was to squander the remainder of his years in hedonistic cavorting.

Penny craved more of the story, but this hardly seemed like the best time to pump her mentor for details. She asked, "What was her name?" She slid her fingers gently against the older woman. Playfully, she prodded the fragile tissues of the witch's bunghole. She spit generously to lubricate the worn orifice.

The Baba replied, "Her name?" She slowly succumbed to the stroking. Her voice softened as if she were lapsing into a dream. "Her name was Phoebe."

Phoebe. The name echoed for a long time in Penny's mind. Phoebe Maxwell. It was likely that Maxwell's people had excised every mention of Phoebe from the newspapers he owned, from the Internet, from history. She would be Max's Achilles' heel. She'd been proof that his heart could be broken. As Penny pondered this new aspect of his life, she lowered her face to the waiting thatch of off-white hair that even now thrust itself upward, eagerly nudging her for attention.

As Penny returned to her studies she yearned to ask how long Max and Phoebe had been married. Yet even without asking, somehow she knew.

They had been married for exactly 136 days.

For respite the Baba rubbed unguent into Penny's raw membranes. The sensual mystic lovingly tucked her into a bed of dried mosses and went out to forage for eggs and mushrooms. She brewed invigorating teas and prompted the girl to drink them from the wrinkled palm of her hag's hand. She taught her student how to grind spiders between rocks to produce a soothing ointment that would enhance Penny's anal sensitivity. So tranquil was her life and so deep their bond that Penny forgot about the legions of evil robots that might be swimming in her bloodstream. She wasn't to forget for long.

As if Max were testing his power, one day Penny felt her nipples grow hard and begin to vibrate. Her nipples and clitoris, they began shaking violently. The old woman had prompted her to orgasm many times that morning before leaving to scavenge eggs and lizards, so the last sensation Penny expected was this. So strange was it that she knew instantly that it was Max's doing. At the time she was sitting alone, cross-legged on the cave floor, sipping a cup of lichen tincture. The next wave of excitement struck her before she could even struggle to her feet.

What felt like a demonic possession overcame Penny. She wasn't in sole control of her body. A separate force seemed to bloom and expand between her legs. Her breasts ached with desire. Her pulse began to accelerate as goose bumps pebbled her skin.

Max had described the physical process so succinctly. Her aroused vagina was extending, growing in length as if to accommodate an erect phallus. It would balloon until it formed a pocket above the opening of the cervix, ideally to trap and hold sperm until they could successfully fertilize an egg. In nature, this was a natural and beautiful process, but what was happening to Penny now was Max's evil remote-controlled handiwork. It was easy to picture teams of microscopic robots ravishing her nerve endings. Even here, with her sequestered in the Himalayas, he could activate them. He was sexting—but with *real sex*. As if arousing her were just an application on his phone! Whatever his method, he was stimulating her the way he'd attacked Alouette onstage. This was some savage satellite-relayed rape.

Moments later, when the Baba returned to the cave, Penny was still wheezing and convulsing with unasked-for pleasure. The aged lamia flung aside her pack of moss and rushed to comfort the figure rolling on the floor.

"Fight it," the Baba urged, kneeling. "What is done to you, you can do in return." She wetted a thin finger in her toothless mouth and began to slide it between the girl's engorged labia. "You are not merely a receiver," the Baba cried. "Return the energy to its vile source!"

At that she shrieked and pulled back a finger that was already bleeding. "What is this monstrous thing?" She peered at a hole lanced in the tip of her shriveled digit. The flow of blood was channeled by the wrinkles and cross-hatchings that centuries had carved in her palms. "What has that devil installed within you?"

Even now Penny's sane demeanor had been displaced by the spirit of a slobbering madwoman. Delirious, she spread her legs and arched her back, pumping her thighs into the air. Her hands roamed her own nude body beyond her rational control, her deranged fingers tweaking and diddling in a frenzy of self-stimulation. Her head tilted back, her mouth hung open, and her tongue lolled thickly around her groaning lips.

The Baba cried out, "Vomit the pleasure or allow it to pass through you as you would excess food or wine."

She grasped the girl's arms and shook her. "A mirror is not burned by the sun!" She screamed, "Reflect back his evil!"

As Penny slipped deeper into an erotic coma she could still hear the old woman's urging. "You would not try to hold all of the water of the world inside your bladder." Muffled by sensation, the aged voice continued. "You wouldn't eat to hoard the entire world within your belly. Pleasure, like food, must pass through you. If it accumulates it leaves room for nothing else. You explode. Your only hope is to replace one pleasure with another. The way food drives waste from your body, you must use love to displace the sex magic Max is practicing. Focus on what you love, and you can deflect his erotic spell."

In desperation, Baba Gray-Beard seized a cluster of antlers and began to gently work it between the suffering girl's loins. "Do not fight the sensations," she urged. "My child, let them pass through you, or you will be killed like so many of my students whose skeletons you see around you."

Penny's eyes rolled. Spittle flew as her lips disgorged a furious stream of obscenities.

"That's it," the Baba exhorted. "Say the words! Release the heat!" Working the antlers gently, rhythmically, she pleaded, "Do not harbor the energy within you!"

Her voice guttural with lust, Penny brayed profanities. Her body intoxicated with pleasure, she rasped and squawked foulness.

"Allow the pleasure to overflow you!" the hag crowed.

Penny gasped. Her torrent of lewdness ceased. Slowly she came back into herself.

The witch tenderly withdrew the antler. "Your torments

will not end," she said. "You will find no peace until you have defeated Maxwell, or he has destroyed you." She began to apply a cooling balm of crushed centipedes to the bruises that were already forming between Penny's legs.

"What I teach you," the Baba said, "you must teach all women in the world so that they might defend themselves against this evil force."

Baba Gray-Beard spoke without bitterness. Nude, she lay back in her commodious bed of moss and feathers, and she parted her legs, shamelessly exposing the wrinkled flesh of her sex. This she began petting, softly flogging herself as she reminisced. Every stroke seemed to elicit memories, as if she were reading the stories from her own gray folds of skin. "I was orphaned at such a cruel age. At dawn I found her—my mother's body lay broken at the foot of a high cliff where she must've been gathering plover eggs." Her blank eyes stared into history. "I lifted my mother's cold hand and placed it against myself, pleading." In this way, the bereft child had eked out a few final hours of nurturance from her lost parent. "For a short while I did not allow the sex energy to leak from me through screams or thrashing."

It didn't take long before the heartless sex seekers of her village discovered that a helpless, unprotected child was theirs for the taking. The first night the young Baba was alone in her hut, they'd attacked.

Her voice husky with nostalgia, the Baba said, "They mapped for me my inner womanhood. With their every violent thrust they taught me about my body." She described how any number of savages might enter her in the night. Many took their wicked pleasure with her tender child's body, but the Baba resolved that she would take something from each of them in return. If she could not stop them, she could learn to control them by increasing or decreasing their pleasure. In her girlhood, she took on a thousand such attackers and used them to her own advantage. Those cruel encounters were her education. From her suffering she gleaned a wealth of incredible sex practices.

"I grew to be eager, my eyes shining with anticipation as they flopped out their meaty penises. I knew each was an opportunity to experiment and perfect my developing sex craft." She closed her eyes in dreamy remembrance. "Among my brutal mentors were women who palmed the back of my head, their fingers interlaced to hold me in place as they bade me lap at them until I neared suffocation." She spoke in a voice without misery. Outside the cave's mouth, a whiteout blizzard raged. Inside, a small campfire warmed a bubbling broth of stewed skinks. The Baba stirred the pot, saying, "This was my childhood, but those were but a handful of years. As my strength grew, the strength of my aging teachers began to fail. By then I'd enslaved them with my erotic skills, for I'd become a rich repository of sensual techniques. They could find satisfaction nowhere else, and I'd learned all they had to teach me. They brought me gold and jewels, things for which I'd no use. Finally, in scenes tinged with mercy and vengeance, I brought each of my former abusers to an ecstasy so great that he or she died."

The Baba's saga continued as she rose and began to pace the floor of the dripping cave. "My reputation as a sex crafter was such that students young and old, male and female, sought me as their guide." As a young sex witch, she was besieged by suitors yearning to acquire the secrets she'd accumulated, her real treasure, earned over countless grappling nights of pain. "To winnow their numbers I retreated to this cave. Here, only the strongest and most youthful can endeavor to reach me. The weak, the old, they die in their pilgrimage, and their bones almost pave the trail to my door." She laughed.

"The Sherpa will not approach me or my home," said the Baba. "The Sherpa believe that I kill my would-be lovers, but those who die do so by their own hands. . . ."

Only the healthiest aspirants reach the cave. There are no cripples among the skeletons. No deformed. These are the skulls of the beautiful with shining straight teeth. They came seeking pleasure for themselves, the Baba explained. "Only Max arrived with the purpose of providing pleasure to others. But once he recognized the power of supplying such pleasure, he was seduced to use it for his own gain!"

She gestured toward the skeletons, her voice windy and hollow. "They waste away and die." Starvation and exhaustion stripped the flesh from them and soon the young apprentices looked more aged than their bemused master. Not long after, the Baba would stagger back from her day's hunt and find them expired.

If she fancied a novel curve in the dead apprentice's iliac crest, the Baba might scavenge it for a new project. Nothing was wasted, for she used the vocal cords and sinews and dried entrails to lash parts together. Thus the young beautiful lovers brought her more pleasure once they were dead. With luck she'd fashion a new pleasure tool before the next student presented herself at the cave opening.

Aghast, Penny asked, "You used them, these bones?"

All Beautiful You products were based on the designs of the Baba. The arc of one tool was that of a rib. The diameter of another toy was based on a human femur.

Pointing to a tangle of ulnas and tendons, her eyes dancing with excitement, the Baba said, "Max once tried to murder me with that one! So great was his skill that he wielded my own creation to spur me to paroxysms of ecstasy so glorious that I almost died!"

She described how Maxwell had challenged her to an erotic

duel. He'd stood, nude, an arrogant young male animal, with his bare legs wide apart. He'd pressed his erection downward, toward his knees, and then released it to spring upward and land a great thwack against his taut belly. A waggish glint in his eye, he'd swiveled his hips to make his member swing from side to side, saying, "Come, old woman, impale yourself. Take your pleasure from this meat you've trained so well!"

Penny asked, "How did you save yourself?"

Smiling at the memory, the old woman said, "The weapon he used flew from my body and shattered. It blasted from me like a cork from a bottle, and the force threw me backward, where my head struck the cave wall. When I awoke Max was gone. He'd absconded with much of my sex-craft technology."

"But how did you free yourself?" Penny demanded.

The Baba touched herself solemnly. "I replaced one pleasure with another. I thought of how beautiful my mother was and how much I adored her. I screamed."

Penny gasped. "From your vagina?"

Almost shouting, the Baba responded, "Child, you can expel energy from any opening of the body!"

Penny sipped her lichen tea and considered the idea.

"This," the sex witch said, plucking something from her wet depths, "this is all I have remaining from my mother." The object she held was brownish, like polished wood, like an unvarnished pencil, and she withdrew it slowly. The extraction made a faint slurping sound. "It was her longest finger," the Baba explained in a hushed voice. "I cut it from her even while the wild animals devoured the rest." She offered it for Penny to examine. The finger gleamed damply, its surface fluted with wrinkles. The narrow end was scabbed with a discolored nail. The blunt end sprouted a shattered, yellowed stub of bone. It felt warm and alive, heavily scented with the Baba's natural oils. Even in the cavern's dim light, it was lovely.

Penny weighed the relic in her palm. It saddened her to think of her own mother nude and spread-eagled, struggling against her bonds in a gritty Nebraska attic. Gibbering in the throes of sexual cold turkey, she'd be writhing against the sweat-soaked sheets like a feverish wild animal. The image filled Penny with despair.

When the girl reached to return the treasure, the Baba did not extend her hand to accept it. Instead she arched her back and pushed forward her ancient pubis. Sensing what the sex crafter desired, Penny spit on the finger to moisten it, and she aimed its gnarled tip at the center of the snowy thatch. As she boldly pressed it home the older woman gasped with enjoyment.

"This is what I must instill in you," vowed the ancient. "I saved myself by channeling Max's contempt back to its source. When I awoke he was gone, the devil, and many of my favorite instruments were missing with him." What Max hadn't stolen he'd re-created from memory—the herbal recipes, for instance, for his unholy salves and enemas. "The way a bullet ricochets off a rock. The way an echo resounds off of a canyon wall. You must redirect his energy."

On one of her last dwindling days in the cave, Penny set aside her tea and searched among the meatless bones and castoff eggshells that covered the stone floor. The Baba would be away foraging for some time, and Penny needed to right a grievous wrong. After rooting through the litter, Penny located what she needed: her mobile phone. An icon on the screen showed that a few moments of power were left in the battery. She dialed a New York City number stored in the phone's memory.

On the first ring a man answered. "Brenda?" He sounded hoarse, as if from months of weeping.

Sadly, Penny replied, "No." Compassionately, she explained, "we met several weeks ago—"

"In Central Park," he affirmed. He sounded crushed, the poor wretch. His fiancée was still among the millions of women who'd dropped out of society.

Penny had to remind herself why she'd called. She'd wanted to apologize and to accept at least partial responsibility for the scourge of Beautiful You. And to promise that she'd do everything within her power to remedy the crisis. She wanted to assure this suffering, lovelorn stranger that she was almost ready to do battle with Cornelius Linus Maxwell. Soon she'd be a full-fledged sex witch, powerful enough to confront and expose Max's nanobot conspiracy. She wanted her kind words to wrap this pitiful man in a comforting cocoon. But at the crucial moment, her courage failed. Instead, she asked, "What's your name?"

Over the phone, the man sniffed. He said, "Yuri." His quavering voice calmed and he asked, "What's yours?" Suddenly his question had an odd, pointed quality to it.

Penny considered saying her real name. She stared guiltily out the cave's mouth, her eyes following the graceful path of a bird against the blue Nepalese sky. Eventually, she said, "I'm Shirley."

A longer silence followed before the man repeated, "Shirley." His voice now had a hard edge to it. "Shirley, why does my phone's caller ID say 'Penny Harrigan'?"

Caught in a lie, Penny froze, speechless and mortified. Her heart rate sped up to 165 beats per minute.

"Don't fool yourself," the man, Yuri, cruelly taunted. "I read the *National Enquirer*!" His tone was steeped in bitterness. "I know Penny Harrigan is claiming ownership of the Beautiful You patents! I saw on the news that you're appearing in court next week!" He brayed a hysterical laugh. "You stole my Brenda from me! You stole the wives from millions of husbands and the mothers from millions of children!"

His ranting had grown so loud Penny was forced to hold the phone at arm's length. The cavern echoed with his threats. She could hear the murderous scorn in his voice. It was unmistakable.

Enraged, Yuri screamed, "Every red-blooded man in New York dreams of killing you!"

Penny's phone beeped to signal that its battery was failing.

"If you dare to show your face at the patent-ownership trial," Yuri vowed, "we will tear you limb from limb. Tonight . . . tonight we will go to burn down your house—"

His threat knocked the wind from Penny. *Monique,* she realized. Monique was alone, incapacitated in her bedroom, equipped with only Pop-Tarts and bottled water. Penny needed to call and warn her. If an angry mob set fire to the town house, Monique would be burned alive.

That was when the telephone battery chose to go dead.

On her long flight from Nepal back to New York, Penny thought of her best friend. When she considered Monique, once so vibrant, now slavishly diddling herself in a darkened, locked room, using a human coccyx modeled out of some space-age polymer, she wanted to cry. Poor Monique with her abused, blistered privates, she was no doubt hovering in some twilight where pleasure yielded to death. Penny prayed silently to the ancient tantric gods that her lovable roommate still drew breath.

To pass the time during the lengthy trip, she practiced the self-satisfaction exercises the Baba had relentlessly drilled into her. She coaxed her hindquarters to the brink of an orgasm, and then replaced that thrilling sensation with thoughts of sincere love for her dad. By tweaking her nipples, she brought herself to the verge of hyperventilating, and then quickly redirected that mounting passion to dreamy thoughts of Abyssinian kittens.

Throughout their days together, the crone had selected erotic weapons seemingly at random from those strewn around the caves. Those rude assemblages of bone and stone and feathers, each she used as a wedge or lever to breach even Penny's most inaccessible tantric hot spots. Once she'd gained access, the witch had repeatedly stimulated Penny to lunatic arousal, always encouraging her to vent the enjoyment in physical thrashing and joyous shouts of vile language. Following each session, she would sponge the sweat from Penny's body using handfuls of fragrant mosses.

Together they would drink lichen tea, and Baba Gray-Beard would expound on the theory that pleasure was a deathless energy that can be directed and channeled. Pleasure, she explained, was attracted to those people who'd trained their receptive organs to welcome it. But, she warned, pleasure could not be held or collected. It must flow through its target, or that target would die.

Brandishing a ram's horn, which she had augmented with many thrill-inducing pebbles and herbal oils, the witch motioned for Penny to lie back, saying, "Shall we recommence your lessons, my dear?"

It was true. Penny's 136 days in Paris with Max had taught her about pleasure without love. But her weeks cloistered in the Baba's dank cavern had taught her that such profound ecstasy could coexist with an even stronger affection. The depth of her attachment to the witch-woman surprised even Penny. She had no idea of it until the final morning she awoke in their shared bed of dried plant matter and realized she had to return to the outside world.

That morning, Penny had quietly breakfasted on a porridge

of coarsely milled snakes. She'd packed her few belongings into a commodious sheep's bladder. Penny had lived day-to-day naked for so long that her Norma Kamali pantsuit felt strange against her body. She'd knelt to kiss the sleeping Baba good-bye. Then she'd begun her harrowing predawn descent down the sheer cliff faces of Everest.

Now, seated alone aboard a chartered private jet, attired head to toe in scrumptious Versace, Penny sipped tea she'd steeped using twigs and yak milk the lamia had gathered. She'd checked her e-mail and found that her patent-rights trial was set to begin in a few days. Her first step in her war against Max would be to contest his exclusive ownership of the Beautiful You designs. She'd force him to confront her, and they would do battle in a public court of law. If she lost, she would be dead. Death held no fear for her, only the hope that she'd someday be reunited with Baba Gray-Beard in an eternity of pleasure.

And if she, Penny Harrigan, won her audacious battle? If she won, and the world was truly liberated from the conspiracy of C. Linus Maxwell, then she would return to live as the old hag had lived: in that isolated cliff-side cavern, inventing endless means to pleasure herself and instructing those students who sought her guidance.

Returning to her Upper East Side town house, Penny found the frosted-glass front door marred by hooligans. Using bright red spray paint, someone had written, "Penny Harrigan Sucks Cocks in Hell!!!" in foot-high letters. The words stretched to deface the elegant stonework facade on either side of the doorway. Long drips ran down from each letter like horror-movie special effects. As she mounted the porch steps she saw that the white-marble stoop was cluttered with stuffed dolls. Roughly the size of baby dolls, each effigy wore miniature Salvatore Ferragamo pumps. Their facial features were stitched and quilted to closely resemble Penny's face. Careful embroidery had given them her warm brown eyes and pink pouting lips. It was unsettling to see how all the dolls were mutilated and bristling with pins. Penny gasped and shuddered, chilled by a realization: These were voodoo dolls.

Heaped among the evil artifacts were a number of decomposing chickens, their throats messily cut, their feathers splashed with gore. Their glassy avian eyes stared back at Penny accusingly. They'd clearly been sacrificed on the spot. The threshold of her home had become an altar for intense hatred. Drawn to the spilled blood were her old nemeses, black houseflies. They hovered above the stubs of burned candles.

Around her, the wail of fire engines echoed from every direction. A pall of black smoke blocked the sky, the stench of it making her cough. A rocket screamed by overhead, like military ordnance, tracing a low arc in the direction of Midtown. It disappeared behind some buildings. A muffled blast followed. The city had become, inexplicably, a battlefield.

Instantly, Penny thought of Monique.

Her roommate and best friend would've been upstairs when whoever had laid siege to the town house. A rush of loving concern displaced Penny's fear, and she quickly kicked aside the elements of the grotesque still life. She fitted her key into the lock.

Inside, broken glass crunched under every step of her Kate Spade kitten heels. The vandals had broken the panes of several windows. Their ammunition—rocks wrapped in paper scrawled with angry messages—lay in the shards. Thank goodness stout security grilles of ornately cast bronze had prevented the attackers from bodily entering.

Rushing up the stairs two steps at a time, Penny shouted, "Monique? Monique, are you okay?"

She wielded a fire ax to bust down the locked door of her roommate's bedroom. Within she found her once free-spirited friend lying across the sodden mattress of her bed, near death. The room stank of drool and stale blueberry Pop-Tarts. Penny nursed the girl, holding a cup of lichen tea to her chapped lips. If the batteries in her Beautiful You products had not failed from overuse, Monique would've died of exhaustion and dehydration long ago. As it was, the once sassy girl responded with hardly a whimper as Penny wiped her frail limbs with a salve made from eagle glands and rich reindeer tallow.

Penny spoon-fed the crippled girl a broth of plover eggs and fermented marrow. When her fallen comrade tried to speak, Penny hushed her. "You mustn't feel ashamed of your hideously degraded circumstances," she said. "You were the victim of primitive pleasures no untrained female could resist."

Penny carried her famished, unresponsive housemate to the media room and arranged her limp form in a comfortable lounge chair. As the two young ladies had done while watching the Academy Awards, Penny popped popcorn and lavished it with salt and butter. She hand-fed Monique kernels, slowly, placing them between the girl's chapped lips as, tonight, together, they watched CNN coverage of the world news.

Spread before them on the high-definition, seventy-two-inch plasma flat-screen was a panorama of global unrest. War and natural disasters were no longer the top stories. The Beautiful You effect had trumped every misfortune. Some men were fast forging new roles for themselves in this rapidly evolving world. Most were not.

Among the first group were slimy lotharios. Self-proclaimed intimacy coaches warned that women who succumbed to Beautiful You products would be unhappy with the ordinary machinations of a human sexual partner. However, any male who could wield a Rotating Relaxation Rod, product number 3447, such a man was never lacking for the companionship of the fairer sex. The cunning pickup line was no longer, "Would you like to see my etchings?" For a successful come-on, a would-be lover need only mention that he possessed one of the rarer BY products. Any laborer who could utilize a power drill or chain saw, he could easily operate the Jiggle Whip or the Trembling Love Snake. Thus, displaced workers from all the construction trades were finding new careers demonstrating Maxwell's personal care tools. In the retail shops. Or selling them door-to-door.

The CNN cameras panned across the showroom inside the Fifth Avenue store. Business was brisk as suave salesmen plied the female shoppers with products. And not just products, there were pricey warranties to sell. And financing schemes, the newscaster explained. Analysts claimed that DataMicroCom was making big money on the financing charges that customers accrued using their bright pink charge cards. Any desperate, libidinous lady wandering into that den of unscrupulous cads, Penny realized, she wouldn't stand a chance! It was the career that every male in the city hotly coveted.

On television, the scene changed. The cameras displayed the miles-long line of shoppers outside the flagship store. Among them, Penny recognized the sales associate from Bonwit Teller, her elegant good looks gone, replaced by a gap-toothed, slack-jawed zombie woman. Likewise, Kwan Qxi and Esperanza, Penny's former roommates, were there, bleary-eyed and clutching well-worn bright pink credit cards.

In recent weeks, according to CNN, the gender composition of the shoppers had shifted. Now an almost equal number of men stood waiting among the women. These were the profiteers.

Among the fastest to adapt, these usurious men sought to buy as many of the new products as possible. They were scalpers who, in turn, sold the toys to females at an astronomical markup. For rich women, crippled women, impatient gals, anyone who couldn't or wouldn't wait in the out-of-doors, it was an expensive godsend. Vibrators and dildos had become the world's new form of underground currency. No day passed without reports of Beautiful You trucks being hijacked for their valuable cargos. Warehouses were looted. Security guards assassinated in drive-by shootings. Deliveries of new stock arrived at stores by armored car. Recent purchasers were targeted by street thugs, who openly stole the merchandise at gunpoint for resale on the black market.

Rival gangs fought over turf. Slave-labor sweatshops flooded the market with counterfeit products that failed to satisfy.

To Penny, the whole situation seemed almost as crazy as Beanie Babies or those Michael Jordan shoes had been. Almost.

As Monique began to listlessly gum her mouthful of calorie-rich corn, the CNN reporter ascended in a helicopter from midtown Manhattan and slowly made his way northward toward a huge plume of black smoke that rose from the Bronx. The New York below them looked, to Penny, like some contested third-world killing field. Mortar rounds seemed to jet across the neighborhoods, igniting fires in high-rise buildings. Police cars and ambulances bathed the streets in flashing red lights. Traffic was gridlocked by burning vehicles.

The camera shot hovered above East One Twenty-second Street, moving steadily toward the Harlem River Drive, slowly crossing into the Bronx. Suspended high above the grid of streets, the helicopter swooped and tilted, dodging some kind of rocket or missile that came jetting directly at it. The weapon looked to be about the size of a bazooka shell. It blazed with flames and trailed an arc of black smoke. Another projectile raced directly at the chopper, and the pilot dived to avoid it.

On the media room television, the skies of the city were crisscrossed with these flaming warheads. Wherever they landed, each burst like an incendiary bomb, igniting buildings, cars, and trees. Turning the island into a war zone. By following the black arc of each, Penny could trace them all back to the source of the black plume.

The smoke rose from the center of Yankee Stadium. There, a massive fire appeared to be raging on the pitcher's mound.

The aerial shot cut to a ground-level news crew broadcasting from the infield. The scene was chaos as mobs of people caroused. Everyone within sight was male, and most wore Promise Keepers T-shirts. Penny could discern long chains of men. These chains snaked toward the bonfire from every direction, spreading to fill the stadium like the spokes of a wheel. They were all-male versions of the customer lines that snaked away from every Beautiful You retailer in the world.

The frenzied men were singing a song Penny recognized from childhood. It was the religious hymn "Kumbaya." Their measured, chain-gang movements were timed to the rhythm of the melody while they passed objects hand to hand. As each item reached the fire it was tossed into the flames.

The cameras drew closer, and Penny witnessed what looked like any male's vision of hell. Innumerable multitudes of severed penises were writhing in the conflagration. Phalluses squirmed in the intense heat, blistering and twisting as if in prolonged torment. Aflame, some suffering man-parts crept, inchworm-like, from the fire as if attempting to escape to safety. They flopped. Flipped. Jumped and twitched. As if in agony. These were caught by the surrounding men and summarily flung back to their doom. Still other dongs erupted in the heat, spouting pink molten lava.

They were all Beautiful You products, Penny recognized. The figures who capered and sang like savages around the inferno, they were men sacrificing their common rivals. As generations before them had torched books and disco records, these men yelped in cathartic abandon, passing the prods and love wands man to man, until they were heaped onto the bubbling, spitting flames. The stench and black smoke of this pyre hung over the streets, acrid as the poisonous reek of an unending tire fire.

Among the phalluses were withering Dragonflies and exploding douches. No product was overlooked. Batteries burst with a high-pitched squeal like butchered baby rabbits.

Other phalluses blasted off like skyrockets. They shot straight up from the bonfire. These, these were the airborne torches that had almost taken down the CNN helicopter. Like incoming missiles, they rained fire on the citizens of the metropolis.

The CNN reporter explained that these pleasure toys had been bought, borrowed, and stolen. Regardless of how they'd come to Yankee Stadium, none of them would leave intact. In every stadium around the world, from huge coliseums to bare-dirt soccer fields, the reporter intoned that hordes of enraged men were fanning the flames of similar love-tool pyres.

Without warning the camera jerked. It veered away from the CNN reporter. Someone, some unseen thug, had commandeered it, forcing the lens to focus on a single bedraggled man. His face was blackened with soot from the burning latex. A scraggly beard hid all of his features except his bloodshot eyes. Only when he spoke did Penny know who he was.

It was Yuri.

"Penelope Harrigan," he ranted from the plasma flat-screen

of her luxurious media room, "soon we will drag you from a courtroom and burn you on this fire like the witch you are!"

The Manhattan that Penny had returned to was a cityscape of men. Only men roamed the sidewalks. No one but men drove the cars and trucks or rode the subways. Every seat in every eatery was occupied by male buttocks. And walking among them, Penny attracted much attention. Her near-starvation diet of organic fungi and her long hours of strenuous self-pleasuring had left her body beautifully sculpted. Every muscle twitched enticingly beneath her thin, smooth skin as she confidently traipsed the streets.

To prevent being recognized she'd donned oversize sunglasses and a baseball cap worn backward. The glasses were by Fetch, and their stylish frames offered the perfect balance of "look-at-me" versus "go-away." She forswore wearing the huge ruby pendant that had become her signature accessory as the Nerd's Cinderella. Despite being incognito, she could too easily imagine a flood of livid vigilantes pouring from the skyscrapers. Men like Yuri. A world of furious, obsolete penises. The same men who had sacrificed chickens on her front steps, they would come streaming down the sidewalks. She pictured them all carrying torches and nooses. If they knew who she was, this all-male lynch mob would hound her as if she were the Frankenstein monster.

The smoke from Yankee Stadium hung over Greater New York like a pall. Blazing dildos shrieked across the sky, and ash fell like black snowflakes. The soot burned Penny's eyes and throat with its acrid stench. Smut, trickling down, clung to the pink flanks of the Beautiful You building. Enshrouding it. Making the tower look like nothing less than a dark parody of the snowy paradise Penny had so recently left behind.

The photocopied posters of missing women continued to paper every available public surface in the city. They climbed like kudzu up telephone poles and walls. But the harsh daylight had begun to fade the smiling photos—these beloved wives and adored mothers. These successful CFOs and CEOs, rain was washing away their career accomplishments. Their names were gradually disappearing. Already, they were half forgotten.

With them, the hard-won political and social progress of all women seemed to be eroding. Vanishing.

On the corner of Broadway and Forty-seventh Penny glimpsed a familiar face. A woman lay splayed on the sidewalk, leaning back against the base of a lamppost. From closer up Penny could see the afflicted stranger wore a gold-and-diamond Paloma Picasso brooch from Tiffany. Her hair was expertly high-lighted although it hung in rank tendrils around the smudged ruins of her once expensively made-up face. She wore the tat-tered remains of a pink Chanel suit, the jacket hanging open, her breasts bared to passersby. Her skirt was wadded up around her waist as she stabbed at her exposed self with a Beautiful You toy. Her legs filmed with grime, she gripped the hilt of the toy in both hands. Her fingernails rimed with dirt, she stirred the smut-stained tool in circles, plunging and withdrawing it. Like an inmate in a Victorian asylum, she giggled and stammered to herself, oblivious to the crowds who passed, averting their eyes.

Approaching this unfortunate spectacle, Penny ventured, "Brenda? Is your name Brenda?"

Without slowing her carnal machinations, the woman looked up at Penny with a faint glimmer of comprehension in her eyes.

"You're engaged to marry Yuri, remember?" Penny held out

her open, empty hands as if she could give the woman back her former life. "You were the CFO of Allied Chemical Corp." The pleasure tool, Penny recognized as Beautiful You product number 2788, the Instant-Ecstasy Probe. Its silicone-and-latex casing was worn and stained almost beyond recognition. Even Yuri would struggle to identify it as the special birthday gift he'd once given so innocently. Penny quickly found Yuri's number in her phone's history. She dialed it and listened to his phone ringing at the other end.

Simultaneously, she went to Brenda's aid, pulling at the remnants of the woman's jacket in an attempt to cover her bared bosom. Trying desperately to save her dignity, Penny insistently tugged the hem of the skirt down Brenda's legs while offering soothing assurances. No one stopped to help. Everyone scurried past. All were men, and they cast furtive, mortified glances at the scene and kept walking. Yuri's phone continued to ring.

"Someone call nine-one-one," Penny pleaded while she tried to match buttons with buttonholes. "Please." She couldn't help but notice that this slathering, maniacal creature wore a double strand of beautifully matched pearls. After her own 136 days among the glitterati, she could recognize that the ice-cube-size sparklers in this stranger's earrings were flawless two-carat diamonds.

In response, Brenda clung tightly to the phallus, bringing her knees to her chest, curling into a ball as if to protect her prize. She bared her teeth in a ferocious snarl.

"Help me!" Penny begged a pin-striped businessman who stared in horror and quickly darted in another direction. She was gently trying to yank the woman's fingers free of their task when she felt a sting in the side of her hand. This crazed stranger had sunk her capped teeth into Penny's skin. Her cheeks smeared with blood, she gnawed at the tender flesh near Penny's thumb like an enraged animal.

A bicycle messenger paused only long enough to say, "Lady, I hope you're current with your tetanus shots . . ." before jetting away.

Shocked and in pain, Penny dropped her phone, but not before she heard a voice on the other end say, "Hello? Brenda?" It was Yuri, but the phone clattered into the gutter, out of reach.

Penny wrestled to escape, but the woman's teeth held fast. Her panting sprayed Penny's blood from the corners of her mouth. Only when Penny launched herself away did she escape the madwoman's toothy grip. Even as Penny fell backward, the lunatic leaped to her feet and scuttled a zigzag retreat. Blood still streaming down her face, Brenda lopped along Broadway, her soiled hands grasping the pink-plastic object of her insatiable obsession. The all-male crowds stepped aside as she scooted past.

The only other females to be found were those haggard zombies standing in the miles-long line that stretched from the doors of the tapered pink tower on Fifth Avenue. The bedeviled wretches looked interchangeable. Their stringy hair had fallen out in clumps, and their fingernails were bitten down to the quick. To a woman, they each carried the same purse, wore identical shoes, dressed in look-alike outfits. These articles of clothing weren't attractive or well made, Penny noted, but they were all products manufactured by DataMicroCom and its subsidiary companies.

A defeated crew of stoop-shouldered men wearing Promise Keepers T-shirts were staging a protest march and vigil near the store's entrance. They trudged in a ragged circle, carrying picket signs that read, "Personal Fulfillment Doesn't Make a

Family!" Other signs declared, "Babies Should Come *Before* Orgasms!" Around and around they shuffled, beleaguered and ignored.

To confront the mob of ladies outside the flagship store, Penny stood with her feet planted wide apart and her shoulders thrown back. Her arms akimbo, she rested a fist on each hip. "Sisters," she shouted. "Hear me, my sister women! You must quit abusing your loins!"

The women squinted, observing her through narrowed, hostile eyes. They clutched bright pink shopping bags to their chests like talismans. No one spoke, but many hissed loudly.

"You're accessing a power you do not understand," Penny called. "An ancient practice of self-stimulation that requires decades to learn and utilize safely without resulting in permanent harm to the user." Penny stared boldly back into their slavering, snarling faces. "Most of you," she continued, "have also been infected with legions of tiny robots."

In response, many heckled. Others spit. In their uniform weakness none could launch an outright attack.

"Tomorrow," Penny decreed, "I shall make public the heinous scheme with which C. Linus Maxwell has plundered the sex secrets of the past in order to enslave all women." In response to their growing catcalls, she shouted, "Beautiful You squanders your endorphins. We must boycott all products made and sold by DataMicroCom." She urged, "I will school you in how to craft safe rudimentary personal care tools from the raw materials provided by nature." She offered, "I bring unguents to soothe your inflamed, overtaxed vulvas!"

Instead of joining her or attacking her, this time the mob turned away. Their jeering dropped to general grumbling. The gambit had failed.

Clearly Penny had misjudged the crowd. Their only interest lay in returning to the mother ship store and acquiring additional products. Reevaluating her strategy, Penny redirected her offense. "Sisters," she cried. "Pleasure is a human right! We must storm the bastions of pleasure and take what is due to us!" She shook a fist in the air, the teeth marks still visible, her hand stained red with her own dried blood.

This drew a positive response. Many in the crowd now cheered.

"Do not wait like passive sheep for your corporate masters to dole out dribs and drabs of ecstasy!" she railed. "Take it! Batter down those doors and take it all!"

Thus Penny rallied the ragtag queue into a rioting army. She whipped their hunger into a frenzied rage. Those thousands of desperate women surged forward and crashed against the pink-mirror facade of the building, hammering at the glass with the clunky heels of their ugly shoes. They wielded their worn erotic tools as truncheons. They beat with their fists until ominous cracks raced in every direction and the windows and doors bowed inward, ready to collapse.

Unnoticed, a black limousine had arrived at the curb near Penny. A rear window of the car rolled down, revealing the high cheekbones of a pale, almost reptilian face. Inside sat Maxwell. Speaking only to Penny, he said, "Get in."

"Hah!" she laughed, indicating her mob. Even now the store's crumbling exterior was crushed underfoot as the angry rioters swarmed inside to loot the shelves and display cases. "You cannot control our numbers, Max!" Victorious, Penny gloated, "We will take what must belong to us!"

In response, the figure seated in the back of the limo lifted a small black device. It was square and could easily be mistaken for a telephone or a gaming system. It was the device he'd been fingering in the audience the night of Alouette's death. He thumbed a few buttons as if composing a text message. He thumbed a few more.

"Go ahead," Penny challenged. "Call in the police. Call your thugs. Even they cannot stem this revolution!"

"Get in, bitch," Max repeated. "This is the last time I'll ask you *nicely*."

"Fuck you!" Penny screamed.

"No," Max said flatly. "Fuck *you,* my dear." At this he pressed a button and the looters all hesitated in their actions.

Some, including Penny, clutched themselves. The knees of most buckled and they fell, gripping their crotches in both hands. Soon all were writhing on the ground, making voracious noises, without human dignity. The army of the revolution broke ranks and collapsed into hedonistic wriggling. In place of the valiant rebels, here was an undulating carpet of human bodies. Their cries of victory dropped to a chorus of sensual moans. These occurred in synch with violent pelvic thrusts skyward.

With the push of another button more women frothed at the mouth and twitched in spasmodic convulsions. They were about to die as Alouette had died, of cardiac arrest or brain aneurysms brought on by too much erotic stimulation.

Even as the crippling spasms of pleasure rippled through her, Penny beseeched, "Set them free!" She began to crawl toward the car. Within her body, she tried to block the erotic force, to block it or redirect it back toward Maxwell. She made an angry, clenched fist of her pelvic floor. She meditated as the Baba had taught her. She tried all the tantric methods, but none seemed to work. Dragging herself across the concrete sidewalk, she arrived beside the car. Defeated, she whispered, "Release them, Maxwell. Spare their lives, and I will go with you now."

The car's door opened, and Max said, "Get in, or I will press another button and they will all die."

Pulling herself into the car's interior, Penny saw her face reflected in Max's polished shoe. *Reflect his power,* she told herself, but nothing happened. Once she was fully incapacitated, shivering and depleted on the car's carpeted floor, Max pulled the door shut and instructed the driver to make a slow circuit of Central Park.

Gradually the unbearable pleasure lessened. Max dialed it back, using his small remote. To any onlooker it would appear he was merely thumbing the buttons of a computer game. No longer subjected to the full brunt of the stimulation, Penny pulled herself up to sit beside him. He poured a glass of champagne at the car's small bar and offered it to her. Pink champagne. She eyed it warily.

"Do not worry, my girl," he crooned. "I don't need to drug you. I already possess complete control over your body."

Penny accepted the glass. The wine tasted so foreign after the many cups of healthy lichen tea and pickled cliff rats. Her vaginal walls relaxed, exhausted. "I know about the nanobots," she gasped. "I know they were delivered inside the Dragonfly."

"Clever girl," Max said. "You'll make an excellent president of DataMicroCom."

"I will not serve as your puppet," Penny swore.

"Poor Clarissa," Max said. "She never wanted to be president. That was something I bullied her into."

He explained how he'd met Clarissa when she was a simple Avon lady selling lipsticks door-to-door. She was nothing to him. A cipher. But he saw how, with the power of life or death, he could bully her into becoming anything. After they'd had their 136 days of romance, it was too late. She was implanted. She no longer had any choice except to be what he wanted her to become—or to die. She'd never wanted to become a senator, much less the president, but if she refused—or if she'd failed in her bids for election—Max would've killed her and begun the process with another woman.

"It was the same with Alouette," he said wistfully. "She was a pretty face, happy to be nothing but a simple fashion model. . . ."

But after being implanted with battalions of nanobots, she had no choice. If she failed to give a brilliant performance, Max would punish her with debilitating levels of pleasure. He would drive her to the brink of insanity by blasting her clitoris with ecstasy for days so she couldn't eat or sleep. Failure ceased to be an option, and Alouette grew terrified of her own genitalia.

"To survive, both women became what I decreed. If either had told anyone about the hold I had over her," Max said, "I would have killed her."

"Is that why you murdered Alouette?" asked Penny.

"She was going to tell you," Max confirmed.

Max's chauffeur steered them in an endless loop through the smoky, war-torn setting. It seemed like centuries since she'd taken the romantic horse-drawn carriage ride with Tad down this same leafy route.

Through the limousine's tinted windows she could see the park. The unchaperoned packs of children still roamed, abandoned by their wayward nannies. The wheelchair-bound geriatrics were still parked like aged Eskimos left to die on arctic ice floes. Standing among them was Yuri, the jilted bridegroom deserted by his pleasure-obsessed fiancée. Bearded, alone in his anger, his clothes disheveled, he continued to leaflet the passing crowds with his pale-green handouts. His photo of Brenda, like his memory of her, would be fainter with every generation of photocopies. Penny yearned to leap from the car and rush to him. She dreamed of showing him the teeth marks on her hand as proof that his beloved was still alive somewhere. Those toothy scars would instill him with renewed hope.

Max followed her gaze to the bereft man. Dismissively, Maxwell shook his head. "I will not let some lunatic murder you." He waved his hand in a sweep that seemed to encompass the entire city. Perhaps the entire world. "Wherever you walk . . . every moment of your life since your birth . . . my security forces have been constantly watching over you. My guards prevented those ruffians from setting fire to your town house . . . once, they saved you from a tornado." Less warmly, he added, "You belong to me. If anyone ends your life, it will be me."

Penny sighed in resignation. "And what is to be my purpose in your grand design?"

Max smiled with a strange mixture of pity and affection. "You will serve as the permanent CEO of DataMicroCom. Every day for the rest of your life you will wear panty hose and carry a briefcase. You will wear your hair as a lacquered helmet and eat salads. You will sit through board meetings so tedious that they will test your sanity."

Max fixed her with a smug smile. "Every woman in the world dreams of becoming my wife."

"Are you hitting on me?" Penny asked, stunned.

"Don't be silly. I'm *proposing*." He shrugged as if to dismiss any argument, "You'll make a stalwart consort. There's no reason why either of us ought to spend our life alone."

The queen of England, the Chinese media baron, the steel magnate, all of his earlier conquests were living similar chaste lives of duty to him and only him. This network of powerful women gave Maxwell dominion over the entire human race.

"Through Beautiful You," Max said proudly, "I've successfully implanted nanobots in ninety-eight-point-seven percent of the adult women in the industrialized world."

This, he confirmed, was how he controlled their buying habits. During television commercials for certain products, those made by DataMicroCom, he'd broadcast a signal that triggered erotic sensations. Be it a shoe or a motion picture or a vampire novel, women quickly associated the stimuli with their aroused response, and they rushed to buy.

"Women are the new masters," Max boasted, "but now I am the master of women."

Penny knew he was telling the truth. At least his own truth.

"Don't reduce this to some playground contest," Max warned. "This isn't about boys versus girls. This is about power. We live in an age when women hold the bulk of the power. In government, in consumer purchase decisions, women steer the world, and their longer life spans have left them in control of the greatest wealth."

He marveled at the black control box in his palm. He turned the device in his hands so she could better see it. The surface was a mosaic of black push buttons, each marked with a letter or number. A keyboard. "Can you imagine if this controller fell into the hands of a thirteen-year-old boy?"

Dryly, Penny said, "It has."

Max's thumbs twitched over the buttons, and she cried out as a spasm of electric arousal ripped through her clitoris.

Suppressing her orgasm, Penny said, "You've created a very effective deterrent to people making babies." She was thinking of the injury done to everyone who'd tried to enter her.

Maxwell smiled enigmatically. "If your labors please me, I might allow you to reproduce. Human beings are incapable of controlling their numbers, so I must do so. In my utopia only the brightest, most productive females will be allowed to bring forth offspring."

Hearing this, Penny could understand why the president had killed herself. Maxwell planned to control the birthrate of the entire industrialized world.

"Overpopulation," Penny said. "So that's why you've placed a dog in the manger."

He nodded with obvious pride. "You're referring to the gatekeeper function. Certain nanobots can deliver a pulse of scorching plasma energy. It was invented to destroy cancer cells, but I find it works equally as well on male erections."

Wryly, Penny said, "You'll be happy to know that it works equally as well on the fingers of Himalayan mystics."

Max raised an eyebrow. "Ah, you sought out Baba Gray-Beard." He smirked, asking, "How is the old girl?"

"She despises you!" Penny countered. Despite how he tried to hide it, she could see the news saddened Maxwell. To press her advantage she added, "The Baba loathes you for how you've stolen the sex secrets of the ancients and used them for your profit."

Without speaking, Max wiggled a toggle on his control, and Penny felt a twinge of heady desire flutter through her.

She flinched but recovered her composure quickly. She narrowed her gaze. "Equipped with her guidance I might prove to be more of a challenge to master than your previous slaves."

Max spied her clenching and unclenching her hands in rage. "You are no longer the weak child whom I tutored in the ways of pleasure. . . . I sense that under the Baba's tutelage you've become something dangerous: a woman." His eyes gleamed with something like admiration. "If you ever consider doing me harm, please know that to kill me would be to unleash consequences beyond your wildest imaginings!"

"After tomorrow," Penny fumed, "the entire world will loathe you." She sipped at her glass of champagne. "In the opening arguments of my patent-rights trial, I plan to expose your entire dirty scheme!"

Max fingered his controls.

Penny felt a shiver of pleasure tease her anus. A warning. She ignored it.

Max toyed with another button, and she felt her nipples begin to enlarge.

"Surely," she taunted, "you can do better than that."

"And I promise I will," Maxwell swore. "If you attempt to expose me I will make you grovel and bark like a mad dog in heat on the courtroom floor. I will drive you insane with passion. And I will kill you."

That night Penny built an altar to the tantric gods of long-ago. She made an offering of tea brewed from a fistful of soil brought back from the cave of Baba Gray-Beard. Using a cool compress of damp lichens, she blotted the feverish brow of her best friend and housemate. This night might be Penny's last on earth, but even death would be better than living as a slave to Maxwell. She pictured the nanobots already massing for their attack in her brain and groin. She telephoned her father in Omaha. Her mother had not improved, but neither was her condition worse. She was heavily sedated and being force-fed through a stomach tube to keep her alive.

Only Tad seemed to believe her. In response to her call he raced to her town house, bringing the legal brief for the two of them to review. Over pizza in the kitchen she had explained about her trip to Nepal. She told him about the gatekeeper lurking within millions of women. That crippling pulse of malevolent penis-lancing plasma energy.

Penny explained everything. Now, only now could they fully and honestly consummate their romantic friendship. Drinking cups of the Baba's sacred dirt tea, they sat at the kitchen table and discussed taking their relationship to that next level.

Tad looked at her, the cooling pizza forgotten between them. His expression was that of a confused, frightened little boy. His eyes round with terror. For months, he'd seen Brillstein limping around the office, obviously in prolonged agony. He swallowed nervously. He didn't seem eager to suffer a similar fate. "I thought you couldn't have vaginal intercourse?"

As the Baba would tell her, Penny's vagina wasn't her only access to power. It no longer mattered whether she was pretty or ugly, thin or fat, young or old. She was already well schooled as a vastly accomplished sex witch. Hers were the skills passed down through a thousand generations of wily sex crafters. She wielded that amazing carnal magic in her hands and mouth. The knowledge was trained deep in Penny's every muscle. Her well-educated rectum alone knew countless methods of giving pleasure.

Penny boasted about none of these natural talents to Tad. Instead, she merely nodded in the direction of the Sub-Zero refrigerator. "There's a bottle of champagne chilling." Her voice furred with erotic suggestion, she said, "Why don't you pop the cork while I go upstairs and slip into something sexy?"

In her bedroom Penny retrieved the negligee of marabou feathers dyed dark purple. Many of the feathers were stiff with dried blood, Brillstein's blood. But the purple perfectly camouflaged that gory evidence from the night she'd seduced and interrogated her evil boss. Donning the plumage, she slipped her feet into her tallest pair of Prada heels and surveyed the results in her dressing room mirror. The memory of the aged senior partner lodged within her, weeping in pain, it made her giggle. The sight of her own magnificent, hairless vulva prompted the bittersweet memory of mounting Alouette's beautiful face in the restaurant toilet stall.

From downstairs, Tad called up, "Champagne's ready."

"Give me one more minute," Penny called down. She rushed to Monique's room. There, her roommate was sleeping soundly, too exhausted to hear Penny collect a sticky armload of much-used Beautiful You products. These she quickly carried into her own bathroom and flung into the shower.

Tad called up, "You ready? I'm bringing the champagne."

"I'm in my bedroom," Penny hollered. She was hurriedly using the shower's handheld attachment to rinse any accumulated residue of old lubricant and dried body fluids off of the various borrowed erotic tools. Now that she knew Max's design secrets she could easily recognize how one product was a plastic version of a human clavicle. Another was clearly a rubberized-fiberglass copy of a scapula. Each of these she blotted dry with a hand towel and flung onto her bed. As Penny heard Tad's footsteps mount the stairs, she had barely enough time to curl her eyelashes, wax her legs, and apply perfume behind her ears.

Doing so, she ransacked her memory for details about the male sexual anatomy. Max had taught her some. Baba Gray-Beard had taught her much more, but Penny had put none of this learning into practice. Her mind reeled with the effort to picture Tad's inferior rectal nerve and his tunica vaginalis.

As a finishing touch Penny walked slowly in a wide circle, scenting the love chamber. The Baba had taught her well how to express the powerful pheromones that naturally accumulated in her Howard gland, and doing so effectively filled the romantic setting with an unmistakable hormonal aroma.

By now Tad was standing in the bedroom doorway, holding the bottle of champagne and two Baccarat flutes. A winning combination of excitement and vulnerability filled his eyes. With a fluttering of marabou feathers, she led him to the bed and quickly undressed him, covertly reviewing his general anatomy. A few gentle caresses located the puboprostatic ligament. Subtly exploring, her fingers teased their way gradually deeper and deeper into Tad's rectum. She traced his inguinal canal to the bulbourethral glands and the ejaculatory duct. If he objected to the liberties she was taking he didn't say so. On the contrary, the virile, brash attorney squirmed with trepidation as he watched Penny combine the pink champagne with the premixed packet of Beautiful You proprietary secret ingredients. Under her touch his youthful flesh quivered with fear and anticipation.

Unknown to him, the blood of her thwarted, would-be lover still stained the mattress where they staged their lovemaking. Fortunately, Penny had thought to flip it over.

Penny savored his goose bumps. This was how Max had felt as he'd dictated her mounting ecstasy. This was power. Gone were the young blue blood's wordy declarations of love. For him nothing existed beyond the erotic sensations he was feeling for the first time. He shuddered with ill-concealed passion as she invaded his frightened sphincter with the syringe's nozzle and the doctored pink wine began to expand and invade his bloodstream. Penny was coaxing his body to a fulfillment which would strain the very framework of his reality.

If Penny herself felt aroused it was on an intellectual level. Tad's groaning and squirming were proof she'd attained a mastery of human pleasure centers. She'd seen so many women acted upon. Grossly manipulated. It felt wonderful to see that she could have an equal effect on a man. Max was right about one thing: This wasn't a battle of boys versus girls. This was about how insight into your own body gave you power over others. Penny had once been the groveling, drooling test subject. Tonight she became the master. She controlled.

Deftly, she compressed his seminiferous tubules in order to suppress spermatogenesis. Penny Harrigan was no longer the shivering slab of meat waiting to be acted upon. Despite her dyed-purple plumage, she was the peerless sex lamia. Her every caress monitored the young lawyer's heartbeat and temperature. He gasped. His heart rate was 197 beats per minute. Tad's pelvic floor surrendered, and she expertly inserted a bright pink phallus chosen from Monique's sizable hoard. Using product number 371, the Daisy Love Wand, she stirred and churned the intoxicating concoction in her boyfriend's bowels. Such machinations quickly sent him into an erotically induced coma—his core temperature dropped below eighty degrees Fahrenheit, his pupils became fixed and dilated—and Penny was compelled to resuscitate him using her own breath. Just as Max had stimulated her to the brink of death, then brought her back to life, Penny resurrected Tad, telling him, "Do not die. Now that you know the joy that is possible for your body, cling to your paltry life. . . ."

This wasn't sex the way Tad had always known sex. The way Sigma Chis knew sex. He didn't ejaculate. Penny's careful tantric touch had suppressed his spermatic artery. Instead of a full-out emission of hot seed, only a clear jewel of seminal fluid trembled on the tip of his exhausted, modestly sized erection. This droplet Penny gracefully collected with the tip of one finger and brought to her tongue. It had the usual fructose sweetness of seminal fluids produced by the Cowper's glands, but beneath that lurked more subtle shadings of flavor.

As she had seen the Baba do, Penny sucked and licked every nuance from the sample. In it, she could read the school-boy affection Tad was harboring for her. She could discern his dreams of their marrying and quickly raising a large, boisterous brood of children. In that single drop of glandular secretions she tasted a suburban ranch house, a pedigreed Irish setter, a seven-passenger minivan. He was as trapped by his small-scale, gender-specific dreams as she had been by hers. Hidden behind all those details was something more elusive. She smacked her lips, savoring the final hints. At last her taste buds recognized the key flavor component. It was shame.

Spent, Tad sprawled on the disheveled bed and returned her

gaze with dread. Even now her hands were tenderly applying a soothing ointment of mashed leeches to the raw, inflamed skin of his scrotum.

The truth of his fluid shocked Penny. But it was unmistakable. Smiling sheepishly at him, she said, "I know your darkest secret. There's no need to hide any longer." As she said the words, Tad closed his eyes, mortified.

She promised, "I won't tell anyone . . . but you didn't go to Yale, did you?"

Hearing that, the ambitious young attorney-at-law dissolved into tears.

Under oath, Penny would speak the truth for those who could not, for Alouette and Clarissa. She would speak for the ragged hordes lining Fifth Avenue. Entering the courtroom, she surveyed the proceedings and panicked. There were no women in the jury box. There were no women among the reporters or spectators in the gallery. Everyone present was male. To be the only woman was thrilling and intimidating. She froze in the doorway a moment too long, just time enough for every eye to find her. Every voice fell silent. She knew she looked breathtaking, her every muscle toned. She lifted a manicured hand and ran her fingers through her lustrous hair, turning her head slightly from side to side so that the long, thick strands bounced and caught the light. Every man was looking at her, and she was looking at no one.

She willed herself to take a step, and the eyes followed. Their hatred felt like a heated fog that swirled around her limbs until she arrived at the plaintiff's table.

Brillstein limped heavily into the courtroom. Wounds like he had suffered were slow to heal in the elderly, and he was clearly still in agony. Wincing, he lowered himself slowly into his seat near Penny, his red-rimmed eyes glowering at her. Only Tad separated the two of them. The firm had agreed that a younger man should question Penny when she was called to testify. The list of witnesses who might be called was short, because Tad planned to subpoena Maxwell's notebooks.

Voices shouted in the hallway outside. Heads in the courtroom turned in the direction of the disturbance. Male voices were shouting, "Maxwell, did you still love Alouette?" A chorus of men was shouting, "How are you holding up in the wake of Clarissa's self-assassination?" It was a near-repeat of the scene Penny had witnessed in the lobby of the BB&B building, when Alouette D'Ambrosia had stepped out of the elevator. Now dozens of journalists and bloggers were fighting for Max's attention. They all held camera phones overhead to capture video of him as he entered the courtroom.

Penny couldn't see him. Max was too closely protected within his scrum of blue-suited bodyguards. But she could see the tiny camera screens that depicted him from multiple angles. He wore a muted Ralph Lauren suit, appropriate for a wedding or a funeral. His pale hands were empty; there was no sign of the control box with which he could torment anyone implanted with the fiendish Beautiful You nanobots. A bemused smirk flitted across his pale lips.

For her part, Penny had worn a durable, stylish Jil Sander pantsuit. She couldn't risk a skirt or dress. She had no interest in repeating the tragically fatal striptease that Alouette had been compelled to perform onstage at the Oscars. She had considered smuggling a gun in her Prada shoulder bag, à la President Hind, but it was too late to murder Max. Courtroom security would be too tight.

The gaggle of reporters trailed Max all the way to his place at the defendant's table. There, a member of his defense team pulled out a chair, and Max took it without so much as a glance in Penny's direction. Even at a distance she could tell that his demeanor today was as cold as his hands had always felt. Gone was the gently smiling, always attentive dinner date who had coaxed her to discuss all of her worries. It was odd to see him without either a pen or a notebook.

True to his word, C. Linus Maxwell had ceased the flow of interest payments from her fifty-million-dollar trust. If she was driven to, Penny knew she could always sell the hefty ruby that dangled from the slim gold chain around her neck. She would squander her last cent to see his downfall.

Everyone stood as the judge made his entrance. He gaveled the trial into session.

Tad stood. "As counsel for the plaintiff," he announced, "I call Penny Harrigan as my first witness."

Every eye was upon her as she stood. Being constantly inspected by the world's rich and famous had left her immune to such public examinations. A thousand strangers were judging her body, her hair, even her character. None of that mattered. She walked like a queen striding toward the guillotine. She placed a hand on the Bible offered to her. Only then did she allow her eyes to meet Maxwell's. He returned the look, his gaze calm, unimpressed. An expression of supreme boredom. His half-closed eyes suggested that he was suppressing a yawn.

As Penny took her seat behind the microphone and stated her name for the record, he reached one pale hand into his suit jacket and removed a small black object. This he held in the palm of one hand and began to manipulate as if he were keyboarding a text message.

Not a text message, Penny thought. This would be a *text massage*.

Whether the effect was psychosomatic or not, Penny couldn't tell, but a soothing rush of warmth flooded her breasts. The general effect was so loving, so nurturing that Penny guessed it was her imagination. It was nothing like the rude sexual assaults he'd menaced her with earlier. This light stroking sensation between her legs was more like the touch of Baba Gray-Beard. Penny squirmed a little. Perhaps these were the feelings which Max broadcast to prompt women to buy certain books and shoes. This was how he could deliver female voters to his choice of candidates. It tickled slightly. The effect reminded her of the phrase her mom had used: "tickled pink."

Rising from his chair, Tad approached. "Miss Harrigan," he began, "are you a virgin?"

Penny wasn't shocked. She knew his entire line of questioning. Their strategy was to make her look like a brilliant coinventor, not a young flower led astray. "No," she answered. "I am not a virgin."

"Were you a virgin when you met Mr. Maxwell?"

Penny shook her head. "No, I was not." The pleasurable sensations continued to course through her. Her heart had begun to beat so heavily that she could almost feel the ruby pendant bouncing against her chest.

Tad fixed her with a stern look. "Did you participate in sexual encounters with Mr. Maxwell?"

Max's fingertips hovered as if waiting for her to betray him. Penny nodded.

The judge interjected, "Let the record state that the witness answered in the affirmative."

Tad continued, "Did you freely engage in the use of tools intended to heighten erotic experience?"

The remote-controlled pleasuring ceased abruptly. The warm buzzing in her nipples and groin, it hadn't been her imagination. It had been a warning. In response to Tad's last question Penny said, "Yes, I permitted Mr. Maxwell to test many of his ideas on me."

Without taking his eyes off of her, Max nimbly touched a series of buttons.

Penny felt her underarms grow damp. Her clothes felt as if the fabric were smoldering, about to catch fire. A trickle of sweat crept down the cleft between her buttocks. A long, sensual moan rose up in her throat but she choked it back.

Tad asked, "Were you compensated for the labor you performed for Mr. Maxwell?"

At the word *labor,* Max laughed quietly, tucking his chin to his chest.

Angered, Penny replied, "No. He gave me specific gifts of a personal nature—haute couture clothes, for example—but I was not formally compensated or recognized as his colleague and coresearcher."

Max glared at her. It was easy to read the rage in his face. How dared she assume equal status with him? He tapped several keys on his control box.

In the same instant, Penny gasped. Her heart stuttered. Her body strained to be free of her snug garments. Every inch of her skin grew so sensitive that even her silken underwear became as binding as barbed wire. Her fingers struggled to subtly undo various buttons and zippers, to find relief without betraying her arousal. She couldn't give Max the satisfaction. Besides, wriggling like a revved-up pole dancer would hardly win her sympathy with the all-male jury.

Tad didn't seem to notice. He asked, "Are you aware of the defendant's alias, 'Climax-Well'?"

Penny quelled a fresh rush of passion. She rotated her hips against her chair in what she hoped was an inconspicuous fashion. She said, "The tabloids called him that. But he *owns* all those *tabloids*!"

Tad continued, "Strictly in your own opinion, Miss Harrigan, what would you say is the chief source of Mr. Maxwell's extensive sexual expertise?"

Here it was, the opportunity to denounce him. Penny quickly swallowed the hot saliva that flooded her mouth. She discreetly lifted a tissue to blot at the beads of sweat that were welling up on her forehead. With the entire world listening, she would explain about Maxwell's journey to Nepal and the apprenticeship he'd served at the knee of the Baba. She'd describe how his truncated tragic marriage had motivated him. And Penny would state for the public record how Beautiful You intimate care products were modeled after the desiccated bones of crazed pilgrims who'd pleasured themselves to death. The world would soon know how Maxwell had looted the sensual secrets of all human history in order to enslave female consumers and control their spending habits. Those degraded ladies were captive to an erotic power beyond their comprehension, and Penny would rescue them. Max would be unmasked.

Even as the words formed on her lips, her breathing grew slow and heavy. Penny's thighs wiggled to be free from her moistened underpants. Her feet kicked off the shoes that seemed to trap them. In subconscious response the male onlookers eagerly edged forward in their seats. Their lustful eyes devoured her.

"Tell us," Tad encouraged. He really looked yummy in his lawyer clothes. Penny couldn't wait to marry him once this ordeal was behind them. Their honeymoon sex was going to be fantastic.

She was only vaguely aware of how Max was pressing buttons, frantically trying to stem her testimony with a larger wave of ecstasy. He might even be trying to kill her with a pleasure-induced stroke or heart attack. He grimly punched keys, never taking his eyes off of her physical reaction.

The nanbots that were implanted within her nervous system, they were most likely feeding Max all of her vital signs.

The black box he held, it would be relaying her heart rate, blood pressure, hormone levels—everything.

His powers went far beyond what she'd anticipated. Max pressed one button, and she instantly tasted phantom chocolate. The best dark chocolate she'd ever known; her mouth was brimming with the delicious flavor. He pressed another button, and Penny smelled the heady perfume of a beautiful rose garden. The nanobots he'd delivered via the infamous Dragonfly, they rallied to stimulate all of her senses. Vast symphonies of violin music played in her ears. The thrilling effects of the pink champagne douche seemed to swell afresh within her.

Still, Penny fought to speak. Her hands roamed unbidden in her hair. Her back arched to thrust her breasts forward. "He's controlling the world . . ." she said in a quavering voice. She pointed a shaky finger. "Look! With his telephone!"

Noticing her distress, Tad cut in. "Your Honor," he addressed the judge, "it appears that the witness is falling ill."

"Please stop him," Penny wailed. "He's controlling my mind!" Of their own volition, her hands were stripping away her blouse. Her violent rubbing and shimmying made her slacks flutter down to collect around her ankles. A cacophony of savory tastes—foie gras and Grand Marnier and caramel lattes—tickled her palate. Deafening Mozart arias rang in her ears. Her sinuses were inflamed with the sweet odors of jasmine and puppies. To the world he looked like he was playing Tetris, but Maxwell was spurring all of these exquisite sensations to occur as his fingers fiddled with keys like a virtuoso concert pianist.

Helpless, Penny felt her body respond to an invisible attacker. Her orifices ached as if she were being violated by hundreds of erect penises. Her legs and lips were forced apart, and she could taste and feel a multitude of unseen tongues invading her. Phantom teeth nibbled playfully at her nipples, and she felt hot panting against her neck.

She screamed, but no one came to her rescue. The court stenographer recorded her pleading. The sketch artists drew her struggles.

Tad stared at her in shocked disbelief. She was no longer the accomplished sex witch. As before, she was the sweaty slab of meat under someone else's erotic control.

The paramedics arrived and lifted her onto a gurney. They asked her for the year, the president. They asked her name and recognized her with delight: "the Nerd's Cinderella."

All the way to the mental hospital one of them kept marveling, "You should've married him. . . ."

Despite a steady downpour of cold rain, a bedraggled line of shoppers stretched along Fifth Avenue. The drops flattened their hair into lank ribbons that hung over their faces, hiding their dulled, glassy eyes. Their ruined shoes stood, brimming, in puddles. Every few minutes a tragic scarecrow would stagger a step forward. One end of the line vanished through the pink-mirrored doors of a shop. The opposite end of the line stretched to the horizon. Here and there a shopper had collapsed, but even those feeble ladies continued to inch forward on their hands and knees.

Few if any of them looked up as a superstretch limousine carried a wedding party to the front of St. Patrick's Cathedral. There, a canopy protected the arriving guests. Among them were world leaders, the queen of England, a Chinese media baron, prizewinning lady artists of every ilk. Legions of journalists crowded the sidewalk. It was the news story of the decade. The world's richest, most powerful man was getting married.

En route to her nuptials, the bride was driven past the miles and miles of haggard shoppers. She kept her veils lowered, hoping that she wouldn't be recognized. She, Penny Harrigan, had failed to save anyone, and now she would pay the ultimate price. She would break no new ground for the next generation of women. She'd open no new frontier for feminism. Adorned in a voluptuous Priscilla of Boston wedding gown, she steeled herself to walk down the aisle and pledge her troth to C. Linus Maxwell.

On every corner, sidewalk newsstands displayed the day's banner tabloid headlines: "Nerd King Marries His Evil Queen." Another headline: "All Hail Queen Penny." Yet other tabloids trumpeted: "Climax Well Plots to Take Over World" and "Corny Maxwell Builds Secret Sex Robots." Only Penny could recognize his strategy. He'd planted these stories in order to present the truth as a ludicrous joke. He was undermining the credibility of her discovery. Now no one would ever believe her.

Her vintage wedding dress was appropriately cumbersome. She was hobbled by its weight of petticoats and flounces. But it was necessary for the mythology taking place. To everyone else in history, this would look like a storybook ending: Cinderella wedding her Prince Charming. Max needed that to bolster the illusion he'd crafted for so many years.

Overall, the inky smoke of burning latex blanketed the city. Flaming dildos continued to pelt down, dealing random death.

The Beautiful You stragglers plodded along like an army in endless retreat from some distant battlefield. Wounded and dispirited. Their sodden clothes streaming, they had no idea that they were pawns in a worldwide plot. Penny had not only failed to help them, she'd been actively complicit in their defeat. It had been in her bed that the weapons of their downfall had been perfected. Penny's feedback had honed the tools that now devastated her gender. So it was only fitting that she must pledge herself to Max.

The most intelligent, talented, determined women in the

world were now subject to his whims. With the push of a button he could put incredible tastes in their mouths. He could make them hear glorious music that didn't exist. He controlled their reality. Today marked the beginning of a dark age for women everywhere, and Penny hoped it would last for only one generation. Once the truth came to be widely known, maybe the next generation would steer clear of Beautiful You products.

But, Penny thought, if the nanobots were self-replicating, each mother might pass the tiny masters to her daughters. Perhaps to her sons as well. Within a generation the entire industrialized world would belong to Max. Evil Max.

If, as he'd said, he'd had a vasectomy, there would be no one to inherit his legacy. Knowing him, Penny assumed the reins of power would eventually pass to a fully automated supercomputer. Soon some software program would be telling everyone what they felt and tasted, doling out artificial orgasms and sweet, faked music via the nervous-system robots.

By then, Penny realized that it wouldn't matter how anything tasted. DataMicroCom could put any ingredients in the foods they sold. Actual flavor and mouth feel wouldn't matter, because the nanobots would control how the consumers perceived all products.

Penny recalled the cab ride to her first dinner date at Chez Romaine. In contrast to walking that first red carpet ignored, this morning a dense wall of newshounds filled the sidewalk, vying to get a photograph of her in her wedding finery. Scores of Max's lackeys carried the train of her dress and held black umbrellas to prevent even a single raindrop from marring her appearance. A scrum of blue-suited bodyguards escorted her through the crowd.

Rushing up the steps of the cathedral, Penny tasted spicy barbecued ribs. She heard sweet birds singing. She knew none of it was real. Max was only putting the perceptions in her head.

To comfort her, she supposed. Her mind would never again be her own.

Entering the foyer of the church she caught sight of three familiar faces but dismissed them as more Max-induced hallucinations. They smiled. She smiled back, asking, "Are you guys for real?"

They were her parents and her housemate. Her mom and Monique looked fragile and emaciated, but apparently Max had given them enough strength to be here today. The two women were less wedding guests than they were hostages brought to ensure the ceremony would go through without a hitch. Penny might attempt another rebellion, but not if the people she loved were in constant danger.

It seemed ironic how not long ago her mom and Monique had been badgering Penny to throw away her birth control and trap Max into marriage. Now she was the one who was trapped. And this morning they looked like mourners at a funeral. They all four hugged warmly.

As the ushers stood ready to seat her parents, Penny's mother whispered, "Here, take this." She pressed something into her daughter's hand. "Read it."

Penny noticed with horror that her mom's wrists were raw with rope burns. Her bare arms were polka-dotted with the red scabs marking hypodermic injection sites. What she offered was a folded square of paper. Smoothing it flat, Penny found it was a yellowed page from an ages-old back issue of the *National Enquirer*. Nervously, she asked a bodyguard whether there was a toilet she could use.

Not one of the parish's pious cleaning ladies had reported to work in weeks, Penny noted with disdain. Maneuvering her gigantic hoop skirt into a filthy toilet cubicle took some doing. Every movement caused the elegant satin to wick up unclean water from the urine-stinking floor. Penny could hear the first strains of the "Wedding March" as her eyes furiously scanned the tabloid page. The headline of the article read, "DataMicro-Com Gambles Big on Cloning Technology." According to the piece that followed, Max's company had made massive investments in researching how to create a viable human embryo and clone it. This research had taken place during the same era as the nanobot research. According to the *National Enquirer*'s science writer, the company's stated long-term goal was to generate a microscopic clone. That clone would be sealed in suspended animation. It could be implanted and gestate to maturity within a surrogate womb.

Penny read and reread the article before flushing it down the toilet.

If Max could sneak mind-controlling nanobots into women, why couldn't he smuggle a suspended embryonic clone into them as well? Including her! Without a doubt this would be a clone of himself. That, *that* was his master plan. To control world population growth . . . to perpetuate his global corporate power . . . like some parasite, he planned to hatch thousands, possibly millions of identical Maxes in the uteruses of unsuspecting women. That was his scheme to bring peace to mankind. His perfect world would be populated by a billion versions of him!

Maxwell was standing at the altar. Her parents were sitting in the front pew, waiting with the hundreds of dignitaries and celebrities for the bride to come down the aisle.

Every woman in the church smiled raptly. Clearly Max was bombarding their senses with every enjoyable sensation imaginable. Penny's mom sighed as if lost in the rapture of fresh-baked brownies. Monique's eyes slowly closed as if she were carried aloft on a magic carpet of waltz music. Only Penny was exempt from whatever pleasures Max was using to keep the other women docile as the ceremony progressed.

Soon she'd become Mrs. C. Linus Maxwell. She'd found her destiny, or it had found her. From this day forward she'd be at the helm of the largest corporation in the world. She'd be wife to the richest man on the globe. Penny took her place at his side. Veiled. Implanted. To love, honor, cherish, but most important—to obey.

The bishop asked, "If anyone here can give just cause for why these two should not be joined in holy matrimony, speak now or forever hold your peace."

A murmur came from the rear of the church. The multitude of elegant necks swiveled to watch as a stooped figure slowly trudged down the center aisle. Its scraggly gray tresses were streaming with rainwater. Its withered body inched along, unclothed. A trailing abundance of gray pubic hair hung so far down it brushed the red carpet. To judge from his expression of surprise and fear, Max knew instantly who this uninvited apparition was. The approaching hag lifted her blind, whitened eyes in his direction and spoke. Her crone's nose sniffing the air, she cried, "Maxwell, I can smell your fear!" Her voice a rusty croak, her toothless mouth bade, "Stop this . . . travesty!"

Warily Maxwell dipped a hand inside his tux jacket and brought forth the black control box. His touch could torture or kill millions.

The ever-encroaching hag commanded, "Tell her, Maxwell!" The witch pointed a gnarled finger and ordered, "If you can wed the girl then tell her the truth! Tell your young bride the true nature of her existence!"

Max's eyes bulged in horror.

Now halfway down the aisle, the ragged cadaver-woman bade, "Tell her the secret which I could not. This knowledge must come from you. Tell her!"

Penny stood, confused, glancing between the ragged accuser and the man who was about to become her husband.

Of course this was the Baba, come all the way from Nepal to New York. Her lips parted and she said, "Tell her why you've dedicated your life to the service of pleasuring women!"

Max lifted his controller for all to see. "Take another step, old mother, and the death of a billion women will be on your head!"

The Baba quelled her progress.

Here Penny interjected. "Baba," she cried boldly, "I know the reason Maxwell stole the sensual secrets of the ancients. I know why he's wagered his lifetime to gain access to the world's best vaginas!"

The women present continued to swoon heavily in their waking pleasure dreams. The male guests seemed nicely surprised to have some unexpected interruption in an otherwise tedious wedding ceremony. If they were aware of the women's pleasure they were studiously ignoring it. These men, for the most part, appeared to be the scurrilous lotharios and black-market profiteers who were exploiting the Beautiful You effect.

As Max's finger hovered over the buttons of a global massacre, Penny announced, "I know about the cloning research. I know that Max has implanted cloned embryos of himself in every user of Beautiful You products, and soon he'll trigger them all to begin gestation." She had the attention of the entire cathedral as she shouted, "The same nanobots that bring pleasure and pain to Max's slaves, those same tiny robots will suppress the immune function that might otherwise reject these foreign fetuses. That army of microscopic robots will protect and defend those fetuses so that hundreds of millions of fertile women will give birth to exact copies of Cornelius Linus Maxwell!"

By the end of her short speech Penny was screaming her words. Wildly waving her wedding bouquet about. As she fell silent, the assembled crowds stared at her in disbelief. Penny, in her fluffy, flouncy gown, waited for the reaction of outrage. She readied herself for Max to begin tormenting her with a few keystrokes. None of that happened.

The Baba turned clouded eyes on her. The old woman tilted her head quizzically and said, "What are you talking about, my dear? That's not it at all."

Somewhere, someone in the cavernous church giggled.

"Another word," Max threatened, "and I'll deliver more suffering than you people can imagine!"

Heedless, Baba Gray-Beard ventured, "The dress you're wearing, Penny Harrigan, it was *her* dress twenty-five years ago. It's the wedding gown Max's long-dead wife wore when she was your exact age!" Her words echoed around the huge stone chapel. "Ask your groom why that dress is such a perfect fit!"

The dress had been an exact fit. From the first time Penny tried it on, the gown had felt as if it were made for her.

Before she could ponder this miracle another moment, Max fingered his device. Unseen, a satellite relayed the signal, and Penny felt a searing jolt of pain shoot through her. Likewise, every female wedding guest shrieked and slumped to the cold floor. Only the Baba remained upright, staring defiantly into Max's outraged eyes. "Tell the girl," she hissed. "She must know the destiny she was born to fulfill."

"Never," Max cried.

Penny was only vaguely aware that the Baba had closed the distance between herself and Maxwell. The two adversaries circled each other, the tuxedo-clad dandy and the emaciated skeleton. Maxwell stashed the control box in the inside pocket of his tux jacket and raised both his empty hands menacingly, ready to lunge at the hag's next words.

The bishop stood over Penny, blushing furiously as she wriggled at his feet, writhing in agony and sensual pleasure, near crazed, with a lunatic's guttural yammering streaming from her mouth.

"You, little Penny," the Baba shouted. "You must reflect his evil energy. It was no accident that you met Maxwell. Only you can defeat him!"

No sooner had she muttered those words than Max sprang forward, grabbing Baba Gray-Beard around her desiccated throat and saying, "Die, wicked sorceress!"

Even as she gasped for her next breath, the Baba said, "Look! Look in his notebook at a date nine months before you were born, Penny!" Her voice reduced to a garbled whisper, she said, "Look and see who he was seducing. . . ."

Penny rolled around in the fluff of her vast wedding dress. She could sense the nanobots scooting about in her veins. She wanted to slice her arteries open and strain her blood clean. The robots would never be at peace. She'd never be free of them. Maxwell's little sentries were alive and inflicting their pain from the inside.

Her neck crushed in Max's cold hands, the Baba was dying. After two centuries of coaching pilgrims to sexual enlightenment, the gentle yogi was expiring in the grip of her greatest pupil. Even as the hands throttled her windpipe, she croaked, "Child, you must rebound his energy. Channel it through yourself and return it with greater force!" She whispered, "No mirror is ever burned by the rays from even the hottest sun!"

To displace the assault of false pleasure, Penny concentrated on her close-knit family and their simple Lutheran faith. She savored the real friendship that had formed between herself and Monique. Penny's mind embraced everything she truly loved in the world. Butter brickle ice cream. Ron Howard. Richard Thomas. With steady meditating, Penny's consciousness began to deflect the signals from Max's control box. The teeming nanobots gradually trickled downward, crowding to a halt within her waiting pelvis.

Simultaneously, a shrill whistle filled the church. Faint at first, the sound grew in strength. The whistle increased to become a siren, a wailing of air-raid volume. The siren built to a bullhorn, so loud it threatened to scramble the brains of everyone present. The guests, the bishop, every person in the cavernous church clamped their hands over their ears and cowered in pain.

Penny was its source. Muffled only by her skirts and crinolines, the trumpeting sound was being emitted from between her legs. It echoed off the masonry walls. The towering stained-glass windows rattled. As trumpets had toppled the great walls of Jericho, thin cracks opened between the cathedral's stones. A dust of mortar drifted down. As the sound built to thunder it exploded through her satin and petticoats, spraying sequins and seed pearls like shrapnel. Shredded lace flew like countless flakes of white confetti, exposing the seat of the bride's power.

Penny focused on the love she felt for the great Baba, and the edges of her sex flared outward, blasting forth a huge noise. It blared, a sonic cannon. The blast extinguished the sanctuary candles.

Without warning, the cathedral's great rose window exploded. Not outward. The window burst *inward,* pelting the wedding party with razor-sharp fragments of red, blue, and green glass, shattered by something flying bullet-fast from the direction of Yankee Stadium.

Like a lightning bolt . . . a ball of fire . . . a molten flaming mass of latex and batteries shot across the vast length of the great sanctuary. With the force of a shotgun blast, this murderous rocket smote Max squarely in the tailored inseam of his designer formalwear. This searing-hot mortar round of burning personal care products, it tore into the groom's private man-parts, doubling him in half at the waist and toppling him backward.

The centuries-old lamia was dead.

Maxwell, he'd been mortally wounded by a weapon from his own arsenal of space-age pleasure tools—an immolating phallus that had launched itself from the Promise Keepers' bonfire! Blood flowed steadily from the torn crotch of his tuxedo. Penny didn't need to look closer to know his genitals were obliterated. Like a character in some Ernest Hemingway book she'd been required to read in high school, his private junk was blown to bits by the blast. Baba Gray-Beard was dead and Max was dying.

The nanobots within her ceased their torment. Slowly Penny and the other women in the church struggled to their feet, blinking dazed eyes. They shook their disarrayed hair out of their faces and opened their purses to begin the long, difficult task of repairing their makeup. And their lives.

The frigid fingers of a dying hand closed around Penny's ankle. It was Max, looking up at her with pleading eyes. His already pale face was bled paper-white, and his lips moved to form words. "Listen," he said. "Look." With his free hand he reached into his jacket pocket and produced a ragged scrap of newsprint. "For you," he said, and held it for her to take.

Penny knelt and accepted it: a newspaper clipping dated

exactly thirty years ago, to the day. It had been saved from the *National Enquirer*. Prominently featured was a black-and-white photograph. It was grainy and faded by the years, but it was like looking into a mirror. It was her face, wearing the same veil and gown she now wore. It was a wedding announcement. Cornelius Linus Maxwell was to marry Phoebe Bradshaw. Stapled to that was a second newspaper article, an obituary dated exactly 136 days later. The young Mrs. Corny Maxwell had died from an allergic reaction to shellfish.

Fear shadowed Penny's heart. She herself was allergic to shellfish. Their first dinner at Chez Romaine, when she'd almost ordered scallop sushi, Max had stopped her. Somehow Max had also known about her severe allergy.

"My wife," he said. Where his penis and testicles had once dangled, Penny saw that there was only a rude wound gushing blood. The same dying hand that had presented the articles now offered his ubiquitous notebook; holding it open to a specific page, he said, "'Test subject number eleven forty-eight, Myrtle Harrigan, March twenty-fourth, 19—. Place: Shippee, Nebraska . . .'"

Penny's mother sobbed quietly as Maxwell read aloud the details of their tryst. Twenty-five years earlier, she had been a small-town newlywed attending a pie social at the local grange hall. In untypically gallant language Max had recorded, "'The test subject seemed bereft as she confided in me about her inability to bear a child. A stranger in town, I must've seemed a safe person with whom to unburden her heart.'" A generation ago, this young Nebraskan woman had spilled out her secret fears to Max just as Penny would on their first date at

Chez Romaine. "'The woman was a hundred and sixty-eight centimeters in height, approximately fifty-four kilograms in weight—'"

A distance away from where Max held his notebook, recounting his past, Penny's weeping mother lifted her face from a handful of tissues and interrupted: "I was only fifty-one kilograms!"

Dying, Max continued. "'In my heart I knew I could do more for this poor, barren woman than provoke her to a gut-wrenching orgasm. It was within my power to give her the baby she so badly wanted.'"

He described how he'd seduced this latest test subject over a slice of pumpkin pie. Her husband was away, attending a Promise Keepers weekend retreat. It took very little charm to persuade this lonely young housewife. Max had consummated the evening in the backseat of his rented Ford Explorer.

"'When her heart rate reached one hundred and sixty-three bpms,'" Max announced flatly, "'I implanted a cloned zygote along with the latest generation of nanobots needed to ensure its survival.'"

Sobbing, Penny's mom insisted, "I've never weighed more than a hundred and twenty pounds, even after you got me pregnant!"

Nine months later, Penny had been born. A seeming miracle.

From his anguished expression Penny knew her father had no idea. Neither of her parents had suspected that they'd played a part in Max's plan to replicate his long-deceased wife. They'd innocently harbored the experiment of a fiend. He could've planted his embryo in any of the many women he'd romanced. He could've implanted embryos in all of them.

More troubling to Penny was the real possibility that she wasn't herself. It was bad enough that impulses were being beamed to her, prompting the arousal of her pleasure centers. Now her very DNA was secondhand, bequeathed to her by a madman genius who yearned to be reunited with his beloved. She, Penny Harrigan, was the genetically resurrected Phoebe Maxwell.

In that shocked, otherwise silent moment, one voice rang out. As spunky as ever, Monique squealed, "Omaha girl! Yikes!"

Farther back in the church, Esperanza, once more a Latin spitfire, shrieked, "*Ay, caramba!*"

"All your life my agents have kept watch over you," Max whispered, blood leaking from the ragged gash between his legs. The church had fallen so silent that everyone present could hear his confession. Penny had only to look at the faded photograph in the obituary to know this was all true.

Her guardian angels, she realized, weren't the helpful agents of Homeland Security. Since infancy, those suited and besunglassed sentries had protected her on Max's behalf. They'd allowed nothing to befall her before she could mature as a replacement for his long-dead wife.

"You are proof that my cloning technology will work," Max continued. "I've spent my life gaining access to every uterus in the civilized world."

As a gesture, even to Penny, it was really quite touching. Maxwell *had* loved her. He'd loved her enough to resurrect her from the dead.

Maxwell crowed, "You with your perfect genitals, my good girl, you will be my gift to all men!"

The Baba's battered corpse lay beside him, so close that his blood washed against it. As the flow of his living juices slowed,

Max's eyes fluttered closed. His lungs exhaled their final breath. "Oh, Phoebe . . . I've missed you for so many years. . . ." And Max was gone.

Alone in her Himalayan cave—nude, of course—Penny sprinkled seasonings into a stewing broth of chopped lizards. She stirred the simmering pot and brought a steaming spoonful to her lips. The taste filled her with a sad nostalgia for the dead Baba. Not an hour after the lamia and Max had expired on the floor of St. Patrick's Cathedral, Penny had boarded a private chartered jet and was winging her way to Nepal. She'd scaled the ragged cliffs of Mount Everest still wearing the tatters of her wedding gown. She'd told no one her destination.

Penny's parents were safe. Monique was delivered from her battery-powered obsession. Monique, to judge from the text messages she blasted on an hourly basis, was engaged to marry Tad. She'd continue to reside in the Upper East Side town house *and* have the adoration of a handsome spouse.

Penny reasoned that perhaps in due time a trickle of students would find her here, lured by the ancient legend of a mystical sex witch who could perpetuate the erotic legacy of the ages. A constant stream of physically perfect specimens striving for erotic education would deliver themselves to apprentice with her. Penny was the heiress to the collected tantric skills of all time, was she not? She, Penelope Anne Harrigan, would accept the torch passed to her by the likes of Baba Gray-Beard and Bella Abzug. She'd liberate women from having to go to men for fulfillment. This legacy—not clothes, not jewelry or practicing law—this was the destiny she had long sought. Hers was a power based on carnal pleasure. Her kingdom a realm beyond interpersonal politics.

Penny had learned what was important. Family was important. Love was paramount.

Slowly she stirred. Concocted according to the Baba's favorite recipe, the soup's surface was garnished with flakes of spicy guano. As Penny squatted beside the cooking pot she enjoyed the gentle warmth of the flames. In the stance of a sumo wrestler, she lackadaisically stroked herself with a short, knurled length of what looked like damp wood. It was the Baba's longest finger, the very finger with which the wise ancient had read all of Penny's secrets. As the old lamia had cut a finger from her own dead mother, Penny had severed this memento mori from her mentor's cooling corpse. Still, the keepsake, even well lubricated with stone-ground rabbit sebum, fell far short of slaking Penny's growing melancholy.

The words *arousal addiction* loomed in her mind, but she shooed them away.

As she dipped her spoon for a second taste, she worried that millions of ladies all over the world were likewise crouched, struggling to achieve fresh self-fulfillment. After the sultry ordeal of Beautiful You it was possible that they might never achieve comparable heights of release.

The rudimentary pleasure tools fashioned by the Baba . . . they were okay. But minus the high-tech vaginal stimulation of Max's hybrids, not to mention the salivating attention of the mass media, Penny felt down in the dumps. Perhaps the eggheads were right. Just as teenage boys clung to their precious video games and skin flicks, Penny longed for her bright pink products. Perhaps arousal addiction was real. Her limbic brain was thirsting for dopamine. Her hypothalamus was completely catawampus! She was suffering withdrawal from the Beautiful You effect. She redoubled her efforts with the desiccated finger but felt little reward.

Leaving the fireside, she waddled across the cave's littered floor in search of something. She cast aside the aged tendons and Prada handbags in her frantic search. At last, she found the object she so feverishly sought.

It was a small black box, no larger than a Game Boy. Max's controller. She'd pocketed it in the final moments of her botched nuptials. After Max had been fatally cut down by a flaming dildo projectile, she'd also made off with his precious notebook. Since then she'd spent the wintery hours deciphering these coded records of his sensual research. The mosaic of black push buttons was cryptically labeled, but she'd taught herself what combinations to press for the best results.

She'd begin with the blizzard winds outside the cave's entrance. Night and day they wailed, a constant annoyance. Quickly Penny utilized the controller to adjust her perception.

She keyed in the first code, and the satellite-relayed result was almost instantaneous. She tasted a flood of red velvet cake with chocolate icing and rainbow sprinkles sliding down her throat. No Swiss clockmaker could've picked out the codes with more dexterity and accuracy. To distract herself further, Penny punched another combination of keys and tasted delicious butter brickle ice cream. Regardless, her busy fingers weren't satisfied. Making quick work, she prompted the nanobots in her brain and bloodstream to create the overwhelming pleasure of Tom Berenger and Richard Thomas kissing her wetly on the lips and breasts.

In the next instant, something shocking occurred. A sound. Someone spoke, and the kissing stopped. It was a familiar voice. A female voice. Penny's eyes scoured the filthy cavern but found no explanation. The disembodied words were vague as a dream. But it was unmistakable: The speaker was Baba Gray-Beard. Hanging in the chill air was the odor of fermented egg yolks, the signature aroma of the lamia's labored sex panting.

Dared Penny hope? Might the great mystic's ghost return to make love magic to her while she slept? A darker possibility was that the nanobots were somehow continuing to shape her perceptions. Faint as a thought, the Baba ordered, "Destroy it!" In words as weak as an echo of an echo of an echo, the spirit warned, "Little one, such power will corrupt you as it did Maxwell. . . ." The spirit urged, "Mash the evil controller device betwixt two large rocks before it *seduces you!*"

In awed response, Penny whispered, "Baba, are you here?"

She waited, listening, hearing only the fierce wind. She sat and contemplated a future of solitude with only the hoary love implements hewn from bone and sinew. She counted to a hundred in fives. She examined the sorry state of her cuticles. After that, she counted to a thousand by twenties. The sex witch's ghost spoke no more. The youthful sex apprentice struggled with the decision of what to do next.

Immediately, inspiration struck. The DataMicroCom satellites were still in orbit. Why couldn't she deliver succor to the legions of gals worldwide who were sharing this same withdrawal from Beautiful You bliss?

Unselfishly, she toggled and keyboarded until these same amazing sensations were bombarding all the women implanted by Beautiful You products. Penny's mom in Omaha. Sassy, spunky Monique. Even Brenda—now Yuri's newlywed bride *and* the CFO of Allied Chemical Corp. Kwan Qxi and Esperanza, too! Wherever they were, they would all be savoring rich desserts and the heavenly bliss of ripe movie-star smooches.

Impulsively, she filled their far-flung nostrils with mango-scented breezes. Let all her sister women rejoice, Penny told herself. Through her they would achieve solidarity.

While their actual circumstances might be grinding poverty

and ignorance, she'd bestow upon them a rich surrogate reality. She'd deliver to their taste buds an unending banquet of gourmet delicacies. An unending repast without a single fattening calorie! She'd replace their mundane thoughts with snippets of inspirational poetry read aloud by the cultured mouth of Meryl Streep.

A few pecks on the right keys, and she'd carpet-bomb them with self-esteem and resolve problematic body-image issues for all time.

She cupped her breasts in her palms and lifted them, examining the nipples with growing awe and wonder. They were astonishing. Her heart, nay, every cell of her swelled in recognition of her own glory and beauty. Following suit, women around the world—tall women, crippled women, fat, old, young and skinny women, they rediscovered themselves. Wherever they were at that moment in their lives—dining at picnics or riding aboard buses or performing intricate brain surgeries—they paused and regarded their bodies with a new, powerful appreciation. Flat-chested, bowlegged, humpbacked, or balding, Penny would force them to recognize their innate beauty. At her satellite-relayed prompting, all women would begin to pet themselves, reveling in the quality of their skin. Penny's electronic urging would compel them to immediately celebrate their bodies with vigorous self-romancing.

This, this was power. She, Penelope Harrigan, would reign over the world, a benevolent lady dictator, awarding well-deserved pleasure to the multitudes. She'd surpassed the power wielded by even her heroes, Clarissa Hind and Alouette D'Ambrosia. To redeem Max's wicked technology, she would singlehandedly bring about world peace and order. She'd reward good behavior and punish the bad.

The generations of females trained too long to look for

insults and injustice, Penny would pummel them with joy and drive them to accept happiness. A happy ending. With stealthy, subtle manipulation of their pleasure centers, she'd gently bully them into achieving their full erotic potential. Lady political activists might bicker over their strategic goals, platforms, and agendas, but Penny would trump their catfighting by giving them tsunami waves of physical thrills.

An ancient truism had once decreed, "Self-improvement is masturbation. . . ." At last the inverse would also be true.

"Baba," she cried out, "rest easy, my guardian! I will not allow the power to overcome me!"

This, Penny whispered to herself, *this would be the best time in history to be a woman.*

She'd give ladies the ultimate zipless fuck. Erica Jong would be so proud of her. This—sex crafting, practicing carnal magic—would be the new frontier for the next generation of young female searchers.

Acting on a generous impulse, Penny pressed the buttons that would bestow a loving, sisterly, long-distance hug on Gloria Steinem.

That accomplished, she scuttled back toward the cooking fire lest her tasty lizards scorch.

Intoxicated with satisfaction, weak from joy, again she referred to Max's notebook of codes. Perfect as this moment was—the precious finger lodged deep inside her, the stewed skinks bubbling deliciously, the flames warming her nude, astonishingly beguiling body—even this scene could be improved upon.

With tired, trembling, happy fingers she punched a few more buttons on the controller.

What took place next was only a nanobot-induced hallucination, but Penny could see it, smell it, feel it.

A robust, strapping figure emerged from the snowstorm and stood brazenly unclothed in the cave's mouth. His dancing blue eyes filled with lust. His impressive, freckled-pink manhood swung heavily between his legs. And a handsome Ron Howard swaggered boldly toward her.

The author would like to acknowledge the following visionaries for their unflagging faith and support of the arts. May the tantric gods visit you with frequent, pulse-pounding, sweat-soaked episodes of full release as you slumber.

Mallory Moss
Katie Dodd
William Klayer
Kasey Bossert
Ian W. Arsenault
Halle Kasper
Megan McCrary
Mandy Boles
Kyle Becker
Adam Stratton
Donald Hugo III
Chuck Crittenden
Peter Wollesen
Stephanie Jean Ray
Nicole Doro
Valeriya Kulchikhina
Meghan Sherar
Angelena Bigham

Zachary Glenn Harbaugh
Andrew G. Gahol
Peter Osborn
Christopher Seevers
Kerstynn Lane
Michael John Silvin
Mandy Marez
Joe Wilson
Wessly Ford
Stephanie Wiley
Patrick D. O'Connor
Henry S. Rosenthal
Brian Manning
Parker Cross
Margaret Dennison
Sharon Leong
Kevin Stevulak
Charlotte O'Neil Golden

Michael Anderson-McGee

Katie McCartney

Jacquelyn Nicole Tawney

Gary Eaton

Mike Parkinson

Dustin Schultz

Gina Chernoby

Michele McDaniel

Jake Richard

Ryan O'Neill

George Washington Anderson III

Aysha Martinez

Trev Pierce

John Hardenstine

Bettina Holbrook

Michael Bowhay

Mark V. Paulis

Kevin Sharp

Patricia Scott Petey Wells

Mike Hardin

Thomas Wayne Harvey

Andrew Greenblatt

Elizabeth C. Nichols

Brian Foster

Bryce Haynes

Tatianna Abastoflor

Ronald Green, Jr.

Alisha Ohl

Cody Maasen

Bryan Kraig Ward

Jessica Dugan

Matthew A. Eller

Meredith Alder

Tiffany Joy Atencio

Kyle Adamski

John Michel

Quentin R. Voglund

James Bendos

Gabriel Cesana

Jason W. Bohrer

Shane Gollihue

Scott Trulock

Aaron Blake Flynn

Brett Kerns

Juliet Walker

Kristina Valencia

James P. Giacopelli

Karen Zacconi

Sean K. Smith

Rita Su

Will Tupper

Michael Pedrosa

Russ Robertson

Tag

Samantha Jade Schnee

Rubyann Baybo

Yassaman Tarazkar

Shereen Lombardi

Ashley Blaike Ralph

Mike Dyson

Lorne Sherman

Patti Vanty-McKinley

Shaun Sharma

Christine Strileckis